THE HUMANISATION OF GLOBAL POLITICS

This book observes a growing humanisation of global politics relating to the appearance of individual human beings in discourses of global politics. It identifies a mismatch concerning International Relations theory and International Law and the study of the humanisation of global politics. To overcome this mismatch, Sassan Gholiagha proposes a novel theoretical framework based on feminist and constructivist International Relations theory and non-statist theories of International Law scholarship. The book applies this interdisciplinary framework together with an interpretative analytical framework to three cases: the discourse on prosecution, studying international criminal law and the work of the International Criminal Court; the discourse on protection, focusing on the Responsibility to Protect; and the discourse on the use of drones in targeted killing operations. Drawing on these case studies and the frameworks, the book identifies how individual human beings as participants in global politics position themselves and are positioned by others in these various discourses.

SASSAN GHOLIAGHA holds a PhD from the University of Hamburg. Having worked at the University of Hamburg, the WZB Berlin Social Science Center, and the Institute of International Relations at the TU Braunschweig, he currently is a Postdoctoral Researcher at the European New School of Digital Studies (European University Viadrina), Frankfurt(Oder), Germany.

STUDIES ON INTERNATIONAL COURTS AND TRIBUNALS

General Editors
Andreas Føllesdal, University of Oslo
Geir Ulfstein, University of Oslo

Studies on International Courts and Tribunals contains theoretical and interdisciplinary scholarship on legal aspects as well as the legitimacy and effectiveness of international courts and tribunals.

Other books in the series:

Mads Andenas and Eirik Bjorge (eds.) *A Farewell to Fragmentation: Reassertion and Convergence in International Law*

Cecilia M. Bailliet and Nobuo Hayashi (eds.) *The Legitimacy of International Criminal Tribunals*

Amrei Müller with Hege Elisabeth Kjos (eds.) *Judicial Dialogue and Human Rights*

Nienke Grossman, Harlan Grant Cohen, Andreas Follesdal and Geir Ulfstein (eds.) *Legitimacy and International Courts*

Theresa Squatrito, Oran R. Young, Andreas Føllesdal, Geir Ulfstein (eds.) *The Performance of International Courts and Tribunals*

Robert Howse, Hélène Ruiz-Fabri, Geir Ulfstein and Michelle Q. Zang (eds.) *The Legitimacy of International Trade Courts and Tribunals*

Marlene Wind (ed.) *International Courts and Domestic Politics*

Christina Voigt (ed.) *International Judicial Practice on the Environment: Questions of Legitimacy*

Martin Scheinin (ed.) *Human Rights Norms in 'Other' International Courts*

Freya Baetens (ed.) *Legitimacy of Unseen Actors in International Adjudication*

Shai Dothan *International Judicial Review: When Should International Courts Intervene?*

Silje Langvatn, Mattias Kumm, Wojciech Sadurski (eds.) *Public Reason and Courts*

Daniel Behn, Szilárd Gáspár-Szilágyi, Malcolm Langford (eds.) *Adjudicating Trade and Investment Disputes: Convergence or Divergence?*

Sondre Torp Helmersen *The Application of Teachings by the International Court of Justice*

Daniel Behn, Ole Kristian Fauchald, Malcolm Langford (eds.) *The Legitimacy of Investment Arbitration: Empirical Perspectives*

Eric De Brabandere *International Procedure in Interstate Litigation and Arbitration: A Comparative Approach*

Chiara Giorgetti and Mark Pollack (eds.) *Beyond Fragmentation: Cross-Fertilization, Cooperation and Competition among International Courts and Tribunals*

Stavros Brekoulakis and Georgios Dimitropoulos (eds.) *International Commercial Courts: The Future of Transnational Adjudication*

Mark Gillett *Prosecuting Environmental Harm before the International Criminal Court*

The Humanisation of Global Politics

INTERNATIONAL CRIMINAL LAW, THE RESPONSIBILITY TO PROTECT, AND DRONES

SASSAN GHOLIAGHA
European New School of Digital Studies (European University Viadrina)

CAMBRIDGE
UNIVERSITY PRESS

CAMBRIDGE
UNIVERSITY PRESS

University Printing House, Cambridge CB2 8BS, United Kingdom

One Liberty Plaza, 20th Floor, New York, NY 10006, USA

477 Williamstown Road, Port Melbourne, VIC 3207, Australia

314–321, 3rd Floor, Plot 3, Splendor Forum, Jasola District Centre, New Delhi – 110025, India

103 Penang Road, #05–06/07, Visioncrest Commercial, Singapore 238467

Cambridge University Press is part of the University of Cambridge.

It furthers the University's mission by disseminating knowledge in the pursuit of education, learning, and research at the highest international levels of excellence.

www.cambridge.org
Information on this title: www.cambridge.org/9781108830140
DOI: 10.1017/9781108909136

First published 2022

A catalogue record for this publication is available from the British Library.

ISBN 978-1-108-83014-0 Hardback

For Veronika, Ezra, and Kian

In Memoriam
Ali-Asghar Gholiagha
1945–2017

Peanut
*/† 2019

Contents

Figures

Tables

Preface

This book is the result of more than ten years of research and work in academia. Its origin lies in my PhD thesis, which I defended in 2016 at the University of Hamburg. While based on the thesis, I revised the book substantially in terms of content, literature, style, and structure. As the book is based on my PhD research, I would like to acknowledge a few people without whom the PhD, and hence this book, would have never seen the light of the day. First of all, I would like to express my deepest gratitude to my PhD supervisor Antje Wiener, who provided an academic environment to grow in, offered constructive feedback, and helped me stay on course during my studies. She also offered invaluable support and advice when it came to turning the thesis into a book. I would also like to thank my PhD examiners and reviewers: Anthony F. Lang Jr, Markus Kornprobst, and Susanne Krasmann. Thanks are also due to my colleagues during my time in Hamburg: Julia Frohneberg, Hannes Hansen-Magnusson, Maren Hofius, Philip Liste, and Jan Wilkens, for valuable discussions, feedback, and companionship during my PhD studies. I also thank Sebastian Kester-Joosten, Birte Gebhart, and Diana Müller, with whom I discussed some of the empirical material studied in this book as part of a reconstructive analysis group and who helped to develop some of the interview questions. Several institutions provided funding for the research undertaken. At the University of Hamburg: the Centre for Globalisation and Governance (today the Center for Sustainable Society Research), the Chair of Political Science, especially Global Governance, the Department 4 (Research Management and Funding), and the Department of Social Sciences. The German Academic Exchange Service and the International Studies Association also provided funding.

Acknowledgements

Writing a book is challenging, even under the best of circumstances. This book was written during the COVID-19 pandemic, which made things a bit more challenging, to say the least. When the pandemic began, my wife and I, like so many others, tried to provide full-time childcare, work two full-time jobs, and have a family life amidst an ongoing pandemic, not knowing how long this would last. While we were privileged both financially and in terms of health, we still struggled with the effects of the pandemic. Like many parents, we were often left alone in the decision whether to send our children to day care or not, to weigh risks, and watching norm collisions between the right to play and the right to health affect our daily life (Gholiagha et al. 2020b).

At the time of writing these words, the pandemic has been ongoing for over two years. Millions have died. And yet, in debates about infection numbers, the number of deaths, reliability of tests, vaccine development and distribution, and large-scale economic and political effects, something has been eerily absent: the dying individual human being. Instead, death is depicted in statistics and curves or visible only in a collective form: images of trucks full of human bodies, makeshift morgues, halls filled with coffins, COVID-19 written on them in bold letters, fields filled with pyres. The individual human being is reduced to being a carrier of a deadly disease or its victim. Human death and suffering have become what Christine Sylvester (2013a: 614) has critically referred to as 'data points'. Sylvester writes about the importance of taking into account individual experience in the context of war. And while the book was written before the Russian war against Ukraine began in February 2022, the pictures of injured and killed human beings I see on my screens while I make final edits to the book are a stark remainder that in all the discussions about power and strategy, about interest and motives, we should never forget the suffering war causes for humans. They are more than data points.

Yet, individuals as data points have also been a familiar figure in political science and legal scholarship. And, if present, individual human beings are often only conceptualised through their relation to other actors or in specific roles. To overcome this way of studying individual human beings in global politics, this book is about the humanisation of global politics, about how scholars can understand and study the growing references to the individual human being in discourses of global politics. It is, however, an academic book that uses the suffering of individual human beings as empirical material. I am not sure that academics can ever do justice to those whose lives we study. We can only hope that by understanding the world better, we can help to make it better.

I am indebted to many people for their support. The following list is certainly not complete, and I hope anyone who is not mentioned but should be can forgive me and knows that I am thankful nevertheless. First of all, I would like to thank my interview partners for their time and insights. I am also thankful to everyone who helped to organise the interviews.

I wrote most of this book during my time as a research fellow at the WZB Berlin Social Science Center, where I was a member of the Research Group on the Governance for Global Health, headed by Anna Holzscheiter. Here I had the privilege to work with Anna Holzscheiter and Andrea Liese in a German Research Council–funded project on norm collisions. I am grateful to both for providing space, time, and resources so I could work on this book. I am also thankful for everything I have learned during our still-ongoing collaboration. Both Anna and Andrea have been great mentors. Our project on norm collision was part of a larger collaborative research group, which studied interface conflicts between international organisations. I profited immensely from discussions with members of the group. After my original contract at the WZB ended, I received funding for another seven months, allowing me to focus on this book and other publications. I am thankful to the WZB for the funding. Thanks are also due to Freifrau Editha von Colberg and Anja Opperman for their help on the funding application.

I am also grateful to my WZB colleagues from the International Politics and Law research area for the many discussions over lunch, in offices, in the WZB backyard, and in the colloquium, all of which shaped my thinking and writing in new and productive ways and helped me clarify my positions. I would also like to thank the WZB's science-supporting staff, especially our research manager Freifrau Editha von Colberg. The WZB library staff did a fantastic job in organising access to the necessary resources. Special thanks goes to Katharina Rötter from the WZB library, who provided me with a detailed literature research. Finally, I would like to thank Martha van Bakel who provided valuable research assistance.

Following my time at the WZB, I joined the Institute of International Relations at the TU Braunschweig as a postdoctoral researcher. I thank Anja P. Jakobi for providing this opportunity. The final work of this book has been conducted at the European New School of Digital Studies (European University Viadrina, Frankfurt(Oder)) which I joined in December 2021. I was also fortunate to join The Writing Academic (TWA), an online writing community. I wrote or edited many pages of the book during writing sessions in TWA's virtual co-working space. Thank you to the founders Katja Günther, Ingrid Scherübl, and Wiebke Vogelaar and to all TWA members.

The book has profited immensely from the following colleagues' feedback: Roisin Cronin, Jelena Cupać, Caroline Fehl, Mark Kersten, Bastian Loges, Neil Renic, Nina Reiners, Mariam Salehi, and Mitja Sienknecht. I also thank the participants of the Global Governance Colloquium at the WZB, the narrative writing workshop at the WZB, and the International Relations Colloquium at the Institute of International Relations at the TU Braunschweig for additional feedback. In addition, other scholars have helped by providing access to literature, sharing their own (at times unpublished) work, or pointing me to relevant literature: Bola Adediran, Alex Bellamy, Oheneba A. Boateng, Jeffrey L. Dunoff, Johannes Gerschewski, Maren Hofius, Marcus Holmes, Anna Holzscheiter, Philip Liste, Frédéric Mégret, Laura Saura, Matthew Weinert, Nicholas Wheeler, and Jan Wilkens. Last but not least, I am also grateful to the three anonymous readers who provided a critical but constructive reading of the original manuscript.

A special mention is reserved to my WZB and now Viadrina colleague and friend Mitja Sienknecht, with whom I shared an office at the WZB for three years and continued to do so virtually once the pandemic forced us to work from our homes. I thank her for her encouragement, chats about academia and life, and always being willing to listen. Mitja also provided excellent feedback on the revision process and she was the one who disovered the image that is now on the book's cover. Another special mention is reserved for my colleague and friend Nina Reiners. I am grateful for her constant encouragement, optimism and for helping me navigate the debates on human rights.

Turning the manuscript into a book was another whole enterprise. Thanks are due to the editors of the *Studies on International Courts and Tribunals* Series, Andreas Føllesdal and Geir Ulfstein. I am also incredibly thankful to the *Cambridge Universitsy Press* Editorial Team, commising editor Tom Randall, content managers Jane Bowbrick and Chloe Quinn, and senior editiorial assistant Gemma Smith for their guidance through the process. I also want to thank Indra Priyadarshini Siddharthan and Sindhuja Sethuraman for their assistance during production. Heather Dubnick provided excellent, constructive, and careful editing of all chapters, proofread the entire manuscript, and created the index. I would also like to thank her for her flexibility. Thanks are also due to Trent Hancock for editing and corrections during the production process.

The book is in much better shape, both in terms of content and style, due to all those mentioned. But of course, all and any remaining errors of facts, interpretation, style, and language are my responsibility.

I want to thank my parents for all they have done for me. Their love and support never withered, and I am grateful beyond words for that and much more. I want to express my deepest gratitude and love to my wife, Veronika, for all her support, in addition to having a full-time job and pursuing her career. She is a wonderful partner, and I am thankful for her love. She is also a great parent to our two children, Ezra and Kian, both of whom I also wish to thank. Ezra's curiosity about how many pages I had already written, his enthusiasm about our world, and his seemingly endless energy provided a much-needed compensation to writing. Born a year into the pandemic, Kian has brought happiness to my life in what has been a truly challenging time. Finally, two humans in my life will never be able to pick up this book and read it: My dad, who passed away in 2017, and our unborn baby, nicknamed Peanut, whom we lost in 2019, a few weeks into the pregnancy. My dad was a wonderful human being who taught me about the need to be kind in this world, open towards others, and to never give up. The baby we never got to know. I dedicate the book to both of their memories.

Materials Used

I wish to acknowledge that some of the material in the book has been previously published. I thank the publisher for the permission to reuse the material here.

Gholiagha, Sassan (2014a). Die Responsibility to Protect und Souveränität. In Volk, Christian and Kuntz, Friederike, eds., *Der Begriff der Souveränität in der transnationalen Konstellation*. Baden-Baden: Nomos Verlagsgesellschaft, 198–214.

Gholiagha, Sassan (2014b). The Responsibility to Protect: Words, deeds, and humanitarian interventions – A review essay, *Journal of International Political Theory*. 10(3), 361–370. https://journals.sagepub.com/doi/abs/10.1177/1755088214541035.

Gholiagha, Sassan (2015a). Individualised and yet dehumanised? Targeted killing via drones, *Behemoth*. 8(2), 128–153. https://ojs.ub.uni-freiburg.de/behemoth/.

Gholiagha, Sassan (2015b). To prevent 'future Kosovos and future Rwandas': A critical constructivist view on the responsibility to protect, *International Journal of Human Rights*. 19(8), 1074–1097. www.tandfonline.com/doi/abs/10.1080/13642987.2015.1082848.

Abbreviations

AL	Arab League
AU	African Union
AUMF	Authorization of the Use of Military Force
BRICS	Brazil, Russia, India, China, and South Africa
CIA	Central Intelligence Agency
ECCC	Extraordinary Chambers in the Courts of Cambodia
ECJ	European Court of Justice
EU	European Union
FATA	Federally Administered Tribal Areas
HRC	Human Rights Council
IAC	international armed conflict
ICC	International Criminal Court
ICCPR	International Covenant on Civil and Political Rights
ICISS	International Commission on Intervention and State Sovereignty
ICJ	International Court of Justice
ICL	international criminal law
ICTR	International Criminal Tribunal for Rwanda
ICTY	International Criminal Tribunal for the former Yugoslavia
IHL	international humanitarian law
IHRL	international human rights law
IL	International Law
IR	International Relations
JSOC	Joint Special Operations Command
LAWS	lethal autonomous weapon systems
MAM	military age male
NATO	North Atlantic Treaty Organisation

NGO	non-governmental organisation
NIAC	non-international armed conflict
OIC	Organisation of Islamic Cooperation
OTP	Office of the Prosecutor
R2P	Responsibility to Protect
RP	responsible protection
RwP	responsibility while protecting
UAV	unmanned aerial vehicle(s)
UDHR	Universal Declaration of Human Rights
UN	United Nations
UNAMIR	United Nations Assistance Mission for Rwanda
UNITAF	Unified Task Force
UNOSOM	United Nations Operation in Somalia
UNSC	United Nations Security Council
UNSMIS	United Nations Supervision Mission in Syria
US	United States
WSOD	World Summit Outcome Document

1

The Humanisation of Global Politics

The Hague, 8 March 2011. Three judges of the International Criminal Court's (ICC) Pre-Trial Chamber II decide on two applications of the ICC Prosecutor on summonses of appearance for six Kenyan individuals, regarding their role in the post-election violence after the 2007 Kenya elections (Commission of Inquiry into Post-Election Violence 2008). The Chamber decides to summon these six individuals to appear before the ICC (ICC 2011b, 2011c).

New York, 17 March 2011. The United Nations Security Council (UNSC) has just passed Resolution 1973, authorising the use of force against Libya under Chapter VII of the United Nations (UN) Charter. Relying on the Responsibility to Protect (R2P), the UNSC authorises member states to use all necessary means to protect the people of Libya, especially in the town of Benghazi, from an impending genocide (UNSC 2011e, 2011f).

A United States military base somewhere in Saudi Arabia, 30 September 2011. Several Predator and Reaper drones, the latter equipped with missiles, fly across the border into Yemen. Having reached their destination, drone pilots, thousands of miles away, fire those missiles, killing Anwar al-Awlaki, a US citizen and leading figure of Al-Qaeda in Yemen (Mazetti et al. 2013).[1]

1.1 THE APPEARANCE OF THE INDIVIDUAL HUMAN BEING IN GLOBAL POLITICS

All three examples described above share that they are concerned with individual human beings in global politics.[2] In this book, I see these episodes

[1] The chapter has profited immensely from constructive comments and feedback by Bastian Loges, Nina Reiners, and Mitja Sienknecht.

[2] I use the term 'global politics' to describe the legal and political relationship between a variety of actors on the global scale. Many scholars use the term 'international relations' instead, and

exemplifying a more significant shift in global politics, namely, what I introduce as the humanisation of global politics. Humanisation denotes the growing reference to and the appearance of the individual human being in global politics. The term highlights that who counts as human in global politics is a contentious issue with strong normative implications (Weinert 2015).[3]

The three examples that opened this book stem from three discourses on prosecution, protection, and targeted killing via drones. Although later discussed in more detail, discourse here refers to utterances by actors manifested in text. It also includes practices or actions. It is a space of sense-making (Holzscheiter 2014: 144). When I thus speak about the discourse on prosecution, I refer to statements and utterances by actors such as the ICC, victims, and alleged perpetrators, and I rely on official documents. I speak about conversations and debates in global politics where different actors discuss issues of prosecution in the context of global politics. And I speak about what takes place at The Hague in the chambers and offices of the ICC. When I speak about the discourse on protection, I refer to debates about politics of protection, R2P, and humanitarian interventions, which take place mainly in fora of relevant regional and international organisations. Here, actors debate about interventions and try to make sense of situations to see whether and how protection should occur. And I speak about interventions and military operations. Finally, when I speak about the discourse on killing or, more precisely, targeted killing operations via drones, I rely on documents such as NGO reports, government documents and speeches, and descriptions of drone strikes in the literature or the media. And I look at how actors talk about drone strikes and try to make sense of them as part of warfare and as part of their experience. I do not claim that the material I use in this book is a

for good reasons. Antje Wiener, for example, speaks of '*inter*national relations' to highlight the 'consideration of relations between different national entities and/or their representatives' (Wiener 2008: 1, emphasis in original). Friederike Kuntz suggest the concept of the international relation. She notes: 'The concept highlights that the international relation is enabled (and constrained) historically as simultaneously non-formal-governmental and formal-governmental and as a self-government *by humans as human individuals*, before all else' (Kuntz 2018: 1–2, emphasis added). My choice of the term 'global politics' is rather pragmatic. I wanted to prevent confusion with the capitalised 'International Relations'. Thus, when using the term 'International Relations' (IR or intermittently 'IR theory'), I refer to the discipline of International Relations. When using 'International Law' (IL or intermittently 'IL scholarship'), I refer to the discipline as well, compared to international law, which refers to the body of law regulating conduct of actors outside the domestic realm.

3 Other scholars talk about individualisation, especially in the context of war (Dill 2019: 1, 4; Welsh 2019b: 13). It sheds light on a specific aspect of global politics that moves away from the collective towards the individual; but for the reasons given, I use humanisation.

complete representation of the discourse. Instead, I posit that these manifestations of the discourse are sufficient to analyse it.

Let me illustrate the aforementioned shift towards the humanisation of global politics by drawing on the three examples from above. I rely on these three examples because the discourses from which they stem are central to the book's three case studies. First, the situation in Kenya before the ICC concerned possible mass atrocity crimes committed against innocent individuals. The ICC aimed to answer the question of who should be held accountable for those crimes. As the case study on prosecution will demonstrate, in the context of international criminal law (ICL), individual humans are positioned or position themselves as innocent victims or guilty perpetrators.

Second, in the UNSC resolution on Libya, Security Council members agreed on the need to protect individual human beings in Libya from a potential genocide. As the case study on protection will demonstrate, in the context of R2P individual human beings are positioned or position themselves as innocent individual human beings, worthy and in need of protection; or they are positioned as guilty individual human beings, as terrorists, who should not receive protection.

Finally, the drone strike described above provides a clear example of warfare directed against specific individual human beings. As the case study on killing will demonstrate in the context of targeted killing operations via drone strikes, individual human beings are being positioned as targets, often with reference to guilt or a future threat they pose. However, survivors of a drone strike or, in case of killed individuals, their relatives, attempt to position individuals as innocent victims.[4] Each of these three cases are examples of the humanisation of global politics.

Numerous International Relations (IR) and International Law (IL) studies, especially in the last two decades, have provided insights into various aspects of the humanisation of global politics (Ainley 2008: 38, 48; Brown and Ainley 2009: 221–222; Teitel 2011; Peters 2014; Weinert 2015; Partzsch 2017; Berenskötter 2018: 816; Welsh 2019b; Holmes and Wheeler 2020: 134). However, as Chapter 2 will demonstrate in detail, the appearance of the individual human being in global politics remains under-theorised. The book holds that a better theorisation of the humanisation of global politics and a different conceptualisation of the individual human being is necessary – and ultimately possible – than the majority of IR and IL offers to remedy this situation.

4 In all three examples, the reference to innocent and guilt should be noted. I return to these notions in Chapter 4.

The objective of this book is to demonstrate how to conceptualise and theorise the humanisation of global politics. The humanisation of global politics manifests itself in the appearance of the individual human being in discourses of global politics (Arendt 1998 [1958]: 198–199; Lang Jr. and Williams 2005: 225).[5] Hence, the book fulfils the objective by studying the appearance of the individual human being in discourses of global politics. Discourse is 'the space where human beings make sense of the material world, where they attach meaning to the world and where representations of the world become manifest' (Holzscheiter 2014: 144).

The book contributes to the study of global politics by systematically studying the humanisation of global politics. In doing so, it contributes to moving away from remaining focused on the state and statist concepts. This move away from states and statist concepts is both helpful and needed as (global) politics is not, as Morgenthau so famously proclaimed, amongst nations (Morgenthau 1954) but people or individuals (Sylvester 2013a, 2013b; Hansen-Magnusson 2020). Thus, the book focuses on the appearance of the individual human being in global politics. And the book contributes to constructivist IR theory by conceptualising the individual human being as a theoretical category of its own.

But why talk about the individual human being and not simply humans or individuals? 'Individual' indicates that the entities this book is concerned with are singular and not collective.[6] 'Human' indicates that this is about humans and not any other singular entity. 'Being' indicates that being, becoming, and appearance matters. Being also indicates, as Matthew Weinert demonstrates, the necessity of 'intersubjective understandings and standards that determine who is human' (Weinert 2015: 2).[7] For these reasons and the fact that the term connects better to related notions such as humanity and human rights than

[5] The term 'appearance' stems from Hannah Arendt's concept of the 'space of appearance'. This space of appearance comes into existence through the 'speech and action' of individual human beings and it is where humans appear (Arendt 1998 [1958]: 198–199; see also Weinert 2015: 44). The space of appearance and the appearance of the individual human being are both constituted by and constitutive of the socially constructed reality in which we live (Berger and Luckmann 1967 [1966]; Arendt 1998 [1958]: 208; Onuf 1989).

[6] I am, of course, cognizant of the collective dimensions of the topics I am concerned with, and I do not deny them. What I do, however, is to focus on the individuals within collectives such as groups. The most obvious example is constituted by my individual-based reading of R2P offered in Chapter 6.

[7] Let me add a semantic clarification: When I use the singular 'individual human being', this indicates a conceptual reference. In contrast, the plural 'individual human beings' indicates an empirical observation.

the term 'individuals', I chose to speak of individual human beings and not individuals or humans.[8]

To study this appearance, I draw on IR and IL to develop an interdisciplinary conceptual and theoretical framework. And I offer a specific conceptualisation of the individual human being in global politics. I suggest conceptualising individual human beings as participants in global politics. In this understanding, they are as much participants in global politics as are states and international organisations. For this conceptualisation, I draw on IL scholarship, primarily the work of Rosalyn Higgins (Higgins 1978–1979, 1978, 1994). I then use the concept of positions to operationalise, that is, make analytically accessible, the participation of individual human beings in discourses of global politics and thus their appearance.[9]

Furthermore, positioning individual human beings in discourses of global politics is constitutive of 'discursive spaces', understood as spaces in which individual human beings can attach meaning to the actions of other individual human beings and interact with others (for different and related uses of the term, see Holzscheiter 2010: 143; Wiener 2014b: 148; Papamichail and Partis-Jennings 2016; Parks 2018). Therefore, the book reconstructs the appearance of individual human beings by studying their (self-)positioning in discourses of global politics. As Markus Kornprobst notes in this context: 'it is still human beings and not structures who come to embark on certain courses of action rather than others' (Kornprobst 2011: 71). And this can either take place through being positioned by others or by self-positioning in the respective discourse.

Notably, while there is an abundance of references to the human or individual in IR theory and IL scholarship, this reference often takes place without any reflection on or conceptualisation and reconstruction of the appearance of the individual human being in discourses of global politics. That is not to say that I do not draw heavily on these disciplines. On the contrary, as will become apparent in this and the following chapters, I draw on feminist and constructivist IR theory and IL scholarship for the book's conceptual and theoretical framework. And I also rely on both disciplines regarding the book's three case studies concerned with prosecuting individual human beings, protecting them, and killing them with drones. I conceptualise

8 The terms have their own respective history and uses in IR, IL, and beyond. I do not engage with those distinctions here in detail but am cognizant of them.

9 While both the notion of positions and participations can be found elsewhere, I draw on IL literature to develop them as concepts. Chapter 3 provides a more detailed discussion.

the debates about these actions as discourses of global politics in which the individual human being appears.

Studying the humanisation of global politics requires problematising the individual human being, as their appearance in global politics remains understudied in both IR and IL. The book, therefore, problematises underlying assumptions existing in scholarship about the individual human being (Alvesson and Sandberg 2013: 5). Problematisation means being 'conscious of the social forces that construct, and thus shape and reshape, the institutions and practices represented' by a term (Wilmer 2002: xii). It means 'to treat "the human" as a question' (Weinert 2015: 22) or, in the case of the book, to treat the appearance of the individual human being in discourses of global politics as something to be studied, not as something given.[10] I demonstrate how, through studying those discourses and the positioning of individual human beings in global politics, scholars of global politics can analyse, conceptualise, and theorise the appearance of the individual human being in discourses and thereby the humanisation of global politics. Finally, by understanding individual human beings as participants and studying their (self-)positioning, the consequences of the humanisation of global politics for global politics come to the fore.

Section 1.2 outlines the humanisation of global politics in more detail, with reference to the book's three case studies, which, as the following will demonstrate, are cases of the humanisation of global politics.

1.2 PROSECUTING, PROTECTING, AND KILLING THE INDIVIDUAL HUMAN BEING

In this book, I study three discourses of global politics, the discourse on prosecution, the discourse on protection, and the discourse on targeted killing via drones. I do so in three case studies, which the present section will introduce. As Audie Klotz argues, 'cases are cases *of* something' (Klotz 2008: 43, emphasis in original). As indicated above, the cases I study in this book are cases of the humanisation of global politics. While I cannot present the 'universe of possible cases' (Klotz 2008: 43) here, some examples that illustrate the humanisation of global politics and the importance of studying it are

10 Rainer Hülsse offers another understanding of the term, referring to actors socially constructing something (he uses money-laundering as his example) as a global problem, which then requires a response on the global level (Hülsse 2007). In this manner, humanisation as such also remains a phenomenon that can and should be problematised. As the case studies will demonstrate, humanisation is not a priori good or bad for the individual human being in global politics or for global politics.

helpful. For example, debates about the protection of civilians in armed conflict (Carpenter 2005; Loges 2013; Willmot and Mamiya 2015; Bellamy 2016), debates about who the subject of human rights is (Celermajer and Lefebvre 2020b), as well as more general work on the role of human rights in global politics (Forsythe 2018) all illustrate the importance of studying the humanisation of global politics. Furthermore, scholars have observed the rise of 'people-centred norms' or 'people-based legitimacy standards' within international organisations (Dingwerth et al. 2019; Dingwerth and Witt 2020). Finally, the humanisation of global politics is also evident when the international community discusses 'foreign terrorist fighters' (United Nations 2014; Welsh 2019b: 19) or identifies the individual human being as the key target of human security in §143 of the 2005 World Summit Outcome Document (United Nations 2005b).

In the context of international law, blacklisting and targeted sanctions provide an excellent illustration of what I mean by the appearance, participation, and positioning of the individual human being in global politics. The most known example of targeted sanctions is the widely discussed *Kadi* case before the European Court of Justice (ECJ). The case itself was concerned with the legality and legitimacy of targeted sanctions against individual human beings due to alleged support for terrorist activities. The decision to target them with individual sanctions was neither communicated nor could they appeal the decision (Isiksel 2010; Kreuder-Sonnen 2020: 81–116). *Kadi* demonstrated how one specific individual human being, Shaykh Yassin Abdullah Kadi, appears as an individual human being in global politics. Through the court case, he participates in the discourse, and he positions himself as someone whose individual rights have been violated. Thus, he becomes a participant together with states, the UNSC, the European Union (EU), the ECJ, and, later on, the Ombudsperson established as part of the UN sanctions regime (Giumelli and Costa Buranelli 2020). The *Kadi* case and the surrounding debate concerned fundamental rights, the international legal order, and the European legal order (Halberstam and Stein 2009; de Búrca 2010; Kumm 2010) and related to questions of global security.

Questions of global security are also at the book's heart, as the three discourses I study are likewise strongly connected to global security.[11] Security is supposedly a 'hard issue' that belongs to the realm of the state or state-based organisations such as the North Atlantic Treaty Organization (NATO). Contrary

[11] The notion of security and the reference to individual human beings raises the question of why I do not begin with a human security approach. As I will discuss in Chapter 2, human security approaches remain focused on the structural conditions to ensure human security and less with the individual human being's appearance and social construction, which is what interests me.

to this assessment, the case studies will demonstrate that the individual human being has a central position within security discourses, making them exemplary cases from which generalisable knowledge about global politics can be drawn by transferring insights from the realm of global security to other realms and issue areas where individual human beings are also central.

The first case study analyses the discourse on prosecution, focusing on ICL and the work of the ICC. The second case study analyses the discourse on protection, focusing on R2P. Finally, the third case study analyses the discourse on killing, focusing on targeted killing via drones. Each case study then analyses the appearance of the individual human being in one of the three discourses, focusing on individual human beings as participants in the discourse. I reconstruct how other participants in the discourse position the individual human being and, where possible and feasible, how individual human beings position themselves.

Due to the shared focus on the conduct and treatment of individual human beings in global politics, all three case studies constitute viable cases to study the humanisation of global politics. The three discourses are all part of an ongoing global discourse about humanity and the humanisation of global politics (Teitel 2011; Barnett 2012; Kettemann 2013: 40; van Beers et al. 2014; Weinert 2015). While debates about individual rights have been the foundation of political change and challenge to existing systems of authority for a long time (Reus-Smit 2013), the scope and degree of connection between these discourses is a relatively new development. The three cases overlap on various dimensions, such as the focus on specific crimes in the case of R2P and ICC/ICL, reference to past conduct in the case of ICC/ICL and drone strikes, and reference to (potential) future threats in the case of ICC/ICL and drone strikes.[12] As becomes apparent through this brief description, all three discourses stem from the realm of global security.

In conclusion, the individual human being and the humanisation of global politics are omnipresent. Yet, as Section 1.3 will show, this observation has not been sufficiently conceptualised and theorised by those studying global politics, leading to a double mismatch.

1.3 THE INDIVIDUAL HUMAN BEING IN IR AND IL: A DOUBLE MISMATCH

There is a double mismatch concerning the appearance of the individual human being in global politics, on the one hand, and the disciplines that study global politics, on the other hand, that is, between IR theory and IL.

[12] For more on these connections see Figure 5.2.

The first mismatch exists between observations in global politics about growing humanisation, on the one hand, and a lack of theorising of this humanisation in IR theory, on the other hand. The observation of a growing humanisation of global politics, noted by many scholars and demonstrated by the examples and the three cases presented above, is neither sufficiently theorised nor adequately conceptualised. While we live in a world of our making (Onuf 1989) and self-creation (Allott 1992: 220; McCorquodale 2004: 484), a world in which we 'produce' or 'make' ourselves and others (Berger and Luckmann 1967 [1966]: 183; Onuf 2013: 3–4; Weinert 2015), the individual human being has so far received insufficient attention with regards to its appearance in global politics. Of course, many IR and IL scholars have studied humans, as Matthew Weinert rightly asserts (Weinert 2015: 18–19). Where I identify a gap is on the conceptual and theoretical level. IR scholars have scrutinised concepts and entities in IR theory, such as the state, international organisations, institutions, or regimes. However, the present inquiry does not take the appearance of the individual human in global politics for granted or for a priori normatively as desirable. Contrary to this, the aforementioned problematisation of the individual human being I undertake in this book will demonstrate that the growing humanisation also negatively affects individual human beings in global politics.

Furthermore, in problematising the individual human being in global politics, I argue that their appearance is something that scholars of global politics must question and analyse. And I hold that IR theory should do so without relying on existing concepts to cover the individual human being in global politics as this risks overstretching existing concepts (Alvesson and Sandberg 2013: 5; Weinert 2015: 22; Welsh 2019b: 10). However, 'any problematisation necessarily takes its point of departure within a specific metatheoretical position' (Alvesson and Sandberg 2011: 252). Therefore, subsequent chapters discuss these positions on the level of literature, theory, and methodology. In addition, problematising the individual human being in global politics allows for a necessary advancement of IR theory to theorise and conceptualise the humanisation of global politics.

From the perspective of many IR approaches, global politics remains dominated by states and collective actors. Does all this talk about individuals in global politics mean that states do not matter? Not at all. After all, states set up the ICC, state representatives sit in the chamber of the UNSC, and states employ drones in targeted killing operations. Furthermore, what states do and what state representatives say matters for understanding what is going on in the discourses I study.

My point is a different one. I do not mean to exchange the individual human being with the state in studying global politics. Instead, I argue and want to demonstrate that individual human beings matter in global politics. Their appearance, while not unnoticed, ought to be theorised and conceptualised by those studying global politics similarly to the way other entities in global politics have been theorised and conceptualised. Does that mean that all individual human beings can participate equally and at all times in global politics? Certainly not.[13] Perhaps we could discern different degrees of participation and different kinds of participation, some more active, some more passive. But I am not interested in measuring or comparing different degrees and kinds of participation of the individual human being in global politics. I am, to reiterate, interested in what comes before, that is, their appearance and how that appearance comes to be.[14] Given the appearance of the individual human being in global politics, its growing importance, and the fact that individual human beings are no longer being exclusively mediated[15] through states or collective actors reveals a limitation: The humanisation of global politics as described above is not analytically graspable for those approaches.

The limitation in grasping this humanisation is due to the fact that many approaches in IR theory focus on grand theorising and macropolitics (Solomon and Steele 2017: 268), which results in the marginalisation or even complete invisibility of individual human beings in global politics (Weinert 2015: 19–20). However, even though much of IR theory is less concerned with the specific issue of the appearance of the individual human being in discourses of global politics, I do not start from scratch. There is no *tabula rasa*. Classical realists focus on human nature to understand the structure of global politics (Morgenthau 1954). In liberal thinking, the focus is often on protecting their rights and liberties in relation to states (Freeden and Stears 2013: 342) or their interests and goals (Moravcsik 2008: 236). And of course, there is a large body of human rights literature, but work on the human in human rights remains limited (Celermajer and Lefebvre 2020a). Furthermore, there is

[13] However, there is much validity in the argument that, normatively speaking, individuals ought to participate in and have access to global politics whenever they are affected by it (Wiener 2018: 1).

[14] All this connects to questions around the notion of agency, which I will take up throughout the book.

[15] Mediation, to briefly explain, refers to the fact that states no longer act as mediators between the individual human being and institutions of global politics such as international organisations (Heupel and Zürn 2017: 4).

growing interest in the emotions of individual human beings (Crawford 2000; Bleiker and Hutchison 2008; Koschut 2020; Loges 2020).

In sum, while humans or individuals have received attention within IR theory (Jacobi and Freyberg-Inan 2015a), many of the approaches concerning the individual human being see the individual human being as given or fixed, or they reduce individual human beings to their human nature. This fixation or assumption of givenness prevents a better understanding of the appearance of the individual human being in global politics. Thus, there is still work to be done regarding the systematic reflection within IR scholarship about the appearance of the individual human being in discourses of global politics. This book intends to overcome the first mismatch by providing a theorisation of the humanisation of global politics.

The second mismatch manifests itself in comparing the two disciplines concerned with global politics: IR theory and IL. While the former misses a theorisation of the humanisation of global politics, the latter has a strong focus on the individual human being in global politics. As Marcus Holmes and colleagues note, there is a growing focus on the 'first image', that is, the individual in IR (Holmes et al. 2021: 214), but no 'grand theory' has developed as part of this focus (Holmes et al. 2021: 218). While I do not necessarily share the view that we need another 'grand theory' in IR, theorising the humanisation of global politics remains a necessary undertaking.

Due to IR theory not having done so, the appearance of the individual human being in discourses of global politics has been primarily framed within debates of IL. Here, more than half a century ago, Hersch Lauterpacht identified the individual human being as 'the ultimate unit of all law' (Lauterpacht 1946: 27). International law now actively intervenes in the life and conduct of individual human beings without the state as an intermediary (Besson 2009: 349), as the cases before the ICC, cases such as *Kadi* before the ECJ (Isiksel 2010), individual sanctions (Eckes 2013), and a growing body of regulations by international organisations concerning individuals' conducts all illustrate (Isiksel and Thies 2013: 151). Chris Brown is, therefore, correct in observing 'the increasing importance of the individual as an international actor, as expressed through the international human rights regime and changing conceptions of international law' (Brown 2002b: 199). Likewise, Kirsten Ainley notes that '[t]he twentieth century saw the unprecedented individualization, legalization, and criminalization of responsibility in international relations' (Ainley 2011: 407; see also Mégret 2017: 33–34).

Studying global politics without studying the humanisation of global politics risks leaving blind spots in its understanding of global politics. As

Jennifer Welsh has argued, there are tensions between the growing rights of individuals and the sovereignty of states in areas such as protection, the use of force, and ICL (Welsh 2019b: 10). Chris Brown and Kirsten Ainley point to the growing importance of individuals with reference to human rights and questions of protection (Brown and Ainley 2009: 222–242), pointing especially to the need for normative theorising (Brown and Ainley 2009: 222). Furthermore, a focus on 'grand theory . . . may direct scholarly attention away from the humanity of politics' (Solomon and Steele 2017: 272). By studying the appearance of the individual human being in global politics, scholars can understand current processes and developments about the individual human being in global politics better.

The growing influence of international law on the individual human being and a growing humanisation of global politics raises critical theoretical challenges. It introduces a high degree of change and innovation into global politics. In other words, international law is highly relevant for global politics and hence for IR scholars. At the same time, institutions of global politics, such as international organisations, and global politics itself matters for international law and hence for IL scholars. By providing an interdisciplinary analysis of the humanisation of global politics, the book overcomes the second mismatch. Table 1.1 summarises the double mismatch identified and outlines how the book overcomes the mismatch.

Understanding the humanisation of global politics is relevant for scholars of IR and IL, regardless of their specific interest, because individual human beings do matter in global politics and, therefore, as this book holds, they matter for IR theory and IL scholarship. Section 1.4 presents the guiding research questions and the book's arguments based on the double mismatch identified.

TABLE 1.1. *A double mismatch*

Mismatch	How the book overcomes the mismatch
Observations in global politics about the growing humanisation of global politics vs. theorising this humanisation in IR theory	Offering a theorisation of the humanisation of global politics.
The discipline of IL has a strong focus on the individual human being in global politics vs. the discipline of IR misses a theorisation of the humanisation of global politics	Providing an interdisciplinary analysis of the humanisation of global politics.

Source: Gholiagha

1.4 RESEARCH QUESTIONS AND ARGUMENTS

Two research questions guide this book: How should we conceptualise the humanisation of global politics? How can the individual human being be included in IR theory as a category of its own? These questions relate to three arguments: theoretical, conceptual, and empirical.

Theoretical Argument: The majority of IR theory concerning the individual human being either presupposes that the individual human being is a given or fixed entity or reduces them to their 'human nature' (Brown 2009; Herborth 2012; Lebow 2012). Both limitations weaken the insights that IR theory can provide into the appearance of the individual human being in global politics and the subsequent humanisation of global politics. I develop a conceptual and theoretical framework with building blocks from feminist and constructivist IR theory and IL to overcome these limitations. As I demonstrate in this book, such a conceptual and theoretical framework can transcend these issues of fixation and givenness and overcome this mismatch.

My point of departure for studying the humanisation of global politics lies in feminist IR theory, which has always spotlighted human beings[16] and in a constructivist ontology. As J. Ann Tickner and Jacqui True have argued, 'the discipline [of IR] came late to feminism' (Tickner and True 2018: 222), challenging accounts of disciplinary history that argue that 'feminism came late to international relations' (Tickner and True 2018: 222). In bringing together feminist and constructivist approaches, I begin my discussions of the literature and my theoretical and conceptual framework with feminist IR literature. Normatively, this book aims to contribute to feminist scholars' call to go beyond studying individual human beings as data points but rather as participants (Sylvester 2013a: 614). Relying on and referencing feminist approaches to IR theory throughout the book, I work simultaneously with a constructivist ontology and constructivist approaches to IR to contribute to the further advancement of constructivist IR theory by including the individual human being into IR theory as a theoretical category of its own.

Conceptual Argument: The book contributes to IR theory by making the argument to conceptualise the individual human being in global politics as

[16] There are of course additional notable exceptions not on the level of approaches but on the level of specific scholarly works, such as Matthew Weinert's *Making Humans* (Weinert 2015); Daniel Jacobi's and Annette Freyberg-Inan's edited volume *Human Beings in International Relations* (Jacobi and Freyberg-Inan 2015a); Jennifer Welsh's work on the individualisation of war (2019b); as well as Marcus Holmes' and Nicholas Wheeler's work on the relevance of studying interaction between individuals for global politics (Holmes and Wheeler 2020). I discuss those and other works in more detail in Chapter 2.

socially constructed. The idea of conceptualising the individual human being as a social construction has been made before by some scholars (Wilmer 2002; Jacobi 2015; Weinert 2015). Others have focused on the role of the individual human being in IR theory (Jacobi and Freyberg-Inan 2015a), the importance of social interactions between individuals (Kornprobst 2011: 84; Holmes and Wheeler 2020), the way the individual requires protection from negative effects of policies implemented by international organisations (Zürn and Heupel 2017), the aforementioned shifting focus of international organisations towards 'people-centred norms' or 'people-based legitimacy standards' (Dingwerth et al. 2019; Dingwerth and Witt 2020), or on the effects of that growing humanisation on war (Welsh 2019b). I offer a reconstruction of the socially constructed individual human being by studying their appearance in discourses of global politics.

I rely on various concepts from both IR and IL for my conceptual framework: gender and body from feminist approaches, participants and positions and human and individual rights and duties from IL, norms and language from constructivist IR. Drawing on these concepts and the theoretical approaches from which they stem, I can analytically grasp the appearance of the individual human being in discourses of global politics and thereby study the humanisation of global politics.[17]

Empirical Argument: The case studies will demonstrate that the appearance of the individual human being in discourses of global politics results from participation in and acts of positioning the individual human being within these discourses (Weinert 2015: 33). The book employs a 'lens of humanization' (Kettemann 2013: 40) to add value to IR theory and IL scholarship by providing a systematic analysis of the humanisation of global politics. It does so by providing detailed case studies of the discourses on prosecution, protection, and targeted killing via drones. Finally, through the three arguments, the book also contributes to constructivist IR theory, which I outline in the following.

1.5 CONTRIBUTION

While employing a constructivist ontology, this book aims to develop constructivist IR theory to include the individual human being as a category of its own. This advancement of constructivist literature is achieved by demonstrating how the appearance of the individual human being can be conceptualised as a social construction, an argument that large parts of the constructivist

[17] See Chapter 3 and Figure 3.1 for a more detailed account of my theoretical and conceptual framework.

literature have neglected (Sikkink 2011b; notable exceptions are Sikkink 2011a; Weinert 2015; Welsh 2019b). In line with constructivist studies, the present enquiry is interested in understanding rather than explaining (Hollis and Smith 1990: 1). For constructivism, this means to ask not only 'how things *are* but ... how they *became* what they are' (Adler 2013: 121, emphasis in original). Therefore, this book offers valuable insight into how the individual being in global politics *is* and how they *became*. This insight is based on the relational assumption that the individual human being in global politics becomes an entity through social interaction (Jackson and Nexon 1999: 293).

Constructivists, by and large, remain focused on collective actors and states (Brown and Ainley 2009: 221). However, as Gert Krell points out, ideas and social structures, central concepts of constructivism need 'carriers', that is, 'humans, who stand for them, who advocate them and, if necessary, enforce them through coercion and force' (Krell 2009: 379, my translation).[18] Gert Krell's point brings up the role of concepts within IR. As Friedrich Kratochwil has argued, only a theoretical conception of something that exists allows us to know what it is (Kratochwil 2008: 82). Likewise, Stefano Guzzini rightly argues that 'categories are the condition for the possibility of knowledge' (Guzzini 2000: 157). Therefore, this book aims to do for the individual human being what constructivists have done for the state, institutions, and organisations. The book provides a theoretical conception of the humanisation of global politics and thereby of the social construction of the individual human being in global politics.

The humanisation of global politics constitutes a real shift in global politics. Although, on the one hand, this is a matter of ethics and theoretical consideration (Brown and Ainley 2009: 222), on the other hand, these developments have real-life implications and effects. Individual human beings are prosecuted, protected, and killed in the context of global politics, and they have become participants amongst others in global politics. Thus, the book contributes to the theorisation of the humanisation of global politics and the humanisation of IR theory. Sections 1.6 and 1.7 outline how the book provides this contribution and conducts the necessary analysis by first presenting the book's abductive research logic, interpretative methodology, and interdisciplinary approach before summarising the subsequent chapters.

[18] The concept of carriers originates of course from Max Weber's theory of social action. For Max Weber, only individual human beings could be seen as 'carriers' of sense making kinds of action (Weber 2015 [1921]: 15). I owe this insight to Maren Hofius. See also the discussion of Max Weber in the context of an internalist approach to the study of global politics provided by Mervyn Frost and Silviya Lechner (Frost and Lechner 2016: 309).

1.6 ABDUCTIVE RESEARCH LOGIC, INTERPRETATIVE METHODOLOGY, INTERDISCIPLINARY APPROACH

Theory in this book appears twice: once at the outset and once at the end. In the beginning, the role of theory is to offer a theoretical and a conceptual framework, a lens to study the humanisation of global politics. I draw on feminist and constructivist IR approaches and IL scholarship for these frameworks. Then, drawing on the results of a first case study for which I employ the conceptual and theoretical framework, I develop a methodological framework to analyse the other two case studies. Thus, the book neither follows an inductive nor a deductive approach. Instead, an abductive research logic is employed, meaning that the book continually oscillates between theory and empirics. Such a research logic facilitates a reflexive research process that draws simultaneously on theoretical and empirical insights, each informing the other. Finally, following the empirical analysis, I return to IR theory writ large and constructivist IR theory. Here I refine the existing constructivist approach (in all its variations) by adding the individual human being as a theoretical category of their own.

To theorise the appearance of the individual human being in global politics, an interdisciplinary perspective combining IR and IL is necessary. It allows overcoming the double mismatch outlined above. Due to the importance of international law for global politics, IR theory should engage more strongly with these developments within international law to provide a better account of global politics. International law is not only the empirical substance to engage with; it is to be understood as a 'language game' (Kratochwil 2014: 74). The ontological status of the individual human being concerns IR theory and IL because the individual human being appears in global politics. To do justice to the 'essential relationship between law and politics' (Higgins 1976, 85, cited in Higgins 1994: 5), this book will employ an interdisciplinary perspective on the humanisation of global politics. This interdisciplinary approach is rewarding for IR and IL, which both IR and IL scholars have noted (Kratochwil 1989: 1; Dunoff and Pollack 2013; Kratochwil 2014). It also allows, as Anthony F. Lang Jr. and colleagues claim, 'to understand interacting and overlapping dimensions of reality' (Lang Jr. et al. 2013: 3–4). IL scholarship is thus an integral part of the theoretical and conceptual framework and the case studies.

This book employs an interpretative methodology to reconstruct discourses to analyse the appearance of the individual human being in them. More specifically, positioning analysis as a well-established sociological method

(Davies and Harré 1990; van Langenhove and Harré 1999) is employed and transferred to the study of global politics. In a nutshell, positioning analysis takes up the middle-ground between micro-level analysis of language in conversation analysis and macro-level analysis, often prevalent in many forms of discourse analysis (but see Holzscheiter 2010 for an approach that combines the micro with the macro). It allows identifying how individuals position themselves within a discourse or are positioned by others.

However, in focusing on the individual human being, I do not engage in methodological individualism. Relying on a methodological individualism risks reifying the individual human being whose appearance in global politics interests me (see Dombrowski 1998: 388 for a similar point). Instead, as I will demonstrate in the case studies in detail, the methodological approach I have chosen allows me to reconstruct the appearance of the individual human being in discourses through the positions they take up or are assigned by other speakers in the discourse (Korobov 2001; Kruse 2014: 500; Lucius-Hoene and Deppermann 2014). Such an approach enables to systematically analyse the appearance of the individual human being in these discourses. In doing so, it provides the epistemological solution to the ontological problem of how we can know that the assumption of the appearance of the individual human being in discourses of global politics holds (Jackson 2011: 27).

More specifically, the case studies discuss the relevance of focusing on the individual human being in each case in more detail, engage with the relevant literature for each discourse, and provide a novel and in-depth analysis of empirical material. In this empirical material (texts), the discourse is manifested. I rely on several sources for these texts. Building on a detailed critical discussion of the relevant secondary literature on each discourse, I select central documents from international institutions, governments, non-state actors, and the media. In addition, I corroborate the analysis through several interviews I conducted in New York and Geneva in 2014. If, as this book posits, the individual human being appears within discourses of global politics, then it will be possible to reconstruct the appearance of the individual human being. Section 1.7 provides a detailed description of the book's chapters, outlining how the book will proceed in this reconstruction.

1.7 OUTLOOK: THE CHAPTERS OF THE BOOK

Chapter 2 – Humanisation in IR Theory and International Law – critically reviews the relevant IR and IL literature. The objective of this chapter is to identify gaps, strengths, and weaknesses of several approaches in both disciplines concerning the book's objective, arguments, and research questions. In addition, it provides an answer to whether alternative approaches to the chosen framework provide a viable pathway to conceptualise the humanisation of global politics. Regarding alternative approaches in IR, I discuss realist and liberal approaches, the literature on human rights and human security, and literature dealing with concepts such as self, identity, and agency. Regarding IL, I discuss, for similar reasons, the notion of mediation and how the individual human being, the international community, and the state relate to each other. And I offer a discussion of international law and the individual human being.

In Chapter 3 – The Social Construction of the Individual Human Being: A Conceptual and a Theoretical Framework – I develop a conceptual and theoretical framework based on feminist and critical constructivist IR approaches and approaches from International Law. To this end, the chapter brings together building blocks drawn from these approaches. The chapter demonstrates the advancement the framework makes possible. Furthermore, it provides evidence for the value each of the approaches and concepts adds to the frameworks and the analysis.

Chapter 4 presents the first of the three case studies: Guilty and Innocent: The Individual Human Being in International Criminal Law. It analyses the discourse on prosecution with a focus on the ICC. In line with the abductive research logic, the position of this first case study before the chapter on the analytical framework is chosen deliberately for two reasons: First, the case study is an illustrative case. The applicability and value added of the theoretical and conceptual frameworks are demonstrated in a case where the existing secondary literature already provides strong support for the results of the empirical analysis. Second, I draw heuristics from this first case study to guide my analysis of the two other case studies, which I embed in a larger analytical framework developed in Chapter 5. While this poses specific challenges in terms of the linearity of writing, it better reflects the non-linear approach of research that underlies this book.

Apart from these theoretical and methodological purposes, the chapter has a substantial purpose, demonstrating how the individual human being appears in the discourse on prosecution and how this appearance matters for global politics. The case study shows how the individual human being appears as a perpetrator or victim. This appearance is based on assertions of innocence and guilt, which makes prosecution and the deliverance of justice to individual human beings possible in the first place. While this is – in this case – not a novel idea, the chapter provides evidence for the humanisation of global politics. Furthermore, it demonstrates the relevance of the appearance of the individual human being in discourses of global politics.

Chapter 5 – Heuristics and Positions: A Framework for Analysing Discourses of Humanisation – discusses what is necessary from a methodological perspective to analyse the appearance of the individual human being in global politics. To this end, the chapter develops an interpretative methodology and presents in more detail the abductive research logic and the method employed in the case studies. As mentioned above, the book draws on positioning analysis and introduces it to the conceptual toolbox of IR scholars. The chapter also outlines the research design and its operationalisation for the case studies. The analytical framework allows overcoming methodological individualism by studying the appearance of the individual human being in global politics instead of studying individual human beings. In doing so, the individual human being is made analytically accessible for scholars of global politics.

Chapter 6 presents the second of the three case studies: Protecting the Individual Human Being from Mass Atrocities. The case study offers a critical discussion of the literature and the development of R2P. The chapter then analyses the discourse on Libya and Syria concerning actions to protect civilians and the potential use of force to do so. The analysis focuses mainly on UN Security Council deliberations. Finally, the chapter demonstrates how the individual human being appears in the discourse on protection as an innocent civilian or guilty perpetrator/terrorist. As will be demonstrated, this matters for enabling a politics of protection. By analysing the debate on the intervention in Libya in 2011 and dealing with the conflict in Syria, mainly focusing on the years 2011–2015, respectively, I demonstrate how these politics of protection play out.

Chapter 7 presents the third of the three case studies: Killing the Individual Human Being via Drones. Here I look at targeted killings and the growing use of drones in this practice. The chapter offers a detailed discussion of the predominantly legal and ethical debate. In doing so, the chapter demonstrates the relevance of an analysis guided by insights from IR theory. But it also discusses legal questions concerning International Human Rights Law (IHRL) and International Humanitarian Law (IHL). The case study engages in detail with the general discourse on drone strikes and targeted killings and provides an in-depth analysis of specific strike types and drone strikes. The analysis demonstrates how the individual human being appears as an innocent civilian who should not be killed (if possible) or as a guilty terrorist who should be killed.

Chapter 8 – The Individual Human Being as a Category: A Conclusion and an Outlook, returns to theory. To this end, the chapter weaves together the results of the case studies and the theoretical and methodological considerations. The chapter, serving as a conclusion to the book, simultaneously summarises the book, revisits the issue of interdisciplinarity, and presents its results. It also discusses the book's contribution and value added. Most importantly, it demonstrates how the results of the empirical case studies are relevant for IR theory and what implications for IR theory, IL scholarship, and the study of global politics can be derived from these results. Finally, the chapter outlines future research based on the book's results.

2

Humanisation in IR Theory and International Law

2.1 INTRODUCTION

Chapter 1 outlined what this book is concerned with: a better understanding of the humanisation of global politics. As developed in the previous chapter in detail, humanisation refers to the growing reference to and the individual human being's appearance in global politics.[1] The obvious question to ask is: Where can we find insights into the humanisation of global politics? This chapter will demonstrate that while specific IR and IL approaches provide a promising pathway towards studying the humanisation of global politics, they all suffer from certain gaps and omissions. Chapter 1 pointed to an interdisciplinary approach bringing together IR and IL literature as especially promising. The present chapter aims to critically assess this potential contribution, carve out relevant insights, and present how IR and IL scholars have dealt with the individual human being in global politics.[2]

Such an assessment is always incomplete and selective. Therefore, I offer neither a history of the disciplines nor a textbook-like systematic overview (for IR theory, see Dunne et al. 2020; for IL, see Shaw 2021). Instead, this chapter's objective is to identify gaps, strengths, and weaknesses of several approaches in both disciplines concerning the book's objective and argument (Cox 1981: 128). To recall, the book's objective is to study the humanisation of global politics. In doing so, it makes a threefold argument. First, it argues that IR theory is currently not sufficiently equipped to understand the individual

[1] The term 'humanisation' is of course used by other scholars with somewhat different meanings. Examples include recognising others as humans, for example, in diplomatic encounters (Holmes and Wheeler 2020: 150), describing how 'dehumanized come to be viewed, accepted, and treated as fully human' (Weinert 2015: 2), and focusing international law towards the individual (Kettemann 2013: 11).

[2] I am thankful for the valuable comments and feedback provided by Nina Reiners.

human being's appearance in global politics. In response, the book develops a theoretical framework that is able to do so. Second, the book argues that the individual human being is socially constructed. Third, the individual human being's appearance in discourses of global politics is to be grasped through the concepts of participation and positions.

This chapter provides the foundation for the conceptual and theoretical frameworks that I develop in Chapter 3. To this end, the chapter provides an overview of how various approaches within IR theory and IL have engaged with the individual human being in global politics. I begin by discussing the humanisation of IR theory and various approaches in IR, namely, feminism, constructivism, realism, and liberalism (Section 2.2). I then discuss specific strands of literature dealing with humans in global politics, namely, the human rights and human security literature. I then provide an assessment of the humanisation of international law (Section 2.3). Here, I present an understanding of IL that moves beyond states, acknowledges the individual human being as a participant, and is cognisant of the individual human being's position. I posit that such an understanding of IL seems especially promising to study the humanisation of global politics. A brief conclusion (Section 2.4) summarises the key insight of this chapter: that most approaches stemming from IR theory rely on what Daniel Jacobi and Annette Freyberg-Inan have called 'auxiliary constructions' (Jacobi and Freyberg-Inan 2015b: 16) and/or rely on fixed assumptions about the individual human being. The conclusion also identifies feminist and constructivist approaches in conjunction with non-statist approaches to international law as a way forward to analyse the humanisation of global politics.

2.2 THE HUMANISATION OF IR THEORY

IR has not been entirely oblivious to the importance of the individual human being in global politics. As the discussion on feminist approaches to IR will demonstrate, calls for a stronger focus on humans in global politics have been made for some decades already. Other approaches have also not been ignorant of humans in global politics. In fact, 'all IR theories hint at a human element in world politics' (Jacobi and Freyberg-Inan 2015b: 26). However, I argue that existing insights and approaches are not sufficiently developed to understand the humanisation of global politics. Realist (and other) approaches rely on a limited notion of human nature. Liberal approaches assume that the individual is already fully constituted before entering any interaction. Moreover, even those approaches open to the idea of social constructions, such as feminism and constructivism, do not think about the social construction of actors 'all the way down' to the individual human being. However, feminist and constructivist scholars' significant contributions are part of the book's conceptual and theoretical framework – developed in Chapter 3 – enabling scholars to understand the humanisation of global politics.

Chapter 1 already demonstrated the growing appearance of the individual human being in global politics in several discourses of global politics. This growing appearance must be understood as part of larger changes, which have been ongoing for some time. They are characterised by the fact that '*[i]ndividuals* and nonstate entities are increasingly able to partake in shaping the international legal order through the forum of the state and are becoming international, indeed transnational, actors in their own right' (Jacobson 1997: 3, emphasis added). There is an 'increasing focus on the *individual*, rather than the state, as the *key agent in international politics*' (Ainley 2008: 38, emphasis added). Therefore, IR theory has acknowledged a more powerful position of the individual human being in global politics, with some even suggesting conceptualising individuals as institutions (Onuf 2016: 127).

However, studies often concern themselves more with the effect of individuals on global politics rather than studying the fundamental development of the humanisation of global politics. Marcus Holmes and Nicholas Wheeler have argued that studies on the effect of individuals on global politics can be grouped into 'three broad domains': 'first, the causal power of dispositions, traits, personality, and experiences of leaders and diplomats; second, the relevance and nature of leaders' beliefs and emotions in decision-making; and third, the interaction between leaders in diplomacy, either in dyads, mediated triads, or larger groups' (Holmes and Wheeler 2020: 138). Other scholars are concerned with 'powerful individuals' who act not in an official capacity, like celebrities or philanthropists (Partzsch 2014, 2017). Studying the human being in global politics in some form is more and more commonplace in IR. Yet systematic accounts are still in the minority (Aalto 2011; Jacobi and Freyberg-Inan 2012; Weinert 2015; Jacobi and Freyberg-Inan 2015a; Holmes et al. 2021). There is one exception: feminist approaches to IR, which have always argued for taking the gendered experience of individuals into account (Grant and Newland 1991: 1). As J. Ann Tickner and Jacqui True note, IR begins to catch up with feminist scholarship (Tickner and True 2018). This book is also to be understood in this fashion. A discussion of feminist approaches will, therefore, be provided both here and in Chapter 3.

One especially notable work concerned with questions similar to mine is Matthew Weinert's *Making Human* (Weinert 2015). In his book, Weinert begins with those who are de-humanised and asks how they can become human again (Weinert 2015: 1). He rightly identifies several sites (Weinert 2015: 3), such as the UN Security Council and international courts and tribunals, as those able to engage in those processes of humanisation. He categorises their conduct into five processes: recognition, resistance, reflection, replications, and responsibility (Weinert 2015: 3). Matthew Weinert is correct in noting that 'we cannot understand one construct (world society, humanity, the cosmopolitan polity, or world order) without understanding the composition and construction of its component parts (human beings or individuals)' (Weinert 2015: 22). Yet, in contrast to Matthew Weinert, I look at the appearance of the individual human being in discourses, not 'being human' as a question of status (Weinert 2015: 25, 207). Humanity, as Adrian Gallagher rightly notes, 'is often portrayed in two ways: humans and humankind' (Gallagher 2016: 344). Matthew Weinert discusses the human in the context of humanity (Weinert 2015: 22). But as the present book's interest ultimately rests with the individual human being in global politics, I leave debates about humanity and humankind to others; in subsequent chapters, however, I will draw on these works as they certainly provide relevant insights into better understanding the individual human being (Owens 2008; Peters 2009; Teitel 2011; Weinert 2015; Gallagher 2016).

The individual human being has been described as a sovereign being (Annan 1999: 81) and as a 'social individual … [which] is at the heart of global politics and, indeed, *both its architect and building block*' (Tétreault and Lipschutz 2005: 165, emphasis added). Yet, as will become apparent, in both the case of the 'architect' and the 'building block', the individual human being has either been reduced to one of their properties, such as 'human nature', 'identity', or 'agency', or they appear fully constituted. Thus, in both cases, IR theory is left with a gap in understanding the appearance of the individual human being in global politics and studying the process of social construction upon which this appearance rests (see Srivastava 2020 for an overview of different types of social construction).

I structure the following presentation of the humanisation of IR theory along the borders of sub-disciplinary categories. Such a structure has one significant disadvantage: it creates boundaries in places where conceptual overlaps exist, as in the case of assumptions about human nature, which can be found in several approaches or sub-disciplines within IR theory. Despite this weakness, the structure has one advantage: it allows reconstructing how IR theory has dealt with the individual human being along the lines of disciplinary history. Related to this is a second advantage. Such a systematic approach can help to overcome the association of IR theory 'with realist, statist, and/or rationalist assumptions' often found in IL scholarship (Dunoff and Pollack 2013: 12). It, therefore, supports IL's development to open up towards liberal and constructivist approaches as well (Dunoff and Pollack 2013: 12). Scholars have also considered feminist perspectives when studying international law (Charlesworth and Chinkin 2000; Charlesworth 2016).

Therefore, the following discussion provides IL scholars with a broader picture of IR in the context of the humanisation of global politics. While I do not follow calls for eclectic theorising connecting to this opening up (Dunoff and Pollack 2013: 12), I believe that IL can indeed profit from a more pluralistic understanding of IR. In sum, the advantages of discussing the humanisation of IR theory by relying on classical ways of structuring overviews of IR outweigh the disadvantage that such a structure creates. As feminist scholars were the first to argue for focusing on individuals' gendered experiences to understand global politics better, I begin my discussion of IR theory with their work.

2.2.1 *Feminist Approaches: Gendered IR and Gendered Global Politics*

Feminist approaches to IR were the first arguing to include the (gendered) individual human being into our understanding of global politics and therefore into IR theory (Whitworth 1989: 266; Hill 1999: 107; True 2009: 237; Prügl 2012: 656). Feminist research has been applied to a wide range of disciplines and fields within the social sciences. Within political science, feminist scholars have contributed to public policy (Ackelsberg 1992), Marxism (Hartsock 1987), and, especially relevant to this book, IR theory (Brown 1988; Birckenbach 1991; Zalewski 1995; Enloe 2014; Steans and Tepe-Belfrage 2016). Two things are important to note when engaging with feminist approaches. First, there are various feminist approaches within IR (Alcoff 1988: 407; Keohane 1991: 41; Weber 1994: 1050; Whitworth 2008: 393; Tickner and Sjoberg 2010: 208). Second, feminist scholars do hold different normative views on political issues. Perhaps the most apparent example is the ongoing debate concerning sex work/prostitution. Activists and scholars on both sides base their respective arguments regarding the regulation of sex work or the abolition of prostitution on feminist scholarship (Doezema 2005; Hahn and Holzscheiter 2013; Lobasz 2019; Holzscheiter et al. 2022).

Feminism delivered the important insight that IR theory and global politics are gendered (Whitworth 1989: 266). Feminist scholars criticised the view of people as objects (Hill 1999: 107) and IR theory approaches that often imagine the individual human being in global politics as a man, not thinking much about women (Grant 1991: 9; Prügl 2012: 656; Enloe 2014).[3] As Terrell Carver notes, in IR 'the generic human appears as apparently de-gendered, but in practice always covertly gendered masculine' (Carver 2016: 63). This vital insight by feminist IR theory is relevant for this book. It clarifies that it does not suffice to use an abstraction of the individual human being in global politics, such as human nature. Instead, it is necessary to 'dig deeper', to assess global politics from below. As Annick Wibben noted: 'Much feminist research aims to recover or highlight voices of those heretofore rarely acknowledged or heard – often women, whose lives are historically underrepresented in IR' (Wibben 2016: 66). To this end, scholars must include studying gender and its role and its effects in global politics. In this book, gender as a relevant category of thinking about and analysing global politics becomes especially evident in the case studies concerning protection (Chapter 6) and killing (Chapter 7).

Furthermore, feminist IR theory offers a more pluralistic and differentiated view on the individual human being (Prügl 2012: 658–659). It provides a distinct non-state-centric view on global politics (Tickner and Sjoberg 2010: 196). In addition, feminist approaches have always seen the human as a construction (Gildemeister 2003: 214–215; Gregory 2012: 341) and hence have been able to reconstruct the individual human being (Grant 1991: 25). Understanding the human as a construction makes research on the individual human being possible in the first place (Tickner 1991: 37). The individual human being, however, whose gender is socially constructed (Harding 1986: 647; Alcoff 1987: 120; Brown 1988: 473; Butler 1993: 8, 1999: 9), often remains a given within feminist approaches. At times, scholars even refer to notions of 'human nature' (Tickner 1991: 37). At the same time, feminist scholars have provided a much-needed analysis of the various roles women play in global politics (Enloe 2014). In the context of the issues this book is concerned with, debates about the 'Women, Peace, and Security' agenda (Shepherd 2011; Tickner and True 2018; True and Wiener 2019) highlight that it is individuals and not only states who should be 'guaranteed security' (Tickner and Sjoberg 2010: 204).

Finally, research on sexual violence in conflicts, rape as a weapon of war, and a broad understanding of gendered violence is also noteworthy and important (Kirby 2015; Sjoberg 2016; Schulz 2018; Agerberg and Kreft 2020).[4]

[3] The distinction between only men and women as a dichotomy is, of course, in itself reflective of the conflation of sex and gender and at times even sexuality (Carver 2016).

[4] In the context of such a broad understanding, Laura Sjoberg speaks of 'gender/violence'. She suggests 'that gender and violence (and conflict) necessarily are paired (where violence is everywhere and always gendered, and gender is everywhere and always violent)' (Sjoberg 2016: 200).

As Laura Sjoberg notes, '*war and conflict are gendered*' as well (Sjoberg 2016: 199). Such research has provided groundbreaking theoretical and empirical work to ensure that the study of global politics became more sensitive towards gender and women's roles (Zalewski 1995). This work has also carved out the importance of thinking about global politics from the individual human being's perspective, which is always a gendered one. Chapter 3 will revisit some of the key insights that feminist approaches to IR offer and further develop gender and body as two central concepts for the book's conceptual framework. I discuss other aspects of feminist scholarship in the respective case studies.[5]

2.2.2 *Constructivist Approaches: Social Constructions, Language, and Norms*

I now turn to the second central approach within IR theory that the book uses: constructivism. This book engages with constructivism in a twofold manner. First, in the present chapter, it offers a critical discussion of constructivist approaches to shed light on the insufficient acknowledgement of the humanisation of global politics and the failure to integrate the individual human being into IR theory as a theoretical category. Second, it uses a constructivist ontology and constructivist insights and concepts – namely, norms and language – to study the individual human being's appearance in global politics (see Chapter 3).

The humanisation of global politics constitutes a considerable change in global politics. Constructivism is well equipped to accommodate the possibility of change (Guzzini 2000: 155). As Peter Berger and Thomas Luckmann noted more than fifty years ago, change is 'brought about by the concrete actions of *human beings*' (Berger and Luckmann 1967 [1966]: 116, emphasis added). Despite this advantage, there are gaps and shortcomings, especially concerning the humanisation of global politics. The following discussion of constructivism demonstrates that while understanding actors as socially constructed, scholars have applied this understanding insufficiently to the individual human being.

Constructivist ontology is founded on the insight that we live in a socially constructed reality (Berger and Luckmann 1967 [1966]: 1). Following this insight, scholars identified the need for an interpretative epistemology (Kratochwil and Ruggie 1986: 775) to capture this social construction.

[5] All this, however, can only do limited justice to the broad research agenda that feminist scholarship has brought to the study of global politics (see Steans and Tepe-Belfrage 2016 for an extensive overview).

Employing such an epistemology meant that scholars began focusing on deliberation and interpretation (Kratochwil 1989: 10–11). Recognising that we live in a 'world of our making', Nicholas Onuf (1989) introduced the term 'constructivism' to IR (Onuf 1989: 1; Fierke and Jørgensen 2001: 5). The world we live in is 'constructed' and 'the human world is one of artifice; *that it is "constructed" through the actions of the actors themselves*' (Kratochwil 2001: 16–17, emphasis added). But the individual as an actor remained somewhat in the background, as constructivist scholars in the 1980s and 1990s focused on identifying their space within IR theory while simultaneously developing constructivism further. Some, like Alexander Wendt, remained linked to certain realist assumptions about the importance of the state (Wendt 1992: 422–424). Others focused on ontological differences between realism and liberalism, on the one hand, and constructivism, on the other hand (Checkel 1998: 327; Risse 2003: 122).

Constructivist research from the 1990s onwards was especially concerned with norms and the importance of language. At the outset stood the insight that rules and norms matter (Kratochwil 1989), with questions of how they matter (Kratochwil 2000) and which norms matter (Legro 1997) appearing on the agenda as well. Similarly, constructivists pointed to the necessity to engage with language in a meaningful sense. The point was most prominently made by Thomas Risse in 2000, who claimed that there was not only 'logic of consequentiality' and a 'logic of appropriateness' (March and Olsen 1989: 160) but also a 'logic of arguing' (Risse 2000: 4; see also Holzscheiter 2017b: 149), and hence he argued for a stronger focus on the role of language (Risse 2000: 2). Thomas Risse, criticising James March and Johan Olsen's approach to explaining actors' behaviour, argued that what was puzzling now was the question 'how . . . actors adjudicate which norm applies?' (Risse 2000: 6). The answer he provided was that they argue (Risse 2000: 6; but see Hanrieder 2011 for a critical account of this argument). Chapter 3 will discuss how language matters as part of the book's conceptual framework.

Next, I want to provide a brief overview of current debates in the literature on norms, as norms constitute the second key concept taken from constructivist research (see Chapter 3). Before doing so, let me briefly make a note on practice theory. It is a label under which scholars with similar interests in questions of normativity and change in global politics then norm researchers have often been gathered (for contributions and critical assessments see Pouliot 2008, 2010; Adler and Pouliot 2011; Ringmar 2014; Frost and Lechner 2016; McCourt 2016; Hofius 2020). While a discussion of practice theory within IR is outside the book's scope, I take it up here because some practice theory scholars have suggested moving away from studying norms.

One recent example is Simon F. Pratt's suggestion to study 'normative configurations' instead (Pratt 2020: 61). However, others have pushed back against this, claiming that norms as a concept are still useful (Evers 2020: 221). I side with those who see merit in studying norms, and Chapter 3 will develop norms as a central element in the book's conceptual framework. For this reason, I provide a broader overview of the IR literature on norms in the following.

A classical way to present the norms literature has been to talk about waves or generations (Pratt 2020: 62–63). However, this temporal approach poses a problem when incorporating recent work that best fits earlier scholarship. Instead of offering a chronology of norms research, I offer a thematically grouped overview of topics with which norms research is concerned. I do this not only for the sake of providing an overview but also because the issues discussed in the following, namely norm emergence and development, norm contestation, and dynamic norm relations, all play a role in the three discourses (and the scholarly debates on them) studied in the book. Therefore, the following paragraphs provide an overview of these different issues alongside illustrations from the case studies.

One key topic constructivists have been concerned with is norm emergence and development (Finnemore 1996; Finnemore and Sikkink 1998; Rosert 2019a, 2019b). Martha Finnemore's and Kathryn Sikkink's well-known norm life cycle has been a central idea in that debate and has received both criticism and support (Krook and True 2012; Rosert 2019a: 1107; Sandholtz 2019: 139; Stimmer 2019). Others study norm diffusion (Risse et al. 1999; Landolt 2004; Almagro 2018; Winston 2018), at times focusing on the global-local divide and/or post-colonial perspectives (Acharya 2004, 2011; Cloward 2016; Zimmermann 2017). Scholars have also studied norm evolution (Hunt 2016). What happens with a norm after being formally validated in a treaty has also been of concern to norms researchers. Here, scholars have engaged with the issue of norm death and degeneration (Panke and Petersohn 2012: 734; Sandholtz 2019: 145) but also with issues such as norm strength and robustness (Percy 2019; Welsh 2019a; Deitelhoff and Zimmermann 2019). These questions of norm emergence and norm development have been central to the academic debate about the emergence and the development of R2P (Chapter 6) and norms related to the ICC, such as non-impunity (Chapter 4).

Norm scholars have also extensively discussed the idea of norm contestation (Wiener 2004, 2007, 2008, 2014a; Wiener and Puetter 2009; Niemann and Schillinger 2017; Zimmermann et al. 2017; Wiener 2018; Deitelhoff and Zimmermann 2020; Orchard 2020). A detailed overview of the contestation literature is outside the scope of this book. What suffices here to say is that within that debate scholars have studied the effects of norm contestation (Stimmer 2019: 272), types of contestation (Wiener 2018; Stimmer and Wisken 2019; Deitelhoff and Zimmermann 2020), and norm-generative effects of contestatory practices (Wiener 2018: 92). While Chapter 3 discusses relevant aspects of the contestation literature for the book's theoretical and conceptual framework, let me briefly point to the literature's relevance for the case studies. Debates have been ongoing about R2Ps application and justification within the contestation literature (Deitelhoff and Zimmermann 2020). Furthermore, debates about the contestations surrounding the norm of non-impunity in the context of ICL (Mills and Bloomfield 2018; Bower 2019) indicate the relevance of this literature.

Most recent norms research has moved away from studying single norms and concerned itself with questions of dynamic norm relations. Such research includes, for example, studying norm linkages (Fehl 2018) and norm hybridisation, that is, 'the merging of different normative ideas into a new, complex norm' (Fehl 2019: 898). Norm dynamics have also been studied by examining the structures in which these dynamic relations manifest, for example, clusters (Lantis and Wunderlich 2018) or bundles (True and Wiener 2019). Relatedly, scholars have engaged with the idea of norm conflicts and collisions (Buitelaar and Hirschmann 2021; Gholiagha et al. 2020a; Holzscheiter et al. 2022). For example, the tension between sovereignty and protection norms (Brock 1999, 2013; Gholiagha 2014a), which are at the heart of the debate on R2P, can be understood as a response to those collisions (Moe and Geis 2020: 395). In a different perspective on norm dynamics, Caroline Fehl has demonstrated the norm linkages between norms of prosecution and protection (Fehl 2019).

Constructivists have also engaged with self, identity, and agency, which constitute relevant concepts to study the individual human being in global politics. However, focusing solely on them would bracket the process of the social construction of the individual human being. This book studies the appearance of the individual human being in discourses of global politics by reconstructing this appearance. This reconstruction is achieved by studying the positions of the individual human being in specific discourses.[6] Notions such as self, identity, and agency require that the individual human being is

6 It is important to distinguish the study of positions I conduct here from work that is interested in subject position (Renner 2013: 125–154; Stern 2016: 38–39; Almagro 2018: 680). Such work on subject positions is often strongly linked to post-structuralist theories and approaches. While there are certainly connections and overlaps, I do not share the underlying theoretical assumptions. My understanding of positions, as I will demonstrate below, is much more linked to IL scholarship.

already there. Contrary to these notions, the book's departure point is the appearance of the individual human being in the discourse, not the moment when they have already appeared. Nevertheless, the following provides a brief discussion of the self, identity, and agency to show scholars have used them to study the individual human being in global politics and demonstrate why they fall short when studying the social construction of the individual human being itself.

The self is a recurring theme in IR theory and represents a specific conception of the individual human being in global politics. It is a 'Western' idea (Neumann 1996: 140) and is linked to the idea of the person, as those can be understood as 'formed selves' (Berger and Luckmann 1967 [1966]: 56). Furthermore, as Nicholas Onuf has pointed out, '[c]onstructivists also tend to treat *self* as an unproblematic primitive term' (Onuf 2013: 75, emphasis in original). Some see it as the 'starting point' for constructivism (Epstein 2013: 288). In addition, the self is 'a position from which we experience ourselves as agents in a given time in a particular space' (Wilmer 2002: 68). Finally, the self is a social construction itself (Davies and Harré 1990: 59). In sum, it requires the individual human being to be already present in 'a particular space' (Wilmer 2002: 68) and cannot be used to understand how it appeared in this space.

Identity is often at the centre of feminist, constructivist, and post-structuralist work (Berger and Luckmann 1967 [1966]: 173; Zehfuß 2001; Wilmer 2002: 68, 211–238; Wiener 2003; Brown and Ainley 2009: chapter 10; Tickner and Sjoberg 2010: 204; Onuf 2013: 75; Epstein 2013: 288). Alexander Wendt's article *Anarchy Is What States Make of It* (Wendt 1992) is a good departure point to scrutinise the notion of identity within constructivism. Wendt has defined identity as relational (Wendt 1992: 397), using this understanding to identify the identity of states and arguing that there is a 'structure of identity and interest' (Wendt 1992: 396). Based on this idea, he concludes that the international system is characterised by 'self-help' and 'power politics' but that these are 'institutions, not essential features of Anarchy. *Anarchy is what states make of it*' (Wendt 1992: 395, emphasis in original).

Maja Zehfuß offers a critique of Alexander Wendt's position on identity. She argues that, for Alexander Wendt, identity is constructed and given at the same time (Zehfuß 2001: 316). Maja Zehfuß also has expressed caution concerning the focus on identity within constructivist research. She is right in arguing that if identity is seen as given, as conventional constructivists often have asserted (Katzenstein 1996: 5), it leads to the effect that 'political questions, for instance about how subjects come to be in the first place, are ignored' (Zehfuß 2001: 341). While this book does not employ the language of subjects (see Section 2.3 and Chapter 3), Maja Zehfuß' point can easily be reformulated to demonstrate that relying on identity does not facilitate studying the appearance of the individual human being in discourses of global politics. Assuming identity as given raises similar problems than a given human nature. Assuming it to be a social construction prevents scholars from going beyond the notion of identity when aiming to include the individual human being into IR theory.

Agency, the third theoretical conception discussed here, is of relevance for this book, as the theoretical and conceptual framework the book employs constitutes a turn towards 'agentic constructivism' (Sikkink 2011a; Lantis 2016; Wiener 2017). Agency can only be discussed of course with its constitutive other, that is, structure (Wendt 1987; Hay 2002: 101–112; Wight 2006: 83). The structure-agency debate showed weaknesses in accounts that were too structuralist, as here 'human action' was lost (Sewell Jr. 1992: 2). This weakness could be somewhat overcome by understanding structure as 'enabling' (Giddens 1993: 169). This enabling understanding then allows scholars to assert that all humans have, 'a capacity for agency' (Sewell Jr. 1992: 20). Within this book, I understand structure and agency as follows '*[S]tructure* basically means context and refers to the setting within which social, political and economic events occur and acquire meaning .... *Agency* refers to action ... to political *conduct*' (Hay 2002: 94, emphasis in original). Agency, which itself is a social construction and always 'socially embedded' (Vetterlein and Hansen-Magnusson 2020: 17) is, without a doubt, a central concept when studying the individual human being in global politics.

Yet studying agency in itself while helping to better understand global politics (Fierke 2013; Epstein 2013; Bucher 2014) does not say anything about the agents' social constructions. Were I to start with agency as a conceptual departure point, I would not understand the processes of social construction. In other words, studying agency says little about the agents bestowed with the agency. Claiming or being assigned agency requires that the individual human being is already there, that is, the individual human being's appearance is presupposed and not further reflected.[7]

In sum, constructivist approaches have provided much insight into the role norms play, into the importance of agency, identity, and normative beliefs of actors to better understand global politics. Yet, despite acknowledging the social constructedness of both the world and the actors in it, the social construction of individual human beings has received very little attention.

[7] In this context, scholars have also engaged with post-human agency and post-human IR (Cudworth and Hobden 2013b).

Instead, constructivism is often guided by the attempt 'to exclude the human as a whole being and to reinclude it as a social agent' (Jacobi 2015: 247). However, this approach leads to constructivist studies that engage with the individual human being already in place (Onuf 1989: 259; Finnemore and Sikkink 1998: 905; Ruggie 1998: 856; Wiener 2014a: 6). To sum up: constructivist scholars fall short of fully developing the constructivist project to understand how the 'carriers' of ideas and identity, who argue and represent ideas (Krell 2009: 377), appear in discourses of global politics.

The failure to study in detail the social construction of the individual human being is striking, given that constructivist scholars have not been ignorant of how actors are socially constructed. In 1999, Alexander Wendt argued that '[c]onstructivist sensibilities encourage us to look at how actors are socially constructed, but they do not tell us which actors to study or where they are constructed' (Wendt 1999: 7). Moreover, Nicholas Onuf noted the social construction of individuals ten years earlier (Onuf 1989: 46). This book's claim and its added value to the constructivist literature are that studying discourses of global politics in which the individual human being appears constitutes an essential move towards a better understanding of 'how the individual unit is constituted' (Fierke 2010: 183).

I will return in Chapter 3 to constructivism and feminism, as these will form a substantive part of the book's theoretical and conceptual framework. Chapter 3 provides detailed discussions about actors' social construction, understanding the individual human being as socially constructed, and the importance of concepts such as norms, language, gender, and body. It also specifies the ontological and epistemological insights taken from feminist and constructivist approaches. Thus, Chapter 3 brings together theoretical and conceptual contributions from feminist and constructivist approaches into a theoretical and conceptual framework. The remainder of this section now turns to realist and liberal IR theory, debates about human nature, individual rights, human rights, and human security, as potential alternative ways of thinking about the individual human being in global politics. However, as will become evident, approaches relying on realist or liberal assumptions about global politics fall short in grasping the humanisation of global politics.

2.2.3 *Realism and the Idea of a Human Nature*

When studying the individual human being in global politics, it would seem obvious to start with human nature. And indeed, human nature is central to various approaches in IR theory (Lebow 2012: 646). However, the reliance on human nature is problematic because it produces analytical weaknesses.

While found in other approaches as well, these weaknesses are most apparent in the realist tradition of IR. Hence, I focus on realism in the following.

Realist approaches assume a stable human nature (Freyberg-Inan 2004: 34; Donnelly 2009: 35). This claim stems from the work of Thomas Hobbes, who outlined in detail in *Leviathan* that all humans share the same nature; humans are all equally strong (or weak), as even a weak person could kill a strong person, either by stealth or cooperation (Hobbes 1966 [1651]: 94). Classical realism, developed by scholars such as Hans Morgenthau (1954), draws broad conclusions for IR and the study of global politics based on this fixed conception of human nature. As Hans Morgenthau wrote, 'for the social world being but a projection of human nature onto the collective plane' (Morgenthau 1962: 7). The individual human being in realist approaches serves as a foundation for understanding state behaviour. Hence, such approaches offer little knowledge about the individual human being in global politics themselves (Cox 1981: 139).

Neo-realism differs from these classical realist approaches in several substantive points. In *Man, the State, and War*, which can be considered the founding work of neo-realism, Kenneth Waltz departed from the realist's focus on human nature, which he called the first image (Waltz 1959: 16–41). Instead, he focused on the 'second image', that is, states' internal structure (Waltz 1959: 80–123). Most relevant for IR was his claim that a true understanding of global politics became only possible by including the 'third image', which contained the understanding of an anarchical world in which states pursue their interest by force, if necessary (Waltz 1959: 159–186). For neo-realists, it is not the state but 'the structure or architecture of the international system that forces states to pursue power' (Mearsheimer 2010: 78). Focusing on the apparent 'anarchical' structure of the international system (Waltz 1979: 39–97, 99–101), they focus not only on human nature but on states and, most importantly, the system of states (Cox 1981: 131; Freyberg-Inan 2004: 72–73).

Critical scholars like Richard Ashley have rightly noted that realist conceptions of global politics place the state '*ontologically prior* to the international system' (Ashley 1984: 240, emphasis in original). The focus on the state, the assumptions on human nature, and understanding of the structure of the international system as anarchical produce a theory that, in the view of critical scholars, whom I follow here, is incapable of accommodating and assessing change within global politics (Ashley 1984: 256; Wendt 1992: 410; Deitelhoff 2006: 183–187).

In addition to this general assessment, there are six reasons not to invoke human nature to understand the humanisation of global politics. First, the focus on structural aspects denies the role of agents and agency (Guzzini 2000: 155;

Wiener 2004: 201). Second, there is no place for community or morality (Freyberg-Inan 2004: 112). Third, as Allen Buchanan notes, a realist perspective sees international law as incapable of contributing to justice (Buchanan 2010: 89). Fourth, the focus on positivist and rational choice–based epistemology (Hay 2002: 103) is incompatible with the interpretative approach chosen in this book. Fifth, approaches working with human nature often borrow their vocabulary from the life-sciences (Jacobi and Freyberg-Inan 2012: 645–646), reinforcing certain 'social stereotypes, especially those concerning race, class, and gender' (Bell 2012: 654). Furthermore 'life-sciences do not represent a unified field and themselves have yet to fully reflect upon their own basic categories and vocabularies' (Jacobi and Freyberg-Inan 2015b: 11). There 'lies real danger [for IR theory] in the unreflective import of the foreign vocabulary as such' (Jacobi and Freyberg-Inan 2015b: 11–12). Reference to the life-sciences, therefore, does not strengthen IR theory.[8]

A final sixth point against relying on human nature is an epistemological one. The idea of human nature is 'ahistorical' (Berger and Luckmann 1967 [1966]: 187) and hence blind to the context or social environments. Furthermore, '[h]uman nature assumptions … fulfil a specific function in keeping theory manageable; by isolating, highlighting, and pinpointing one single aspect of what allegedly constitutes human distinctiveness' (Herborth 2012: 661). Likewise, as Peg Birmingham correctly notes, an assumption of a fixed human nature leads to the 'loss of the human' (Birmingham 2003: 97). Based on this critique, Benjamin Herborth is right to argue that epistemologically human nature 'end[s] up saying very little about either human beings or their interrelations' (Herborth 2012: 661). As human nature tells us very little about the individual human being, the alternative is to 'take seriously the 'human element' in the study of global politics [which] means to take seriously the social and historical conditions of individuation' (Herborth 2012: 663). Similarly, Felix Berenskötter has pointed out that 'references to human nature allows theorists to fix ontology and 'interests' qua assumptions', thereby leaving out the possibility of a 'reflexive human' (Berenskötter 2018: 823).

Having demonstrated that realist approaches and the notion of human nature do not provide a viable pathway for this book's endeavour, Section 2.2.4 turns to liberal political theory, liberalism, and the conception of the constituted individual human being found therein.

[8] An assessment of whether this statement holds concerning the rise of 'quantum IR' (Wendt 2015) in the last years is outside of the book's scope and aim. But I would like to point to a critical assessment regarding the conception of the human being and human beings (Michel 2018) and to a critical reading of the quantum approach from a feminist perspective (Sjoberg 2020).

2.2.4 *Liberalism and the Constituted Individual Human Being*

Liberalism is a broad term, which can refer to 'a popular political philosophy . . . a political movement . . . and a phenomenon in global politics' (Freeden and Stears 2013: 342). For one, liberalism is partly about shielding individuals from too much state power (Freeden and Stears 2013: 321). However, states can also protect individuals and ensure their well-being, for example, by providing welfare (Freeden and Stears 2013: 335). The state and the individual thus become the 'two primary agents' in 'liberal political theory' (Tétreault and Lipschutz 2005: 18). This double focus on the individual and state is brought together in what Andrew Moravcsik calls a 'bottom-up perspective' (Moravcsik 2008: 236): 'Functionally differentiated individuals and groups define material and ideational goals independently of politics, then seek to advance those ends through political means' (Moravcsik 2008: 236).

Liberalism as an IR theory is concerned *inter alia* with issues of modernisation and cooperation, with the individual at the centre of these processes (Grieco et al. 2019: 86–88). The individual 'is a universal subject, with, ultimately, the same kind of interests, wherever he and she is located across time and space', and liberalism centres on the well-being of that individual (Brown 2002b: 185). Individuals are autonomous (Lebow 2003: 343) and 'are free to cooperate, even to the extent of entering contracts that will significantly constrain their own autonomy' (Freyberg-Inan 2004: 164). In terms of analysing the individual human being's appearance in global politics, this book's concern, liberal IR theory, does not provide a viable path. This is for two reasons: the conception of the individual offered in liberal IR theory and the focus on the state when it comes to analysing global politics.

Concerning the conception of the individual human being, liberalism perceives individuals often as fixed or 'fully constituted' (Ruggie 1998: 866–867) before social interaction, thereby upholding a substantive and not a relational approach to global politics (Jackson and Nexon 1999: 293). Often, as Anne Brown notes, 'liberal approaches seem deeply constrained by the character and the pervasive dominance of the models of "the person" and "the community" with which they operate' (Brown 2002a: 46). However, such a conception of an already constituted individual human being prevents any attempt to understand the humanisation of global politics, as processes of appearance cannot be grasped analytically and methodologically. In addition, liberal scholars rely on a specific idea about human nature (Onuf 1989: 164; Tétreault and Lipschutz 2005: 19; Russett 2010: 96). More specifically: 'Liberal theorists . . . saw individual consciousness and self-interest as evident characteristics of every person and, consequently, thought they must be the starting point of any theory of politics' (Tétreault and Lipschutz 2005: 19). As is the case within realist approaches, a reliance on liberal approaches to human nature leads to similar analytical weaknesses when attempting to study the humanisation of global politics.

Concerning liberalism's preoccupation with the state, liberal IR theory is ultimately interested in 'variation in socially determined state preference' (Moravcsik 2008: 235). The individual, however, does not act on their own in global politics. Instead, states act on behalf of the individual (Brown 2002b: 61; Moravcsik 2008: 237). Thus, liberalism is unable to answer questions about the social construction of individuals in global politics due to its focus on structural aspects of global politics (Herborth 2004: 65) and its interest in the creation and functioning of collective institutions, such as states and international organisations, and cooperation of these institutions (Sterling-Folker 2010: 117).

Finally, liberalism often is less interested in the 'dark side' of the centrality of the individual human being in global politics. This omission comes especially to the fore when liberal scholarship focuses on the positive impacts of individualisation and humanisation, on rights and liberties (Burchill 2009: 68–72; Forsythe 2018: 7, 43–44). Of course, this literature, as will become apparent, also acknowledges failures of human rights in the practice of global politics, but it does not problematise the individual (see Chapter 1). Nevertheless, human and individual rights matter for understanding and analysing the discourses, in which this book is interested. Therefore, I provide a discussion of human rights and individual rights in the following. Here I also pay attention to the notion of human security.

2.2.5 *Human Rights, Individual Rights, and Human Security*

Human rights are about the individual human being (Higgins 1978–1979: 29; Brown 2002a: 15; Hopgood 2017: 289), and 'the unit of human rights discourse is the individual human being' (Yeatman 2000: 1507). The following provides a brief overview of the human rights literature. A substantive review is neither possible nor feasible. Therefore, I focus on key works that provide useful overviews themselves (for a brief audit, see Hopgood et al. 2017b: 8–15). A cursory read allows us to identify work on human rights' origin and history (Hunt 2007; Reus-Smit 2013: 13; Moyn 2014; Hopgood et al. 2017b: 4–5). Despite a missing consensus on the human rights' history and origin, scholars usually point to the centrality of the Universal Declaration of Human Rights (UDHR). The UDHR, irrespective of its non-binding nature, is the main reference point in the post–World War II human rights discourse (Hunt 2007: 205;

Hafner-Burton 2013: 46). From this book's perspective, the UDHR is also of relevance due to 'its aspiration to protect all individuals at all times – not just in war – and make states accountable for this protection' (Hafner-Burton 2013: 41).

Scholars also debate the future of human rights (Hopgood et al. 2017a), questions of implementation (Hafner-Burton 2013: 67–85 for an overview), and the role of human rights within international organisations (Zürn and Heupel 2017) and within global politics more generally (Forsythe 2018). The universality of human rights, agreed upon by states during the 1993 World Conference on Human Rights in Vienna (OHCHR n.d.b), remains the subject of debate (Donnelly 2007; Forsythe 2018: 65). There are also discussions concerning the relationship between individual rights, human rights, and rights of citizens (Yeatman 2000; Reus-Smit 2013; Peters 2016; Kjeldgaard-Pedersen 2018: 71), studies on the question of how human rights matter for the right bearers (Ignatieff 2017), and questions about failures of human rights (Hunt 2007: 209). Furthermore, the question of whether to define human rights formally or substantively remains an issue (Peters 2016: 440–441). A human rights perspective can also be fruitful for understanding human rights violations, including the mass atrocity crimes of the 1990s and institutions and norms to prevent or prosecute such violations, such as the ICC and R2P. These were 'all significant developments in the law and compliance regime of human rights' (Hopgood et al. 2017b: 6).

When it comes to the relationship between human rights and the individual human being from the book's view of the humanisation of global politics, two perspectives are of interest. One focuses on the individual and the other on the state. While different, they do not necessarily exclude each other, as both perspectives are concerned with human rights and their implementation and enforcement. Where they differ is in their focus – and as Anne Brown rightly notes, '[t]he categories of the state and the individual produce each other' (Brown 2002a: 200).

In the first perspective, the individual human being is the bearer of human rights (Yeatman 2000: 1498). Through human rights, humans become the subject of these rights (Yeatman 2000: 1505). As Hunt notes, human rights have also been used to discursively exclude humans based on ethnicity, gender, sex, and religion. Simultaneously, human rights were necessary to speak out against such exclusion and, more importantly, atrocity crimes (Hunt 2007: 212).[9] The majority of the literature does not ask many questions about the human in human rights. The notable exception is work concerned with

[9] For a discussion of the relationship between de-humanisation and human rights, see Marie-Luisa Frick (2021).

questions of rights for specific groups of humans. The development of rights for various subjects of human rights and (Celermajer and Lefebvre 2020b) and new human rights standards (Mutua 2016) are necessary. Acknowledgement of new subjects and the development of new standards is also necessary, as Makau Mutua rightly reminds us, because '[t]he state of being – the human condition – that occasions a violation is not fixed or frozen in time. But the state of being is both physical and metaphysical. It is constantly evolving, and with it the complex ways in which abuses can occur' (Mutua 2016: 2). In studying questions concerning human rights with regards to children (Holzscheiter 2010), migrants at sea (Moreno-Lax and Papastavridis 2017), the elderly (Holzscheiter 2017a), refugees (Gorlick 2000; Orchard 2014), indigenous peoples (Navarrete-Frías and Thoumi 2005; Pfeiffer 2013; Burger and Kapron 2017), or LGBTQI (Johnson 2016; Langlois 2018), scholars have contributed to a better understanding of how, when, and why individual and human rights are granted to certain individual human beings, or how, when, and why this is not the case.

However, on a more abstract level, the human as a bearer of rights appears as already constituted or analytically bracketed. The individual human being as the bearer of those rights is already constituted. At the same time, assigning human rights to someone means that they are identified and constituted as humans (Yeatman 2000: 1498; Kratochwil 2014: 200). But who counts as a bearer of human rights is subject to change as is what counts as a human right (Krook and True 2012: 110), with the debates about the right to water being perhaps the most recent example (Reiners 2021a, 2021b).

The second perspective focuses on human rights as something that binds governments (Hafner-Burton 2013: 52) and focuses on states' role in human rights discourse (Hafner-Burton 2013: 16–17). But suppose no government feels responsible for an individual human being or a whole group. In that case, problems arise, a point most forcefully made by Hannah Arendt in *The Origins of Totalitarianism* when discussing the need for political membership as the foundation for holding and more importantly claiming rights and their protection (Arendt 1951: 288; Volk 2010: 193).

In a nutshell, human rights matter for the individual human beings in global politics, but the human rights literature has largely been concerned with the 'rights' part of human rights (Celermajer and Lefebvre 2020a: 1), either from a perspective of right holders or from a perspective of those who ought to protect these rights. A relatively recent overview of human rights and global politics, such as David P. Forsythe's *Human Rights in International Relations* (Forsythe 2018), for example, engages with a multiplicity of perspectives on the status of human rights both on the level of politics (Forsythe 2018: 32–33) and on the level of law (Forsythe 2018: 15–16) but does not discuss the 'human' part of human rights. As Danielle Celermajer and Alexandre Lefebvre note, this is not uncommon (Celermajer and Lefebvre 2020a: 1).

While scholars are cognisant of questions about the subject of human rights, that is, the human (Yeatman 2000), and have noted that '[t]o consider what we might mean by "human rights" involves questioning the broad conceptions of "the human" and of "political community" that underpins approaches to rights' (Brown 2002a: 21), systematic studies on the 'human' in human rights are rare. A recent exception is an edited volume on *The Subject of Human Rights.* (Celermajer and Lefebvre 2020b). Here, several authors engage with how human rights produce the subject of human rights, the human. But here as well the authors focus on 'the subject of human rights' and not the individual human being itself (Celermajer and Lefebvre 2020a: 2–3).

Studying the appearance of the individual human being in global politics through a human rights lens certainly would yield results, as humans clearly appear in that discourse on human rights. They are positioned in the discourse as bearers of rights, and they position themselves in the discourse, for example, through right claims (Holzscheiter 2016). Studying human rights violations enables us to learn more about the human. Using the example of targeted killing, the most radical instance of rights violations with which this book engages, the following theoretical argument can be made: only by positioning the individual human being as a target in the discourse (as will be demonstrated in Chapter 7) does the individual human being appear in the discourse of targeted killing and become killable at the same time (Gholiagha 2015a; Wilcox 2015: 156).

Considering human rights highlights the role of human rights and human rights violations in the cases I study. Then why not make use of a human rights perspective to study humanisation? As Helmut Aust has argued, 'the ideal of human rights is based on notions of human agency' (Aust 2017: 2). Put differently, the social construction of the human being comes before the questions of who has which human rights (Hunt 2007: 27). Hence, taking human rights into account provides a more holistic picture of the humanisation in a specific case but provides fewer insights into the process of social construction that led to the appearance of the individual human being in a specific position, for example, as a rights-bearer, in the first place.

The notion of human security can be discussed in a manner similar to the debate on human rights and individual rights. Here as well, the individual human being, or rather their well-being and security, are at the centre. The concept was first formulated in the Human Development Report (UNDP 1994). The concept broadened the notion of security, focusing on the security of individual human beings and not only on the security of states. In doing so, the report also broadened the meaning of security (Weinert 2015: 117). The value added to the concept, as Matthew Weinert notes, lies in the fact that 'it adds the human being' (Weinert 2015: 126). In doing so, it 'becomes a useful analytical tool to gauge effects of political, social, and economic processes – whether local, national, or transnational – on human welfare and livelihood' (Weinert 2015: 115). Here it becomes clear that human security offers another valuable perspective on the humanisation of global politics. What also becomes clear is that human security says little about the social construction of the human, whose security is the key reference point (Buzan and Hansen 2009: 206). And while more detailed discussion of the broad literature of human security is outside the book's scope, there are important discussions about human security, for example, feminist works on the ethics of care (Robinson 2008) as well as constructivist (Newman 2001) and critical (Owens 2012) perspectives on human security.

To sum up this long discussion about the humanisation of IR theory, we can note that some of the approaches discussed offer useful insights and concepts for a conceptual and theoretical framework, for example, the focus on the social construction of actors found in constructivist approaches and the importance of individuals' (gendered) experience found in feminist approaches. Having provided an overview of the humanisation of IR theory, Section 2.3 turns to the humanisation of international law.

2.3 THE HUMANISATION OF INTERNATIONAL LAW

In this section, I discuss the humanisation of international law. I begin with a discussion of mediation to provide some context on the changing environment in which the individual human being in international laws find themselves. I then focus on how scholars have dealt with and conceptualised the individual human being in international law. Here, I also discuss the relation of the individual human being to the state and the international community.

IL scholars have engaged with the individual human being, humanisation, and humanity for some time (Meron 2006; Bumke 2009; Peters 2011, 2016; Teitel 2011).[10] Developments in many fields of international law have led to a direct interaction between international law and the individual human being. The most prominent example of this development is ICL, discussed in detail in Chapter 4. Should the task of theorising the individual human being's

[10] It should be noted here that such an assessment is not unchallenged. As Anne Peters points out, it has been questioned by scholars and states (Peters 2016: 2, 4).

appearance then not be a task for legal scholars? This book contests the argument that the humanisation of global politics is a purely legal topic. While conceding that in many instances of the humanisation of global politics international law and its institutions have played a dominant role, as is obvious when cases concerning individual rights and violations of them are deliberated and adjudicated before international courts and tribunals, such as the ECJ or the ICC, I hold that while courts can find legal solutions for these issues, questions of politics and normativity remain unanswered by them, or they are at least hesitant to engage with them (Birkenkötter 2020: 336; Birkenkötter and Kaya 2022).

The issues and developments many scholars have observed and described take place outside jurisprudence with direct implications for the conduct between people, states, collective actors, and the individual human being. They are, in other words, profoundly political, both in their nature and in their implications. Hence, these are not purely questions of *de lege lata* or *de lege ferenda*. IL scholarship does matter and is relevant. It provides important concepts to think about the individual human being in global politics. And given the focus of the case studies, IL scholarship provides the necessary tools to understand the discourses at hand, especially in the cases where questions of international law are central, for example, in the case study on ICL and the case study on drone strikes. States and the international community play a role in all of these debates and developments. Therefore, the following engages with the relation between the individual human being, the international community, and the state through the notion of mediation.

2.3.1 *Mediation: The Individual Human Being, the International Community, and the State*

International law recognises states, the international community, and non-state actors as well as individuals. The individual human being, while central, is not alone in international law. Likewise, the social construction of the individual human being cannot be grasped without looking at other entities, actors, and institutions in global politics. Therefore, this section casts a closer look at the state and the international community and, most importantly, the position the individual human being takes up in relation to them.

The term 'mediation' captures this relation. As Knut Ipsen and colleagues note, 'this *mediation of the individual* means that the human being on the international legal plane becomes relevant primarily as a subject of a state' (Ipsen et al. 2004: 94, my translation, emphasis in original; see Peters 2016: 54–55, for a critical account of the term). Scholars have identified the rise of international organisations and their direct influence on individuals affected by this system of mediation. As Michael Zürn and Monika Heupel argue: 'In this case, states lost their role as mediators between their citizens and the international level' (Zürn and Heupel 2017: 14). Legal scholars have argued that the system of mediation has become dysfunctional, leading to an imbalance in the international legal system (von Arnauld 2011: 506–507; but see Peters 2016 for a critical account). Two related issues, which follow from this assessment, warrant further scrutiny. First, does the international community simply replace the state? Second, could one not argue that states prosecute, protect, and kill individual human beings, making the focus on the individual human being this book pursues seem unwarranted? To engage with both issues, the following paragraphs discuss the international community's idea and the role of the state in global politics concerning the individual human being.

The term 'international community' has been referred to by various actors so often that Bruno Simma and Andreas Paulus already spoke of 'an almost inflationary' use nearly twenty-five years ago (Simma and Paulus 1998: 267). They argue that international law provides the 'necessary normative structure to this community', while at the same time, it affirms its existence (Simma and Paulus 1998: 267). But while many references to an international community can be found in both primary sources as well as academic work (ICJ 1951; Tomuschat 1993; de Wet 2006; ICJ 2007; Teitel 2011), the more fundamental questions about the construction and constitution of communities (Vetterlein and Wiener 2013: 81–84) remain mostly unanswered. Antje Vetterlein and Antje Wiener offer a sociologically informed critique of IR theory's usage of the term 'community', arguing that it is based on the problematic assumption that there is a liberal community in place (Vetterlein and Wiener 2013: 87). Based on their critique and the lack of a clear understanding of what the international community is and how it is constituted, I argue that a reference to the international community does not help provide insights into the individual human being's appearance in discourses of global politics.

That is not to say that the international community and its many institutions do not matter – an insight demonstrated by Matthew Weinert when analysing the importance of institutions 'sites' in 'making humans' (Weinert 2015: 3). As Jennifer Welsh notes, 'there remains strong evidence for the continued influence of forms of collective authority, agency and subjectivity both in theory and in practice' (Welsh 2019b: 18). Yet, as Welsh also notes: 'As a result of individualisation, however, the value of state consent is arguably being eroded, or in some cases counter-balanced, by imperatives to protect individual human rights' (Welsh 2019b: 20). Somewhat to the contrary, from a perspective of international law, Anne Peters argues that 'states remain the primary and indispensable agents of individuals' (Peters 2016: 6). However, Chapter 1 already demonstrated the growing appearance of the individual human being in global politics disaggregated from the state. While states clearly still play a role in global politics, this book is not primarily concerned with them. States play a part in the conduct and the treatment of the individual human being in global politics; however, they are neither the only actor nor ontologically prior to other actors. But what this book ultimately is interested in is the appearance of the individual human being in global politics, in which states, international organisations, and non-state actors of course exist.

IL scholarship has always been aware of the individual human being and its position in international law (Norgaard 1962; Higgins 1978–1979; Randelzhofer 1999; Gorski 2011; Parlett 2011). Section 2.3.2 discusses how scholars have tried to include the individual human being in international law.

2.3.2 *International Law and the Individual Human Being*

With the end of World War II, the founding of the UN, and the rise of ICL, international law increasingly 'exert[ed] moral force on individuals, to whom rights accrue, and who are obliged by it' (Kettemann 2013: 76). These rights are often rights vis-à-vis the state (Walter 2012: 5). IL scholars have argued for some time for the importance of including the individual human being into international law on its own (Higgins 1994: 50–51; Buchanan 2010: 87; Dixon 2013: 128–130; Hakimi 2014: 247).

Individual human beings have become the 'authentic carriers of the law' (Peters 2011: 421, my translation). An example of such an understanding can be found in the *LaGrand* Judgement of the International Court of Justice (ICJ) (ICJ 2001) and its reading of §36 of the Vienna Convention on Consular Relations (Peters 2011: 432–433). Ruti Teitel has criticised Peters' view as state-bound (Teitel 2011: 31, 2013: 233). Despite this valid criticism, Peters' view remains an accurate description of the development of international law concerning the growing importance of individual human beings. The concept of subjects allows the integration of the individual human being in the existing system of international law. However, scholars have questioned the subject-object dichotomy, suggesting the term 'participants' (Higgins 1994; McCorquodale 2006; Peters 2016: 21; Kjeldgaard-Pedersen 2018: 37–38). Chapter 3 will return to this notion in more detail.

Furthermore, scholars such as Ruti Teitel have pointed out the importance 'to pay attention to human-centered legal discourse *because* of and not despite its role in politics, given that it is being used by a variety of actors, parties, and movements to make specific claims with an impact on global governance' (Teitel 2013: 233, emphasis in original). At the same time, '*individuals* may also be bound by international law, with or without their own state' (Besson 2009: 365, emphasis in original). Due to the parallel development of rights and duties, new issues arise for the individual human being, who is confronted with a plurality of legal orders (Peters 2016: 57), which may contest each other (Thies 2013: 239; Isiksel and Thies 2013: 151; de Wet and Vidmar 2013: 217).[11] Despite all positive developments within international law, the critical remark by Kratochwil that '"law" might have become part of the problem rather than the solution, and this problem requires further analysis' (Kratochwil 2014: 2) must be recognised.[12] This will be part of the discussion within the case studies. In the following, the historical developments towards the current status of international law will be sketched out.

One paramount event of the development to include the individual human being in international law was the prosecution of high-ranking members of the German Nazi Regime in the Nuremberg Trials. While the development of ICL will be assessed in more detail in Chapter 4, Nuremberg demonstrated that the individual human being matters. In line with this, Samantha Besson reminds us 'that the moral position of individuals cannot be ignored' (Besson 2009: 360). With the end of the World War II, the individual human being began to emerge as a subject of international law more clearly (Randelzhofer 1999: 232; Dixon 2007: 123; Isiksel 2010: 565; Parlett 2011: 343). However, others have argued against the view that the rise of the individual in international law really is new.

[11] This of course also relates to larger debates about the fragmentation of international law (Fischer-Lescano and Teubner 2004; Michaels and Paulwelyn 2011). Relatedly, in political science, scholars have noted a growing regime-complexity (Alter and Meunier 2009; Gómez-Mera 2016). Most current research has begun to move 'beyond fragmentation' (Meggido 2019). One recent attempt, which I participated in, focused on questions of managing conflicts between overlapping legal orders, international organisations, and regimes (Alter 2020; Birkenkötter 2020; Faude and Fuß 2020; Flonk et al. 2020; Gholiagha et al. 2020a; Kreuder-Sonnen and Zürn 2020; Krisch et al. 2020; Mallavarapu 2020; Moe and Geis 2020).

[12] Of course both IL and IR scholars have studied 'politics of law' (Liste 2020: 7) and the relationship between politics and law (Kennedy 2016). A systematic engagement with the relationship between politics and law and the understanding that 'law is politics' (Tushnet 1991: 1517) can be found in the critical legal studies (CLS) movement, that developed in the United States, especially in the 1970s (Kennedy 1988; Kennedy and Klare 1984; Frankenberg 2011). A more detailed engagement with this stand of literature is unfortunately outside of the book's scope.

Indeed, notions of the individual human being as a subject of international law can already be found in the work of legal scholars of the 1940s and 1950s (McCorquodale 2006: 310). International law in such contexts understands the world as created by individual human beings (Allott 1992: 220). Robert McCorquodale rightly points out that 'individuals are at the very core of the international legal system, no matter how that system is defined' (McCorquodale 2006: 310). Likewise, Samantha Besson states that, 'international law … directly regulates the life of individuals alongside domestic law' (Besson 2009: 349). For others, like Christian Walter, individuals are only partial subjects (Walter 2012: 5). However, this perspective has been convincingly challenged because either someone is a subject or not (Besson 2010: 172–173; Gött 2013: 3).

Similarly, Christoph Schreuer suggests that '[i]nternational law has always accepted certain actors in addition to states, at least for certain purposes. They include … individuals. However, the dominant role of States has never really been questioned by these additional actors. They were either established and controlled or at least tolerated by the States' (Schreuer 1993: 449). Likewise, Astrid Kjeldgaard-Pedersen has pointed to many scholars in the early twentieth century who took a clear position against a 'state-only' view regarding international legal personality (Kjeldgaard-Pedersen 2018: 30). Anne Peters has made a related point. She argues that the individual is the 'natural person of international law' (Peters 2016: 431), asserting that it is already customary international law that individuals are subjects of international law (Peters 2016: 419).

Let me briefly discuss the notion of international legal personality in this context. It is a key concept in international law to establish whether an entity is recognised in international law (Nijman 2004). Notably, the list of entities with international legal personality has been continuously expanding, including international organisations and other non-state actors. Most importantly perhaps, legal scholars such as Anne Peters have argued that individuals not only have international legal personality but also have a human right to it (Peters 2016: 430). International legal personality is often understood to be only in place when the entity also has a law-making capacity (Kjeldgaard-Pedersen 2018: 42). Contrary to this, Anne Peters argues that this is not the case as '[i]nternational legal personality precedes the ownership of rights. It is filled by specific rights and/or duties but is not constituted by them' (Peters 2016: 58). The move towards recognising and protecting the individual human being through international law can furthermore be traced back to the 1948 UDHR (UNGA 1948b; Wenzel 2008: 404).

The discussion of IL scholarship in this chapter has demonstrated that debate exists on grasping the individual's position in international law. Scholars have applied notions and concepts such as subject, international legal personality, actor, and participant, trying to capture various aspects of the individual human being and their place in international law. As Chapter 3 will demonstrate, it is the notions of participants and positions that are of specific value for the book's endeavour. Participation implies a more active role of the individual human being than the use of the object-subject dichotomy. Positions say something about the place of the individual human being in global politics.

2.4 CONCLUSION

The chapter's task was to critically assess the potential contribution of IR and IL scholarship to study the humanisation of global politics, carve out relevant insights, and provide an overview of how scholars of IR and IL so far have dealt with the individual human being in global politics.

In its assessment, the chapter has provided further evidence of the double mismatch that characterises IR and IL theory when studying the humanisation of global politics. While cognisant of the human being in global politics, IR has not analysed the process of the social construction of the individual human being. IL provides relevant insights into the individual human being's position but can profit from feminist and constructivist scholars' insights about the humanisation of global politics. Most IR theory has primarily taken the individual human being for granted and given. As Daniel Jacobi and Annette Freyberg-Inan rightly note 'positivist IR scholar ... rely on auxiliary constructions' (Jacobi and Freyberg-Inan 2015b: 16) of the individual human being. But as this chapter has demonstrated, the reliance on 'auxiliary constructions', to borrow Daniel Jacobi and Annette Freyberg-Inan's terminology (2015b: 16) can also be identified in post-positivist IR scholarship, where concepts such as identity, the self, agency, or gender are frontloaded. That is not to say that these concepts and notions do not matter. The contrary is the case. Nevertheless, I believe that they should not be the sole departure point for studying the social construction of the individual human being. While acknowledging the need to include the individual human being conceptually into international law, IL scholarship has not provided a clear and adequate conceptualisation. Instead, it offers a plethora of concepts to grasp the individual human being or some aspect of the individual human being.

More specifically, despite claiming the importance of individual human beings in constructing social reality and acknowledging that the individual human being is equally socially constructed, constructivist scholarship has not yet delivered a consistent analysis of the social construction of the individual human being in global politics. Most constructivist approaches study the social constructions of other actors in global politics. If they study individuals, they do so as constituted beings, with little interest in the processes of social construction. However, due to its acknowledgement of the social construction of the individual human being, constructivist approaches offer a pathway towards including the individual human being in IR theory. Nevertheless, further developments are necessary, especially concerning the issue that the state as a mediator loses its relevance. To this end, feminist approaches that successfully demonstrate the need to bring people into the analysis of global politics are helpful.

Taken together, feminist and constructivist scholarship both provide a valuable pathway towards a theoretical and conceptual framework to study the humanisation of global politics and to acknowledge and recognise the individual human being as a central theoretical category in IR theory. All that is not to say that there is nothing but the individual human being in global politics. There is always a historical, social, or institutional context (Onuf 1989: 46), and there are always other actors, both state and non-state.

It is here that IL scholarship is especially helpful. IL scholarship offers important insights into the place of the individual human being in global politics, and the relation between the individual human being, on the one hand, and states and the international community, on the other hand. However, it could profit from a perspective that sheds more light on the political and normative dimensions of the humanisation of global politics. We find important debates about these dimensions in the literature on (human and individual) rights and duties.

Chapter 3 suggests overcoming the shortcomings identified within singular approaches by synthesising several approaches into a theoretical and conceptual framework that provides the necessary theoretical and conceptual means to study the humanisation of global politics.

3

The Social Construction of the Individual Human Being

A Conceptual and a Theoretical Framework

3.1 INTRODUCTION

Chapters 1 and 2 have demonstrated two things. First, the individual human being's appearance in discourses of global politics, a process that I call the humanisation of global politics, has shifted global politics (at least partially) away from states and collective actors towards the individual human being. Second, while cognisant of human beings in global politics, large parts of IR theory have remained focused on states and collective actors. When they have taken up the notion of the individual human being, they have done so by relying on ideas about human nature or a fixed conception of the individual human being. It seems that large parts of IR are 'at the end' (Wight et al. 2013), at least when attempting to understand the humanisation of global politics.[1]

Yet not all hope is lost. As already noted in Chapter 2, some of the IR and IL approaches offer useful concepts and theoretical insights to study the humanisation of global politics. Building on these approaches and concepts identified, this chapter provides the conceptual and the theoretical framework for analysing and understand the humanisation of global politics. Therefore, the present chapter has two tasks: to develop a conceptual framework and to develop a theoretical framework. A conceptual framework is defined 'as a network or a "plane" of interlinked concepts that together provide a comprehensive understanding of a phenomenon or a phenomena' (Jabareen 2009: 51). A theoretical framework 'is comprised of the different theories and theoretical constructs that help explain a phenomenon' (Pacheco-Vega 2018). In the following, I discuss three different theoretical approaches: feminism, constructivism, and IL.[2] In conjunction, they provide the

[1] The chapter has immensely profited from feedback provided by Jelena Cupać.

[2] I am aware of course that International Law is not a theory or an approach and that legal theory contains various approaches. But for the sake of the chapter's structure, I rely on the term

theoretical framework for the book. From each approach, I draw specific concepts, which, taken together constitute the book's conceptual framework. The theoretical framework provides the ontological and epistemological guidance for the book. The conceptual framework provides specific concepts that will help me study and understand the individual human being's appearance in global politics.

To make all this less abstract, let me provide examples. The first theoretical approach I will discuss can be summarised under the heading of 'feminism'. In terms of ontology, feminist approaches in IR assume that we live in a world where gendered beings and their gender matters. In terms of epistemology, this means that we must overcome the 'gender bias' (Grant 1991) of IR by asking: what role does gender play? (Zalewski 1995). These are the theoretical insights of feminism on which I rely. There are, of course, many more, but I focus on those. I also take two concepts from feminist IR: body and gender, which help us conceptualise human beings in global politics and play an essential role in understanding what is happening in the book's case studies.

Combining the theoretical and conceptual frameworks enables me to engage with the humanisation of global politics and the manifestation of that humanisation: the appearance of the individual human being in discourses of global politics. In the following, I discuss the relevant concepts in the context of the theoretical approach from which they stem. To demonstrate the usefulness of the theoretical approaches and the theoretical framework, I focus on the insights these theories and my framework offers. I take note of both ontological (what we believe the world is made of) and epistemological (how we can learn about the world) insights. It is important to note that the frameworks aim to understand rather than explain (Hollis and Smith 1990; Jabareen 2009: 51), meaning I will not draw hypotheses from the theories or test them. Instead, I use the frameworks to make sense of my cases and reconstruct the individual human being's appearance in discourses of global politics. In Chapter 4, the book's first case study, I offer an extended empirical illustration of the frameworks' applicability by demonstrating what can be seen by reading the field of ICL and cases before the ICC through the conceptual and theoretical lens the frameworks offer.

As discussed earlier, this is an interdisciplinary work, combining IR and IL approaches. I therefore briefly want to provide my understanding of interdisciplinarity. Interdisciplinarity refers to using 'a range of lenses to understand interacting and overlapping dimensions of reality' (Lang Jr. et al. 2013: 4). The interdisciplinary approach of courses poses a challenge, as I come to the IL as an outsider, without a legal scholars' formal training and education. Thus, there are certainly omissions in

International Law to summarise the various ontological and epistemological insights taken from the International Law scholarship.

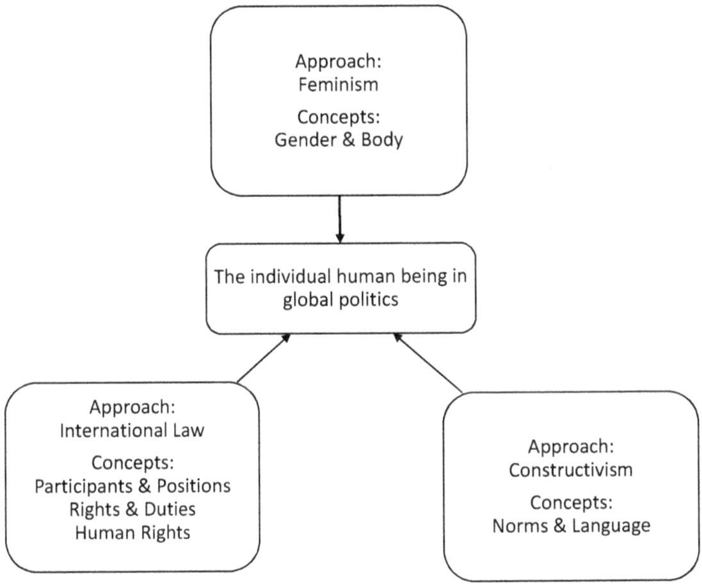

FIGURE 3.1 Theoretical and Conceptual Framework[3].
Source: Gholiagha

my portrayal of IL scholarship. As Emily Hafner-Burton rightly notes 'that is the nature of interdisciplinary scholarship on real world problems' (Hafner-Burton 2013: 10). In all that diversity and interdisciplinary there is, however, a common ground. All approaches rest on a common ontological foundation: all approaches are post-positivist and agency-oriented. They all assume reality is socially constructed, that the individual human being is a relevant participant in global politics, and that language is constitutive of social reality. Figure 3.1 presents both the theoretical and conceptual framework. I use the three theoretical perspectives (feminism, constructivism, and IL) to study the individual human being's appearance in discourses of global politics. Within each box containing the theoretical approach, I list the concepts derived from each of the three approaches.[4] Following this overview of the chapter, I now turn to the first approach: feminism, with two concepts: gender and body.

[3] While concepts and theoretical approaches are presented hear as clearly separated, they are connections and overlaps between them, as the discussions in the previous and the present chapter demonstrate.

[4] As Herbert Blumer noted in 1954: 'Theory is of value in empirical science only to the extent to which it connects fruitfully with the empirical world. Concepts are the means, and the only means of establishing such connection, for it is the concept that points to the empirical instances about which a theoretical proposal is made' (Blumer 1954: 4).

3.2 FEMINISM: INDIVIDUAL HUMAN BEINGS, GENDER, AND BODIES

Let me begin by briefly recalling the three key points discussed in Chapter 2, which established feminist scholarship as a valuable theoretical point of departure for this book. First, the idea of a socially constructed individual human being can be found throughout feminist scholarship (Grant 1991: 25; Gildemeister 2003: 214–215; Gregory 2012: 341). Second, feminist IR theory provides a distinct non-statist view on global politics, moving away from more structurally and state-focused accounts. Feminism demonstrates the importance of moving towards individuals' experiences and perspectives (Pettman 1992: 58; Tickner and Sjoberg 2010: 196; Sylvester 2013a, 2013b). Third, feminist accounts of IR offer a more pluralistic and differentiated view on the individual human being (Prügl 2012: 658–659). I now turn to the insights and concepts offered by feminist scholarship.

As the ontological insight and the two concepts – gender and body – are closely connected, I discuss them together, rather than individually. I begin with the ontological insights of the socially constructed individual human being. Feminist scholars were the first to note that gender was a social construction (Ackelsberg and Diamond 1987: 506). Therefore, feminist research yields several highly relevant insights into the social construction of the individual human being. Feminist approaches (whose variation and diversity I discussed in Chapter 2) all share certain views, such as the importance of gender for studying global politics and the idea that gender is socially constructed (Harding 1986: 647; Alcoff 1987: 120; Brown 1988: 473; Butler 1993: 8, 1999: 9).[5]

If gendered individual human beings are the result of processes of social construction, and their gender and their individual (gendered) experience matters, what follows from this in terms of epistemology? It requires us, also normatively speaking, to engage with the individual human being beyond being 'aggregated into data points' (Sylvester 2013a: 614). Christine Sylvester makes this point, especially in the context of war, arguing for the need for a bottom-up approach to study war (Sylvester 2013a: 619–620). In a similar fashion (and with reference to Christine Sylvester and others), Ty Solomon and Brent Steele have emphasised the importance of feminist work that turns to what they call 'micropolitics', which is constituted *inter alia* by returning to

[5] An excellent example on how a feminist perspective and taking gender into account can provide new and better insights into global politics is to be found in the work of the *Centre for Feminist Foreign Policy*.

the 'humanity of politics' and a renewed focus on agency (Solomon and Steele 2017: 272) They also mention constructivist work that focuses on the local level (Solomon and Steele 2017: 272–273).

In the present inquiry, this move to micropolitics is achieved by asking how the individual human being has appeared in the respective discourse studied and how this appearance matters for global politics. Having established the theoretical insights drawn from feminist scholarship, I now present the two concepts from feminist IR theory I employ in this book: gender and body. Gender is a vital concept to understand the social construction of the individual human being in global politics. Considering the individual human being's body when studying global politics is a second key concept provided by feminist IR scholarship for this book's aims and objectives.

Gender, as Rebecca Grant and Kathleen Newland noted over thirty years ago, 'constitutes one of the most basic sources of division and definition in political society' (Grant and Newland 1991: 2). Put differently, including gender provides a more encompassing picture of politics. Leaving gender aspects outside of the analysis leads to gaps, because '[g]ender roles ... reflect the way that humans understand their place in the world' (Grant 1991: 8). And as this book argues, we cannot understand global politics without looking at the individual human being in global politics. What follows from this is that '[e]very human experience – even that of international politics – has gender content because gender is one of humanity's major socializing forces' (Grant 1991: 23).

The second key concept drawn from feminist approaches to IR is the body. Feminist scholars demonstrated a long time ago that body politics matter significantly if we are to understand certain developments and practices that affect the body and if we are to analyse how bodies affect politics (Butler 1993; Wilcox 2015: 29). Here, I would like to introduce an important distinction offered by Karin Fierke between the 'flesh-and-blood body' vs. the meaning of the body depending on context (Fierke 2013: 62). As Lauren Wilcox reminds us, IR more often than not has only focused on the body in the biological sense (Wilcox 2015: 2). And even in constructivism, this biological determinism remains the dominant line of thinking about the body when scholars presuppose the body inasmuch as they presuppose the individual human being (Wilcox 2015: 3, 35; see also Chapter 2). A clear example of such a position can be found in Nicholas Onuf's work, when he writes: 'The identity of a human being depends, as a necessary condition, on having a body of one's own' (Onuf 2013: 82).

In my case studies on R2P and drones, I use feminist scholars' insight into the political dimension of the human body, looking at bodies in context and how bodies are socially constructed, and in doing so, move beyond constructivist assumptions about the body. The importance of considering bodies is especially evident when studying practices such as drone strikes (see Chapter 7). In drone strikes, targets are often identified by analysing their body, both in the sense of flesh-and-blood (body structure, movement) and the context-sense (where is the body, what other bodies are visible, what is in the environment of the body). Furthermore, drone strikes directly affect the body, destroying or harming it (Wilcox 2015; Auchter 2016). The importance of considering the body is also evident in the context of R2P (see Chapter 6), where individual human beings are often reduced to 'pure bodies in need, human "matter" waiting to be rescued' (Mégret 2010: 49).

Let me conclude with a note on a more abstract level. Drawing on Marysia Zalewski's seminal text on feminist scholarship in IR published in 1995 in *International Affairs* (for a recent discussion of it see Kinsella and Shepherd 2019) the question is not: 'Well, what is the feminist perspective?' (Zalewski 1995). As Marysia Zalewski made clear, the questions ought to be: '"What work is gender doing?" and: "What about women?"' (Zalewski 1995: 341), with the question on gender being the more difficult but more important one (Zalewski 1995: 356). So, instead of answering the question of what a feminist approach contributes to my book, let me conclude this section by outlining what the questions: 'What work is gender doing here?' and 'What about women?' contribute to the book. As will become apparent in the case studies on R2P and on drones, gender can be understood 'as epistemology' (Zalewski 1995: 341). It helps us to understand who is protected and who is killed. Who is deemed innocent and who is guilty.

Moreover, the question about women equally turns up when it comes to analysing situations in which groups of civilians are separated based on who is considered a man and who falls into the category of 'women and children' (Carpenter 2005). To summarise, feminist approaches to IR offer four things for this book: First, understanding humans as socially constructed. Second, the gender-lens for understanding global politics. Third, insights into the role of the body in global politics. Fourth, support for the normative argument that IR scholars need to include the individual human being in the analysis of global politics.

3.3 CRITICAL CONSTRUCTIVISM: NORMS AND LANGUAGE

Constructivism provides – similar to feminist approaches to IR – ontological assumptions about our world's social constructedness. It combines this insight with insights about the co-constitutiveness of structure and agency

(Onuf 2016: 126). The key ontological insight constructivist scholars provide is that we live in 'a world of our making' (Onuf 1989). While not denying the material reality, our world needs to be made sense of, requiring intersubjective agreement to be socially consequential. The epistemological viewpoint that follows from this is that for scholars to study this social construction and sense-making, we need to 'make sense' of the 'world making' (Onuf 2013). Making sense can best be achieved through an interpretative epistemology, as Friedrich Kratochwil and John Ruggie (1986) argued over thirty-five years ago. Building on these key theoretical insights, two crucial concepts emerged from constructivist approaches, which I will employ in my conceptual frameworks: norms and language.

3.3.1 *Norms*

Norms research is a substantive dimension of this book's focus on the humanisation of global politics (a point Weinert 2015: 10, also makes in his analysis of humanisation). And it is an important aspect of the book's central theoretical claim that the individual human being is socially constructed. More generally, the focus on norms is part and parcel of the constructivist focus on international relations' social dimension. Thus, norms play a significant role in constructivist research (Kratochwil 1984b: 343, 1989a: 11). The importance of norms for the book's endeavour is also evident in Antje Wiener's observation that social facts and social practices 'sharpened the view for the *social construction of actors* in world politics' (Wiener 2003: 133, my translation, emphasis added). Norms relevant to the individual human being are made by international organisations, regional actors, and states (Isiksel and Thies 2013: 151). Furthermore, 'with increasing frequency international legal norms directly address and engage individuals' (Peters 2016: 1). Understanding how norms work and what norms are, therefore, is essential to understand the humanisation of global politics and study the appearance of the individual human being in global politics.

Norms are 'value-based collective expectations for the appropriate behaviour [of actors] in specific types of situations' (Gholiagha et al. 2020a: 293, emphasis removed).[6] Furthermore, norms have different qualities; they

[6] I depart from the classical definition of norms as 'standard of appropriate behavior for actors with a given identity' (Finnemore and Sikkink 1998: 891) for several reasons. First, the definition requires a given identity and a given community, both assumptions that have been rightly criticised (Zehfuß 2001: 316; Towns 2010: 33; Vetterlein and Wiener 2013: 87). Second, they often do not acknowledge the situation-dependence of norms. Third, and in line with new work, the definition used opens up the concept of norms, taking both into account in the

'enable, constrain, guide and give meaning to human action and choice' (Stone Sweet 2011: 228) at the same time, and there are various norm types (Jurkovich 2020: 694). Norms play a paramount role in global politics, and any meaningful study of global politics must account for them. Therefore, the case studies will focus on the relevant norms within the specific discourses studied.

However, norms do not exist a priori to human social interactions, as constructivist work on questions of norm development, emergence, and diffusion has demonstrated (Finnemore and Sikkink 1998: 895; Keck and Sikkink 1998; Risse et al. 1999). Such work often takes a structural and linear, sometimes even teleological, perspective (Flynn and Farrell 1999: 510–511; for critical perspectives see Landolt 2004; Ulbert 2012: 132; Daase 2013: 43–44). The criticism of the linear and diffusion focused literature (led to the development of more critical norms research and, hence, critical constructivism (Engelkamp et al. 2012, 2013; Hofius et al. 2014; Wiener 2014a: 41; Engelkamp et al. 2021).

Critical constructivists argue that the norms do not have a fixed meaning. Instead, the meaning of a norm can only be understood with reference to a specific problem (Winston 2018: 3), context (Wiener 2007: 69), or situation (Gholiagha et al. 2020a: 293). There, their *meaning-in-use* (Weldes and Saco 1996: 373; Wiener 2004: 217; Gholiagha et al. 2021) comes to the fore when articulated by actors. Understanding norms hence requires looking at what actors say about norms and do with them. The prohibition of torture and the contestation of this norm by liberal democracies following the attacks on 11 September 2001 (hereafter 9/11) is a case in point, as it shows how actors attempted to change the meaning of norm-prohibiting torture in a specific situation, the so-called war on terror (Liese 2009; Schmidt and Sikkink 2019). Besides, norms have a dual quality, as they are socially constructed and at the same time are constitutive of the actions of actors (Wiener 2003: 150, 2007: 48).

Compared to conventional constructivism, a critical constructivist approach is better equipped to study the individual human being's appearance in discourses of global politics. The approach highlights the role of interaction between actors, their agency, and norms. Critical constructivism is also aware that norms are being constituted by and constitutive of actors. Moreover, the inclusion of a critical constructivist view on norms into the theoretical framework allows me to focus on human agency, as such approaches take into account actors' actions in relation to the norm (Sikkink 2011a: 2; Lantis 2016;

situation in which actors apply a norm and underlying values guiding actors (Winston 2018). The definition used here, was developed – in a slightly different form – in the context of a co-authored publication with Anna Holzscheiter and Andrea Liese (Gholiagha et al. 2020a).

Zimmermann et al. 2017; Wiener 2017). The book's case studies will demonstrate the relevance of such a critical constructivist understanding of norms by reconstructing how actors use references to norms to position the individual within discourses. The analysis will also demonstrate that the contestation of norms (Wiener 2018; Deitelhoff and Zimmermann 2020), their *meaning-in-use* (Wiener 2004: 217; Gholiagha et al. 2021), and dynamic norm relations (Fehl 2018; Gholiagha et al. 2020a; Holzscheiter et al. 2022) all matter for analysing the respective discourses and the appearance of the individual human beings in them. For this, the interaction between actors, their agency, and norms matters. Discourses are closely related to language. Section 3.3.2, therefore, introduces language as the second building block drawn from constructivism.

3.3.2 *Language*

Language is the second concept taken from constructivist scholarship. As Peter Berger and Thomas Luckmann note, 'language marks the co-ordinates of my life in society and fills that life with meaningful objects' (Berger and Luckmann 1967 [1966]: 22). Analysing language helps us understand social constructions, as language is constitutive for the social construction of reality (Doty 1993: 302). This was also a key insight from the 'ZIB Debate'.[7] In Harald Müller's view, there would be no society and no politics without language (Müller 1994: 39). However, the debate lacked a focus on specific actors or actor-constellations (Jaeger 1996: 318; Zangl and Zürn 1996: 361). Revisiting the debate more than twenty years later, Anna Holzscheiter, building on Friedrich Kratochwil (1989), rightly points out that language must also be understood by the participants in a discourse (Holzscheiter 2017b: 146). This points to the 'social nature of language' (Fierke and Jørgensen 2001: 4), a feature of language often not taken up in debates about deliberation and arguing (Wiener 2003: 147).

Language not only has a constitutive function for the social construction of reality but also constitutes and constructs the speakers, that is, the individual human being, at the same time (Doty 1993: 302; Edkins and Pin-Fat 1999: 3). This usually takes place within discourse (Milliken 1999; Holzscheiter 2010: 30–31). As Anna Holzscheiter notes, it is also within discourse that norms are being created, which are then referred to by speakers and 'are a constitutive factor for the social context in which international actors speak and act'

[7] The debate took place in the mid-1990s in the German *Zeitschrift für Internationale Beziehungen*, abbreviated as ZIB; hence the name of the debate.

(Holzscheiter 2017b: 146). Therefore, a critical constructivist perspective on language must include studying how language constitutes the individual human being as part of constituting the socially constructed reality. Here, Anna Holzscheiter's claim that, within discourse, subjects make meaning and meaning makes subject is essential, as it clarifies that to reconstruct the appearance of the individual human being in global politics scholars need to study discourses in global politics (Holzscheiter 2010: 30–31). Within these discourses, the individual human being is positioned or positions themselves. Chapter 5 will provide a detailed discussion of discourse and positions from a methodological perspective. However, the idea of positions can also be found on a theoretical level in IL scholarship. Section 3.4 develops this concept, together with the concept of participants. Here, I focus solemnly on the concepts of participants and positions, leaving aside debates about the philosophical underpinnings of IL, as others have done so much more skilfully (Besson and Tasioulas 2010).

3.4 INTERNATIONAL LAW PARTICIPANTS, POSITIONS, HUMAN AND OTHER RIGHTS, AND DUTIES

In this section, I provide an overview of the concepts of positions and participation. I also discuss questions about the duties and rights of the individual human being in global politics. Regarding rights, I offer an account of what Anne Peters has identified as two groups of individual rights: 'ordinary' rights and human rights (Peters 2016: 436). The international law approaches I use can be described as 'non-statist' (Dixon 2013: 20). The section on international law is structured in three sub-sections. In Section 3.4.1, I revisit the concepts of subjects and objects of international law and introduce the concept of participants. In Section 3.4.2, I talk about the concept of positions. In Section 3.4.3, I discuss rights (human rights and individual rights) and duties of the individual human being in international law.

3.4.1 *Individual Human Beings as Subjects, Objects, and Participants in International Law*

IL scholars have not provided a coherent conception of the individual human being. Instead, they have identified a 'multiple personality' and a multiplicity of images of the individual human being (Bumke 2009: 125, 148, my translation). As discussed in Chapter 2, the individual human being is typically introduced into IL as another subject of international law. However, the underlying object-subject dichotomy is not without problems, as Rosalyn

Higgins (1994: 49–50) points out. Therefore, she suggests speaking of participants instead of subjects (Higgins 1994: 50). For her, 'the whole notion of "subjects" and "objects" has no credible reality . . . no functional purpose. We have erected an intellectual prison of our own choosing and then declared it to be an unalterable constraint' (Higgins 1994: 49). To be clear, for Rosalyn Higgins there are only participants in international law. States, IOs, NGOs, and individuals all participate in international law (Higgins 1978: 5).

This idea about participants is embedded in an approach that thinks about international law as a 'decision-making process' (Higgins 1994: 50), originating from the so-called New Haven School, that advocated 'sociological "policy-oriented" jurisprudence' (Peters 2016: 21). Rosalyn Higgins' suggestion has drawn some criticism, with scholars fearing a 'loss of legal precision' (Walter 2012: 7) and arguing that the term is 'underdifferentiated' (Peters 2016: 21). However, Rosalyn Higgins' suggestion for the term 'participant' also finds support in the legal literature, although there is disagreement regarding the underlying idea about law as a decision-making process (Nijman 2004: 403; McCorquodale 2004: 481, 2006: 328, 2017: 751–753; Kjeldgaard-Pedersen 2018: 41). In the classical definition of the New Haven School, participants are those who play some role (formal or informal) in the decision-making process (Kjeldgaard-Pedersen 2018: 37–38). Robert McCorquodale, however, points out that the notion 'has been used by other jurists' who are not part of the New Haven School (McCorquodale 2017: 754), such as Christoph Schreuer (1993: 449). Christoph Schreuer observes that '[t]he gradual diffusion of powers among different types of participants casts doubts on our traditional conception of international law' (Schreuer 1993: 453).

In this book, I build on the notion of participants but remain agnostic about how international law is to be understood. The notion is useful because it allows for a more inclusive notion of international law (McCorquodale 2004: 481–482). Robert McCorquodale notes that the 'binary opposition between "subject" and "object" has been rightly criticized, not least because it privileges the voices of states, since all potential participants are compared to states, and it silences alternatives voices' (McCorquodale 2004: 481). As Hilary Charlesworth and Christine Chinkin (2000: 48) demonstrate, women are one example of such marginalisation or silencing. I choose the term 'participants' over alternatives, such as subjects or actors, to be able to refer to the individual human being in global politics that recognises the agency of the individual and moves beyond an understanding of global politics that begins with the state. The term participants thus captures the appearance of the individual human being in global politics on a conceptual level.

The idea that international law is something in which various actors participate and interact provides additional support for claiming that the research on discourses of global politics should focus on the individual human being. Furthermore, such views on individual human beings as participants can be fruitfully combined with the work of Jutta Brunnée and Stephen Toope (2010a), who focus on the theme of interaction in international law. These interactions are taking place at an individual level and are linked to the development of international law. Conceptualising international law as interactional (Brunnée and Toope 2010a: 354) also allows Jutta Brunnée and Stephen Toope to provide alternative criteria of the legality of norms, based on the work of Fuller (1964: 164). For interactions to be possible, the inclusion of all participants (Higgins 1994) is necessary and, at the same time, ensures an inclusive legal system (McCorquodale 2004: 482). Additionally, the focus on interaction and a conception of norms as shared understandings (Brunnée and Toope 2010a: 350) fits well with critical constructivist work on norms and IL scholar's work on participation, because here too the interpretation of actors and the question of how they perceive a specific situation are foregrounded.

Individuals thus participate in global politics. They may participate themselves, for example, when they appear as defendants before the ICC (see Chapter 4). But at times they participate through being referred to by other participants. In any case, they appear in global politics as participants. The concept of participants thus constitutes another building block of the book's conceptual framework, enabling me to grasp the appearance of the individual in a more meaningful sense and in relation to other participants in international law. To operationalise this participation, I rely on a second concept drawn from IL, that of positions.

3.4.2 *The Position of the Individual Human Being in International Law*

Individuals have appeared in discourses of global politics. We can conceptualise this appearance through the term participant. The question remains how to operationalise this appearance and this participation, that is, how to enable me to operationalise the idea of individuals as participants. The answer can be found in IL's engagement of the 'position of individual' (Kettemann 2013: 5). The term 'position' usually refers to the physical location of something or someone and can be stated in relation to the position of others. In the context of international law, the term originates from 'interposition', which is used 'to describe the positioning of one entity (or of a legal field) between two others' (Kettemann 2013: 5). As Matthias Kettemann rightly notes, the question of the individual human being's position remains unsettled in international law (Kettemann 2013: 5). However, while states in the view of scholars like Malcom Shaw will remain dominant, there is a development within international law towards a world in which 'individuals may acquire rights free from the interposition of the state' (Shaw 2003: 722). Positions hence tell us something about the place of the individual human being in global politics.

Building on this, I use the term 'position' to operationalise the concept of participants and the participation of the individual human being in discourses of global politics.[8] An individual human being's position in a discourse relates to their position as a participant in the discourse and others recognising this participation (Davies and Harré 1990: 46). To give an obvious example from ICL: Here individuals have appeared in the discourse right from the beginning and they participate, for example, as victims or defendants. This places them in specific positions within the discourse vis-à-vis other participants. Studying their position in the discourse, and more specifically how they are positioned or position themselves, allows me to reconstruct how they participate and in doing so understand the appearance of the individual human being in the discourse of ICL.

3.4.3 *Human Rights, Other Rights, and Duties of the Individual Human Being*

As we already saw in Chapter 2, IL as a discipline has been at the forefront of recognising the individual human being in international law and global politics. This individualisation (Peters 2016) or humanisation (Meron 2006) of international law manifests in the growing number of rights and duties for the individual human being. A key focus has been on human rights (Hunt 2007; Hafner-Burton 2013; Hopgood et al. 2017a; Sikkink 2017; Forsythe 2018). Building on the discussion of the human rights literature in Chapter 2, we can draw several relevant conceptual and theoretical insights.

Most importantly, the cases discussed in this book are closely connected to human rights questions; they are either concerned with violations of specific human rights or protection of specific human rights. Therefore, the case studies will be cognisant of the respective human rights. That the individual human being matters in global politics as a right-bearer, and has become more

[8] More on the specifics of this operationalisation is provided in Chapter 5.

and more independent of states, is another relevant observation the human rights literature offers (Brown 2002b: 199). However, for most humans, these rights were not granted or recognised by governments for a long time. Women, BIPoC, LGBQTI, and many others were not – and in many countries are not – granted full human rights. In other words, the question of who has what kind of human rights is contested.

Concerning the human rights individual humans have, it is worth recalling that assigning rights and duties to individual human beings was confined to the state for most of human history. Today, states remain key players in protecting these rights (Hafner-Burton 2013). Yet individual human beings have pathways to remedies outside their state or in cases of state failure. This is especially the case for those living in states that have ratified the European Convention on Human Rights, with the European Court of Human Rights acting as a guardian of the Convention. There are also individual complaint mechanisms under several international treaties and covenants (OHCHR n.d. a). Nevertheless, this system is far from perfect or complete. As Anne Peters argues, a '"right to rights" independent of the state . . . is fundamental to an up-to-date international legal order' (Peters 2016: 435).

Anne Peters, in her seminal study *Beyond Human Rights* and the earlier published German work *Jenseits der Menschenrechte* (2014, 2016) offers an excellent account of rights and duties of the individual human being in international law. She points to the existence of rights arising from international responsibility (Peters 2016, 167) and offers a detailed study of rights across a wide range of areas of international law. More importantly, she argues that in her view individual rights can be divided into two groups, 'human rights and ordinary (simple) international individual rights' (Peters 2016: 436). Both kinds of rights matter for understanding the humanisation of global politics, as both provide reference points in the discourse about the individual human being and both matter for international law and the individual human being (Peters 2016: 8).

Apart from rights (human and otherwise), it is essential to note that international law also imposes duties on the individual human being (Peters 2016: 113, 408). These duties or obligations can be of a primary or secondary nature (Peters 2016: 61). Examples include the 'obligations to refrain from genocide, war crimes or certain military activities' or 'to participate in suppressing the trade in blood diamonds and drug smuggling' (Peters 2016: 62). In conclusion, rights (human rights and ordinary ones) and duties are key concepts for understanding the humanisation of global politics.

3.5 CONCLUSION

By combining concepts taken from several IR theories and IL approaches, a fruitful conceptual framework for studying the appearance of the individual human being in global politics is now in place. These concepts are embedded in a theoretical framework, bringing together feminist and constructivist theories with various approaches in International Law. Table 3.1 summarises the conceptual and theoretical framework.[9] Taken together, they constitute the foundation from which I engage with specific cases of humanisation of global politics in the sucbsequent chapters.

It is important to note that the following chapters are not about testing these frameworks or using them to explain a specific outcome. Instead, they are used as a lens through which I study the appearance of the individual human being in discourses of global politics. To recall, in this book, I aim to provide a theoretical conception of the humanisation of global politics and the social construction of the individual human being in global politics. Hence, the book's objective is to demonstrate how to conceptualise the humanisation of global politics. This objective is fulfilled by studying how the individual appears in discourses of global politics and theorises this appearance as a process of social construction. As demonstrated above in the discussion on the various approaches and concepts, they all enable me to study specific aspects or central elements of the humanisation of global politics. In addition, the interdisciplinarity of the frameworks reflects the interplay between politics and law in global politics. This interplay between political issues and legal issues also comes to the fore in the case studies.

The frameworks guide my engagement with the case studies through the ontological and epistemological insights. The role of theory in this book is neither to be tested nor to develop hypotheses. Instead, theory guides the analysis by providing lenses of analysis. Combining various approaches and disciplines allows me to close gaps and compensate weaknesses in individual approaches and disciplines, providing a holistic and robust framework for the analysis I conduct.

With the theoretical and conceptual framework in place, one problem remains: an epistemological one. As Patrick T. Jackson (2011: 27) reminds us, beginning with ontology – as I did – raises the question of whether ontology (and if so, what kind of ontology) can be put first in any scientific inquiry and what this means for scholarly work. In his view: 'If someone makes

[9] For a detailed discussion of all these approaches, a more differentiated picture of the various approaches within each theory, and more detail on the theoretical insights, see also Chapter 2.

TABLE 3.1. *Overview of the theoretical and conceptual framework*

Approach	Concepts	Theoretical insights
Feminism	Body Gender	• Humans are socially constructed • Gender is important in studying global politics • Importance of the human perspective and experience • The human body beyond mere biology as a relevant category to study global politics
Constructivism	Norms Language	• Social construction of global politics and its entities • A relational approach to IR • Humans as speakers • Humans as carriers of norms • Norms as inherently contested • Language constitutes the individual human being in discourse • Relevance of agency
International Law	Participants Positions Rights Duties Human Rights	• Importance of the individual human being in international law • The relevance of human rights, individual rights, and duties of the individual human being in international law • Human right norms as an important category of norms in the case studies

Source: Gholiagha

an ontological claim about something existing in the world, then we are faced with an intriguing *epistemological* problem of how possibly to know whether that claim is true, and the equally intriguing problem of selecting the proper *methods* to use in evaluating the claim' (Jackson 2011: 27, emphasis in original).

Chapter 5 will provide a detailed answer to this 'epistemological problem'. It will do so in the form of an analytical framework. The analytical framework is defined as 'a model that helps explain how a certain type of analysis will be conducted' (Pacheco-Vega 2018, emphasis removed). In following the abductive research logic, that analytical framework is based partly on insights drawn from empirics.

Therefore, Chapter 4 turns to the first case study, which is concerned with the prosecution of individual human beings under ICL. More precisely, I study two discourses concerning the situations in Kenya and Libya, both of which ended up before the ICC. The analysis will illustrate that the theoretical framework allows me to grasp the individual human being's appearance in ICL discourses and better understand how the individual human being is socially constructed. Furthermore, it allows me to develop innocence and guilt as two heuristics. These will then be integrated into the analytical framework offered in Chapter 5. While not unusual in doing research, such an approach is still rare when presenting research results. I invite the reader to follow me through the oscillation between the three frameworks (theoretical, conceptual, analytical) and empirics. I believe and I hope this allows a better understanding of what this book does.

4

Guilty and Innocent

The Individual Human Being in International Criminal Law

New York City, February 2011. The UN Security Council has just passed Resolution 1970, asking the ICC to investigate the situation in Libya. Only two weeks later, the ICC opens an investigation. In May 2011, the Office of the Prosecutor (OTP) requests arrest warrants for Muhammad Gaddafi, his son Saif Al-Islam Gaddafi, and Abdullah Al-Senussi, which the court grants in June 2016. As Mark Kersten remarks, this is a 'remarkable turnaround time' (Kersten 2016: 117). Furthermore, it seems that the ICC will move forward quickly, as the old regime topples, because of the NATO intervention (discussed in Chapter 6) and the prospect of arresting the three individuals becomes more likely. However, the reality is different. Opposition forces kill Muhammad Gaddafi; Saif Al-Islam is captured and held by a militia group in Libya, with neither Libyan authorities nor the ICC having access. Later, he invokes amnesty due to a new Libyan law, a move that remains contested in Libya and does not change his case before the ICC. Al-Senussi sits in a prison in Tripoli, sentenced to death (Trahan 2017: 820). Here, the ICC decided in July 2014 that the case is not admissible to the ICC, with Libya being both willing and able to put Al-Senussi on trial (Trahan 2017: 818; ICC 2020b). The dock of the ICC's courtroom remains empty again (Kersten 2018: 159).

A man dances happily in the street somewhere in Kenya, it is December 2014. Around his neck hangs a self-made sign that says 'UHURU INNOCENT', a little Kenya flag is attached to it (Aljazeera 2014).[1] Others are not happy: '"It is a victory for the president, but a heartbreaking loss for the victims of the violence," said 43-year old David Mongeri, a lawyer in Nakuru, some 150km north of the capital Nairobi' (Aljazeera 2014). On 5 December 2014, and roughly 10,000 kilometres away in The Hague, Netherlands, the

[1] This is my description of a picture in the article that appeared on Aljazeera.

then ICC Prosecutor Fatou Bensouda has asked the Trial Chamber V(B) to withdraw the charges against Uhuru Kenyatta as well as some of his associates. They had been charged with crimes against humanity in the context of post-election violence in Kenya in 2007 and 2008. The violence took place, there are perpetrators and victims for sure, but the ICC will, at least for some of the accused, not continue to investigate the situation and the alleged crimes any further. Whether the investigation will be reopened again at a later stage against others is not clear. A few years earlier, the ICC Prosecutor, then Luis Moreno Ocampo, had decided to bring the situation before the court *proprio motu*, that is, 'on one's own initiative' (ICC 2020a). No one is – at least for now – convicted for these alleged crimes.[2]

Violence took place, victims and perpetrators exist. Yet, in the narrow and strictly legal sense of the word, neither those in Kenya nor those in Libya were found guilty before the ICC. But does that mean they are innocent? Guilt and innocence are two central categories in ICL. And while the ICC and other courts and tribunals use them in a narrow legal sense, other actors within the discourse on prosecution use them in a much broader sense. In that broader sense, the term 'innocence' often refers to victims, who ought to be protected. The term 'guilt' often refers to perpetrators, who ought to be held accountable, not necessarily legally but perhaps politically or morally. The short stories about Kenya and Libya that opened this chapter already indicate, and this chapter will show, that the terms innocence and guilt are used more widely than in the narrow legal sense. For this reason, the chapter engages with the notions of innocence and guilt in ICL. To this end, the chapter zooms into the situations in Kenya and Libya before the ICC. It demonstrates how innocence and guilt matter in the discourse of prosecution outside and inside of courtrooms. In doing so, the book's interdisciplinary nature comes to the fore.[3] The chapter attempts to weave together insights from IR and IL hoping that meaningful patterns emerge that help us gain a more holistic picture of the individual human being in the discourse on prosecution.

4.1 INTRODUCTION

In 1946, Hersch Lauterpacht, in his discussion of Grotius' work, remarked that '[t]he individual is the ultimate unit of all law' (Lauterpacht 1946: 27). Nearly

[2] I am indebted to Caroline Fehl for extremely valuable feedback for this chapter. The chapter also profited immensely from a discussion with Mark Kersten. He had also pointed out to me during a conversation that the Kenya and Libya cases I discuss here are interesting because, legally, no one was found guilty before the ICC.

[3] See Mark Pollack (2020) for an overview of IR perspectives on international courts.

fifty years later, in 1995, the International Criminal Tribunal for the former Yugoslavia (ICTY) noted that '[a] state-sovereignty-oriented approach [of international law] has been gradually supplanted by a human-being-oriented approach' (ICTY 1995: 97). Jennifer Welsh has described the recent developments in ICL as 'the move to both establish and act upon individual liability in the conduct of armed conflict' (Welsh 2019b: 15), pointing out that the establishment of the ICC constitutes another 'key aspect of individualisation' (Welsh 2019b: 16–17). Scholars, while being cognisant of the political nature of international courts and tribunals and their respective political power (Rajkovic 2010: 31), have also identified these developments as part of 'the unprecedented individualization, legalization, and criminalization of responsibility in international relations' (Ainley 2011: 407). This chapter takes up the development of the 'criminalization of responsibility' (Ainley 2011: 407) and the corresponding rise of the non-impunity norm (Mills and Bloomfield 2018: 102). The development of ICL, especially since the end of the Cold War, indicates a growing focus on the individual human being in ICL (Bower 2019: 90) or the humanisation of ICL. Finally, international courts and tribunals are without doubt an integral part of global politics (Forsythe 2018: chapter 4, offers a human rights–based overview of international courts and tribunals; see Føllesdal 2020 for a survey article on their role and their legitimacy). They 'have ... become new social actors, ones that contribute to evolutions in the state of human consciousness and actions' (Sands 2016b: 889).

Against this backdrop, Chapter 4 presents the first of the three case studies in which I analyse the discourse on prosecution with a focus on the ICC. In line with the book's abductive research logic, I have chosen the first case study's position deliberately and for two reasons: First, the case study is illustrative, demonstrating the applicability of and the value added by the conceptual and theoretical framework. Second, I draw heuristics from this first case study to guide my analysis of the two other case studies (Kruse 2014: 151). In addition to these theoretical and methodological purposes, the chapter has an empirical purpose. It answers the following two research questions: How does the individual human being appear in the discourse on prosecution? How does this appearance matter for global politics?

The chapter demonstrates that the individual human being appears and therefore participates in the discourse on prosecution either as a victim or a perpetrator. This appearance occurs by positioning the individual human being as innocent or guilty within the discourse on prosecution. I argue that this matters for global politics because it opens a discursive space in which discussions about and enactment of the punishment of those guilty of the most serious international crimes become possible in the first place. Furthermore, it allows – at least potentially – to deliver justice to the victims of such crimes. Given this chapter's results, it should be evident to those familiar with ICL that the case study is an 'easy' case. Neither do I claim innovation nor a high degree of novelty in this analysis. However, it is precisely for this reason that it constitutes an ideal case to demonstrate the applicability of the theoretical and conceptual framework and develop heuristics following the abductive research logic. To enable me to follow this abductive research logic, I transfer insights from one field (Lynch 2014: 21), ICL and the ICC's work regarding the prosecution of individual human beings, to two other fields: the discourse on protecting the individual human being in the context of R2P (Chapter 6) and the killing of individual human beings via drones (Chapter 7).

To this end, the chapter is structured as follows: I begin by providing an overview of ICL and the ICC (Section 4.2). Section 4.3 then provides an empirical analysis of the situations in Kenya and Libya before the ICC. Building on both sections' insights, I then develop in Section 4.4 the heuristics of innocence and guilt as analytical tools. In concluding the chapter, I offer, in Section 4.5, a summary of the chapter and an answer to the chapter's guiding research questions.

4.2 INTERNATIONAL CRIMINAL LAW AND THE ICC

This section aims to provide a foundation for the analysis in Section 4.3 and provide a discussion of the position and the participation of the individual human being in ICL. I structure the section into four parts, beginning with a presentation of the development of ICL and then moving on to an overview of the ICC's development and current work. I highlight the relationship between the ICC with Africa, as both cases I study later in the chapter are concerned with African states. I then focus on the individual human being in ICL and before the ICC on a conceptual level, discussing first how individuals appear before the ICC and then the categories of victim and perpetrator and the idea of individual criminal responsibility.

4.2.1 *The Development of International Criminal Law*

ICL assigns rights and responsibilities to the individual human being outside the state (Robinson 2013: 147), making it part of the environment in which the individual human being as 'bearer of international rights and duties' finds themselves (Campbell 2013: 163). Prosecution of war crimes, including the prosecution of heads of states (Parlett 2011: 234–241), predates the modern version of ICL in which this book is mainly interested. The first international tribunals defining and dealing with war crimes, Nuremberg and Tokyo, were created only after World War II. These tribunals acknowledged individual criminal responsibility for international crimes, with duties arising for the individual human being from those responsibilities (McCorquodale 2004: 487; Walter 2012: 2; Fehl 2019: 900).

The idea of a permanent court for international crimes stalled during the Cold War (Forsythe 2013: 479), and the idea to use prosecution as a 'means to redress human rights violations' remained contested (Cacciatori 2018: 390). The atrocities committed in Rwanda and (former) Yugoslavia in the 1990s led to a renewed interest in institution building in the context of ICL.[4] The international community dealt with Rwanda and Yugoslavia via specialised ad-hoc tribunals, namely, the International Criminal Tribunal for Rwanda (ICTR) and the ICTY. The work of these tribunals and others, such as The Special Court for Sierra Leone and the Extraordinary Chambers in the Courts of Cambodia (ECCC), nourished the discussion on a possible permanent international criminal court. These tribunals and special courts have been discussed widely in the literature. Here, scholars have identified their strengths and weaknesses (Rajkovic 2010; Kaleck 2012; Forsythe 2013; Renner 2013; Weiss and Burke 2014; Simmons and Jo 2019: 25–28). In the following discussion, I sometimes refer to certain cases or the scholarly work I rely on has focused on one or several of these tribunals. However, beyond that, I do not discuss them but rather focus on the ICC.

One key point that, however, is shared across all those international courts and tribunals is the social construction of the individual human being as a victim and perpetrator. Sometimes, for example, in the case of child soldiers, the individual human being is constructed as a victim-perpetrator (Clarke 2009: 91; Renner 2013: 125–154). An extraordinary example where the label of victim and perpetrator overlap is Dominic Ongwen, a Ugandan national and member of the Lord's Resistance Army (Kersten 2016: chapters 4 and 5 offer a detailed discussion of the situation in Uganda before the ICC). Ongwen, a former child soldier, was found guilty of war crimes and crimes against humanity on more than fifty counts (ICC 2021c). On 6 May 2021, he was sentenced to twenty-five years of imprisonment (ICC 2021d). As of March 2022 the the case is in its appeal phase (ICC 2021b). A detailed discussion of the Ongwen case and related questions concerning the conviction of former child soldiers, themselves victims of a crime, are outside the chapter's scope.

[4] Chapter 6 provides details on these atrocities.

However, I would like to point to an excellent online symposium on the *Justice in Conflict* blog, which provides comprehensive analysis and discussion (Kersten 2021). What is important to note is that not only is the appearance as victim and perpetrator the result of a process of social construction but that the same individual human being at different points of time might be a victim and a perpetrator. Thus, for example, the 'crafting' of both victims and perpetrators through the ICC (Clarke 2009: 89–116) is clearly illustrated by the fact that victims can become perpetrators (Renner 2013: 124–125; Welsh 2014: 218).

To conclude this section, I would like to highlight that the development of ICL is part of the movement towards the prosecution of international crimes by the international community (Bonafé 2013: 339). Scholars have identified it as a significant development in international law (Forsythe 2013: 475). ICL is an important case for this book, as individual perpetrators commit international crimes against individual victims (Mégret 2010: 35; Welsh 2014: 217; Peters 2016: 117–120, for a historical overview), a point I revisit later in the context of debates about international criminal responsibility. ICL and the work of the ICC provide relevant insights into how legal orders develop and how the individual human being is positioned within legal orders, as Beatrice Bonafé reminds us (Bonafé 2013: 316). Because we already know about the centrality of the individual human being in ICL from both the historical development and the scholarly work, the case is also ideal for illustrating what we can learn about the discourse of prosecution by reading it through the lens offered by the conceptual and theoretical framework. Let me begin by offering some more background on the ICC, given that both situations I study below in detail were situations before the ICC.

4.2.2 *The International Criminal Court: Development and Current Work*

Following the end of the Cold War and the varied experience with ad-hoc tribunals for specific countries (Kaleck 2012: 50–66; Weiss and Burke 2014), the idea of a permanent international criminal court gained new motion, culminating in the Rome Conference. In 1998, after long and difficult negotiations (Schiff 2008; Deitelhoff 2009; Forsythe 2018: 174–151; Schabas 2020), the Rome Statute of the International Criminal Court (hereafter Rome Statute) was agreed upon (Rome Statute 1998). Four years later, the required sixty ratifications were reached, the Rome Statute came into force (Dixon 2007: 124), and the ICC started its work as a permanent court.

The ICC is concerned with what Article 1 of the Rome Statute calls 'the most serious crimes of international concern' (Rome Statute 1998: Article 1). Article 5 list the crimes that fall under the ICC's jurisdiction. These are the crime of genocide, crimes against humanity, war crimes, and the crime of aggression (Rome Statute 1998: Article 5).[5] Furthermore, the Rome Statute lists three different ways to bring a matter before the ICC (see Kersten 2016: 6–8, 163–165, for a discussion). The first one is the referral of a situation by a State Party (Rome Statute 1998: Article 14).[6] The second allows the Prosecutor to initiate investigations *proprio motu* based on information on crimes within the ICC's jurisdiction (Rome Statute 1998: Article 15[1]). The third one is through a UNSC referral (Rome Statute 1998: Article 16).[7]

A critical factor in deciding whether a case is brought before the ICC is the complementarity norm: while previous ad-hoc tribunals had been placed above national jurisdiction (Nichols 2015: 5), the ICC operates with the principle of complementarity (Preamble, Article 1, and Article 17 Rome Statute). While complementarity and the related issue of admissibility are not the main focus of the chapter, it is worth briefly discussing them (for a detailed discussion and excellent analysis see de Vos 2020). Questions concerning complementarity and admissibility played a role in both the Libyan and Kenyan situations before the ICC (see Section 4.3).

The principle of complementarity has been described as the 'corner stone' of the Rome Statute (Kaukoranta 2010: 16). As a result of the Rome Statute, many states have created domestic legislation or have claimed universal jurisdiction for international crimes (Buchanan 2010: 84; Wernicke 2014). This complementary system of ICL also means that 'criminal law cannot operate in complete isolation from domestic legal orders' (Bonafé 2013: 317). Individual human beings are faced with a plurality of legal orders (Bonafé

5 At the time of the Rome conference, no definition was agreed upon for the crime of aggression. Hence Article 5(2) of the Rome Statute reads: 'The Court shall exercise jurisdiction over the crime of aggression once a provision is adopted in accordance with articles 121 and 123 defining the crime and setting out the conditions under which the ICC shall exercise jurisdiction with respect to this crime. Such a provision shall be consistent with the relevant provisions of the Charter of the United Nations.' The definition was agreed upon during the Kampala Review Conference 31 May–11 June 2011 in Kampala, Uganda. Following the ratification of the amendment by more than thirty states, the ICC's Assembly of State Parties decided that the ICC has jurisdiction over the crime of aggression beginning on 17 July 2018; however, only over those states that have ratified the amendment (ICC 2019b).

6 While Article 14 speaks of referring a situation to the ICC through a State Party, in practice states have self-referred cases concerning their own territory to the ICC. As Mark Kersten notes: 'The idea behind state referrals as a trigger mechanism was that states would refer each other and not themselves to the Court . . .. But these "self-referrals" were useful for the new institution and the OTP recognized their potential political utility' (Kersten 2016: 7).

7 As of March 2022 there are – according to the ICC website – three ongoing preliminary examinations (seven have been conducted and closed with the decision not to proceed), seventeen investigation, and thirty cases (one appeal, nine closed, ten in pre-trial, four reparation/compensation, six on trial).

2013: 319), 'there is no shield to the prosecution of international crimes and, if States [*sic*] are unable or unwilling to prosecute, then the ICC can take over the task' (Hobbs 2020: 346). Strictly speaking, complementarity is understood as negative, as admissibility requires that the state in which the crime occurred or a state that has jurisdiction of the crime is either unwilling or unable to investigate the crime (Rome Statute 1998: Article 17,1(a) and (b); see Trahan 2017: 813, for an overview of debates on Article 17).

However, in its practice, the ICC has begun to develop what has been called positive complementarity (Burke-White 2008; Office of the Prosecutor 2013: 23; Nichols 2015: 29–44; Kersten 2016: 149). It was promoted at the Kampala review conference (Chandler 2010: 12) and aimed to increase the number of domestic prosecutions compared to international ones (Nichols 2015: 6). It is possible that ICC intervention would create pressure on states to investigate crimes within their states.[8] William Burke-White defines positive complementarity as situations in which 'the OTP would actively encourage investigation and prosecution of international crimes within the Court's jurisdiction by States [*sic*]' (Burke-White 2008: 62). An OTP policy paper from 2013 seems to define positive complementarity in that sense. However, it takes a careful approach, stating that '[t]he Office will engage with national jurisdictions provided that it does not risk tainting any possible future admissibility proceedings' (Office of the Prosecutor 2013: 24).

To sum up, the ICC functions as a regular judicial body amongst others, but it is also 'filling a gap' by prosecuting heads of states and senior government officials (Interview A7: 467–468).[9] The same interview partner remarked that the ICC is there 'to ensure that *every individual* that commits a crime is held accountable' (Interview A7: 469–470, emphasis added). In the word of one interview partner, the ICC 'changed the landscape of international relations' (Interview A8: 24–25), as, in the past, peace often was made via amnesties (Interview A8: 30–33).[10] Ending impunity through prosecution and complementarity is, for some, the greatest achievement of the ICC (Interview A7: 103–104; Interview A8: 41). Similarly, Kirsten Ainley calls the ICC one of 'the most important innovations in human rights protection for decades' (Ainley 2015: 37). However, the ICC has not been free from criticism.

8 I owe this insight to Caroline Fehl.

9 Here it is important to note that while the ICC enables the prosecution of heads of states and governments, its jurisdiction is not limited to those or senior government officials. In some cases, investigations are even targeted only against individuals fighting the government, as is the was the case with the Lord's Resistance Army in Uganda (Kersten 2016: chapters 4 and 5)

10 On the issue of amnesties in ICL and in the context of the ICC, see Jospeh Close (2020) and Michael Scharf (1999).

A large point of contention has been the relationship between the ICC and African states. The relationship between the ICC and Africa as a continent and, more specifically, the relationship between the ICC, on the one hand, and the African Union (AU) and African states, on the other hand, is of particular interest to this book. Both the situations I study in more detail, Libya and Kenya, concern African states. It is also of interest because the bone of contention in the debates is how to deal with certain individual human beings, heads of states and governments, who have a specific position in global politics.

4.2.3 *The ICC and Africa*

Since the beginning of the ICC's work, critics have argued that the ICC is de facto a 'Court on Africa', claiming that its focus is entirely on African countries (Ambos 2013; Endoh 2020). In this context, critics have described the ICC as a new form of colonialism (Quashigah 2010: 94) and an 'instrument of Western politics or an impediment to regional solutions' (Stahn 2015: lxxxv). Others have conceptualised the problematic relationship between (some) African countries and the ICC as a 'normative problem', pointing to the contestation and non-cooperation as an indication of norm contestation (García Iommi 2020: 105, 115–116). The structural set up with the UNSC's permanent members has also fed into this criticism. For one, UNSC permanent members can defer investigations against themselves or allies indefinitely. Even though China, Russia, and the United States are not State Parties to the ICC, they can refer others to the ICC who are also not a State Party to the ICC.

The Kenya situation (to be discussed below in detail) and the debates around the arrest warrants against Sudanese President Al-Bashir further illustrate these tensions. Following the opening of the investigation against several Kenyan political leaders, including Uhuru Kenyatta and William Ruto, who had been elected as president and vice president in 2013, the AU expressed its concern against this decision (for an overview, see Maunganidze and Du Plessis 2015). It furthermore regretted the decision of the ICC not to refer the investigation back to Kenya (African Union Assembly 2013: 13–14) and supported Kenya in a (failed) attempt to have the UNSC defer the case (Endoh 2020: 14).[11] The AU had raised similar criticism earlier concerning the two arrest warrants issued against Al-Bashir in 2009 and 2010 (ICC 2009, 2010b;

[11] Deferrals were built into the Rome Statute as a response to the peace vs. justice problem. Article 16 of the Rome Statute authorises the UNSC to defer an investigation or prosecution for up to twelve months if the UNSC passes a resolution under Chapter VII (Rome Statute 1998:

Quashigah 2010: 95; African Union Assembly 2013: 13–14; Cacciatori 2018: 394–397). In the case of Al-Bashir, the critique had also manifested through clear violations of their duties to arrest suspects by those African states who are party to the Rome Statute but did not arrest him when he visited the respective states, which include 'Chad (in 2010, 2011 and 2013), Malawi (in 2011), South Africa (in 2015) and Jordan (in 2017)' (Endoh 2020: 19).[12]

The changing and at times strained relationship between the ICC and African countries has led to calls for African states' withdrawal, with some states initiating that process. As of March 2022, only Burundi has withdrawn, with South Africa and Gambia having to rescind their withdrawal for various political and legal reasons (Mills and Bloomfield 2018: 116, 123).[13]

In response to the critique of the ICC as a 'court on Africa', scholars and practitioners alike have made three counter-arguments against this critique. First, African countries have been particularly involved in creating the ICC and are still a major part of it today, as State Parties, and providing judges and staff (Ambos 2013: 516; Kaul 2013: 5–7). Second, scholars have pointed out that despite the criticism of African countries against the ICC, there is no 'single African voice' (Ambos 2013: 516) on the ICC, and in fact, several states, as well as African civil society organisations, are strong supporters of the ICC (Ambos 2013: 516; Mills and Bloomfield 2018: 108, 121). Third, there are good reasons for the predominant focus of the ICC on African situations. First, several situations the ICC is involved with were brought before the ICC through self-referrals. From the currently seventeen situations under investigation (as of March 2022), ten concern African countries. But five of the ten are self-referrals (ICC 2020c). Second, there are 'legal and policy' reasons (Ambos 2013: 516), explaining the high number of African cases and situations before the ICC (Ambos 2013: 508–524). The 'legal and policy' reasons argument Ambos makes has been phrased much more directly by then-deputy ICC Prosecutor Fatou Bensouda, '[a]nytime I hear this about ICC targeting Africa, ICC doing double justice, it saddens me, especially as an African woman, also

Article 16), which means that the UNSC must deem the investigation or a prosecution as a threat to peace and security (Kersten 2016: 55).

12 The visit to South Africa is perhaps the most interesting one, as here the South Gauteng High Court 'in response to an application by the South African Litigation Centre, ordered the government to temporarily prevent Bashir from leaving South Africa until a full hearing could be held on the request to arrest Bashir and send him to The Hague. During the hearing, which took place the next day the court 'adjourned for an hour at the request of government lawyers .... Minutes later, Bashir was allowed to leave on his plane, which had been moved from a civilian airport to a military base' (Mills 2015).

13 The Philippines have also withdrawn from the ICC.

knowing that these conflicts, most of these conflicts are happening on the continent of Africa' (cited in Stearns 2011). Similarly, her predecessor Ocampo had pointed out that while there were African accused, there were also African victims (Gevers 2020: 190). Scholarly work supports this view by the two former Prosecutors of the ICC (Endoh and Mbao 2016; Endoh 2020: 32).

The critique of an African bias is part of a larger debate on the ICC's politicisation (Kaul 2013; Schabas 2013: 396–402). Scholars such as Christopher Gevers (2020) emphasise the need to read the current critique against a much longer and colonial history of Africa's relationship as a continent with ICL. Some scholars have argued that the ICC should not be politicised. Others argue that politicisation is inevitable, so there is a necessity to deal with it (Schabas 2013: 404–405). Mark Kersten points out that 'it is often maintained that the biggest threat to the ICC is "politicization". The fear of politicization manifests itself primarily through the discourse on the Court's independence' (Kersten 2016: 166). What we can observe in practice, Mark Kersten notes, is that 'the ICC's decision-making reflects a negotiation of the Court's own interests with the interests of those political actors upon which it depends. The Court may be used and instrumentalized by states or state-based organizations such as the Security Council' (Kersten 2016: 168). Nikolas Rajkovic even goes further concerning the issue of politicisation, arguing that law, including ICL, is 'a practice of government aimed at directing human conduct' (Rajkovic 2010: 31). In his work, Nikolas Rajkovic suggests understanding practices such as prosecuting international crimes as ruling through the law instead of a manifestation of the rule of law (Rajkovic 2010: 31). His point is well taken. The analysis conducted in this chapter demonstrates how political actors such as the UN Security Council and its members use their power to refer cases to the ICC to facilitate individual human beings' prosecution.[14]

The critique of the ICC as a court on Africa can also be seen in the context of a more general critique concerning the ICC's selectivity (Kaleck 2012: 119–122). Wolfgang Kaleck suggests distinguishing 'horizontal selectivity', that is, only some crimes are being prosecuted over time, and 'vertical selectivity', that is, only certain people are prosecuted (Kaleck 2012: 14–15). One example is how the ICC has dealt with potential war crimes by the United States in Afghanistan since 2003. It took a long time before, on 5 March 2020, the Appeals Chamber authorised the ICC Prosecutor to begin an investigation (ICC 2021a). Generally, the selectivity of international criminal courts and

[14] As Chapter 6 demonstrates with reference to Syria, this politicisation can also lead to a case not to be referred to the ICC.

tribunals remains an unsolved issue. However, as the late ICC Judge Hans-Peter Kaul remarked, the selectivity towards specific individuals he labelled as 'leading perpetrators' is part of the ICC's work (Kaul 2013: 8). Nevertheless, a double-standard critique remains valid when considering a more extensive historical view of African countries' relationship with ICL (Gevers 2020: 179). I now turn to the question of how the individual human being appears before the ICC in terms of legal questions. But as will become evident, that process also profits from an interdisciplinary perspective that combines the study of law and politics.

4.2.4 *Appearing before the ICC*

Regarding whom can be charged, Article 25(1) of the Rome Statute limits the criminal responsibility to natural persons (Rome Statute 1998: Article 1; see also Gorski 2011: 7; Peters 2016: 143) and thus binds the individual human being directly. While this point was relatively uncontested, the question of how the process of charging individual human beings would take place was the subject of heavy debates amongst delegates negotiating the Rome Statute. As Nicole Deitelhoff explains, two positions had developed in the negotiations. The first position, heralded by the 'like-minded-group' and NGOs, demanded a completely independent prosecutor. The second position, held by the five permanent UN Security Council members and several other states, required prosecutions to be opened only at the request of the Security Council or states (Deitelhoff 2006: 258). The results of these negotiations led to the current system, with a prosecutor able to bring charges on their own initiative against states who have ratified the Rome Statute with the condition that a Pre-Trial Chamber accepts those charges. For states who are not members of the ICC, investigations are only possible following a referral by the UNSC. Argentina and Germany introduced the idea of a relatively independent prosecutor in March 1998 (Deitelhoff 2006: 258). However, the Security Council retains the right to defer an investigation for up to twelve months and renew this deferral if deemed necessary without any limitations (Rome Statute 1998: Article 16).

The Prosecutor is also responsible for the act of charging (Jacobs 2013: 208). Dov Jacobs notes 'that the ICC statute itself does not use the "indictment" terminology, as is the case in other international tribunals, but rather refers to a "document containing the charges"' (Jacobs 2013: 206). The related question here then is: what constitutes a charge? The ICC's preferred interpretation is 'that a charge is composed of two elements, a factual description of the crimes and legal characterisation of the facts' (Jacobs 2013: 207). Article 53 of the

Rome Statute outlines the details of initiation of an investigation, with the Prosecutor having to consider several factors. A central factor is the gravity of the crime (Rome Statute 1998: Article 53,1[c]).[15] The Rome Statute does not define gravity further. As a result, the ICC has developed its own understanding (SáCouto and Clearly 2008; deGuzman 2012). The OTP's approach to gravity is to assess it not only quantitatively, that is, in terms of the number of victims but also qualitatively (Office of the Prosecutor 2013: 15). This qualitative assessment includes considering the 'nature of the crimes' and 'their impact' (Office of the Prosecutor 2013: 15–16). Some scholars argue that there is a shift towards more qualitative factors (Schabas 2013: 399–401).

Regardless of how the OTP measures gravity, it always constitutes an integral part of whether charges are brought forward or not. Relatedly, to be able to hold an individual accountable, two core principles are at work: personal culpability of the perpetrator and legality, that is, the action must be declared as a crime and that declaration must take place before the crime, that is, there is no retroactivity (Robinson 2013: 132–133). The principle of culpability is of particular interest here, as culpability requires positioning the individual human being as a perpetrator. This positioning in the discourse and the shift in the ICC towards a more qualitative approach requires a careful reading of situations and consideration of legal and political developments and context. Therefore, an interdisciplinary, interpretative, and reconstructive approach, such as this book presents, helps understand and analyse developments in ICL and the work of the ICC, both in a general sense and in specific situations and cases. The necessity and usefulness of such an interpretative approach also become evident in the following discussion on victims, perpetrators, and individual criminal responsibility.

4.2.5 *Victims, Perpetrators, and Individual Criminal Responsibility*

There are many different actors in the courtroom (judges, defence lawyers, witnesses, victims, the accused, the prosecutor), either in person or represented through lawyers or written documents. Here, I am primarily interested in the alleged perpetrators, who can also be referred to as the accused or the defendant. Nevertheless, for two reasons, I want to start with the victims. The first reason is a normative one: while ICL is concerned with holding those

[15] Another factor that must be weighed against the gravity of the crimes and the 'interest of victims' is the 'interest of justice', if an investigation does 'not serve the intertest of justice' (Rome Statute 1998: Article 53,1[c]), the prosecutor shall not initiate an investigation (see Scharf 1999: 524, for a brief discussion).

accountable who are criminally responsible, victims ought to be heard and to be seen, as ICL is ultimately about delivering justice to them.[16] The second reason is a methodological one: perpetrators and victims are co-constitutive of each other; in the discourse, they are often identified together or with reference to each other. Assessing one often requires studying the other.

What is a victim? A comprehensive definition of the term 'victim' is offered in the *United Nation's Basic Principles and Guidelines on the Right to a Remedy and Reparation for Victims of Gross Violations of International Human Rights Law and Serious Violations of International Humanitarian Law* (United Nations 2005a). Victims are defined as

> *persons who individually* or collectively *suffered harm,* including physical or mental injury, emotional suffering, economic loss or substantial impairment of their fundamental rights, through acts or omissions that constitute gross violations of international human rights law, or serious violations of international humanitarian law (United Nations 2005a: 5, emphasis added).

From this definition, two points should be noted. First, victims are individual human beings who have been harmed. Second, individuals are being harmed by perpetrators.[17] One requires the other. Therefore, positioning one individual human being as a victim requires another individual human being to be positioned as a perpetrator. However, we may not always be able to put a name or face to the latter or the former.

Victims are furthermore within ICL more generally but especially in the context of the ICC 'individual rights-bearers' (Sehmi 2018: 583). In its practical work, the ICC distinguishes between victims of the case and victims of the situation: 'a "victim of the case" is a person who can establish a causal link between the harm suffered and the person responsible for the crimes. Victims who are unable to establish this link are deemed to be victims of the situation' (Sehmi 2018: 575–576). Most importantly, perhaps, victims can declare themselves as such, for example, through victim declaration forms, thereby taking up a specific position in the discourse that allows them to participate in the proceedings (Sehmi 2018: 578). This idea of self-positioning compared to positioning through others will be revisited in Chapter 5 on the analytical framework and analysed in more detail in the subsequent case studies and the

[16] An idea that is reflected in the preamble of the Rome Statute and the provisions concerning victim participation and protection, laid out *inter alia* in Article 68 of the Rome Statute (Rome Statute 1998: Article 68).

[17] On the concept of harm in international relations and IR Theory, see the work of Andrew Linklater (2011). On a discussion of harm in the context of the ICC, see Matthew Weinert (2015: 154).

analysis in this chapter. Having provided a brief overview of victims in ICL and within the ICC,[18] let us turn to the perpetrators.

There are two original approaches to perpetrators[19] in criminal law theory: the objective one and the subjective one. The former requires that the perpetrator 'performs the *actus reus* of the crime', that is, the 'guilty act'. The latter focuses on the *mens rea*, that is, the 'guilty mind' (Ohlin 2015: 519). Midway between these two is Claus Roxin's control theory (Roxin 2008) based on the concept of 'organized power structures' (Roxin 2011: 198). As Jens Ohlin elaborates, '[u]nder Roxin's control theory, the perpetrator is defined as the individual who has control or "hegemony" over the act, who decides whether the criminal transaction will occur' (Ohlin 2015: 520). While there has been some critique of this control theory (Ohlin 2015: 527–531), it presently constitutes the ICC's preferred approach (Gil, Gil, and Maculan 2015: 352; Smeulers 2020: 394). Furthermore, according to Elies van Sliedregt, Article 25(3) of the Rome Statute supports this approach (Rome Statute 1998: Article 25(3); van Sliedregt 2015: 499). In this context, crime, Ruben Reike argues, 'strongly emphasizes individual agency and responsibility, and largely ignores the role of collectives or social grievances' (Reike 2014: 453). Regarding ICL, he argues that it is 'fundamentally based on the principle of individual criminal responsibility' (Reike 2014: 455).

Scholars such as Toni Erskine have criticised this focus on the individual, claiming that certain acts and developments lie outside individuals' power; hence, assigning responsibilities to them is difficult (Erskine 2008: 701). Similarly, Kirsten Ainley has criticised this focus on the 'evil' individual human being (Ainley 2008; see also Kersten 2016: 42). She argues that an 'individualistic view' on evil is based on a too simplistic classification of 'good' vs. 'evil' and 'leads us to believe that little or nothing can be done to prevent evil' (Ainley 2008: 60–61). Other scholars are more supportive of the notion of 'evil', basing their argument on Arendt's descriptive use of the term (Owens 2007: 49).

A related argument is that the conception of the individual human being as evil is not representative of real-world behaviour, claiming that it focuses too strongly on individual moral agency (Ainley 2008: 68; Hoover 2012: 233–234). Mark Kersten, referring to these debates, points out that '[s]ome scholars have

[18] See Anne Peters (2016: 270–274) for further analyses of victims in the context of the ICC.

[19] I primarily use the term 'perpetrator' as I find it to be the most encompassing, working inside and outside of the courtroom. At times, especially in reference to the literature I discuss, I use more legal-technical terms such as 'defendant' or 'accused', which I have taken from Frédéric Mégret's work on the topic (Mégret 2018, 2019).

argued that the individualization of guilt in this context is not a strength, but a weakness of international criminal justice' (Kersten 2016: 26). However, as Liam Murphy rightly argues, this 'does not mean that all responsibility is, in the end, individual responsibility. It means ... that the point of view of individuals cannot be ignored' (Murphy 2010: 301). In response to this, one can consider the critique raised by Kirsten Ainley that the focus on jurisprudence is not enough and that we need a conception of political responsibility in addition to legal responsibility, allowing 'to process collective alongside individual accountability' (Ainley 2011: 422–423). While I agree with Kirsten Ainley that a broader conception of responsibility would be useful, this does not diminish the need for a better understanding of the position of the individual human being within the context of ICL and the ICC. Doing this requires consideration of individual responsibility.

I am, of course, not alone in my argument to focus on individual criminal responsibility. As Frédéric Mégret notes, it has 'assume[d] a domineering position' within ICL (Mégret 2017: 32). Yet assigning individual criminal responsibility in the context of international crimes remains a challenge (Smeulers 2020: 379), due to the features of these crimes as 'manifestations of *collective* violence ... system criminality ... [and] that they are in essence political crimes' (Smeulers 2020: 381–382). In a critical assessment of the relationship between 'collective violence and individual punishment' Mark Drumbl (2005) offers a detailed discussion of the problems arising from the fact that focusing on few individuals indicates 'that a number of selected guilty individuals squarely are to be blamed for systemic levels of violence' (Drumbl 2005: 542).[20] Similarly, Miriam Aukerman asks, '[i]s ordinary crime really an appropriate analogy for massive human rights atrocities ...?' (Aukerman 2002: 41). These are important questions, but this is not the space to discuss them (Aukerman 2002 offers a detailed discussion of the question). What matters for the chapter's focus is that the crimes are committed by individuals who have 'different positions, roles, and motives' (Smeulers 2020: 389). In sum, the central position of the individual human being as a participant in ICL is characteristic of a system that is 'constrained by respect for the autonomy, dignity, or agency of the *individual*' (Robinson 2013: 133, emphasis added).

20 Mark Drumbl also offers a careful analysis of the in his view rather weak theoretical foundation for punishing those individuals, however 'it does not follow that international criminal law should shirk the construction of a doctrinal method or starve the development of a penological purpose that truly is its own' (Drumbl 2005: 608). As I note further below, I do not deal with those questions here or with the different rationales for why we punish, e.g., retribution or deterrence (Drumbl 2005: 577). For an additional analysis of the question of punishment, see the work by Miriam J. Aukerman (2002).

Despite these insights, Frédéric Mégret has convincingly demonstrated that most scholarship on perpetrators focuses on them as objects within ICL (Mégret 2019: 402–403). Identifying this as a research gap, Frédéric Mégret suggests thinking about perpetrators as subjects who have agency and play a part in shaping trials through their agency in the courtroom (Mégret 2018: 433, 2019: 404). This suggestion is noteworthy, as it leads to relevant insights about guilt and innocence, concepts at the core of this chapter and this book. While remaining within the language of subjects and objects, Frédéric Mégret refers to defendants as participants as well (Mégret 2019: 471). In another publication written with Damien Scalia, there is a reference to perpetrators' position in the discourse (Mégret and Scalia 2019: 103). In her work on the '"ideal" perpetrator', Sofia Stolk (2018) provides an equally interesting and relevant analysis. Studying opening statements of several cases before international criminal courts, she demonstrates how language is us when the 'defendant is presented as well as created' (Stolk 2018: 681).[21]

A final point I want to draw attention to from this kind of scholarship is the discussion of what Sofia Stolk has called '[t]he paradoxical (in)humanity of perpetrators' (Stolk 2018: 678). She points out that 'both humanizing and dehumanizing qualities are simultaneously assigned to the defendant' (Stolk 2018: 679). Relatedly, Frédéric Mégret has argued that a defendant may want to be recognised as a human again by displaying remorse. Using the case of Duch, the former Khmer Rouge Chairman, in front of the ECCC, Frédéric Mégret notes: 'In a sense, therefore, his confession was meant to make him "human" where he had so often been described as a "monster," exposing his complexity and redeemability' (Mégret 2018: 437). Humanisation and dehumanisation take place simultaneously, 'defendants are located both inside and outside the all-encompassing community that is invoked and created at international criminal courts and tribunal' (Stolk 2018: 678). In terms of innocence and guilt, the perpetrator as a defendant is positioned in the discourse as guilty, thereby appearing in the discourse of prosecution and participating in it. But, as Sofia Stolk notes, despite the fact of having committed or at least being charged with having committed inhumane crimes, the perpetrator remains human. They must remain human to be charged for violating norms (Stolk 2018: 678). As Matthew Weinert notes, ICL humanises both victims and perpetrators (Weinert 2015: 143, 154–155).

What about the collective dimension of crimes? What about groups as victims and perpetrators who commit their crimes as part of a larger

[21] Thanks are due to Caroline Fehl to alerting me to this work.

enterprise? Taking up an argument by Mark Osiel, mass atrocities will always oscillate between 'individuating' and 'collectivizing' (Osiel 2014: 282–283). Furthermore, the aforementioned control theory also supports a focus on the individual human being. However, one should not leave out the context in which these crimes occur (see Smeulers 2020, for a criminological analysis of the control theory). Here, it is essential to note that this act of assigning is one that other individual human beings do. Importantly for this book, the control theory provides a theoretical foundation on which an individual human being is constructed as a 'perpetrator' in the discourse on prosecution, especially concerning international crimes. It is, also, on a level of practice, what the ICC does, as it defines individual criminal responsibility in Article 25 (3) of the Rome Statute (Rome Statute 1998: Article 25[3]). Thus, little doubt exists that the practice of prosecution conducted by the ICC is aimed at individual human beings and not at states (Osiel 2014: 249; Vasiliev 2014: 42) and therefore it constitutes a viable case for this book.[22]

The literature and the existing studies on specific cases say less about the positions and social constructions, norms and language, how individual experience matters, and how notions of guilt and innocence are used outside of the strict legal sense. This chapter hopes to contribute to the theoretical and conceptual work on ICL and the ICC from an interdisciplinary perspective. To this end, the Section 4.3 engages with two situations before the ICC in the early 2010s: Libya and Kenya. The cases are read and analysed with the theoretical and conceptual framework as a lens. Following an abductive research logic (outlined in detail in the following Chapter 5), Herbert Blumer's notion of 'sensitizing concepts' (Blumer 1954: 7; see also Hofius 2015, 2020: 179), and drawing on the idea of 'sensitizing reading' (Wiener 2018: 5) or 'sensitizing questions' (Gillespie and Cornish 2014), I use the conceptual framework to guide me through the interpretation of the empirical material and to develop the notions of guilt and innocence as heuristics (Section 4.4).[23] In sum, such a reading allows me to focus on the relevant discourses for the

[22] Of course states matter for and in ICL as well. As Jennifer Welsh rightly notes: 'While international criminal law (seeks to determine the criminal responsibility of an *individual* offender, it is underpinned and enabled by a state-centric system: it is states which ratify the relevant treaties establishing this body of law; it is states that must enforce international criminal law, by apprehending indicted individuals and collecting evidence; and, it is states that have privileged access to the international institutions (like the Security Council) that are crucial for operationalising accountability' (Welsh 2019b: 18, emphasis in original). In this context it must be noted that the ICJ has dealt with cases concerning mass atrocity crimes as well (ICJ 2007, 2021).

[23] With thanks to Maren Hofius pointing me to some of the references used here.

book's overall argument. In more concrete terms, I look for direct or indirect references to central concepts in this book's conceptual framework, such as norms and language and positions and participations.

4.3 THE SITUATIONS IN LIBYA AND KENYA BEFORE THE ICC

Let me begin by briefly saying something about why the analysis focuses on Libya and Kenya. They both share links to the debates on R2P, which I discuss in Chapter 6.[24] They both failed in the sense that no one ended up being convicted. However, they led to substantive political debates, which provides reasonable grounds for analysing the discourse on prosecution both inside and outside of the courtroom. In terms of differences, the most important one is that the Kenya investigation was opened following an investigation *propiu motu* (ICC 2010a), and the Libya investigation was referred to the ICC through the UNSC (UNSC 2011d).[25] In both situations, the facts presented are accurate as of March 2022. Before engaging in the analysis, readers should know that the following analyses do not aim to deliver a full account and detailed discussion of these two situations.[26] The analysis I conduct should provide sufficient material to fulfil the chapter's objective, illustrating how the theoretical and conceptual framework can help us make sense of what is happening beyond strictly legal and procedural questions. Furthermore, the material analysed provides enough insight into the notions of guilt and innocence.

4.3.1 *Documents for the Analysis and Time Frame of Analysis*

For the analysis, I rely on ICC documents, the ICC website, documents of the UNSC, government documents, media reports, and secondary literature. The analysis is corroborated through several confidential expert interviews with

[24] On the potentially problematic relationship between the ICC and R2P, see Mark Kersten (2018).

[25] As I will use these cases to demonstrate what we can learn through the application of the theoretical and conceptual framework, and for developing heuristics for the analysis of the case studies on R2P and drone strikes, I am not concerned here with questions of case selection and research design necessary for comparative case analysis.

[26] For more detailed analyses of these situations, I kindly direct the reader to the vast amount of literature available on those situations. While not offering a full literature review in the following analysis, the literature cited should provide sufficient detail for those who like to learn more about the situations, cases, and specific legal and procedural questions concerning them.

diplomats, NGO representatives, and UN staff conducted in 2014.[27] Table 4.1 provides an overview of the central documents used in the analysis. I refer to more documents in the discussion of the situations of course. Concerning the time frame, I focus on the early phase of both situations but refer to more recent developments where necessary.

4.3.2 *Libya*

The situation in Libya before the ICC has its origins in the UNSC Resolution 1970 (UNSC 2011d) when the Security Council referred the situation in Libya to the ICC. The referral was necessary to begin the investigation as Libya was and still is not a State Party to the Rome Statute. The situation was also the first with direct links to R2P. Shortly after the referral, the UNSC authorised collective actions under Chapter VII of the UN Charter with reference to R2P (see Chapter 6). Carsten Stahn sees in this link the manifestation of the ICC as an instrument of deterrence and, 'not solely an ex post facto mechanism' (Stahn 2012: 326). Relatedly, Caroline Fehl points to the possibility of positive norm linkage between prosecution norms under ICL and protection norms such as R2P (Fehl 2018: 4).

In the following analysis, I primarily focus on the early phase of the situation in Libya, starting in 2011 in which both the referral of the UN Security Council and the decision of the ICC to issue arrest warrants against Muammar Mohammed Abu Minyar Gaddafi, his son Saif Al-Islam Gaddafi, and Abdullah Al-Senussi took place. I do so for several reasons. First, they fall in the same time frame and context as the NATO-led intervention authorised by the UNSC in 2011 (see Chapter 6). Second, they provide ample material to demonstrate the usefulness of the conceptual and theoretical framework in making sense of what is happening in these cases regarding the individual human being's appearance in discourses of prosecution for international crimes. In short, the material is illustrative of the humanisation of ICL, which has been in the making at least since Nuremberg. Third, they provide excellent material to develop the heuristics of innocent and guilt. As the analysis will demonstrate, there have been various developments concerning the situation in Libya. And while I take note of them and present them with reference to the ICC's decision, media reports, and secondary literature, the actual analysis is limited to a few key documents.

[27] See Chapter 5 for more details on the interviews. The appendices includes a list of all interviews.

TABLE 4.1. *Documents for the analysis of the discourse on prosecution*

Document name	Source	Date
UNSC Resolution 1970	UNSC	26 February 2011
Record of the 6491st Meeting of the UNSC	UNSC	26 February 2011
Decision on the 'Prosecutor's Application Pursuant to Article 58 as to Muammar Mohammed Abu Minyar GADDAFI, Saif Al-Islam GADDAFI and Abdullah ALSENUSSI'	ICC	27 February 2011
Report of the Commission of Inquiry into Post-Election Violence	Commission of Inquiry into Post-Election Violence	15 October 2008
Decision on the Prosecutor's Application for Summonses to Appear for William Samoei Ruto, Henry Kiprono Kosgey and Joshua Arap Sang	ICC	08 March 2011
Decision on the Prosecutor's Application for Summonses to Appear for Francis Kirimi Muthaura, Uhuru Muigai Kenyatta and Mohammed Hussein Ali	ICC	08 March 2011
Situation in the Republic of Kenya	ICC	11 April 2015
Interview A2	Interview by author	March/ April 2014
Interview A3	Interview by author	March/ April 2014
Interview A5	Interview by author	March/ April 2014
Interview A7	Interview by author	March/ April 2014
Interview A8	Interview by author	March/ April 2014
Interview A10	Interview by author	March/ April 2014

Source: Gholiagha

4.3.2.1 Resolution 1970: The UNSC's Referral of the Situation in Libya to the ICC

In the following analysis, I begin with the UN Security Council debate on Resolution 1970 before moving on to several relevant court documents concerning Libya's situation. Following the uprisings across Western Asia and North Africa, which would become known as the 'Arab Spring', in February 2011, citizens in Libya took to the streets to protest the Gaddafi regime. Mark Kersten offers a description of one essential demonstration:

> In the eastern capital of Benghazi, protests escalated on 17 February, named the Day of Rage, with demonstrators calling for political reforms. The largest demonstrations against the regime in decades quickly turned bloody as Libyan security forces opened fire on protesters who, in turn, resorted to violent measures. Despite attempts to contain the proliferation of protests and the fomenting unrest in Libya, images of bloodshed spread rapidly, instigating greater – and much less peaceful – agitation against the regime (Kersten 2016: 116).

These 'images of bloodshed' also reached the UN and several regional organisations such as the AU. I will provide a detailed account of the debates that followed in Chapter 6. For now, let us observe what took place in the chambers of the UN Security Council in New York following these protests before moving on to the courtroom of the ICC in The Hague and Libya's capital Tripoli. The international community's reaction to the situation that unfolded in Libya in early 2011 is atypical for many reasons. The 1990s had been full of similar situations: civil protests turning bloody at the hand of a regime, of genocides or threats thereof, of horrendous human rights violations, but often the reaction was too little, too late (see Chapter 6 for more on this). One event is perhaps most emblematic of how unique the Libyan situation was or would become. On 21 February 2011, the deputy representative of Libya to the United Nations, Ibrahim Dabbashi, made the following statement in New York at a press conference:

> Gaddafi's regime has already started the genocide against the Libyan people since January 15. His soldiers and the mercenaries being flown into the country were ordered to shoot to kill .... We are calling on the UN to impose a no-fly zone on all Tripoli to cut off all supplies of arms and mercenaries to the regime .... We call on the UN Security Council to use the principle of the right to protect to take the necessary action to protect the Libyan people against the genocide .... We call on all countries in the world not to permit Gaddafi to escape to their territories and call on

> them to watch carefully for any amounts of money which may be flowing outside Libya .... We also call on the Prosecutor of the International Criminal Court to start immediately investigating the crimes committed by Gaddafi (du Plessis and Louw 2011: 1–2).[28]

A high-level Libyan diplomat had broken ranks with his government, calling directly on the international community to help. As scholars have observed, this plea for help was decisive for the UNSC and the ICCs quick reaction (Kersten 2016: 116). It took the UNSC five days to react to this call. On 26 February 2011, the UNSC adopted Resolution 1970, referring Libya's situation to the ICC (UNSC 2011d).[29] It is important to note that several regional organisations and the Human Rights Council already had condemned the violence in Libya (UNSC 2011d). As we will see in detail in Chapter 6, this was important to lay the groundwork for future resolutions and understand the international community's swift response. For now, I want to focus on Resolution 1970 and the debate on it, looking at two aspects: (a) very briefly, perspectives on the ICC and its role in Libya and (b) the way the individual appears in the discourse on Libya within the UNSC debate. For both, I rely on the official verbatim meeting record of the relevant UNSC session (UNSC 2011a) and on interviews.

In the statements made by Council members after the Council passed Resolution 1970, two views on the ICC can be identified. The first view refers to the deterrent effect for future crimes that an ICC investigation will have, as pointed out by India (UNSC 2011a: 2). Statements by the United States, Columbia, Portugal, France, Germany, Bosnia and Herzegovina, Brazil, and Libya pointed to the end of impunity as an important effect and aim of the referral (UNSC 2011a: 5–6) as well as to the fact that those responsible must be held accountable (UNSC 2011a: 3, 5). These two views also appeared in the literature on the ICC (Ainley 2015: 47–53; Nichols 2015: 12–14) and were further expressed by many interview partners.[30] I now move on to the second

[28] There seems to be no official record of the press conference, I am therefore relying on a quote found in du Plessis and Louw (2011). I first came across the text by Max du Plessis and Antoinette Louw elsewhere (Kersten 2016: 117).

[29] Mark Kersten (2018: 155–157) demonstrates how politicised this mandate was right from the beginning.

[30] See Interview A2: 176–177; Interview A7: 103–104; Interview A8: 41; Interview A3: 209–213, 236–238; Interview A10: 253. One interview partner however expressed strong doubts about the ICC's preventive capacity (A5: 273–274). A much more detailed analysis of the effect of the ICC's investigation can be found in Mark Kersten's excellent work *Justice in Conflict* (Kersten 2016: chapter 6).

aspect I wanted to focus on, the way the individual appears in the discourse on Libya within the UNSC.

The debate on Resolution 1970 and the statements made by UNSC in their explanations of vote, clearly demonstrates that individuals in the discourse appear as either innocent or guilty. The individual human being is either a victim or a perpetrator. While the language of innocence and guilt is to be expected in court documents, the use of such language outside of court documents is noteworthy. In methodological terms, it is an indication that 'something is going on here' (Schwedler 2013: 28),[31] which both justifies and requires further analysis.

The following statements by member state representatives indicate that they had identified several individuals as perpetrators guilty of punishable crimes and others as innocent and as victims. Ms Rice, the representative of the United States, stated that '[t]hose who slaughter civilians will be held *personally accountable*' (UNSC 2011a: 3, emphasis added). The Portuguese representative, in his statement, made clear that '[t]he Council thus was united in sending a clear, swift and *strong message to the perpetrators* of heinous crimes taking place in Libya' (UNSC 2011a: 5, emphasis added). The clear focus on perpetrators of the alleged crimes committed is also visible in the statement by the French representative: 'We have also decided to impose an embargo on arms – the *arms that President Al-Qadhafi has chosen to turn against his own people*. We have, finally, *decided to sanction the individuals* who are at the head of a regime that has chosen to commit atrocities' (UNSC 2011a: 5, emphasis added). And the Russian representative even speaks of 'those *guilty* of violence against the civilian population' (UNSC 2011a: 4, emphasis added).

As these quotes demonstrate, the UN Security Council members first identified individuals responsible for atrocities as 'perpetrators' and talked about 'sanctioning' them, holding them accountable, and as being 'guilty of violence' (UNSC 2011a: 3–5). At the same time, other individual human beings were identified as innocent. The South African representative, Mr Sangqu, recalled the Libyan delegation calls to end the 'killing of *innocent people*' (UNSC 2011a: 3, emphasis added). Ms Rice of the United States of America talked about 'atrocities … committed against *innocents*' (UNSC 2011a: 3). Using the language of 'innocents' and 'innocent people' (UNSC 2011a: 3) and juxtaposing them to those guilty and those perpetrating crimes, the UNSC members discursively construct these individual human beings as innocent victims of specific crimes.

[31] Thanks are due to Mariam Salehi for pointing me to Jillian Schwedler's work.

This brief analysis has already shown that the terms 'guilt' and 'innocence', and the use of the term 'perpetrator' to position individuals, were key themes in the debate. Representatives relied on this terminology to justify the referral of the situation in Libya to the ICC. The use of these terms is, of course, taken from the legal discourse on ICL. Notably, however, the use of these terms by UNSC members, while not being a legal categorisation *stricto sensu*, is still based on legal concepts.[32] It is, therefore, necessary to look at how the ICC dealt with the situation.

4.3.2.2 The Situation in Libya before the ICC

Before the ICC opened its investigation, the ICC's then-Prosecutor Moreno Ocampo gave a press conference, in which he stated that Muammar al-Gaddafi (amongst others) had been identified as having 'authority on the security forces who allegedly committed the crimes' (cited in Kersten 2016: 181). As Mark Kersten notes, '[t]his early invocation of the responsibility of Gaddafi, his sons, and key officials was legally questionable ... and was subsequently raised by defence counsel at the ICC' (Kersten 2016: 181). Nevertheless, the Pre-Trial Chamber decision following the Security Council's referral confirmed the charges and decided to issue arrest warrants. It took only three months from the UNSC referral to the ICC arrest warrants, an unprecedented speed for the ICC until then (Kersten 2016: 111, 162).

In the ICC's decision, we can find a justified assumption that the Prosecutor's application for arrest warrants for Muammar Gaddafi, Saif Al-Islam Gaddafi, and Abdullah Al-Senussi is valid (ICC 2011a: 3). The ICC assumes that the crimes committed fall under the ICC's jurisdiction and that the three named individual human beings bear responsibility for those crimes (ICC 2011a: 6–7). Specifically, it stated: 'From 15 February 2011 onwards, *GADDAFI, as indirect perpetrator, and SAIF AL-ISLAM and AL-SENUSSI, as indirect co-perpetrators*, committed crimes against humanity in the form of persecution across Libya' (ICC 2011a: 6, emphasis added).[33] Here, it is clearly visible how those individuals appear in the discourse as responsible and

[32] Frédéric Mégret offers an interesting definition of guilt. Talking about accused who have not been convicted, he says they can be guilty '[i]n the sense of having committed the crimes they are accused of' (Mégret 2019: 450).

[33] Mark Kersten offers an explanation of the starting date of the investigation: 'It would thus appear that the restriction of the ICC's jurisdiction to allied crimes committed after 15 February 2011 was included in order to shield key Western states from having their affairs and relations with Libya exposed or perhaps even investigated' (Kersten 2016: 121).

accountable for the crimes mentioned above. At the same time, the ICC stated:

> There are also reasonable grounds to believe that, on 17 February 2011, in the eastern Libyan cities near Benghazi, such as Al-Bayda, Derna, Tobruk and in Ajdabiya, *at least 29 peaceful demonstrators* were killed as a result of violent attacks by Security Forces (ICC 2011a: 15, emphasis added).

By making these claims, the 'peaceful demonstrators' appear as innocent victims of crimes. Within the preliminary documents produced by the ICC, the leading figures of the Libyan regimes are identified as responsible and accountable for certain crimes. From this follows that those victims of the crimes were seen as innocent.

While the ICC withdrew the arrest warrant against Gaddafi following his death in November 2011 (McElroy 2012; ICC 2020b), problems with the arrest warrant arose earlier. The AU voted not to follow the indictment, as the arrest warrant, in their view, would hinder diplomatic efforts towards peace in Libya (African Union Assembly 2013: 13–14; Forsythe 2013: 487). Such issues are nothing new within the debate of ICL, and scholars have been discussing them for a long time under the heading of 'peace vs justice' (Kersten 2016, chapter 2, offers a review of the debate). From a perspective of norms research, scholars have pointed to the 'complex and contested' relationship between military and judiciary intervention (Fehl 2019).

Concerning Saif Al-Islam Gaddafi, the ICC had ruled that the case was admissible in May of 2013 (Kersten 2016: 152; Trahan 2017: 818). The ICC dismissed further requests asking the court to declare the case not admissible by the Libyan government and Gaddafi himself (ICC 2019a; de Vos 2020: 77). However, Saif Al-Islam Gaddafi remained in the custody of a Libyan militia. A court in Tripoli sentenced him to death through a video-link trial, which was widely criticised (Stephen 2015; Trahan 2017: 820). In addition, the case raised the question of whether (in)admissibility should go beyond the strict question of unwillingness or being unable as laid down in Article 17 of the Rome Statute, that is, whether to include issues such as human rights of the defendant or questions of a fair trial (Trahan 2017). There is nothing in the Rome Statute that would allow a defendant to have his trial moved to the ICC due to due process and fair trial issues (Heller 2006; Mégret and Giles Samson 2013: 573–574). Others have pointed out that 'the concern was not that Libyan authorities were unwilling to prosecute Saif Al-Islam Gaddafi and al-Senussi, but rather that they were too willing' (de Vos 2020: 91).

According to media reports, Saif Al-Islam Gaddafi was released by the militia in June 2017, claiming that he fell under a general amnesty law. However, doubts remain whether this is true and whether the law applies to him (Jawad 2017). However, what seemed certain right away was that an amnesty in Libya would not end the trial before the ICC (Trahan 2017: 822–823). And in fact, the Pre-Trial Chamber of the ICC argued that the amnesty law did not apply to Saif Al-Islam Gaddafi and held the case was admissible (ICC 2019c; Close 2020). Saif Al-Islam Gaddafi appealed against the decision. The Appeals Chamber ruled on 9 March 2020 that the case was admissible (Close 2020; ICC 2020d).

There was some debate regarding these trials. As Mark Kersten notes: 'The debate has been characterized by a polarizing battle between proponents of trying Saif and Senussi in Libya on the one hand, and those who believe that only the ICC can do so impartially and legitimately, on the other' (Kersten 2016: 147). As of March 2022, Saif Al-Islam Gaddafi is not in the ICC's custody and the ICC arrest warrant is still in place (ICC 2020b).[34] The Saif Al-Islam Gaddafi case illustrates debates surrounding complementarity and admissibility (Kersten 2016: 148; de Vos 2020; Hobbs 2020: 368) and jurisdiction (Stahn 2012: 336–347). Concerning the proceedings against Abdullah Al-Senussi, the Appeals Chamber decided in October 2013 that the case was inadmissible before the ICC (ICC 2013).

Before providing a brief concluding remark, let me summarise the situation of Libya before the ICC. As of March 2022, there are three cases, five warrants of arrest, and three people at large connected with the situation in Libya (ICC 2020b). The three current cases are all at the pre-trial stage and concern Mahmoud Mustafa Busyf Al-Werfalli, Saif Al-Islam Gaddafi, and Al-Tuhamy Mohamed Khaled. I have not discussed the cases against Al-Werflli and Khaled (ICC 2020b; see also Saba and Akbarzadeh 2021: 92). Instead, I focus my analysis on the earlier phase of the conflict in Libya and other cases before the ICC.

In conclusion, I want to briefly discuss what the Libya cases meant for both Libya and, more generally, to understand the humanisation of global politics. Going beyond the specific issues, the ICC's involvement in Libya also raised questions about the ICC's role in conflict and post-conflict situations (see Kersten 2016 and Chapters 6 and 7 for a detailed discussion of these

[34] In 2018, there were media reports that Saif Al-Islam wanted to run in elections for the Libyan presidency, which as of March 2022 supposed to take place in June 2022 (Crilly 2018, Hammady 2022). There was also a noteworthy Interview with Saif Al-Islam in the New York Times in 2021 (Worth 2021).

questions). For now, it seems that the ICC settled on the narrative to sell this as a case of 'positive complementarity' (Kersten 2016: 148). Regarding the humanisation of global politics, Kersten notes several actors, including the ICC and the National Transition Council of Libya, shaped the underlying narrative of an 'evil Gaddafi' and the 'good rebels'. It remained the dominant narrative about the conflict in post-Gaddafi Libya (Kersten 2016: 124, 129, 143, 160). The power of that narrative became evident in the case of allegations of genocide by Libyan opposition forces that were not included in the ICC's dealing with the situation in Libya (Kersten 2016: 155). In terms of the effect the investigation had on the conflict, Mark Kersten identifies three effects, most notably for this chapter, he points to the focus on and labelling of individuals by the ICC:

> ICC interventions shape conflict narratives in three ways: by labelling indicted individuals as 'evil' and thus delegitimizing them as negotiation partners; by making the conflict narrative about particular individuals, namely those indicted by the Court; and by focusing on the dynamics, rather than the causes, of the conflict. The ICC's intervention into Libya had all of these effects (Kersten 2016: 118).

Before moving on to the situation in Kenya, let me conclude the analysis with reference to the concepts the book employs. We have seen here, both in the debates within the UNSC and in the discourse of the ICC, that it matters whether someone is positioned in the discourse as a perpetrator. And this positioning matters for how the individual human beings in question can participate in the whole process inside and outside the courtroom. It also became clear that actors refer to innocence and guilt as central categories to position individual human beings. In short: language matters. It also became clear that norms matter: I identified several debates about norms, such as complementarity, immunity, and human rights norms. In addition, the rights and duties of all participants involved must be considered when attempting to make sense of what is going. Section 4.3.3 deals with the situation in Kenya before the ICC to provide additional illustrations of these and other points.

4.3.3 *Kenya*

The situation in Kenya as the second situation discussed here is also not an arbitrary choice. First, it has been at the centre of criticism by African regional organisations and several African states (Ambos 2013: 503). Following post-election violence in December 2007, which led to at least 113 persons killed and more than 350,000 displaced (African Union Assembly 2008; Commission of Inquiry into Post-Election Violence 2008; Nichols 2015: 47; Endoh and Mbao 2016; Hillebrecht 2020: 473–477), a peace treaty was negotiated (Juma 2009; Lindenmayer and Kaye 2009). Second, like the Libyan case, it has a close link to R2P. In this case, to prevent future violence and assist the government in preventing atrocity crimes (Lindenmayer and Kaye 2009). The following analysis focuses on the time between the outbreak of the election violence in 2007 to March 2015, when the cases came to an end for various reasons discussed below.[35]

In response to the post-election violence, the Kenyan government set up the Commission of Inquiry into Post-Election Violence. The Commission published the so-called Waki-Report, named after the chairman Justice Waki (Commission of Inquiry into Post-Election Violence 2008). The report did not identify perpetrators by name. However, the Commission handed a sealed envelope with a list of alleged perpetrators to the Panel of African Eminent Personalities headed by Kofi Annan (Commission of Inquiry into Post-Election Violence 2008: 18). The Commission recommended that a special tribunal be set up (de Vos 2020: 203). Should this recommendation not be followed, the Panel of Eminent Personalities should forward the envelope to the OTP at the ICC (Commission of Inquiry into Post-Election Violence 2008: 18).

Following two years of examination of events, and despite the threat of passing the list of alleged perpetrators on to the ICC's Prosecutor, the Kenyan Parliament failed to set up such a tribunal, despite three attempts in 2009 (Nichols 2015: 69). The commission report still affected the situation in Kenya, as it 'created great interest and demand for accountability across Kenya' (de Vos 2020: 123). Once it had become clear that there would be no special tribunal for Kenya, the OTP became active (de Vos 2020: 125, 171). The OTP received the envelope with the list of alleged perpetrators. It then filed a request for a *proprio motu* investigation under Article 15 of the Rome Statute on 26 November 2009 (Rome Statute 1998; ICC 2010a: 4).[36]

The Pre-Trial Chamber discussed the necessary conditions of opening an investigation based on the Prosecutor's request at length (ICC 2010a: 7–30). On 31 March 2010, the Chamber authorised 'the commencement of an

[35] As of March 2022, there remains only three cases in the Kenyan situation open, two at the pre-trial stage and one at the trial stage. All three concern witness intimidation charges, which I do not analyse here (ICC 2020a).

[36] Lionel Nichols (2015: 257–264) provides a detailed timeline of the events in Kenya, from 27 December 2007 until 7 October 2014.

investigation into the situation in the Republic of Kenya in relation to crimes against humanity within the jurisdiction of the ICC committed between 1 June 2005 and 26 November 2009' (ICC 2010a: 83). As the dissenting opinion of Judge Kaul demonstrated, the case was contested within the Chamber (ICC 2010a: 84–163; Hiéramente 2013: 190; Kaul 2013; Schabas 2013: 393). On 15 December 2010, the Prosecutor then applied to the Pre-Trial Chamber in two separate applications to issue summonses to appear against six individuals. The reason that there were two separate applications was that the first one ('Kenya I') included supporters of the Orange Democratic Movement, whereas the second one ('Kenya II') included supporters of the Party of National Unity supporters (Nichols 2015: 82).[37]

The 'Kenya I' application requested summons to appear for Wiliam Samoei Ruto, Henry Kiprono Kosgey, and Joshua Arap Sang (Office of the Prosecutor 2010b). The 'Kenya II' application requested summons to appear for Francis Kim Muthaura, Uhuru Muigai Kenyatta, and Mohammed Hussein Ali (Office of the Prosecutor 2010a). The Pre-Trial Chamber, by majority with Judge Kaul dissenting, followed the prosecutor's applications and issued summonses of appearance for the six individual human beings (ICC 2011b, 2011c), who became known as the 'Ocampo Six', named after the ICC's Prosecutor at that time, Luis Gabriel Moreno Ocampo (BBC 2010; Nichols 2015: 1). I focus on the most prominent cases concerning Kenyatta and Ruto, as they would become leading figures in the Kenyan government, which complicated the case further. Kenyatta and Ruto were elected president and vice president in the 2013 elections (Endoh and Mbao 2016). Their election immediately brought 'questions of diplomatic immunity to the fore' (Bower 2019: 94). The fact that the two previous opponents had joined in what has been referred to as the 'Jubilee Alliance' (Cacciatori 2018: 397–400) led to an essential role for politics in how the cases would develop and ultimately fail (Mburu 2018).

Initially, Kenya seemed to cooperate. One sign of cooperation was that Ruto and Kenyatta appeared before the Court giving statements, thereby taking up a position as defendants or suspects and participating actively in the case. Mégret points out that this may have been strategic to close the case and ideally resume their political careers (Mégret 2019: 437), which is precisely what happened. Things turned less co-operative, with Kenya claiming that they would investigate these cases on the national level, requesting all evidence from the ICC to be turned over. The ICC denied those requests

37 The Orange Democratic Movement and the Party of National Unity had been the two conflicting groups following the election in 2007 (Nichols 2015: 47).

(Bower 2019: 94). Kenya also submitted admissibility cases to the ICC but had no success (de Vos 2020: 75).

These six individual human beings, like the Libyan case, appear in the discourse as perpetrators. Interestingly, those accused publicly opposed their appearance in the discourse as perpetrators and engaged in self-positioning. For example, Kenyatta, one of the accused, positioned himself as a hero (Hiéramente 2013: 197), which stood in stark contrast to the accusations by the OTP. Yet, as mentioned above, he did not defy the court but engaged with it (Mégret 2019: 437). As Frédéric Mégret points out, such engagement can be accompanied by even 'strongly worded statements of innocence', as made by Ruto during his appearance (Mégret 2019: 437). Similarly, Sofia Stolk notes that 'Sang is explicitly portrayed as a faithful Christian by himself and by his lawyers, which attempts to account for his *innocence*' (Stolk 2018: 693, emphasis added). Such a portrayal constitutes another instance of self-positioning.

The Kenyan situation remains one of the most controversial and problem-ridden situations before the ICC. The case against Kenyatta was closed upon the Prosecutor's request to withdraw the charges on 5 December 2014 (ICC 2014), which the Court decided upon on 13 March 2015 (ICC 2015). In its request, the Prosecutor was 'citing the inability to access evidence and insufficient state cooperation to support a successful prosecution' (Bower 2019: 98–99). The case against Ruto and Sang, which had already reached trial stage, was likewise closed, but in this case the charges were vacated based on an application by the defence. In both cases, the court declined to confirm the charges against the other individuals (ICC 2020a).

There are certainly lessons to be drawn from the situation in Kenya for the ICC (Kersten 2014b), and the effects on the ICC of these cases are not fully clear, but this is not the place to discuss them in detail; three brief references shall suffice: in terms of justice, Anushka Sehmi has argued that the end of the cases 'marked the end of the quest for justice for thousands of victims of the Kenyan post-election violence' (Sehmi 2018: 572); Adam Bower has studied the effect of the Kenya cases on the non-impunity norm (Bower 2019); and David Forsythe points out that despite the failure of the case in the end, it may have prevented further violence in the future (Forsythe 2018: 29).

For the book and this chapter, the situation in Kenya before the ICC serves as a second illustration of the book's conceptual and theoretical framework. Again, we find central concepts such as the role of language and norms and the relevance of positions and participation in the discourse. We also find questions concerning the rights and duties of those participating, such as the Kenyan State, the accused, and the victims. As in the Libyan case, we find individual human beings in a position of perpetrators being charged with crimes and victims deemed innocent. Again, guilt and innocence play an essential role in the language and discourse used inside and outside the courtroom. The case also shows the amount of contestation regarding these acts of positioning.

Moreover, we see norm contestation, for example, in debates about the non-impunity norm and other ICC/ICL related norms, including human rights norms concerning a fair trial and the right to life (Trahan 2017; Simmons and Jo 2019; Bower 2019: 92). Additionally, we can learn from the Kenya case study that assessment of guilt and innocence may change either in light of evidence or lack thereof and hence – while rooted in facts – remain subject to debates and changing social constructions. The appearance of an individual human being in discourse and their position is thus neither fixed nor given.

Both Libya and Kenya also answer the book's question on how the individual human being appears in discourses of prosecution. Here, however, there is little surprise. The individual human being appears as innocent or guilty, which is what one ought to expect from a discourse deeply embedded in a legal context and taking place (at least primarily) within legal institutions such as courts and within the context of ICL. As both examples demonstrate, an individual's mere appearance within discourse as a perpetrator and even perhaps evidence of crimes committed does not always lead to a verdict in the courtroom.[38] However, the debates within the UNSC concerning Libya have demonstrated that the appearance opens a discursive space in which a possible and potential prosecution moves into the realm of possibilities. Furthermore, within this discursive space, questions of state sovereignty and immunity of heads of state are open to debate, as the conflict between the AU and the ICC has aptly illustrated (Maunganidze and Du Plessis 2015).[39]

4.4 DEVELOPING HEURISTICS OF INNOCENCE AND GUILT

As the analysis above has demonstrated, the concepts of guilt and innocence are at the core of the discourse on prosecution. The abductive research logic outlined in the introduction facilitates the application of insights from the first case study on prosecution to the case studies on protection and killing, thereby ensuring reflexivity. Using heuristics based on data allows focusing on the

[38] If accused perpetrator are found guilty in the strict legal sense than punishments await them. As mentioned earlier, I do not deal with this part of the criminal process here (but see Jessberger and Geneuss 2020 for an overview on the topic).

[39] Such conflicts can also be framed as norm collisions (see Chapter 2).

relevant issues within documents for a research project while not closing the possibility of discovering alternative interpretations (Kruse 2014: 151).

In this book, 'innocence' and 'guilt' will be used as heuristics. As Cecilia Lynch argues in this context, abduction refers to applying certain concepts from one field to another (Lynch 2014: 21). In line with this, these are not theory-based heuristics, but they stem from the case study on prosecution, similar to what Herbert Blumer has called 'sensitizing concepts' (Blumer 1954: 7). I will discuss in more detail the use of heuristics from a methodological and analytical perspective in Chapter 5. For now, I want to make some etymological and conceptual remarks on the terms and present some debates about these terms in the literature.

Etymologically, the word 'innocence' stems from the Latin *nocere* meaning 'harm' and the prefix *in* meaning 'not'. Thus, innocence (*innocere* in Latin) can be understood etymologically as 'unable to do harm' (Harper 2021b).[40] This can be juxtaposed etymologically with the notion of 'guilt', as innocence also refers to not being guilty (Harper 2021a). Here one could argue for using responsibility as a heuristic instead of guilt. However, as Anthony F. Lang Jr. and John Williams explain with reference to Hannah Arendt, 'while guilt is *individual*, responsibility can be corporate' (Lang Jr. and Williams 2005: 229, emphasis added). As this book focuses on the individual human being, guilt serves as a better heuristic. The subsequent case studies will demonstrate the feasibility of using innocence and guilt as heuristics in detail.

To provide further conceptual grounding of the concepts of innocence and guilt, I want to revisit some of Frédéric Mégret's work, which I already discussed earlier in this chapter. Studying perpetrators as active subjects or participants allows to us shed light on their self-positioning within the discourse. Defendants can plead guilty themselves (Mégret 2018: 432). In doing so, they position themselves within the discourse as guilty. At the same time, they can then identify victims as innocent, as happened, for example, in front of the ECCC (Mégret 2018: 436).

I mention all this for two reasons. First, it shows how the notion of participants rather than subjects helps grasp the actions and the agency of individual human beings in the courtroom. Second, Frédéric Mégret connects these utterances of innocence or guilt, or acts of self-positioning in this book's language, to larger ideas about the individualisation and humanisation of ICL. Frédéric Mégret argues that uttering remorse brings to the fore the individual agency of the defendant (Mégret 2018: 441), by conceptualising it as

40 Helen M. Kinsella (2011: 58) offers further discussions on the etymology of the term. See also Chapter 7 for further references on the term in the context of IHL.

'a performance of individualization' (Mégret 2018: 438) and by describing it as an 'attitude of an accused' who recognises their individual guilt (Mégret 2019: 440, 450).[41] Finally, being acquitted can also be used for statements of innocence by the acquitted (Mégret 2019: 442) and for 'conferring innocence on all those involved on their side of the conflict' (Mégret 2019: 443). Or – as we saw at the beginning of the chapter – by their supporters.

These additional conceptual insights strengthen the chapter's argument that innocence and guilt and the humanisation – or individualisation as Frédéric Mégret calls it – are constituted through discourse, through the language individual human beings and other actors in global politics use. The Chapter 5 will embed the notions of innocence and guilt as heuristics in a larger analytical framework.

4.5 CONCLUSION

To recall, the purpose of the chapter was threefold. First, the case study illustrated that the theoretical and conceptual framework can be used to make sense of the debates and the discourse on prosecution. Second, following the abductive research logic, I developed two heuristics – innocence and guilt – to guide my analysis of the two other case studies (Kruse 2014: 151). Apart from these theoretical and methodological purposes, the chapter had a third, substantial purpose, answering two research questions: How does the individual human being appear in the discourse on prosecution? How does this appearance matter for global politics?

Concerning the first purpose, this chapter reconstructed the appearance of the individual human being in the discourse on prosecution, focusing on the debates about the situation in Libya at the UNSC and before the ICC and the situation in Kenya before the ICC. The two case studies demonstrated that the individual human being appears in the discourse as either an innocent victim or a guilty perpetrator within the discourse on prosecution. For the courtroom, this is to be expected. After all, Justicia weighs innocence and guilt in her scales (Kratochwil 2014: 4).

However, the analysis also illustrated the different uses of the terms inside and outside of the courtroom. While there is no space to discuss these different usages and their effects in detail, that they are being used differently

[41] In several articles Frédéric Mégret (at times with co-authors) offers a set of possible 'dispositions' of the accused and links them to 'typical attitudes', namely: defiance, sacrifice, participation and repentance (Mégret 2019: 411–412). While extremely insightful, I cannot discuss them here in detail (Mégret 2018, 2019; Mégret and Giles Samson 2019; Mégret and Scalia 2019)

by different actors is still noteworthy. And in analysing discourses of protection, scholars ought to be aware of these different usages and their effects. For this chapter and the book, it is essential to note that the different usages are all part of what I have labelled throughout the chapter as the discourse on prosecution. Innocence and guilt are used both in political debates and in legal deliberations. Analysing them together and not separately is an important task, which requires an interdisciplinary approach, such as the one the chapter has suggested.[42]

The result of the reconstruction of the discourse on protection demonstrated that the appearance of the individual human being in discourses of prosecution as innocent victims and guilty perpetrators is the result of social construction in which individual human beings are discursively positioned or position themselves. Here, the theoretical and conceptual framework helped make sense of the discourse on prosecution, provide a better understanding of the interplay between politics and law, and highlight the role language, norms, rights and duties, positions, and participation played.

Furthermore, while the cases studied here have not engaged with questions of gender and the human body, they have demonstrated the importance to turn to the individual experience of individual human beings in global politics (Sylvester 2013b), as victims or as perpetrators, to be able to draw a more conclusive picture about ICL. Nevertheless, questions of gender matter on a general level for the analysis of ICL and the work of the ICC. As Doris Buss notes:

> Feminist activism and scholarship on international criminal courts have tended to pursue three main directions: raising the visibility of sexual violence against women as a component of war; expanding the range of gendered harms recognized and prosecuted; and exploring and pushing the limits of international criminal law as a mechanism for ensuring women's inclusion in the post-conflict transition (Buss 2016: 162).

When studying ICL and the work of the ICC or other criminal courts, feminist scholarship is especially important when it comes to sexual and gender-based violence, rape as a weapon of war (including prosecuting it as acts of genocide or crimes against humanity), and concerning questions of gender justice (Bensouda 2014; Buss 2016; Chappell 2016).

[42] I thank Caroline Fehl for pushing me to say a bit more about the different usages here.

Concerning the second purpose, innocence and guilt as clearly established concepts in the discourse on prosecution were developed as heuristics based on secondary literature and the empirical analysis of the two case studies on Libya and Kenya. The analysis demonstrated how the individual human being appeared in the discourse as innocent or guilty. However, such an appearance is based on the use of specific language and references to specific norms. There is nothing natural or given to appear in a discourse as an innocent or guilty individual human being. Instead, it is a process of social construction, which can be grasped with the help of the frameworks developed in Chapter 3. This social construction takes place by referring to the innocence or guilt of individual human beings.

Concerning the third purpose, the chapter has reconstructed how the individual human being appears in the discourse on prosecution as a victim or a perpetrator. This appearance and the positioning that leads to it matter for global politics by making it impossible to ignore atrocities and crimes. We have the language to describe the conduct of an individual human being grounded in ICL and its institutions. The ICC's Prosecutor has the power to open investigations. This may not always lead to verdicts, and justice may still not be served, but it is a clear indication of the growing humanisation of global politics, in which no longer only states matter (Crawford and Watkins 2010: 284). Individual human beings have direct duties within international law (Hailbronner 2007: 219), and impunity is – while still occurring – no longer unchallenged. Individual human beings can be held accountable without the state as a mediator (McCorquodale 2006: 315; Hoover 2012: 255). The following quote from the trial judgement of the ICTY in *Prosecutor v. Dragoljub Kunarac Radomir Kovac and Zoran Vukovic* aptly describes this shift:

> *Individual criminal responsibility* for violation of international humanitarian law *does not depend on the participation of the state* and, conversely, its participation in the commission of the offence is no defence to the perpetrator (ICTY 2001: 159–160, emphasis added; see also Teitel 2011: 60).

To conclude, the individual human being appears in the discourse on prosecution only through the positioning as victim or perpetrator, as either innocent or guilty. Through this appearance, a discursive space is opened that facilitates the further development of ICL and chances of prosecuting those responsible for atrocity crimes. Chapter 5 builds on these insights to develop the book's analytical framework.

5

Heuristics and Positions

A Framework for Analysing Discourses of Humanisation

5.1 INTRODUCTION

This chapter[1] develops an analytical framework to analyse the case studies in the two subsequent chapters. The analytical framework is based on the theoretical and conceptual frameworks presented in Chapter 3 and the results of the prosecution case study presented in Chapter 4. The first three chapters of this book have engaged with the humanisation of global politics on a theoretical and conceptual level. They have made a case for an interdisciplinary framework that brings together feminist and constructivist approaches from IR with IL approaches that focus on the individual human being as a participant and are cognisant of the individual human beings' position in international law.

Chapter 4 provided an initial assessment of those claims by studying the discourse on prosecution and reconstructing the individual human being's appearance as an innocent victim or a guilty perpetrator. Chapter 4 revealed that these categories are not always clear-cut or dichotomous in practice, as in the case of former child soldiers committing atrocities. Chapter 4 also demonstrated that different actors use these terms differently inside and outside of the courtroom. Nevertheless, guilt and innocence are central concepts in ICL. As Chapter 4 demonstrated, they help understand how the individual human being participates in the discourse on protection, either by self-positioning themselves as innocent or guilty or by being positioned by others as innocent or guilty.

In short, in these chapters, I have been putting forward ontological claims about global politics and the humanisation of global politics. The analytical framework in this chapter now offers a solution to the epistemological

[1] This chapter has immensely profited from comments by Mariam Salehi.

problem of knowing whether ontological assumptions are true (Jackson 2011: 27). The analytical framework consists of an interpretative methodology, an abductive research logic, and heuristics, all of which I present in Section 5.2. I also offer a coherent research design in Section 5.3, discussing case selection, sources, and data gathering.[2] I also present my understanding of discourse as it pertains to this book. In this section, I also revisit the concept of positions introduced in Chapter 3, and I introduce 'positioning analysis' as a specific method for the reconstructive analysis of the empirical material I undertake.[3] The framework provides a structure and guidance for the analysis of the two subsequent case studies. Section 5.4 provides a conclusive summary of the chapter.

5.2 INTERPRETATIVE METHODOLOGY, ABDUCTIVE RESEARCH LOGIC, AND HEURISTICS

This book aims to further develop constructivist IR theory to include the individual human being as a theoretical category. This inclusion is accomplished by answering the question of how we can conceptualise the humanisation of global politics. To this end, I employ an interpretative methodology, which focuses on meaning and context (Lynch 2014: 13) as it allows 'understanding events by discovering the meanings human beings attribute to their behaviour and the external world' (Della Porta and Keating 2008a: 26). Interpretative research is more open than positivist approaches towards the material studied (Blatter et al. 2007: 24). This openness towards the material allows remaining open towards new insights generated by the analysis and continuously feeds them into the analysis. Thus, there is no outside viewpoint from which to approach the world and the data we collect about the world. Researchers are always part of this world (Jackson 2011: 35–37; Lynch 2014: 17) and need to reflect both the research and their own position (Guzzini 2000; Suddaby 2006: 640; Hofius et al. 2014: 88; Lynch 2014: 17).

In studying the humanisation of global politics, I aim to make the individual human being analytically accessible to IR without employing methodological individualism or an individualist ontology (Jaeger 1996: 320; Ruggie

[2] The term 'data' to many indicates a positivist mode of analysis. However, as like other interpretative researchers (Fujii 2018: chapter 5), I believe that the material we research, collect, systematise, and analyse is as much data as the data used by colleagues employing more positivist modes of analysis.

[3] Methodology is 'the study of the differing methods of gaining knowledge relative to the object of inquiry' (Wight 2006: 259). Methods constitute the means of data gathering and data analysis.

1998: 869; Della Porta and Keating 2008b: 2; Fierke 2010: 180–181). I also do not rely on the equally criticised distinction of levels of analysis (Wilmer 2002). Neither is the individual human being the object of study nor the level at which this work is analytically located. Rather, I reconstruct the appearance of the individual human being in discourses of global politics, demonstrating that this is a process of social construction in which the individual human being is understood as socially constructed through their position in the discourse. I use positioning analysis to study these discourses to overcome methodological individualism and transcend levels of analysis. Similarly to others studying processes of humanisation, I am also 'traversing the levels of analysis' (Weinert 2015: 25). Thus, positioning analysis constitutes a useful approach for scholars to study the individual human being participating in global politics.

An abductive research logic constitutes the foundation of the interpretative methodology developed in this chapter. I rely on abduction as presented within IR literature (Friedrichs 2009; Hofius 2015: 88–91, 2020: 179).[4] Here, abduction is understood as a logic of inquiry that allows collecting and analysing data with a theoretical framework in mind and moving between theory and empirical material. Therefore, abduction is conceptualised as 'reasoning at an intermediate level' (Friedrichs 2009: 647) between induction and deduction. As part of such a logic, insights from the data analysis are continuously fed back into the theoretical framework and the next steps of the data analysis (Friedrichs and Kratochwil 2009: 709; Kruse 2014: 134–146).

An abductive research logic can help to generate new knowledge in those cases where something appears that cannot be explained with the given knowledge within a field (Kruse 2014: 143–145). This is the case for the book's central research focus, the humanisation of global politics, which, as an observable phenomenon (Chapter 1), cannot be adequately conceptualised with the given theoretical approach available in IR theory (Chapter 2). It is important to note that this does not mean studying global politics free of any theory, starting with a clean slate, as that is impossible (Kruse 2014: 104). Instead, abductive reasoning requires a foundation from which to start. Chapter 3 provided this theoretical foundation in the form of a theoretical and conceptual framework. To briefly recall, the theoretical framework brings together feminist and constructivist approaches in IR theory with IL scholarship, which is especially interested in individual human beings' participation and position in international law. The conceptual framework draws on the theoretical framework for the central

[4] For a more detailed discussion of abduction as originally developed by Peirce, see the work by Igor Douven (2011) and Kuni Fann (1970).

concepts the book works with: norms, language, gender, body, positions, participants, human and individual rights, and duties.

As this book aims to theorise the humanisation of global politics, it is necessary to reconstruct the discourses in which the individual human being appears (Flick et al. 2003: 13; Franke and Roos 2013: 13). To this end, data is approached with a theoretical sensitivity in place, which refers to the existence of 'useful heuristic concepts which allow identifying theoretical relevant phenomena within the data' (Kelle 1996: 32, my translation). Heuristics serve here as a guiding element through which the empirical material is read, similar to what social theorists have identified as 'sensitizing concepts' and IR theorists have employed in their work, often as part of an abductive research logic (Blumer 1954: 7; Kruse 2014: 111; Hofius 2020: 179).

In line with the abductive research logic, I use innocence and guilt as heuristics, which I developed from the empirical analysis of the discourse on prosecution conducted in Chapter 4. Using empirically drawn heuristics allows me to compare the processes of humanisation across the chapters and guide my analysis without pre-determining the results of the analysis. The use of such an abductive approach combined with empirically developed heuristics generates insights of which purely theory-driven deductive or purely data-driven inductive approaches are less capable.

More specifically, I use heuristics to evaluate the individual human being's position in the discourses I analyse.[5] As the two subsequent case studies show, innocence and guilt appear directly or indirectly in utterances of self-positioning and when others position the individual human being in discourses of protection or killing. How the individual human being participates is also related to these notions of innocence and guilt. Those perceived as innocent receive protection or are not identified as legitimate targets for drone strikes, as the respective analyses in Chapters 6 and 7 demonstrate. Subsequently, those perceived guilty are not seen as worthy of protection or are identified as drone strike targets. The chapters will discuss the validity and legitimacy of these positions in more detail. Figure 5.1 summarises this abductive research logic and presents the book's overall structure, guided by this abductive research logic.

To recall the discussion in the introduction (Chapter 1) and in the case study on protection (Chapter 4), I oscillate between theoretical and conceptual discussions, on the one hand, and empirical analysis, on the other hand, throughout the book. While the concepts of innocence and guilt are to be

5 I am thankful to Mariam Salehi for helping me clarify my thinking here.

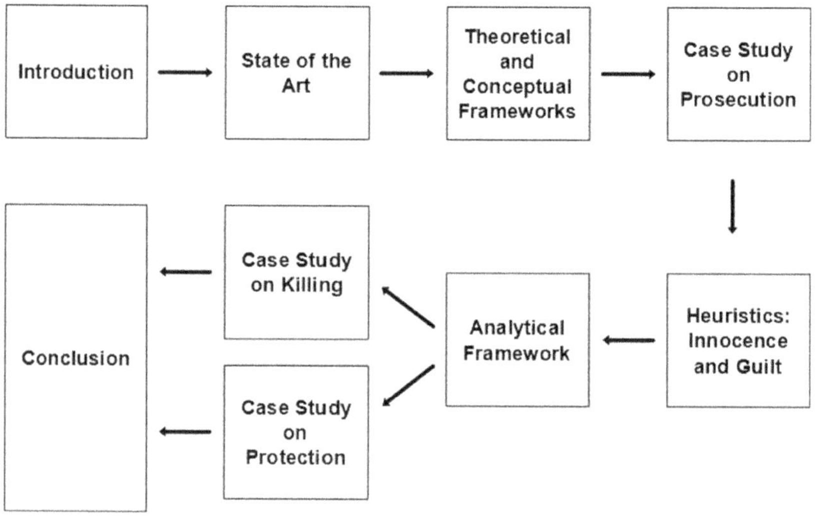

FIGURE 5.1 Abductive research logic of the book.
Source: Gholiagha

expected in discourses of prosecution, its application for studying the discourse on protection and the discourse on drones and targeted killing constitutes a novel approach. Section 5.3 outlines the research design for the case studies.

5.3 RESEARCH DESIGN

The following develops the research design for the case study in five steps.[6] The section begins in a first step with selecting cases, discussing normative issues and the interconnectedness between cases. The second step turns to sources and data gathering. Step three discusses the term 'discourse' as it pertains to this book. The fourth step introduces the concept of positions within discourses and demonstrates how 'positioning analysis' as a method is applied in this book. Here the related notion of participants is taken up again. The fifth step offers a description of the steps undertaken in the case studies to guide the reader.

5.3.1 *Step 1: Case Selection, Normative Issues, and Interconnectedness*

To recall the brief introduction to the cases in the introduction of this book, 'cases are cases *of* something' (Klotz 2008: 43, emphasis in original). All three cases discussed in this book are cases of the humanisation of global politics.

[6] For a discussion of research designs, see Uwe Flick (2003), Joachim Blatter et al. (2007: 23), and Philippe Schmitter (2008).

Due to this shared characteristic, all three case studies in this book deliver specific answers to the question of how the individual human being appears in discourses of global politics, thereby providing insights into the 'specific meaning' and the 'generalizable knowledge' of each case (Vennesson 2008: 226). Furthermore, as the cases are embedded in an abductive research logic, they are 'interpretative cases'. Interpretative cases use 'theory to explain a case and then refin[e] theory' (Della Porta and Keating 2008b: 13).

The case studies in this book provide the empirical foundation of the theoretical advancement this book undertakes to conceptualise the humanisation of global politics and strengthen IR theory and our understanding of global politics. As already discussed, the first case study on prosecution (Chapter 4) has a unique position and function in the book. Regardless of this unique role, the case study nevertheless analyses a specific case of the humanisation of global politics, thus constituting a 'normal' case study. The following discussion, therefore, relates to all three case studies in the book.

The normative relevance of all three cases I study in this book is constituted by the fact that, due to the weakened role of the state as a mediator and the position the individual human being takes up in global politics, they are now more powerful and more vulnerable at the same time than before (Brown and Ainley 2009: 221–222).[7] Such a focus on the appearance of the individual human being in discourses of global politics allows IR theory to provide a normative assessment of the humanisation of global politics. This humanisation of global politics presents itself most clearly in these three cases. Within the cases, the individual human being is the focal point.

I also selected the three cases based on conceptual and empirical similarities and the degree of their interconnectedness. The cases share several similarities: All three cases are located within the context of security as they concern the life and death of individual human beings, and constant reference to security is made within the discourses studied. All three cases relate to global issues, that is, they are not limited to a particular state or region. Furthermore, all three cases have a political and legal dimension. Most importantly, all three cases are specific cases of the individual human being's appearances in global politics.

7 Chris Brown and Kirsten Ainley speak of an increased vulnerability of the individual human being because 'they cannot rely on a strong state to protect their interest' and of an increased power because 'they can demand certain rights not as a result of their status as citizens of a particular state but because of their identity as a *human being*' (Brown and Ainley 2009: 221–222, emphasis added). Others have made similar or related points of the negative effects on the individual human being through the 'expansion of international institutions' (Schreuer 1993: 465) or through actions of states (Buzan and Hansen 2009: 206).

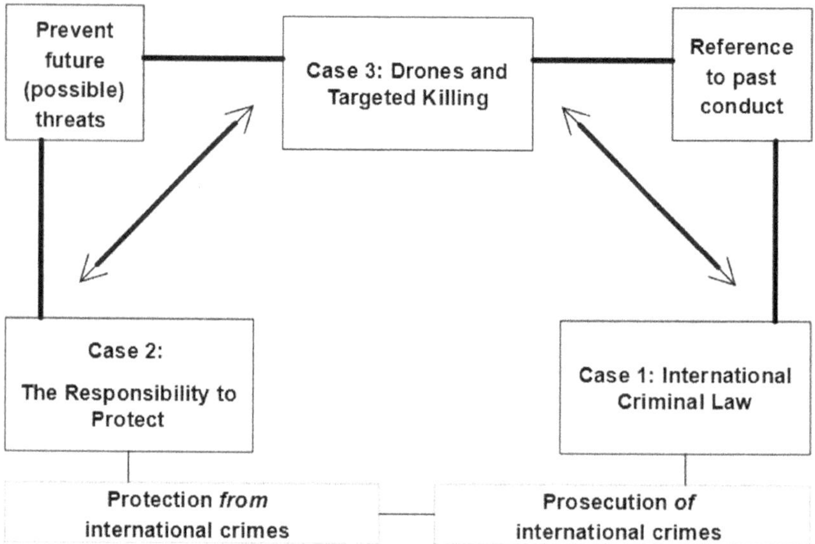

FIGURE 5.2 Relationship between the three case studies.
Source: Gholiagha

In addition to these similarities, there is a strong connection between the cases. The cases of killing and prosecution share a reference to past conduct of individual human beings, that is, they are prosecuted because of actions in the past, or they are selected as a target because they have conducted behaviour deemed a threat to the security of others in the past. The cases of protection and prosecution are positioned diametrically to each other. Often, those prosecuted have committed international crimes such as genocide, war crimes, or crimes against humanity, from which other individual human beings had to be protected. Killing is opposed to protection, as the latter aims to preserve life while the former aims to end it. Furthermore, prosecution is a non-lethal form of stopping harm and imposing punishment and, therefore, it is opposed to killing, which constitutes a lethal form to stop harm and punish.[8] Figure 5.2 visualises these connections and relationships between the three cases.

[8] Jennifer Welsh identifies a similar relationship in her discussion of the individualisation of conflict, when she suggests that 'the individualisation of conflict forces us to confront the status of individuals in at least three different capacities: 1) as subject to violence but deserving of protection; 2) as liable to attack because of their responsibility for attacks on others; and 3) as agents who can be held accountable for the perpetration of crimes committed in the course of conflict' (Welsh 2019b: 10).

5.3.2 *Step 2: Sources and Data Gathering*

The second step of the research design deals with the issue of sources and data gathering. Each case study identifies 'canonical texts or monuments' (Neumann 2008: 67) to collect sufficient documents to generate insights but limit the number so they can be analysed in an interpretative case study. The limitation to selected documents will be paired with a defined time frame for each case (Neumann 2008: 67). The text selection is furthermore guided by the criteria of intertextuality, that is, the connection of texts with each other (Hansen 2006: 82–87). Additionally, the selected documents provide a variety of viewpoints on the respective cases. Such an approach has the advantage of covering a large part of the discourse while keeping the number of documents manageable with a view to reconstructive approaches to text analysis used in this book.

The documents I use in the analyses include UNSC resolutions, resolutions of other relevant international or regional organisations, records of meetings, press releases, government documents, speeches by government officials, newspaper articles, and blog posts. Due to international law's relevance in all three cases, I also refer, where applicable, to international treaties and conventions, courts' and tribunals' judgements, international treaties, and secondary literature from legal scholars. Additionally, I rely on interviews that I conducted during two research stays.[9] The first took place in March and April 2014 in New York, where I interviewed diplomats, UN staff, academic experts, and NGO representatives. The second one took place in May 2014 at a UN expert meeting in Geneva on Lethal Autonomous Weapon Systems. In this context, I also conducted on-site interviews with diplomats and talked more informally with conference participants. During both research stays, I also collected field notes and wrote memos.[10]

Interviews constitute one central method of gathering data, especially in interpretative research (Helfferich 2011; Gubrium et al. 2012; Kruse 2014; Efrat 2015; Fujii 2018). Depending on the research objectives and what researchers

9 On research stays and field work as specific modes of data gathering, see, for example, the work by Asif Efrat (2015) and William Neuman (2006).

10 An anonymised list of interview partners can be found in the book's appendix. The full names and contact details of all interview partners as well as audio records and transcripts of the interviews are on file with the author.

want to learn, various interview forms exist (Helfferich 2011: 36–37, 45; Morse 2012; Kruse 2014: chapter 2). I conducted expert interviews, which are generally understood to generate insight into a field by interviewing people with knowledge about the field (Kruse 2014: 168–169). Expert interviews facilitate gaining insights into the specific discourses studied, allowing the analysis to provide additional insights beyond available documents and corroborate the analysis of the documents.

Expert interviews can be explorative, systematising, and theory-generating (Bogner et al. 2014: 22–23; Kruse 2014: 169–170). I conducted theory-generative expert interviews, as the abductive research logic applied in this book aims to generate knowledge and work towards theorising the humanisation of global politics. Theory-generative expert interviews are characterised by providing factual knowledge and any kind of knowledge relevant to gain a deeper understanding of the field in which the interview partner is an expert (Bogner and Menz 2009: 66; Bogner et al. 2014: 25). This allows the assessment of facts, ensuring a high degree of validity. Interviewing experts from different institutional contexts (diplomats, UN staff, representatives of NGOs, academics) provided for further cross-checking and validation of the data and the analysis. The validation was further enhanced by asking interview partners about their assessment of past events and future developments (Kruse 2014: 169–180). Finally, I conducted interviews to gain a deeper understanding of the studied discourse beyond what can be found in the documents (Patton 1990: 278).

Regarding the selection of interviews, I began by researching relevant interview partners through their respective institutional websites.[11] Furthermore, I used snowballing, that is, the suggestion of additional interview partners through identified interview partners (Helfferich 2011: 156). I conducted ten interviews in total. While some interview partners agreed to be identified by name, others opted to remain anonymous. Taking the strictest request for confidentiality as a benchmark, I use the same level of identification for each interview partner.

Following the selection of interview partners, interview questions were developed for semi-structured interviews. To ensure that relevant facts would be retrieved and that the format of the questions was consistent with an

[11] It is important to note that I selected interview partners instead of sampling them, meaning that, based on my research questions and interest, I chose who to contact and who to interview, which also is an iterative process (Fujii 2018: 38).

interpretative research methodology, I applied an iterative process to design the questions and develop a guideline for the interviews (Helfferich 2011: 182–190; Kruse 2014: 230–240). In terms of the interview structure, I opted for semi-structured interviews. Because I interviewed actors from various backgrounds and at times asked interviewees questions about more than one of the three cases, I developed, based on the general questionnaire, a questionnaire specifically geared towards the interview partner and the time available for the interview. The semi-structured interview format also allowed me to ask ad-hoc questions or follow-up questions to clarify interview partners' statements and better understand events or topics discussed (Fujii 2018: 60–67). I transcribed the interviews verbatim using a basic transcription style, including all questions (Dresing and Pehl 2015). Subsequently, the transcripts were used as a written source in the analysis of each case study.[12]

5.3.3 *Step 3: Discourse*

This book claims that the humanisation of global politics is best studied by focusing on the appearance of the individual human being in discourses of global politics. Therefore, it is necessary to discuss the term 'discourse'. The role of language has been discussed in Chapters 2 and 3 from a theoretical and conceptual perspective, outlining the close relationship between language and socially constructed reality (Doty 1993: 302; Fierke 2001: 118). Language, in the form of discourse, also plays a pivotal role in this book from a methodological viewpoint. The social science literature offers various definitions and understandings of discourse (Fairclough and Wodak 1997: 276; Milliken 2001: 139; Neumann 2002: 630; Holzscheiter 2005; Keller 2005; Holzscheiter 2014). Discourse is understood as both constitutive and constituted (Fairclough and Wodak 1997: 258; Renner 2013: 5), which in this book means that it is both constituted through the individual human being and constitutive of the individual human being.

Anna Holzscheiter offers the most useful definition of discourse for this book, which fits well with the book's claim about the social construction of the individual human being in global politics. Anna Holzscheiter defines discourse as 'the space where human beings make sense of the material world, where they attach meaning to the world and where representations of the

[12] For a similar approach to using the transcript of interviews as material for the analysis alongside other documents, see the work by Laura Shepherd on *Gender, UN Peacebuilding, and the Politics of Space* (Shepherd 2017: 27–29).

world become manifest' (Holzscheiter 2014: 144). The definition is valuable for this book because it refers to the fact that through discourse, social reality, including human beings themselves, is constructed and that this construction entails a moment of social interaction. In line with the definition above, this book does not refute the material reality of the individual human being but argues that we can only make sense of the individual human being in global politics through discourse, as this is how social reality is constructed. The following step clarifies how a focus on positions of individual human beings in discourses provides an analytical access point to study their appearance in these discourses.

5.3.4 *Step 4: Positions, Positioning, and Positioning Analysis*

As noted throughout this book, the individual human being has appeared in discourses of global politics. The notion of appearance introduced in this book may, at times, present itself as somewhat elusive. Therefore, Chapter 3 introduced the concept of participants to describe in somewhat more concrete terms what I mean when I talk about the appearance of the individual human being. However, neither appearance nor participation on its own help much to answer more specific questions about how exactly the individual human being appears in the discourse or participates in global politics. International Law's notion of position – also introduced in Chapter 3 – is helpful here, insofar it places the individual human being in relation to other participants.[13] This chapter provides the final piece of this book's approach to study the individual human being's appearance in discourses of global politics. In this fourth step of the research design, I introduce the method of positioning analysis. Positioning analysis allows analytical access to the appearance of the individual human being in discourses of global politics. In other words, in this book I use the term 'position' to operationalise the concept of participants and to analytically access individual human beings' appearance in discourses of global politics. In Section 5.3.4.1, I first discuss positions from a methodological perspective before presenting positioning analysis as a specific method to study positioning.

[13] This use of the term 'position' should not be confused with the concept of subject positions that is central to poststructuralist approaches to IR (Towns 2010: 35; Almagro 2018: 680). Instead of taking up a poststructuralist notion of language and discourse, I retain a critical constructivist perspective on both (see Buzan and Hansen 2009: 199, for a good discussion of the difference).

5.3.4.1 Positions and Positioning

Looking at positions enables us to study the appearance of the individual human being in discourses of global politics in terms of how such discourses refer to the place where entities appear within a discourse. Furthermore, positions constitute the speaker, one could also say the participant, within a discourse (Kruse 2014: 510–511). It is necessary to analyse interactions to study the individual human being's appearance in discourses of global politics. Without interactions, humans cannot make sense of their world or 'figure out what to do' (Kornprobst 2011: 84). These interactions may occur in real time, for example, during debates at the UNSC or in a courtroom. But they may also be taking place across space and across time. For example, various actors debate the appropriate response to a situation and refer to each other's positions in their statements.

Therefore, positioning oneself and others within discourse is understood here as a specific form of interaction (Lucius-Hoene and Deppermann 2014: 196). The following three features of interactions must be considered to study interactions: 'i. the moral position of the participants and the rights and duties they have to say certain things, ii. the conversational history and the sequence of things already being said, iii. the actual saying with their power to shape certain aspects of the social world' (Harré and van Langenhove 1999b: 6). The positioning analysis conducted in each case will take these features into account by providing the background of all actors and the context in which they speak through discussing the relevant literature on each case study and contextualising all documents analysed.

Positioning can take place both '*directly and explicitly* or *indirectly and implicitly*' (Lucius-Hoene and Deppermann 2014: 199, emphasis in original, my translation); therefore analysing positions requires an interpretative methodology, as quantitative approaches or approaches based on a priori defined codes would not be able to identify indirect or implicit positionings. Furthermore, positioning always includes self-positioning and the positioning others undertake (Lucius-Hoene and Deppermann 2014: 196; Kruse 2014: 511). Within interviews, this occurs when interviewees position themselves in their stories against other actors (Kruse 2014: 511). All interviews I conducted therefore included questions on the positioning of interviewees and the positions of others. Such an approach is based on a relational understanding of positioning (Harré and van Langenhove 1999b: 1; Lucius-Hoene and Deppermann 2014: 200). To sum up, analysing positions and acts of positioning within discourses creates insights into the individual human being's appearance in those discourses and their participation in global politics that would otherwise remain invisible.

5.3.4.2 Positioning Analysis

Positioning analysis refers to a specific method to study positioning (Hollway 1984; van Langenhove and Harré 1999: 16). Methodologically, positioning analysis sits between conversation analysis and discourse analysis and provides a *via media* between micro-linguistic analysis and macro-level analysis of language (Kruse 2014: 510). This means that while I study discourses, I do not work explicitly with discourse theory. Instead, I present a method to reconstruct the individual human being's appearance in discourses of global politics.[14]

More specifically, positioning analysis allows the analysis of 'the different linguistic forms used to position oneself within different topics, during different interactive situations' (Korobov 2001: 33). The appearance of the individual human being in discourses can only be grasped through identifying the position in which someone appears, as Section 5.3.4.1 has demonstrated. Thereby, the method of analysing positioning provides an operationalisation of the notion of appearance used so far in this book, allowing me to analytically access the individual human being's participation in discourses of global politics. This operationalisation and analytical access is based on the assumption that the individual human being is constituted discursively (Scott 1991: 793), a notion Anna Holzscheiter has identified as a structural notion of discourse, where '*meaning makes subjects*' (Holzscheiter 2010: 31, emphasis in original). At the same time, a more agentic understanding of discourse exists, in which '*subjects make meaning*' (Holzscheiter 2010: 31, emphasis in original).

While this discussion does not engage in discourse analysis the way Anna Holzscheiter does in her work, her distinction remains helpful for this book. I study discourses through which subjects' appearance becomes meaningful and their participation in global politics can be analysed. To this end, positioning analysis, as developed in this section, provides valuable insights into the appearance of the individual human being in global politics.

Positioning analysis practically focuses on several language elements that indicate positionings, such as personal pronouns, which participants use to speak about themselves or others (Kruse 2014: 511). Also, a close reading of a document allows identifying sections, paragraphs, or sentences about specific participants. Therefore, in addition to looking for personal pronouns in the text, I analyse sentences as the smallest sense-making unit of language,

[14] It should be noted that what I present here is a version of positioning analysis amended and developed for the specific purpose of analysing discourses of global politics. It therefore may differ from other versions of positioning analysis presented in the literature (Harré and van Langenhove 1999a; Korobov 2001; Kruse 2014: 499–503).

focusing primarily on acts of (self-)positioning through the speaker. Thus, I study how individual human beings position themselves and how individuals are positioned by other participants in discourses of global politics (Davies and Harré 1990: 62). To conclude, studying the positioning of the individual human being in discourses allows for reconstructing the social construction of the individual human being that takes place through the interaction with others. In a final step, I now present a structure for the two subsequent case studies.

5.3.5 *Step 5: Structure of Each Case Study*

The research design presented in this section will now be applied to the two subsequent case studies. To guide the reader through the analysis and the empirical material, I structure them similarly. In Sections 1–3 of each case study, I provide an overview of the discourse and scholarly literature. In both case studies, I then present the empirical material used for the analysis before engaging in the actual analysis using the analytical framework presented here. Both chapters conclude with a final section evaluating the analysis. To relate the specific analysis of the case studies with the overall research question this book is concerned with – that is, how IR theory can conceptualise the humanisation of global politics – I have developed specific research questions for each of the three case studies. Table 5.1 presents these case study specific research questions.

TABLE 5.1. *Research questions in the case studies*

Case study	Research question 1	Research question 2
Guilty and Innocent – The Individual Human Being in International Criminal Law (Chapter 4)	How does the individual human being appear in the discourse on prosecution?	How does this appearance matter for global politics?
Protecting the Individual Human Being from Mass Atrocities (Chapter 6)	How does the individual human being appear in the discourse on protection?	How does this appearance matter for global politics?
Killing Individual Human Beings with Drones (Chapter 7)	How does the individual human being appear in the discourse on targeted killing via drones?	How does this appearance matter for global politics?

Source: Gholiagha

5.4 CONCLUSION

This chapter aimed at providing a solution to the epistemological problem of how we can know whether ontological assumptions, presented so far in this book, are true (Jackson 2011: 27). To this end, the chapter developed an analytical framework complementing the theoretical and conceptual frameworks developed in Chapter 3. This conclusion summarises this analytical framework and demonstrates how theory, methodology, and method are connected in the book. In addition, the conclusion outlines how the analytical framework developed constitutes a novel contribution to the methodological toolbox available to scholars studying global politics.

In Section 5.1, the chapter developed an interpretative methodology based on an abductive research logic. This abductive research logic is necessary to collect and assess data openly enough to provide new insights and generate new knowledge while at the same time providing sufficient structure to be able to conduct research.[15] The abductive research logic developed in this chapter constitutes a foundational part of the methodological framework for this book.

In Section 5.2, the chapter offered a coherent research design for the case studies and outlined the different steps. The chapter also offered a structure for the case studies. As part of the research design, the chapter also introduced positioning analysis as a specific method to reconstruct the individual human being's appearance in discourses of global politics as a participant in those discourses. Positioning analysis allows one to study of how individual human beings position themselves or how others position the individual human being.

This approach then constitutes a novel contribution to the methodological toolbox available to scholars studying global politics and the individual human being as part of global politics. The framework and the method developed therein allow overcoming methodological individualism without relying on theory-based fixed concepts of the individual human being in global politics.[16] Furthermore, this approach transcends the levels of analysis on which

[15] I am indebted to the late Jan Kruse for the idea that qualitative research must always be open enough to find new things and structured enough to not get lost in the material (Kruse 2014).

[16] See Chapter 2 for a detailed discussion on the weaknesses of such fixed conceptions.

research is often placed. With a theoretical, a conceptual, and an analytical framework in place, the following two chapters now return to empirics: studying the humanisation of global politics in the context of protecting the individual human being from mass atrocities (Chapter 6) and killing the individual human being via drones (Chapter 7).

6

Protecting the Individual Human Being from Mass Atrocities

Kigali, 1994: 'There will be no rescue, no intervention force. We can only save ourselves. Many of you know influential people abroad, you must call these people. You must tell them what will happen to us . . . say goodbye. But when you say goodbye, say it as though you are reaching through the phone and holding their hand. Let them know that if they let go of that hand, you will die. We must shame them into sending help' (George 2004). This is a fictional quote from the movie *Hotel Rwanda*, but the events described are real. As the genocide unfolds in Rwanda, the world watches on CNN but does not intervene. The international community fails to lend a helping hand. And when they reach out again, it is too little and too late.

Five years later, in 1999, NATO conducts airstrikes against Serbia, aiming to prevent ethnic cleansing and perhaps a genocide in Kosovo. The heads of states and government of the NATO member states see in the events in Kosovo 'a fundamental challenge to the values for which NATO has stood since its foundation: democracy, human rights and the rule of law. It is the culmination of a deliberate policy of oppression, ethnic cleansing and violence pursued by the Belgrade regime under the direction of President Milosevic. We will not allow this campaign of terror to succeed. NATO is determined to prevail' (NATO 1999b).

Twelve years later, in New York, the UN Security Council president's gavel hits the table. The Council has just passed Resolution 1973. A press release on the evening of that day reads: 'Demanding an immediate ceasefire in Libya, including an end to the current attacks against civilians, which it said might constitute "crimes against humanity", the Security Council this evening imposed . . . a no-fly zone . . . and tightened sanctions on the Qadhafi regime and its supporters . . . . the Council authorized Member States . . . to take all necessary measures to protect civilians under threat of attack in the country, including Benghazi' (UNSC 2011f). This chapter tells the story of these events and developments as part of a discourse on protection: the analysis shows how governments and international organisations have at times failed and at times succeeded to protect the individual human being from mass atrocities, and how in all of this, we ought to shift the focus on the participant that matters most when it comes to mass atrocities: the individual human being.[1]

6.1 INTRODUCTION[2]

Discussions about protecting individual human beings from war crimes, crimes against humanity, genocide, and ethnic cleansing – in short, mass atrocities – often focus on state sovereignty and its potential violation by military interventions (Brock 1999, 2013; Wheeler 2006; Benhabib 2007; Fabri 2008). However, according to this book's main research objective, this case study takes a different approach: it begins with the individual human being (Peters 2009: 535) and proceeds to analyse the discourse on protection. To that end, it engages with the Responsibility to Protect (R2P). Accordingly, this case study asks two specific research questions:[3] First, how does the individual human being appear in the discourse on protection? Second, how does this matter for global politics? To answer these questions, the remainder of this chapter is structured as follows.

Section 6.2 provides an overview of the development of R2P as a contribution to the politics of protection. Section 6.3 provides a critical discussion on the literature of R2P, based on a categorisation I have developed elsewhere (Gholiagha 2014b). Section 6.4 then offers a reading of R2P from the individual human being's perspective, proving a foundation for the empirical analysis, presented in Section 6.5, of the positioning analysis of the discourse on protection in two specific situations, Libya and Syria. Section 6.6 conclusively answers the specific research questions of this case study. With a view to the results of the previous case study and the analytical framework, it is to be expected that the individual human being appears in the discourse on protection either as innocent and therefore worthy of protection or as guilty and therefore unworthy of protection. I argue that this matters for global politics because herein lies R2P's normative advancement: that is, this positioning

[1] I am thankful to Bastian Loges for providing valuable feedback on this chapter.

[2] Some of the discussions, analyses, and ideas presented in this chapter draw on several articles and chapters I have published elsewhere (Gholiagha 2014a, 2014b, 2015b; Gholiagha and Loges 2020).

[3] See Chapter 5 for an overview of the case study–specific research questions and how they were derived from the overall research question.

creates the possibility of a politics of protection independent from the state in which an individual human being who needs protection happens to be in.[4]

6.2 THE DEVELOPMENT OF R2P

This section provides an overview of the development of R2P, with reference to the debate on the relationship between sovereignty, human rights, and the principle of non-interference. I also discuss the humanitarian interventions of the 1990s, zooming in especially on Kosovo as a turning point of the discourse on protection. Furthermore, this section presents the lessons the international community drew from Rwanda and Kosovo and offers a history of R2P and an overview of R2P cases.

6.2.1 *R2P: Sovereignty, Human Rights, and Non-interference*

Given that the sovereignty norm, human rights norms, and the norm of non-interference are at the core of the debate on R2P, I want to discuss their application and their *meaning-in-use* (Wiener 2009). Sovereignty is a key concept in IR theory and IL (Bartelson 1995; Weber 1995; Biersteker and Weber 1996; Krasner 1999; Brown 2002b; Cohen 2004; Jackson 2007; Zaum 2007; Peters 2009). There are different types of sovereignty (Krasner 1999: 9); for the debate on R2P, 'Westphalian sovereignty, referring to the exclusion of external actors from domestic authority configurations' (Krasner 1999: 9) is the most relevant one. IR theory today often defines sovereignty as authority over a clearly defined territory (Diez et al. 2011: 215), but historically, sovereign authority has been heavily contested (Krasner 1993: 261). And while many link the idea of sovereign nation-states to the Peace of Westphalia (Diez et al. 2011: 215), concepts such as self-determination, the prohibition of war, and the idea of sovereign equality stem from the UN Charter and have not been part of the Treaty of Westphalia (Krasner 1993: 260, 1996: 236; Cohen 2004: 12). Furthermore, the Treaty of Westphalia only applied to very few European powers at that time. The critical constructivist perspective on sovereignty in this book highlights constant changes of the meaning of sovereignty, conditional on actors, time, and context (Reus-Smit 2001: 256, 526, 638; Zaum 2007: 27).

4 For a more general discussion of the concept of responsibility in IR, see Hannes Hansen-Magnusson and Antje Vetterlein (2020). For a discussion of conflicting responsibilities, see Mitja Sienknecht (2021).

The UN Charter provides in Article 2(1) for sovereign equality for all its members,[5] and Article 2(4) prohibits the use of force except for self-defence (Article 51) and collective action under Chapter VII. Simultaneously, the Charter spells out a solid commitment to the protection of human rights in Article 1(3) (United Nations 1945). However, the Charter requires human rights protection within each state's jurisdiction but does not allow the use of force by others to enforce these rights. Hence, human rights protection and non-interference are in tension (Brock 1999; Wheeler 2006: 42; Gholiagha 2014a; Peltner 2017; Stimmer and Wisken 2019: 517). Yet these norms and principles – while at the heart of the post–World War II international order (Bellamy 2009: 8–9) – are aimed at preventing inter-state war (United Nations 1945: UN Charter Article 1(1); Tomuschat 2014: 15). Thus, they say little about protecting human rights in inner-state conflicts. During the Cold War, the tension between human rights protection and sovereignty did not come to the fore, partly because either the United States or the Soviet Union exercised their veto regularly.[6] As a result, only very few military interventions to protect human rights took place. Most known are Vietnam's action in Cambodia against the Pol Pot Regime in 1979 (Wheeler 2002: 79, 89–100, 136; Smith 2010: 88–99; Rodley 2015: 782–783) and India's engagement in East-Pakistan/Bangladesh in 1971 (Smith 2010: 81–88; Rodley 2015: 781–782). Furthermore, Tanzania used military force in Uganda in 1979 to overthrow Idi Amin (Gray 2008: 33; Rodley 2015: 782). Neither India nor Uganda used humanitarian arguments; only Vietnam did in Cambodia, but other states rejected these claims (Dixon 2007: 324; Gray 2008: 34).

The view of the relationship between sovereignty and human rights protection began to change in the 1990s (Smith 2010: 105). In this context, Andreas von Arnauld argues that binding human rights treaties and the UN's commitment to consider human rights violations in domestic conflicts may lead to a right to be protected (von Arnauld 2009: 14; see also Forsythe 2018: 78). Anne Peters, however, suggests that human rights law does not provide grounds for the obligation of third-party states to protect human rights when they 'do not have effective control over the persons or territory concerned' (Peters 2016: 239). Hence, for Anne Peters, R2P goes beyond extraterritorial human rights protection as human rights do not provide a right to be protected by third-party

5 Sovereign equality includes the right for each country of non-interference in its domestic affairs. This was spelled out explicitly in the *Friendly Relations Declaration* (von Arnauld 2009: 11).

6 De jure, the UN Charter does not provide a veto for the permanent members of the UN Security Council, but rather requires that all permanent members agree on Chapter VII Resolutions. De facto, this of course constitutes a veto.

states (Peters 2016: 247). While I follow Anne Peters in her assessment, it is still necessary to discuss human rights as actors refer to them in debates.

Following the end of the Cold War and the tension between sovereignty and human rights protection moving towards prioritisation of human rights protection over sovereignty concerns, a steady rise in military interventions aiming to protect human rights could be observed (Bellamy and McLoughlin 2018). Furthermore, these interventions were conducted more often in the international community's name than as interventions by individual states (Smith 2010: 105, 179; Diez et al. 2011: 95). With the use of humanitarian arguments in the justification of such interventions, scholars began to refer to these interventions as 'humanitarian intervention' (Holzgrefe and Keohane 2003), suggesting the term 'expansion of humanity' (Finnemore 1996: 170) for this development, referring to the growing use of humanitarian language,[7] which was explainable through changing norms (see also Finnemore 1996: 153–154; Weiss 2007: 38–39). More specifically, the understanding of who deserved protection widened and encompassed all human beings (Finnemore 1996: 184). Others have described this process with reference to state sovereignty with the image of the 'armour' of sovereignty having become penetrable (von Arnauld 2009: 16, my translation). The landscape of global politics had begun to shift from concerns about states to concerns about protecting individual human beings. Section 6.2.2 engages with the failures and successes of humanitarian interventions in the 1990s. It prepares the ground for a more detailed discussion of the Kosovo intervention and a history of R2P.

6.2.2 *Humanitarian Interventions: Failures and Successes of the 1990s*

After the Cold War, the Security Council became more active in terms of human rights protection. The first authorisation of collective action for protecting human rights was the conflict in Iraq in 1991. Resolution 688 (UNSC 1991) established a no-fly zone intending to protect the Kurdish civilian population in Iraq (Wheeler 2002: 139–171).[8] In 1992, Resolution 767 (UNSC 1992a) was the first one in which the Security Council avowed that 'grave violations within a country or severe emergencies could be evaluated as a threat to peace or international security' (Tomuschat 2014: 17, my

[7] Interventions, as such, conducted for a variety of reasons and with different motives, however, have always been part of global politics (Krasner 1996: 246).

[8] Notably, possible spillover effects of the conflict into the region also played a role in the resolution, which means that the resolution was not only concerned with events in Iraq.

translation). Operation Restore Hope by the Unified Task Force (UNITAF) in Somalia, which was authorised unanimously through UN Security Council Resolution 794 (UNSC 1992b), demonstrated that the shifting views might also result in the use of force, including ground troops. In the resolution, 'humanitarian claims were being advanced and legitimated by members as justification for the use of force' (Wheeler 2002: 185). It seemed that governments were willing to use their soldiers to protect foreign populations (Wheeler 2002: 173).

In terms of the sovereignty norm, Somalia remained an exception for many states. They saw sovereignty only de jure and not de facto violated because the Somali government's authority had collapsed (Wheeler 2002: 187). On 26 March 1993, the UN mission in Somalia was renewed through Resolution 814 (UNSC 1993a). Despite the mission, the situation deteriorated further, and an attack of US forces against the Somali National Alliance led to a disaster with hundreds of people killed (Wheeler 2002: 188–200; Smith 2010: 140, 147; Bellamy 2011a: 5). This was also the end of the UNITAF mission. It was followed by the United Nations Operation in Somalia (UNOSOM II), which remained active until early March 1995 (United Nations 2003b).[9]

In 1994, the situation in Rwanda escalated. Fuelled by ethnic tensions between Hutu and Tutsi, in about 100 days 800 000 civilians, most of them Tutsi, were killed. In responding only reluctantly and too late, the international community did not prevent the genocide. Lack of political will, especially after the events in Somalia, partly explains this reluctance (Smith 2010: 179; Orend 2014: 237). Today, there is little doubt that a fast and robust military response would have prevented the genocide (Wheeler 2002: 209–219). The authorisation of the United Nations Assistance Mission for Rwanda (UNAMIR II) through Resolutions 918 and 925 (UNSC 1994a, 1994b) did not suffice. The intervention turned out to be 'too little, too late' (Annan 1999). The Security Council authorised the French Opération Turquoise, aiming to bridge the gap until UNAMIR II was fully deployed, but this also had little success (Wheeler 2002: 227–235; Smith 2010: 173–176). However, the memories of Somalia were only part of the explanation for the inaction in Rwanda. The question of how to classify what happened on the ground was another. The United States and European states avoided calling the events genocide (Smith 2010: 154–167) out of fear that this would trigger obligations under Article 1 of the 1948 Genocide Convention, entered into force 12 January 1951, which obligates states to prevent and punish genocide.

9 Its predecessor the United Nations Operations in Somalia (UNOSOM I) had been in place from April 1992 to March 1993 (United Nations 2003a).

The ICJ later confirmed with reference to Bosnia in its 2007 judgement on the Genocide Convention (UNGA 1948a) that Article 1 indeed triggers legal obligation (ICJ 2007; for a critical assessment, see Lang Jr. 2011).

In July 1995, a massacre, killing at least 7,414 Bosnian men and boys in Srebrenica during the war in Bosnia, constituted another failure of the international community to protect individual human beings from mass atrocities (Smith 2010: 105–141). What makes this mass atrocity crime especially heinous is that it happened under the eyes of UN soldiers, who had been sent there to establish and secure a 'safe haven', authorised by UN Resolution 819 (UNSC 1993b; Wheeler 2002: 253–255; Smith 2010: 123–129). Again, the international community failed to prevent mass atrocities. The 'expansion of humanity' (Finnemore 1996: 170) did not lead to a consistent practice of interventions to protect human rights, as Karen Smith notes (Smith 2010: 105).[10] However, Karen Smith does identify what she calls a 'liberal consensus' towards moving away from an absolute position on non-interference (Smith 2010: 179). When, four years after Rwanda, the situation in Kosovo, then a Serbian province, worsened and reports about civilian casualties surfaced, this growing consensus came clearly to the fore. Section 6.2.3 discusses in some detail the events and the consequences they had, demonstrating how the reaction to Kosovo was a turning point for the international community and how it wanted to handle the tension between state sovereignty and human rights protection in the future.

6.2.3 *Kosovo: A Turning Point*

In Kosovo, a similar pattern to the conflicts described above could be seen: a conflict fuelled by ethnic tensions led to an outbreak of violence. Kosovo raised the question 'to what extent and how the international community has the right or even the obligation, to intervene in inner-state conflicts, in which grave human rights violations are looming or already being committed' (Brock 1999: 323, my translation). This question of intervention for humanitarian reasons by the international community had come up before. The crucial difference in Kosovo was that, despite a consensus or authorisation by the UNSC, NATO conducted military airstrikes against Serbia (NATO 1999a; Renic 2020: 151–154).[11]

10 Several scholars offer discussions about R2P in relation to humanity (Papamichail and Partis-Jennings 2016; Radice 2016; Jarvis 2018).

11 Neil Renic has noted how the decision to only employ high-altitude bombing had a problematic side, as 'NATO's commitment to force protection during the conflict did not so

In early 1998, the conflict between Serbian forces and an armed non-state actor, the Kosovo Liberation Army, escalated. Between February and September 1998, about 1,000 civilians were killed during the conflict, but it remains contested whether the acts of violence in Kosovo did amount to genocide (Lang Jr. 2009: 196; Smith 2010: 188–202).[12] The estimates for September 1998 to March 1999 are somewhat lower. During the conflict, 400,000 civilians sought refuge outside of Kosovo (Smith 2010: 183–184). Very early on, diplomatic negotiations with Serbia attempting to end the violence included a threat to use force if necessary (Smith 2010: 184–186). Passing Resolution 1199 (UNSC 1998) in September 1998, the UN Security Council identified the events in Kosovo as a 'threat to peace and security in the region' in Resolution 1199. However, the Council did not authorise the use of force. But when attempts for a political solution failed, NATO nevertheless opted for military force.

As Christine Gray notes, NATO's arguments were political and moral, and there was no legal basis for the intervention (Gray 2008: 40). Despite the apparent violation of the UN Charter, a draft resolution condemning NATO for violations of international law only received three votes in favour (Russia, China, and Namibia), with twelve UN Security Council members voting against it (Wheeler 2006: 44). In sum, the reaction to the NATO operation was ambivalent. While the Organisation of Islamic Conferences (since 2011, Organisation of Islamic Cooperation) supported the actions (Farer 2003: 70), the G77 criticised it (Byers and Chesterman 2003: 184; Gray 2008: 35).

Later, the Independent International Commission on Kosovo concluded that NATO's actions were illegal but legitimate (Independent International Commission on Kosovo 2000; Farer 2003: 68). To Allen Buchanan, this illustrates a growing consensus 'that there is an unacceptable gap between what international law allows and what morality requires' (Buchanan 2003: 130). While some supported this view, speaking of 'emergency relief', legitimised through international law (Habermas 1999, my translation), others were more critical, arguing that what was needed was a reform of the existing law (Hehir 2012: 171). Regardless of how one assesses the intervention in Kosovo (see Nuñez-Mietz 2018 for a critical analysis of the legal discourse), there is no doubt it constituted a turning point in the debate on state sovereignty and intervention. Kosovo shed light on the fracturing of the 'dualism of the current

much eliminate physical risk as *transfer* it to the vulnerable noncombatants on the ground' (Renic 2020: 20).

[12] It must be noted here that both NATO and the Kosovo Liberation Army also caused civilian casualties.

international legal order as a *law of states and human rights order*' (Brock 1999: 323, emphasis in original, my translation). The debates and developments in the 1990s demonstrated that state sovereignty could no longer be used to shield states from all outside interference, especially in cases of mass atrocities (von Arnauld 2009: 16).

This development can be explained by constructivist norms research suggesting that what changed in the 1990s was who or what was worthy of protection. Human beings were identified as worthy of protection independent of their location and citizenship (Finnemore 1996: 184; Wheeler 2006: 48). Ruti Teitel identifies the reasons for this change, arguing that '[c]ivilians, not soldiers, are increasingly recognized as the primary targets and victims of modern war; civilian suffering is often the direct objective of military action' (Teitel 2011: 100). This focus on civilians was possible only by making a specific assumption, namely, that 'the people on whose behalf the military was to intervene had in some way to be seen as *worthy of the effort, as human*' (Zehfuß 2001: 331, emphasis added). Therefore, Kosovo, where those favouring the intervention identified the individual human being as worthy of protection, signifies a significant shift in the discourse on protection. As the following will demonstrate, Rwanda and Kosovo led to renewed debates about the relationship between sovereignty and human rights protection, preparing the ground for R2P.

6.2.4 *Lessons from Rwanda and Kosovo*

The main effect of the events in Rwanda and Kosovo consisted of an enhanced debate about sovereignty: the understanding of state sovereignty as the right of non-interference and the international community's growing focus on human rights protection led to a more comprehensive debate about the meaning of sovereignty. A short piece, written by then–Secretary General Kofi Annan and published in the *Economist*, kicked off the debate. Entitled 'Two Concepts of Sovereignty' (Annan 1999), Kofi Annan criticised both lacking political will in Rwanda and the unauthorised use of force by NATO in Kosovo. However, on Rwanda, he wrote:

> Imagine for one moment that, in those dark days and hours leading up to the genocide, there had been a coalition of states ready and willing to act in defence of the Tutsi population, but the council had refused or delayed giving the green light. *Should such a coalition then have stood idly by while the horror unfolded* (Annan 1999: 81, emphasis added)?

For Kofi Annan, actors should not circumvent the Security Council, nor should genocide occur (Annan 1999). Put differently: there should neither be 'future Rwandas' nor 'future Kosovos' (Bellamy 2006: 143). Using the term 'individual sovereignty', he pointed to the complementarity of state sovereignty and the protection of human rights. The idea of conditional sovereignty was already put forward in the term 'sovereignty as responsibility' (Deng et al. 1996) and, as Oheneba Boateng (forthcoming: 14) has demonstrated, even much earlier: in 1957, Ako-Adjei, at that time, Ghana's Minister of Interior and Justice, gave a speech to the UN General Assembly. As Oheneba Boateng notes: 'At the centre of this speech was the idea of sovereignty as responsibility and humaneness, that a state can be considered truly sovereign only if it treated its citizens with responsibility and humanness according to domestic and international obligations' (Boateng forthcoming: 15). Several authors have also argued for conceptualising sovereignty in that manner (Peters 2006; MacDonald and Alston 2008: 2; Bellamy 2009: 14).

At the dawn of the twenty-first century, the relation between state sovereignty and human rights protection began to move from tension to complementarity. The Canadian sponsored International Commission on Intervention and State Sovereignty (ICISS) (ICISS 2001; von Arnauld 2009: 17; Brunnée and Toope 2010b: 194) accelerated that development with its report on 'The Responsibility to Protect' (ICISS 2001; see Cunliffe 2016 for a critical reading of the report). The R2P was born. Section 6.2.5 presents a history of R2P. Before doing so, let me be transparent here: it is one way to tell the history of R2P, which is similar to many others; but it does not take up a more postcolonial perspective, which places R2P 'as part of an older and much wider global history of interventionism' (Mallavarapu 2015: 319). Similarly, it does not begin with debates amongst African states about interventionism that can be traced back to the late 1960s (Boateng forthcoming: chapter 6). I can only point to others who provide such histories (Mallavarapu 2015; Boateng forthcoming) and acknowledge that mine is one of many perspectives.

6.2.5 *Establishing R2P*

The ICISS report moved away from debates about a potential 'right of humanitarian intervention' to the idea of a 'responsibility to protect' (ICISS 2001: vii–viii; von Arnauld 2009: 33). There are several characteristics where R2P differs from humanitarian interventions (Thakur 2016: 418). Three of the characteristics are central from the book's perspective. First, R2P begins with the perspective of the person to be protected, the (potential) victim of mass atrocities crimes, while humanitarian interventions focus on the intervener

(Wheeler 2002: 1; von Arnauld 2009: 33; Thakur 2016: 418). Second, states hold the primary responsibility to protect their populations, thereby strengthening sovereignty (Welsh 2016b: 5). Third, R2P includes rebuilding and prevention. Neither aspect is part of humanitarian intervention (von Arnauld 2009: 33).

The ICISS report identifies the UNSC as the institution vested with the authority to decide whether a state failed its responsibility and, therefore, to decide whether and how the international community should act (ICISS 2001: 13–14, 47–50).[13] The report distinguishes between a 'responsibility to prevent', a 'responsibility to react', and a 'responsibility to rebuild' (ICISS 2001: 19–29, 29–38, 39–46, respectively).

Following the report, R2P was discussed during debates of a UN Reform in 2004. Furthermore, the 2005 Secretary-General report refers to R2P (von Arnauld 2009: 17–19). During the World Summit 2005, R2P was added to the World Summit Outcome Document (WSOD) (United Nations 2005b; Bellamy 2006; Strauss 2009). Notably, the definition of R2P in the ICISS report and the WSOD differ. The primary focus of the 2005 version of R2P is on each state's responsibility to protect its population from genocide,[14] war crimes, crimes against humanity, and ethnic cleansing. Only when a state is 'manifestly failing' to act accordingly should the international community intervene (United Nations 2005b: Articles 138 and 139). Furthermore, there is no list of criteria for possible military intervention (Brunnée and Toope 2010b: 197; Rodley 2015: 788–792).[15] The Security Council is supposed to act on a case-by-case basis (United Nations 2005b: Articles 138 and 139). As this constitutes the understanding of R2P the book works with, I cite it once here in full:

> 138. Each individual State has the responsibility to protect its populations from genocide, war crimes, ethnic cleansing and crimes against humanity. This responsibility entails the prevention of such crimes, including their incitement, through appropriate and necessary means. We accept that responsibility and will act in accordance with it. The international community should, as appropriate, encourage and help States to exercise this responsibility and support the United Nations in establishing an early warning capability.

[13] For a discussion of this transfer of responsibility, see William Bain (2010) and Andreas von Arnauld (2009: 27–29, 2015: 60–62).

[14] A detailed discussion on genocide within IR and its relations to R2P is provided by Adrian Gallagher (2013).

[15] For a discussion on advantages and disadvantages of such a criteria-based approach, see, for example, the work of Hajo Schmidt (2015) and Daniel Peters (2015).

> 139. The international community, through the United Nations, also has the responsibility to use appropriate diplomatic, humanitarian and other peaceful means, in accordance with Chapters VI and VIII of the Charter, to help to protect populations from genocide, war crimes, ethnic cleansing and crimes against humanity. In this context, we are prepared to take collective action, in a timely and decisive manner, through the Security Council, in accordance with the Charter, including Chapter VII, on a case-by-case basis and in cooperation with relevant regional organizations as appropriate, should peaceful means be inadequate and national authorities are manifestly failing to protect their populations from genocide, war crimes, ethnic cleansing and crimes against humanity. We stress the need for the General Assembly to continue consideration of the responsibility to protect populations from genocide, war crimes, ethnic cleansing and crimes against humanity and its implications, bearing in mind the principles of the Charter and international law. We also intend to commit ourselves, as necessary and appropriate, to helping States build capacity to protect their populations from genocide, war crimes, ethnic cleansing and crimes against humanity and to assisting those which are under stress before crises and conflicts break out (United Nations 2005b: Article 138 and 139).

Prima facie, the WSOD version of R2P does not seem to change how the international community should respond when witnessing grave human rights violations in domestic conflicts. In the end, there is no automatism, and the ultimate decision lies, as before, with the UNSC. Whether this version of R2P would be able to prevent 'future Rwandas' or 'future Kosovos' (Bellamy 2006: 143) remained unclear, which is why some scholars refer to the WSOD version of R2P as 'R2P-lite' (Bellamy 2008: 616; Weiss 2014: 15). Yet the international community has agreed upon this narrow version, and Jennifer Welsh, for example, has argued that it helps to clarify the question of responsibility in the face of mass atrocities (Welsh 2016b: 5).

Another, and from the perspective of this book more important, difference between the ICISS and the WSOD version is that while the ICISS report speaks of citizens, and thus limits itself to a particular group of individual human beings within a state, the WSOD speaks of the more encompassing term of 'populations' (United Nations 2005b: Articles 138 and 139). Thus, it is not citizens but populations who are placed at the centre of the debate. The term populations can be understood as a catchphrase, referring to every individual human being within a state's territory. An interpretation supported in the following quote, which also points to the importance of talking about populations instead of citizens:

> Well, citizens have to … be recognised by their governments so. *And populations we're talking you could have refugees, you could have asylees, you could have all kinds of people* with different statutes in terms of citizenship … and the government if they're within your borders you have to protect them *so that's … a very big distinction that was made during the World Summit Outcome Document* (Interview A2: 319–323, emphasis added).[16]

Following the 2005 World Summit, R2P was referred to in UNSC resolutions, for example, in the Resolutions 1674 and 1706 (UNSC 2006a, 2006b). With regard to Resolution 1706, which was on the situation in Darfur, Jess Gifkins notes that 'R2P was highly disputed … and it took six months to find agreement, even with the abstentions from China, Qatar, and Russia' (Gifkins 2016: 156). And it was not until 2009 that then–Secretary General Ban Ki-Moon suggested a three-pillar version to operationalise R2P within the UN system (Ban 2009). The first pillar is each state's responsibility to protect. The second pillar is the international community's responsibility to support states. The third pillar refers to the international community's responsibility to act if a state fails its responsibility and may include the use of force (Ban 2009). Many states supported and accepted that operationalisation in statements during the 64th UN General Assembly (ICRtoP 2009). The verdict on these debates and, more generally, the acceptance of R2P differ starkly. While some suggest that the acceptance displayed during the debates was relatively weak (Hehir 2011), others provide a more positive assessment concerning R2P's acceptance (Kurtz and Rotmann 2016: 15). Scholars, however, all note one thing: R2P, while slowly consolidating, remains contested and inconsistently applied (Bellamy 2010: 144, 2011a: 68; Hunt and Orchard 2020a; Crossley 2020).

Since 2005, different actors in various situations referred to R2P, but others did not always accept their views. One example is the invocation of R2P by France in response to the regime in Myanmar seemed unable and unwilling to deliver humanitarian aid to its population after the 2008 cyclone Nargis (Selth 2008; Bünte 2009; Haacke 2009; Weiss 2014: 11). Other states equally rejected Russia's invocation of R2P as a legitimisation of its military conflict with Georgia, pointing to the need to protect the Russian population in Georgia (Kranz 2008; Luchterhandt 2008; Glanville 2014: 156–157). In other instances, references to R2P found broader support. R2P has been frequently

[16] Others are, however, more critical of the notion of population due to a population being an 'object' of concern (Conley-Zilkic 2014: 442). Such a critique, however, remains within the subject-object dichotomy criticised in Chapters 2 and 3.

referenced in UNSC Resolution and Presidential Statements (Global Centre for the Responsibility to Protect 2021 offers an overview). At times this has included diplomatic efforts, sanctions, or military support through UN Missions (UNSC 2013a, 2013c; Ainley 2015: 51). The preventive effect of R2P came to the fore when Kofi Annan successfully negotiated a peace agreement in Kenya, after the election in December 2007 led to violence (Juma 2009; Lindenmayer and Kaye 2009; Babbitt 2017: 433; Bellamy and McLoughlin 2018: 73–93). The situation in Libya – discussed below in detail – constitutes the first instance of the UNSC invoking R2P to authorise force against the state's expressed will (UNSC 2011e).

Moving on from this discussion of the development of R2P and its application since 2005, Section 6.3 provides a critical discussion of the R2P literature. The aim is to provide an overview and typology of the literature, identify shortcomings and gaps, and highlight the usefulness to think about R2P through the lens of the conceptual framework the book provides.

6.3 A CRITICAL DISCUSSION OF R2P LITERATURE

Since the ICISS report, legal scholars and political scientists have discussed R2P widely, with Google Scholar listing more than 99,000 results for the term 'Responsibility to Protect'.[17] But even twenty years after the ICISS report was published and more than fifteen years after the states agreed on a definition of R2P in the WSOD, scholars still grapple with how to conceptualise R2P. R2P has been described with reference to international law (Arbour 2008; Verlage 2009; Welsh and Banda 2010; Verlage 2013) as a political promise (Bellamy and Reike 2010: 269), a norm (Glanville 2016; Labonte 2016; Deitelhoff and Zimmermann 2020), a concept (Orford 2011: 212), a regime (Orchard 2020), and a provisional duty (Roff 2013). How scholars conceptualise R2P affects their research perspective and what they can say about R2P. As others have done, this book subscribes to the idea that R2P needs to be acknowledged as a 'complex norm' and its different parts require a differentiated analysis (Bellamy 2010; Welsh 2013).

This section offers a typology and a critical assessment of the R2P literature. Others have provided such typologies (Loges 2013: 116–127; Kurtz and Rotmann 2016; Thakur 2016). I argue that there are three types of literature: advocacy, critical, and analytical.[18] While recognising weaknesses in R2P,

[17] https://scholar.google.com/scholar?q="Responsibility+to+Protect" (14 March 2022).

[18] These categories stem from a review essay I published some time ago. The discussion of the literature provided also draws on this essay (Gholiagha 2014b). The review essay focused on

advocacy literature aims to strengthen R2P and its implementation through analysis and policy suggestions (Weiss 2011; Bellamy 2011a; Weiss 2014; Bellamy 2015; Thakur 2015; Glanville 2016; Bellamy and McLoughlin 2018). Critical literature focuses more on the failure of R2P (Dunford and Neu 2019: 1085, offers a brief overview). The criticism ranges from a stern rejection of R2P as Western imperialism to more differentiated discussions. In the latter case, scholars identify failures inherent to R2P or its inability to deliver on the promise to end mass atrocities or at least significantly reduce them (Chandler 2004; Alvarez 2008; Hehir 2010, 2011b, 2012; Cunliffe 2016; Morris 2016; Hehir 2018a; Dunford and Neu 2019).

Analytical literature focuses on deepening the understanding of R2P without taking a normative position a priori (Arbour 2008; Brunnée and Toope 2010b; Bain 2010; Orford 2011; Garwood-Gowers 2015; Ralph 2018). Such analytical literature can conclude with a normative position on R2P (see, for example, Orford 2011: 41). Two things must be noted. First, these categories are not exclusive, meaning that a specific piece of scholarship may fit into more than one category. Second, these different perspectives on R2P can be brought together fruitfully (Hehir and Pattison 2016).

This chapter and the analysis provided therein fall into the analytical category, offering an interdisciplinary perspective on the interplay between politics and law (Kratochwil 2014) in the context of R2P. In line with the book's conceptual and theoretical framework, I discuss questions of language and norms and take up issues of authority and decision-making and the more general issue of the usefulness of R2P for the protection of individual human beings from mass atrocities.

In the debate about R2P, scholars at times distinguish words and deeds, rhetoric and practice, or rhetoric and reality (Bellamy 2011a; Orford 2011: 2–3, 10; Hehir 2012; Welsh 2016a). I do not find this distinction very helpful. As Nicholas Onuf noted more than thirty years ago: 'saying is doing: talking is undoubtedly the most important way that we go about making the world what it is' (Onuf 1989: 59). Scholars more critical of R2P, such as Aidan Hehir, claim that language does not play an important role (Hehir 2012: 127–128), and

three central works published around that time: Alex J. Bellamy (2011a), *Global Politics and the Responsibility to Protect* (Oxford; New York: Routledge); Aidan Hehir (2012), *The Responsibility to Protect* (Houndsmill: Palgrave Macmillan); Anne Orford (2011), *International Authority and the Responsibility to Protect* (Cambridge: Cambridge University Press). I have revised the text here substantively and added additional and newer literature, yet the three central pieces by Alex Bellamy (for advocacy literature), Aidan Hehir (for critical literature), and Anne Orford (for analytical literature) remain central to the discussion, as they are good representations of their respective type.

if it is employed as a 'discursive means', its effect is weak (Hehir 2018b: 81). Contrary to such a critical perspective, others have pointed to R2P's rhetorical power (Stamnes 2009; Thakur 2015; Glanville 2016; Babbitt 2017: 432). A clear example of a language-focused analysis is reflected in Ramesh Thakur's analysis of the Libyan intervention: '*R2P was the discourse of choice* in debating how best to respond to the crisis and the Security Council for the first time invoked R2P under the coercive chapter VII of the Charter' (Thakur 2015: 19, emphasis added; see also Gifkins 2016: 150). Luke Glanville offers a middle position, agreeing with scholars such as Aidan Hehir that it is not about the '*frequency* of invocations of R2P' but rather about '*how* such language about the imperative to protect populations is deployed and how it is received by relevant audiences' (Glanville 2016: 190, emphasis in original). Whether words matter is also a question of who says them and on whose behalf (Orford 2011: 138).

I hold that a critical constructivist understanding of the role of language and discourse as presented in the previous chapters can help us assess whether and how references to R2P matter. However, it is essential to note that using the language of R2P does not automatically lead to anything but provides a framework to discuss a situation to offer protection from mass atrocity crimes (Gifkins 2016: 151). Scholarship on R2P, including my work, has included such a focus on language and discourse (Welsh 2013; Weiss 2014; Ainley 2015; Gholiagha 2015b; Thakur 2015; Gholiagha and Loges 2020; Deitelhoff and Zimmermann 2020).

Another core theme in the literature on R2P is concerned with the question of what exactly R2P is. The question about R2P's ontological status may irritate at first, given that the heads of states and governments agreed on a definition over fifteen years ago at the 2005 World Summit. However, the issue is far from settled (Orford 2011: 106; Bellamy 2011a: 84–86; Hehir 2012: 29; Peters 2016: 238), and as discussed above, several terms and concepts are used. Like many others, I understand R2P as a norm. However, I differ in the often-read qualification of R2P as 'emerging' (Brunnée and Toope 2010b: 192). Christopher Daase has rightly pointed out that the classification of R2P as 'emerging' is part of a 'liberal narrative' and he rightly problematises the term, as it already assumes 'what the right norm is that stands at the end of the norm emerging process' (Daase 2013: 47, my translation). This perspective of R2P as an agreed upon norm remains present in some of the literature. Yet this book's conceptual framework suggests, as other constructivist scholars have done, that the ongoing contestation of R2P is to be expected (Wiener 2009: 176, 2014a: 66–68; Gholiagha 2015b). Furthermore, contestation in a 'proactive' form (Wiener 2018: chapter 2) can strengthen and further legitimise R2P (Gholiagha and Wiener 2013; Wiener 2014a: 66–68). Finally, scholars have observed a simultaneous consolidation and contestation (Hunt and Orchard 2020b).

Yet, despite insights on norms being inherently contested and moving away from a linear understanding of norms in large parts of the norms literature, R2P literature often remains loyal to such linear notions (Bellamy 2011a: 9; Tacheva and Brown 2015: 438).[19] Instead, as many have suggested, R2P as a norm remains contested, and its meaning is sizable when studying its '*meaning-in-use*' (Wiener 2009; Gholiagha et al. 2021). When studying norms, we cannot examine them independently, as the literature on norm dynamics discussed in chapter two has demonstrated. Scholars have also made this point about R2P and related norms such as the Protection of Civilians norm (Rhoads and Welsh 2019: 615) or the prohibition of aggression (Fehl 2019: 908). In the case of R2P, we also need to take a closer look at the norm's complex structure (Welsh 2013; Hunt 2016). As Jennifer Welsh explains:

> R2P in its three-pillar form thus represents what I call a 'complex' norm, containing more than one prescription. This complex structure also creates a situation in which the *breach* of one of the components of R2P (failure on the part of a national government to protect its population) is meant to act as a trigger for *fulfilment* of another component (the international community's remedial role in protecting) (Welsh 2013: 384, emphasis in original).

This book works with this complex understanding of R2P. However, the claim that R2P is a complex norm does not settle the question of the effect of this complex norm on states' behaviour. The issue of how norms affect states is, of course, not limited to R2P (Legro 1997; Kratochwil 2000). Still, it is a central aspect of the literature on R2P. While scholars such as Luke Glanville argue that R2P influences states' behaviour in various ways (Glanville 2016: 185, 196), others are much more critical, speaking of R2P as a 'hollow' norm (Hehir 2018a). As I will demonstrate in the analysis, R2P affects the discourse of protection, as diplomats use it to position the individual human being in discourses of protection.

But even with a better understanding of what R2P is and with the conclusion that it does matter, a crucial question remains: who decides if R2P applies in a situation and, if so, what should happen then (Orford 2011: 182–184; Hehir 2012: 140–144)? Looking at the WSOD, it seems clear: states are primarily responsible for protecting their population from mass atrocities, and if they fail, the international community, through the UNSC, steps in. And the

[19] See Chapters 2 and 3 for a detailed critical discussion of linear norm-development models.

debates about Libya and Syria demonstrate that, at the moment, there is little doubt that in practice, authority currently lies with the UNSC. However, when the UNSC fails to act, one can wonder whether it is the right actor for the job (Hehir 2012: 146). Therefore, scholars have explored possibilities of circumventing the UNSC via actions based on the Uniting for Peace Resolution from 1950 (UNGA 1950), especially following the inaction by the Security Council on Syria (Arbour 2013; Gallagher and Ralph 2013; Gholiagha 2013; Nahlawi 2019). A critical constructivist perspective on R2P enables analysing and understanding debates of R2P's contested application better, showing the importance of considering the specific situation and meaning actors attach to R2P (Deitelhoff and Zimmermann 2020). However, even if there is agreement on applying R2P, it is unclear if it does any good.

A critical assessment to R2P's effect is offered by Aidan Hehir when he points to 'two fundamental and related issues which have manifestly not been resolved; the permissibility of actions taken without Security Council authorisation, and what to do to ensure greater consistency in Security Council decision making' (Hehir 2012: 77). For Aidan Hehir, it remains unclear what advantage R2P contains (Hehir 2012: 11). He claims that it has failed as it did not deliver what it promised, that is, 'to improve the international community's capacity to respond to looming and/or actual intra-state mass atrocity crimes' (Hehir 2018b: 71). Proponents of R2P counter such arguments by pointing out that '[w]e can recognize the impact of a norm both in instances of compliance and violation' (Glanville 2016: 189) and that in fact 'atrocities have declined over the past few decades and that international activism against them is increasing' (Bellamy and McLoughlin 2018: 34). In a similar vein, Alex Bellamy argues for strengthening various aspects of R2P (Bellamy 2011a: 122–142, 187). Anne Orford offers a middle position between the negative view heralded by critics such as Aidan Hehir and the affirmative view scholars such as Alex Bellamy provide. For Anne Orford, protection is a political question (Orford 2011: 212). Similarly, Jenifer Welsh suggests that R2P has 'helped to forge political consensus and … has helped to build new institutional capacity' (Welsh 2016b: 4).

The theoretical and conceptual framework of the book suggests that an answer to the question of whether R2P as a norm has an effect and whether it ought to be applied or not can only be answered by studying the discourse of protection more closely, reconstructing how R2P and the discourse of protection matter for the individual human being. It requires assessing the position of the individual human being as a participant in that discourse. Only then can R2P's *meaning-in-use* (Wiener 2009; Gholiagha et al. 2021) be analysed. To this end, the remainder of the chapter analyses the appearance of the individual human being in the discourse on protection by providing, first, a reading of R2P with a focus on the individual human being, and second, an analysis of debates about the R2P in Libya and Syria. In doing so, the various ways individual human beings are positioned and position themselves in the discourse on protection comes to the fore.

6.4 THE INDIVIDUAL HUMAN BEING IN R2P

War and violence have primarily been studied on a systemic or state level in IR, as feminist scholars have critically noted (Sylvester 2013b: 1–2). Christine Sylvester has argued for the need to consider the personal experience of war in general (Sylvester 2013a: 619–620). In the context of R2P, Jennifer Welsh has argued that R2P is part of a development 'to make the individual – and his or her rights – one of the central reasons or causes for armed conflicts' (Welsh 2019b: 14). Grant Marlier and Neta Crawford claim that R2P is about the 'suffering of people on the individual level' (Marlier and Crawford 2013: 410). And Anne Peters sees R2P as part of a 'paradigm shift . . . towards the needs, and possibly even the rights of the individual' (Peters 2016: 236). Relatedly, Samuel Jarvis has pointed to the need to further study the 'concept of humanity' 'as the moral source of the Responsibility to Protect's motivational capacity' (Jarvis 2018: 107). Finally, R2P's focus on individual rights also becomes apparent on the level of the crimes it aims to prevent. While often discussed on the levels of groups and collectives, these crimes also matter for the individual human being, even for crimes with a strong focus on groups.

The most obvious case of a group-based crime is genocide. The Convention on the Prevention and Punishment of the Crime of Genocide (hereafter Genocide Convention) defines genocide in Article II as 'acts intended committed with intent to destroy, in whole or in part, a national, ethnical, racial or religious group, as such' (UNGA 1948a).[20] What becomes immediately apparent is the focus on a group of a certain kind. This focus has partly to do with the historical development of the concept by Raphael Lemkin, as David Luban notes (Luban 2010: 574; see Sands 2016a for a fascinating account of the history of the Genocide Convention). However, when looking at the specific acts,[21] these are at least partly about individual

[20] Karen Smith has rightly pointed out that there are two norms against genocide: a narrower one to be found in the Genocide Convention and a broader social or non-legalised norm that takes into accounts genocidal crimes that fall outside the narrower legal definition of the Convention (Smith 2010: 6).

[21] These acts are: '(a) Killing members of the group; (b) Causing serious bodily or mental harm to members of the group; (c) Deliberately inflicting on the group conditions of life calculated to

human beings. Christopher Macleod is correct to point out that 'genocide's distinctive harm should be characterised either in terms of *damage to individuals* or *damage to groups targeted by genocide*' (Macleod 2012: 197, emphasis in original). Group-based perspectives on genocide assume 'that groups as such possess value over and above the value of all the individuals in them' (Luban 2010: 574). Individual-based accounts assume that 'the distinctiveness of genocide is the harm done to its individual victims, or the intention to do the harm' (Lee 2010: 335–336). Such an individualist account is grounded in the understanding that the act of genocide is especially harmful to individual human beings because of the intention to kill all members of the group the specific individual is a member of (Lee 2010: 341–342).

Bridget Conley-Zilkic has pointed out that when 'posing "groupness" . . . as the subject of atrocities it is too easy to fall into the traps of naturalizing, simplifying, homogenizing, and assuming too much based on group identity' (Conley-Zilkic 2014: 440). In line with this, Robert Pape has argued that 'attacking a group is immoral not because the group matters most but because the individuals do' (Pape 2012: 48). Here, it is helpful to recall Hannah Arendt's description of genocide. She describes it as 'an attack upon human diversity as such, that is upon a characteristic of the "human status" without which the very words "mankind" or "humanity" would be devoid of meaning' (Arendt 1963: 247; on the 'human status', see also Weinert 2015: 44–54). Discussing this Arendtian understanding, Christopher Macleod points out that for Hannah Arendt 'there was a high number of individual murders, violations of human dignity and heinous acts, but there was also some further evil, over above these individual crimes committed on individual people' (Macleod 2012: 197). In sum, while genocide always has a collective element, the acts committed are crimes against individual human beings (Kinsella 2011: 167, notes the dehumanising effect genocide has on both collectives and individuals). Furthermore, those who participate in genocide as perpetrators are individual human beings, too (see Chapter 4).

The argument for an individual-based account of R2P is even stronger concerning the other crimes that fall under R2P, that is, war crimes, crimes against humanity, and ethnic cleansing. Crimes against humanity, according to the definition of the Rome Statute, include crimes of murder, extermination, torture, and rape. War crimes include wilful killing and torture. These

bring about its physical destruction in whole or in part; (d) Imposing measures intended to prevent births within the group; (e) Forcibly transferring children of the group to another group' (UNGA 1948a: Article II).

are all crimes committed against individual human beings (Rome Statute 1998: Articles 7–8).

Due to the connections between ICL and the ICC, on the one hand, and R2P, on the other, discussed in Chapter 4, we can observe a growing use of crime language in the context of R2P. Such language identifies (potential) victims of crimes as the beneficiaries of R2P (Lucas 2014: 35). Mark Osiel has pointed out that this raises the issue of individualisation vs. collectivisation of victims (Osiel 2014: 290) leading to the need to discuss who the parties to mass atrocities are (Osiel 2014: 296). Therefore, the argument can be made that crimes that fall under the R2P scope and R2P itself can be understood from the perspective of the individual human being as the primary beneficiary of the politics of protection and the sole victim of these crimes. Collective entities are not victims of crimes; individual human beings are, and, as Yossarian reminds us in *Catch-22* (Heller 1961), this is the only thing that matters to them.

Simultaneously, a focus on the well-being of the individual human being as the beneficiary of preventing such crimes is present in the discourse on protection. As Mark Kersten rightly notes, 'R2P was intended to place *the human experience* at the very heart of decision-making in international relations' (Kersten 2014a, emphasis added). Likewise, Jennifer Welsh, at that time the UN Special Representative on R2P and the Prevention of Genocide, recalls that R2P is about protecting '*individuals* inside the jurisdiction of a particular state' (Welsh 2013: 368, emphasis added), a point both political scientists and legal scholars have echoed (Tacheva and Brown 2015: 460; von Arnauld 2015: 64; Wilcox 2015: 173; Peters 2016: 237). In this context, Lauren Wilcox has suggested that R2P produced three 'subjects': 'a subject to be saved, a subject that can do the saving, and an inhuman subject that can be killed in order to save others' (Wilcox 2015: 174; see also Dunford and Neu 2019: 1087, on the killing of people as a result of interventions and other negative effects). In this chapter, the focus lies on the first of the three subjects or participants.

Jennifer Welsh furthermore notes that 'when individuals inside a sovereign state are subjected to such extreme violations of their basic security [...] they can no longer even be said to have rights as members of the community' (Welsh 2013: 396). Jennifer Welsh thus points out that those rights are lost because such extreme violations coincide with a de facto loss of membership in a political community. What should, therefore, lie at the heart of the analysis of R2P is whom R2P aims to protect, that is, the individual human being (Peters 2009: 535; Chandler 2010: 9). And, of course, in these situations, international human rights and individual rights gain relevance as normative reference points for protection. Additionally, such a focus on the individual human being can further develop R2P (Luck 2015: 501–502).

We already find this focus on the individual human being in the early debates on the 'Protection of Civilians in Armed Conflicts' in the UN Security Council (Loges 2013: 221, 317).[22] Even Aidan Hehir, a critic of R2P, acknowledges that '[t]he question posed by intervention and sovereignty is certainly concerned with protecting the weak but it is weak *individuals* rather than states' (Hehir 2012: 189, emphasis in original). Those being protected under R2P are 'human beings as such' (Stone Sweet 2012: 57) and the issue is one of 'human protection' (Paris 2014: 571; Bellamy and McLoughlin 2018: xxxvii; Crossley 2020: 475). Scholars have noted a shift in political speeches regarding interventions towards more 'human-centric justifications' (Teitel 2011: 35), 'rights of vulnerable people' (Weiss 2014: 9), and the '*defense of others*, namely, the *persons* who are victims of unjustified violence by their own governments' (Téson 2014: 63, emphasis in original). All this demonstrates the necessity for a stronger focus on the individual human beings' appearance in the discourse of protection. To better understand this appearance, Section 6.5 analyses the individual human being's appearance in the discourse on R2P in two specific situations beginning in 2011: Libya and Syria.

6.5 R2P IN LIBYA AND SYRIA

So far, this chapter has offered a history of humanitarian interventions and a discussion on the development of R2P and a critical discussion of the existing literature on R2P. This section answers how the individual human being appears in the discourse of protection by analysing the conflicts in Libya and Syria in the early 2010s and R2P's role in them. While the first case, Libya, was the first situation in which the UNSC referred to R2P in a Chapter VII resolution, the second situation, Syria, has been subject to a decade of debate with few results, ongoing suffering bloodshed, and human rights violations. Nevertheless, scholars often discuss it under an R2P heading and in comparison to Libya (Morris 2013; Kersavage 2014; Stahn 2014; Weiss 2014).

The two situations share some common factors, such as time – both conflicts began in 2011; context – both conflicts emerged as part of the so-called 'Arab Spring' (Hehir and Pattison 2016); and region – both countries are

[22] The Protection of Civilians however is distinct from R2P, even though the two discourses are being mixed and intertwined at times (Willmot and Mamiya 2015: 381–382). Protection of Civilians is often referred to in peacekeeping missions, which are not necessarily R2P-guided missions (Willmot and Mamiya 2015: 375).

in the Western Asia and North Africa region. However, the international community's response, especially comparing the early phases of the conflicts, could not be more different. As the following analysis will reveal, this becomes understandable by focusing on the individual human being's position within each of the discourses and by looking at the participation of individual human beings. In line with the abductive research logic developed in the previous chapters, guilt and innocence provide a heuristic for the analysis. As will also become evident, the concepts of gender and body that form part of the book's conceptual framework play a part in analytically grasping certain aspects of the discourse on protection. And, of course, human and individual rights of the individual human beings matter too. I have structured the analysis into three parts. First, I identify and contextualise the documents on which the analysis rests and define a time frame for the analysis (Section 6.5.1). In Sections 6.5.2 and 6.5.3, I analyse the discourse on Libya and Syria, respectively.

6.5.1 *Documents for the Analysis and Time Frame of Analysis*

Table 6.1 provides an overview of the documents I analyse. The analysis focuses primarily on UNSC resolutions and meeting records and documents by other relevant international organisations. I corroborate the analysis through interviews, media reports, and secondary literature.

For both Libya and Syria, I mainly focus on the early phases of the conflicts. For Libya, I zoom into the debate leading up to the authorisation of the use of force in 2011 and briefly discuss the aftermath of the intervention. For Syria, I expand the time frame somewhat wider, considering events such as the use of chemical weapons in 2013 and debates about humanitarian aid up to 2015. As the situation in Syria has evolved into a full-blown civil war with several external actors, the more recent developments, including the fight against the so-called Islamic State, are briefly acknowledged but not discussed in detail. I also cannot provide an exhaustive analysis of all debates and all UNSC documents. However, the analysis provides sufficient material to better understand the individual human being's appearance in both situations.

I now turn to Libya. Before delving into the analysis, a note on the structure of the analysis: In the following analyses, rather than separating the presentation of facts from the analysis, I interweave the description of facts, the interpretation of these facts, and the positioning analysis based on the interpretation. Recalling the previous chapters, the use of conceptual terms such as 'positions' and 'participants' and the reference to the heuristics of innocence and guilt point to the analysis.

TABLE 6.1. *Documents for the analysis of the discourse on protection*

Document	Author / Source	Situation	Date
UNSC Resolution 1970	UN Security Council	Libya	26 February 2011
Meeting Record for Resolution 1970	UN Security Council	Libya	26 February 2011
Organisation of Islamic Cooperation Statement on Libya	Organisation of Islamic Cooperation	Libya	8 March 2011
AU Statement on Libya	African Union	Libya	10 March 2011
Arab League Statement on Libya	Arab League	Libya	12 March 2011
UNSC Resolution 1973	UNSC	Libya	17 March 2011
Meeting Record for Resolution 1973	UNSC	Libya	17 March 2011
UNSC Presidential Statement	UNSC President	Syria	3 August 2011
Draft Resolution on Syria	UNSC	Syria	4 October 2011
Meeting Record UNSC on Draft Resolution	UNSC	Syria	4 October 2011
Draft Resolution on Syria	UNSC	Syria	4 February 2012
Meeting Record UNSC on Draft Resolution	UNSC	Syria	4 February 2012
Resolution 2139	UNSC	Syria	22 February 2014
Meeting Record for Resolution 2139	UNSC	Syria	22 February 2014
Resolution 2165	UNSC	Syria	14 July 2014
Meeting Record for Resolution 2165	UNSC	Syria	14 July 2014
Resolution 2235	UNSC	Syria	7 August 2015
Resolution 2254	UNSC	Syria	18 December 2015

(continued)

TABLE 6.1. (*continued*)

Document	Author / Source	Situation	Date
Resolution 2258	UNSC	Syria	22 December 2015
Interview A1	Interview by author	Syria/ Libya	March/ April 2014
Interview A2	Interview by author	Syria/ Libya	March/ April 2014
Interview A3	Interview by author	Syria/ Libya	March/ April 2014
Interview A4	Interview by author	Syria/ Libya	March/ April 2014
Interview A5	Interview by author	Syria/ Libya	March/ April 2014
Interview A6	Interview by author	Syria/ Libya	March/ April 2014
Interview A10	Interview by author	Syria/ Libya	March/ April 2014

Source: Gholiagha

6.5.2 *Libya*

Following the UN World Summit in 2005, the UNSC took six years to pass a resolution under Chapter VII authorising the use of force with reference to R2P when it passed resolution 1973 in March 2011 (UNSC 2011e).[23] The resolution and the subsequent intervention were seen by scholars supportive of R2P as a significant event (Bellamy and McLoughlin 2018: 94–95). The international community responded to Libya swiftly, partly because, as one interviewee pointed out, the language of Gaddafi was so 'reminiscent of Rwanda' (Interview A2: 200–202), an explanation also to be found in the literature (Paris 2014: 586; Weiss 2014: 13; Bellamy and McLoughlin 2018: 98). Hence, actors feared that a genocide was in the making.

[23] As one interview partner remarked, this somewhat refutes the argument that R2P was to serve as a Trojan horse for Western imperialism (Interview A6: 180–182).

The support of regional actors[24] provided further grounds for a swift UNSC decision (Bellamy and McLoughlin 2018: 104).[25] Several regional organisations supported actions to protect individual human beings in Libya: the Organisation of Islamic Cooperation[26] (OIC) (Organisation of Islamic Cooperation 2011), the AU (African Union Peace and Security Council 2011), and the Arab League (AL) (Arab League 2011). Furthermore, as Alex Bellamy and Stephen McLoughlin state, 'Libya's lack of friends', a 'short window of time', and 'lack of effective alternatives' are additional reasons to explain why Resolution 1973 passed so quickly (Bellamy and McLoughlin 2018: 101–104). The situation in Libya has been described as a 'perfect storm' (Peters 2015: 161, my translation). As Thomas Weiss noted, 'Libya was unusual: the legal, moral, and political/military dimensions all merged to create the perfect conditions for intervention under the Responsibility to Protect' (Weiss 2014: 13).[27] The following offers a detailed analysis of the early phase of the conflict in Libya and the response by the international community.

The Organisation of Islamic Cooperation was the first regional actor to make a statement on Libya. As a communiqué from 8 March 2011 states: 'The participants at the meeting extended their condolences to the families of the *martyrs of the peaceful demonstrations* and their *sympathies to the wounded* and expressed their regrets over the *heavy loss of lives* of the Libyan people' (Organisation of Islamic Cooperation 2011, emphasis added). Here the killed and wounded individual human beings were the focal point of action. The meeting also called for an end to target civilians. Two days later, on 10 March 2011, the AU gathered for the 265th Meeting of the Peace and Security Council (see Aning and Edu-Afful 2016 for a discussion on African agency and R2P). The Peace and Security Council pointed to the necessity of protecting Libyans and 'migrant workers'. Furthermore, the Council 'conveys its condolence to the families of the victims and wishes early recovery to those

24 Bolarinwa Adediran (2017) offers a good discussion of the role of regional actors and a potentially more important role for them when it comes to R2P.

25 Additional explanations and analyses are also provided in the literature (Bellamy 2011b; Welsh 2011; Seibel 2013; Adler-Nissen and Pouliot 2014). These analyses focus on debates within the UNSC, including specific analysis of members voting behaviour, and discussion of the effect of the Libya decision on R2P.

26 Formerly Organisation of the Islamic Conference.

27 It was, however, partly a carefully orchestrated storm. Leaked documents reveal a rather active role by France and the United States in choosing who would then be recognised as the legitimate representatives of the Libyan government (Pecquet 2015). As Ayça Çubukçu, in her critical analysis of the Libyan intervention, demonstrates, this is not without problems, as it can be understood as part of what she calls 'the imperial themes in the Responsibility to Protect framework' (Çubukçu 2013).

who have been injured' (African Union Peace and Security Council 2011: 5, emphasis removed). Note the clear focus on individual human beings as victims, clearly positioning them as innocent. This positioning is reinforced by stating that the armed rebellion began because of the targeting of 'pacifist demonstrations' (African Union Peace and Security Council 2011: 5). Alexander de Waal offers a detailed account a meeting of several African leaders with Gaddafi later that month, with the no-fly zone already in place:

> At that meeting, Gaddafi insisted that his country was a victim of aggression and that Africa should stand on his side. He spoke at length about his unhappiness with the 10 March PSC [Peace and Security Council, SG] communiqué and rejected accusations that his army and security services had killed civilians. Instead, he accused the demonstrators of being drug addicts, criminals and Al-Qaeda-linked terrorists ... the four presidents insisted that the communiqué was fair and that attacks against civilians had to stop (de Waal 2013: 372).

I cite this here because it contains several acts of self-positioning and positioning of others worth highlighting. First, Gaddafi sees his country as a victim, positioning the protesters as criminals and as terrorists, thus as the guilty party in this conflict. He also positions his army and security services as not being guilty of the accusations. Put differently, they are, in his view, innocent. The AU leader rejects these positionings. Due to the material I primarily use in the analysis, there is a bias towards speech acts and utterances where positioning through others occurs, at least when it comes to those in Libya. That should not be read as an indicator that self-positioning does not take place.

Following the AU meeting, the AL met in Cairo. Likewise, they supported the establishment of a no-fly zone and safe areas (Arab League 2011). They directly point to the need to protect 'the Libyan people and foreign nationals residing in Libya' (Arab League 2011), which is explicitly mentioned. With this statement, the individual human beings in Libya are positioned as worthy of protection, regardless of their legal status. Put differently, this is about protecting the population.

Following the meetings of these regional actors, the UNSC, on 17 March 2011, passed Resolution 1973 (UNSC 2011e). In doing so, it took note of regional actor's decisions, referred to Resolution 1970 (UNSC 2011d),[28] and

[28] There is a close link between R2P and the ICC (Kersten 2018; Saba and Akbarzadeh 2021), with some even describing the ICC as part of the 'R2P toolbox' (Weerdesteijn and Holá 2020). Others offer a more critical reading of the relationship, especially in the Libyan case and the clear indication for the politicisation of the ICC in dealing with the situation in Libya (Kersten 2018).

begins by expressing 'grave concern' about the 'heavy civilian casualties', thus placing the well-being of individual human beings in Libya at its centre. This is followed by a reference to the responsibility of the Libyan government to protect its population. The reference to R2P is a good point to linger on for a bit. It is this phrase that those, including myself, arguing that Resolution 1973 and Libya was a case of R2P always point to (Bellamy 2011b: 263; Weiss 2011). Yet others have questioned this reading on various grounds (Kurtz and Rotmann 2016: 18; Shesterinina 2016: 812). Gerrit Kurtz and Philipp Rotmann, for example, argue that 'it was primarily the shadow of the international failure to prevent genocides in Rwanda and Srebrenica that influenced the quick-paced decision making in spring 2011' (Kurtz and Rotmann 2016: 18). Others provided a similarly critical assessment (Kersten 2015; Hehir 2016). In this context, Mark Kersten points out an interesting discursive omission:

> In both Resolutions 1970 and 1973, the UNSC invoked only half of the R2P equation. The resolutions made clear that UNSC member states agreed that Libya had a responsibility to protect its citizens and that, in the absence of doing so, international intervention was appropriate. Missing from the resolutions, however, was any justification of military intervention on the basis of the international community itself bearing a responsibility to protect Libyan citizens. (Kersten 2018: 154)

What should we make of these more critical readings of the Resolution? Relying on a narrative reading of central documents for R2P (the ICISS report, the WSOD, and the Secretary-General's 2009 report) and the meeting record where Resolution 1973 was passed, together with my colleague Bastian Loges, we demonstrated that while the term 'responsibility to protect' may not be mentioned verbatim, the way events and reactions are presented demonstrate that the speaker refers to one or several of the public narratives on R2P. In other words, R2P mattered for the deliberations and ultimately for the decision in the UNSC to pass Resolution 1973 (Gholiagha and Loges 2020). But irrespective of how one reads Resolution 1973, the Libyan intervention remains an important case for studying R2P, as both supporters and critics of R2P refer to it (Glanville 2016: 192; Malito 2017; Bellamy and McLoughlin 2018: chapter 4). Now, let us return to the text of the resolution.

Acting under Chapter VII, the Resolution '[d]emands the immediate establishment of a cease-fire and a complete end to violence and all attacks against, and abuses of, civilians' (UNSC 2011e: 2). This statement clearly positions individual human beings as innocent victims of violence who have not done any harm, that is, who are innocent and thus need to be and should be protected. This positioning also comes to the fore in UNSC members' statements. While this is expected by those who supported the resolution, notably those who abstained, they engage in a very similar positioning act. In short, UNSC members shared the positioning of individual human beings in Libya. Brazil's statement is illustrative of this: '*[H]er delegation's vote today should in no way be interpreted* as condoning the behaviour of the Libyan authorities or *as disregard for the need to protect civilians and respect for their rights*' (UN DPI 2011, emphasis added). The German representative made a similar statement (UN DPI 2011; UNSC 2011b).

Shortly after the resolution passed, NATO began an intervention, enforcing the no-fly zone, including airstrikes against military targets of the Libyan army. The intervention shifted the balance in Libya. As Jutta Brunnée and Stephen Toope aptly summarise, 'NATO not only established no-fly zones, but also provided general support to rebel forces, attacked Libyan military assets and ultimately precipitated regime change in the country' (Brunnée and Toope 2014: 15). NATO's involvement also facilitated Gaddafi's death (Paris 2014: 582), thereby playing a part in the subsequent regime change.

The issue of regime change and R2P is a contentious issue (Pattison 2011: 273; Glanville 2014: 162; Bellamy and McLoughlin 2018: chapter 5; Malito 2019). While proponents of R2P argue that at times regime change is the only way to stop mass atrocities (Bellamy and McLoughlin 2018: 121), it is not an official part of R2P as agreed at the 2005 World Summit. The ICISS report is a little bit more open, when it states: 'Overthrow of regimes is not, as such, a legitimate objective, although disabling that regime's capacity to harm its own people may be essential to discharging the mandate of protection – *and what is necessary to achieve that disabling will vary from case to case*' (ICISS 2001: 35, emphasis added). Some scholars have argued that R2P includes an inherent tension 'between the protection of civilians and regime change' (Akbarzadeh and Saba 2019: 537) as keeping the two apart may prove difficult in practice, as 'military intervention, by a third party against a regime . . . alters the balance of power on the ground' (Akbarzadeh and Saba 2019: 541). This, of course, is precisely what happened in Libya. And it is perhaps a little surprising, given that that the political leaders of the United States (Barack Obama), the United Kingdom (David Cameron), and France (Nicolas Sarkozy) declared in an op-ed that appeared in several international newspapers: 'It is not to remove Qaddafi by force. But it is impossible to imagine a future for Libya with Qaddafi in power' (Obama et al. 2011).

Even before Gaddafi was killed, both permanent and non-permanent Council members raised a critique about NATO's implementation of Resolution 1973. The BRICS (Brazil, Russia, India, China, and South

Africa) also voiced their concerns (de Waal 2013: 368, for South Africa's critique; Shesterinina 2016: 812, for arguing that China's abstention had little to do with R2P; Job 2016: 902–903, offers an analysis of the BRICS votes).[29]

One outcome of the operational criticism towards R2P was the proposal of 'Responsibility while Protecting' (RwP) by Brazil and China's suggestion of 'Responsible Protection' (RP) (Dalhaus 2015: 217; Hunt 2016: 882; Job 2016: 903–904; Bellamy and McLoughlin 2018: 151–161; Akbarzadeh and Saba 2019: 550). As Roland Paris notes, 'Brazil sought to establish additional safeguards against the future 'misuse' of the Responsibility to Protect doctrine' (Paris 2014: 589), thereby aiming at further developing the operational phase of military actions under R2P. Such an ongoing assessment and inclusion of all relevant actors during the operational phase of R2P will be an essential step for further developing R2P (Tourinho et al. 2016). Similarly, China coined the term RP (Gegout and Suzuki 2020: 386–388).

Many have argued that the criticism raised following R2P's application and especially NATO's implementation in Libya under UNSC Resolution 1973 made things difficult for the way the UNSC dealt with the situation in Syria (Glanville 2014: 153; Ainley 2015: 40–41; Hunt 2016: 881; Akbarzadeh and Saba 2019: 541–542). The implementation of Resolution 1973 also created the need for 'confidence building' by the P3, i.e., the United Kingdom, the United States, and France, that 'R2P is not all about regime change', as one interviewee remarked (Interview A10: 121–132). As the comparison between the discourse on Libya and Syria I offer further below will show, there is an additional factor, and perhaps a decisive one, that explains the difference between the way the international community dealt with Libya and Syria: the way the individual human being is positioned in the discourse.

The analysis of the UN Security Council deliberations on Libya demonstrates that the positioning of individual human beings in Libya by Security Council members as innocent and worthy of protection facilitated the intersubjective agreement to protect individual human beings from mass atrocities, using the R2P, including the use of force.[30] However, NATO's Operation 'Unified Protector' was also criticised (Conley-Zilkic 2014: 442; Paris 2014:

[29] The role of the BRICS or 'emerging/rising powers' in relation to R2P more generally has been also discussed in the literature (Baranovsky and Mateiko 2016; Cunliffe and Kenkel 2016; Fung 2020; Gegout and Suzuki 2020; Hunt 2016).

[30] Rebecca Adler-Nissen and Vincent Pouliot have a somewhat more strategic-based explanation for the agreement, 'in the struggle to look competent, other Council members could not counter P3 moves and resources. As one diplomat said, countries such as Russia were "skeptical at first, but they also didn't have sufficient information to say that [the P3 narrative] was a lie"' (Adler-Nissen and Pouliot 2014: 901).

585). Gaddafi loyalists, who were perceived as civilians, were killed (Capasso 2014: 393).[31] A report by the International Commission of Inquiry on Libya presented at the Human Rights Council on 8 March 2012 describes these events (Human Rights Council 2012). What does the incident tell us regarding the position of the individual human being in the discourse on Libya? Individual human beings who were not perceived as worthy of protection, because they participated in the conflict on the side of the regime, were not part of the protection under R2P. This is no judgement on the legality or legitimacy of those killings. Instead, such incidents demonstrate that how others position an individual human being in the discourse on protection has, for better or for worse, a real-life effect.

Overall, the literature assesses the intervention in Libya as ambivalent both in terms of its effect on Libya and on the effect on R2P (Bellamy 2014: 166; Brunnée and Toope 2014: 15; Todorov 2014: 52; Weiss 2014: 8; Brockmeier et al. 2016: 114; Zambakari 2016). Following the intervention, different secular and religious groups remained in violent conflict (Capasso 2014: 382, 392, 396). And even over ten years after the intervention, Libya's situation remained dire, with the country torn by civil war and political conflict (Pedde 2017; Bellamy and McLoughlin 2018: 107–115). Only recently, in October 2020, the warring parties agreed to a peace deal (United Nations 2020). In January 2021, there was an agreement on transitional government (Aljazeera 2021), with the new government taking over in March 2021 (Africanews 2021). Whether the intervention is to blame for the developments and whether things would be better or worse without the intervention falls in the realm of counterfactuals. But some suggest that without NATO's intervention, there 'would have been a very lengthy bloody civil war between Gaddafi forces and the rebels, somewhat akin to the situation in Syria' (Pattison 2017: 221).[32] The actions by the international community stopped a possible genocide in Benghazi (Pape 2015: 10), but this does not mean that this is followed automatically by a peaceful transition, regardless of the manifold calls for such a transition (Arab League 2011; African Union Peace and Security Council 2011; Organisation of Islamic Cooperation 2011). Section 6.5.3 analyses the situation in Syria.

[31] Recall the argument by Lauren Wilcox that we need to differentiate between subjects to be protected, subjects to do the protection, and subjects who need to be killed to save others (Wilcox 2015: 174). It is this last category that Matteo Capasso's description falls into.

[32] Counterfactuals are always a challenge but especially in the case of military interventions. As Robin Dunford and Michael Neu note, they are characterised by 'radical uncertainty' (Dunford and Neu 2019: 1088). A new dataset may be able to shed some light on this question in future research (Gromes and Dembinski 2019).

6.5.3 *Syria*

At the time of writing, the conflict in Syria has been ongoing for more than ten years. When violence erupted in early 2011 in the wake of the 'Arab Spring', some expected a development for Syria similar to what had happened in Libya: once it became clear that the Syrian regime was not upholding their R2P, the international community would take over. As we know, this did not happen. A few years into the conflict, 'years of killing and mayhem' (Haddad 2015), observers began to point out that 'Syria is not Libya' (Schoch 2014: 132) or 'Syria is bigger than R2P' (Interview A2: 241). Indeed, an utterly different image became visible when comparing Libya and Syria (Kersavage 2014: 33).[33]

This section casts a closer look at the early phase of the conflict in Syria. Since 2012, the UNSC has passed Resolutions on Syria every year, nearly thirty resolutions in total as of the July 2021. I focus primarily on resolutions, draft resolutions, and presidential statements in 2011 and 2012 and consider the debates surrounding the chemical weapons attack in 2013. I also look into discussions about humanitarian access to Syria in the following years. But I do not study those or other resolutions passed in the subsequent years with the same level of scrutiny. The analysis provided here instead zooms into debates in the UNSC about protecting individual human beings in Syria and debates about R2P and its application or non-application in the early conflict phase. As a result, this section does not aim to analyse Syria's current situation, the years of civil war, nor terrorist activities, especially by the so-called Islamic State (sometimes also referred to as ISIS or Daesh). Neither do I study the multiplicity of conflicts and actors within the territory and across Syria's borders. Others have done so (Gerges 2016; International Crisis Group 2019; Hinnebusch 2020; Hinnebusch and Saouli 2020; Phillips 2020).[34]

After protests began in Syria on 26 January 2011, the government's security forces responded with violence. In reaction to this violence, the Human Rights Council (HRC) adopted a Resolution on 29 April 2011 raising concerns about human rights violations (Human Rights Council 2011). Roughly a month later, on 25 May 2011, the United Kingdom, France, Germany, and Portugal put forward a draft resolution. However, it included language some UNSC members were critical of, and thus there was no vote on it (Security Council Report 2018). The president of the UNSC issued a statement on 3 August 2011. The statement expresses profound regret at the death of many

[33] A detailed analysis of Syria is offered by Alex Bellamy in a forthcoming book entitled: Syria Betrayed: Atrocities, War, and the Failure of International Diplomacy (Bellamy forthcoming).

[34] With thanks to Jan Wilkens for pointing me to these references.

hundreds of people, supports political reforms, and asks to ensure humanitarian access (President of the Security Council 2011). On 4 October 2011, France, Germany, Portugal, and the United Kingdom put forward another draft resolution (France et al. 2011). The draft recalled the 'Syrian Government's primary responsibility to protect its population', and it condemned human rights violations (France et al. 2011). Russia and China exerted the first of many double vetoes on Syria (Security Council Report 2018).

Several Council members strongly criticised the veto (UNSC 2011c). The French representative Mr Araud stated that the veto showed 'disdain for the legitimate aspirations that have been so bravely expressed in Syria for the past five months. It is a rejection of this tremendous movement for freedom and democracy that is the Arab Spring' (UNSC 2011c: 3).[35] But the text of the draft and the statements supporting the resolution went beyond condemning the violence against individual human beings. Portugal's representative Mr Cabral stated that 'violent repression against its population and the ongoing violations of human rights and fundamental freedoms must cease immediately. We regret the *huge loss of life* and strongly condemn the widespread human rights violations' (UNSC 2011c: 6, emphasis added).

In these statements, UNSC members position the individual human being within Syria as a victim of violence and human rights violations as innocent and thus worthy and in need of protection. The draft resolution was supposed to prevent 'further bloodshed', as the Portuguese representative noted (UNSC 2011c: 6). Sir Grant, the representative of the United Kingdom, found even more powerful words in support: '[T]he regime continues to brutally repress its people. It has killed *almost three thousand civilians*. It has used disproportionate force and has *arbitrarily detained many thousands of people*. Its actions may amount to *crimes against humanity*' (UNSC 2011c: 7, emphasis added). Such language, including the references to crimes against humanity, positions government officials representing the regime as participants in a conflict in which they are seen as perpetrators guilty of crimes against innocent civilians as victims of such crimes.

In contrast, the positioning undertaken by Mr Churkin, the Russian representative, could not be more different. For Russia, Syria's situation was about issues of terrorism:

[35] Concerning the use of vetoes, Anne Peters has suggested that while R2P does not produce legal obligations, it 'does provide a procedural obligation to justify non-intervention, especially an obligation of the permanent members of the Security Council to justify their veto in that body' (Peters 2016: 240).

> Recent events convincingly show that *the radical opposition* no longer hides *its extremist bent* and is *relying on terrorist tactics*, hoping for foreign sponsors and acting outside of the law. Armed groups supported by smuggling and other illegal activities are providing supplies, taking over land, and killing and perpetrating atrocities against people who comply with the law-enforcement-authorities (UNSC 2011c: 4, emphasis added).

For them, those protesters participated in the conflict in a manner that legitimised the violence against them. Mr Ja'afari, the Syrian representative, claimed that there was an 'international campaign to intervene in Syria *under the pretext of human rights and the protection of civilians*. Those countries [who are part of this campaign] continue to reject the existence of the armed terrorist groups in Syria, for reasons that are known to all' (UNSC 2011c: 12, emphasis added). These two distinct positionings of individual human beings participating in the conflict, either as suffering civilians who are innocent or as terrorists who are positioned as guilty and need to be fought, remain present in the discourse on Syria to this day.

A second draft resolution, tabled with support by many more states, including regional actors, was tabled on 4 February 2012 (Bahrain et al. 2012).[36] The draft spoke of a 'grave concern at the deterioration of the situation in Syria, and profound concern at the death of thousands of people' (Bahrain et al. 2012). Furthermore, the text condemned 'the continued widespread and gross violations of human rights and fundamental freedoms by the Syrian authorities, such as *the use of force against civilians, arbitrary executions, killing and persecution of protestors*' (Bahrain et al. 2012, emphasis added).

The draft also spoke out against violence from all armed groups and included a call to hold those actors accountable who were responsible for violence and violations of human rights (Bahrain et al. 2012). Nine UNSC members voted in favour, but with four abstentions and two vetoes (Russia and China), the resolution did not pass. Again, UNSC members who had supported the resolution strongly criticised China and Russia. The French representative Mr Araud said, 'this is a sad day for the Council; it is a sad day for the Syrians; and it is a sad day for all the friends of democracy' (UNSC 2012a: 3). Addressing China and Russia, he said, 'I know the arguments that will be made by those who today opposed the Council's action. I have already heard them say that only a few more days would have sufficed for us to reach an

[36] Bahrain, Colombia, Egypt, France, Germany, Jordan, Kuwait, Libya, Morocco, Oman, Portugal, Qatar, Saudi Arabia, Togo, Tunisia, Turkey, United Arab Emirates, the United Kingdom, and the United States all co-sponsored the draft.

agreement. How can one speak of a few more days when *hundreds of Syrians are dying every day*?' (UNSC 2012a: 3–4, emphasis added). On behalf of the United States, Ms Rice called the veto 'disgusting' (UNSC 2012a: 5). In these statements, the individual human being is positioned as a victim of violence and human rights violations, as innocent and in need of protection.

Sir Grant, speaking for the United Kingdom, reiterated the view that the protests in Syria were about the individual and human rights of the Syrian people when he said that '[i]t has been 10 months since the *Syrian people bravely demanded their universal rights*, and 10 months since the Syrian regime responded by violently repressing and killing its own people' (UNSC 2012a: 6, emphasis added). The statement juxtaposes the claim for universal rights of individual human beings in Syria with killing these individual human beings by Syria's government. The UK representative positions these individual human beings as innocent and the Syrian government members as guilty. As before, the Russian statement focused on terrorism, rejecting the positioning undertaken by others as the real issue in Syria. While Mr Churkin supported calls to end violence, he also said:

> The sponsors of the draft resolution did not take into account our proposed amendments to the draft resolution to the effect that *the Syrian opposition must distance itself from extremist groups that are committing acts of violence*, and calling on States and all those with any relevant opportunity to use their influence to stop those groups committing acts of violence (UNSC 2012a: 9, emphasis added).[37]

To summarise, we can see a precise positioning of individual human beings as innocent victims by those in favour of the Resolution and individual human beings positioned as guilty terrorists by those UNSC members who spoke out against the Resolution.

In 2012, the UNSC did pass three other resolutions concerning the situation in Syria. Resolutions 2042 and 2043 (UNSC 2012b, 2012c) recalled the ongoing humanitarian crises. It supported attempts by the former UN Secretary General Kofi Annan, who served as a special envoy, to find a solution for the conflict. Resolution 2042 furthermore authorised an observer mission, the United Nations Supervision Mission in Syria (UNSMIS) (UNSC 2012b), which was later expanded to 300 observers through Resolution 2043 (UNSC

[37] As noted by Shahram Akbarzadeh and Arif Saba (2019) justifications for vetoes were sometimes delivered outside the UNSC. China, for example, justified its vetoes outside of the Council with references to the Libyan experience and regime change.

2012c). The third resolution, 2059, renewed the Mandate of UNSMIS for 'a final period of thirty days' (UNSC 2012d).

A chemical attack with sarin gas on 21 May 2013 in the Ghouta suburbs near Damascus killed between 281 and 1,729 people, with numbers varying in different sources. Each side in the conflict blamed the other for the attack. But the attack also put the possibility of a military intervention back on the table (BBC 2013; Stahn 2014: 25; Aistrope et al. 2018; Price 2019). Shortly after the incident, Syria joined the Convention on Chemical Weapons in September 2013 (OPCW 2015). Following intense negotiations (Security Council Report 2018), Security Council Resolution 2118 demanded that Syria destroy all chemical weapons (UNSC 2013b). And while US President Obama drew a 'red line' regarding chemical weapons, he did not follow through with it in the end (Aistrope et al. 2018: 6). In terms of positioning, there was less debate about the fact that they were innocent victims of an illegal attack. The contention was instead on the question of the perpetrators of the attack. While not being able to settle this, some compromise was possible due to the type of weapon used and the fact that there were innocent victims.

A situation in the town of Homs, an important location of resistance against Assad, serves as an additional illustration for the dichotomy of innocent civilian and guilty terrorists. As a result of negotiations in Geneva, 1,100 civilians were allowed to leave the city (Miliband 2014). When they left, the Syrian authorities took 300 men and boys away for questioning (What's in Blue 2014). This raised concerns with the UN Human Rights Commissioner (BBC 2014). Taking only boys and men can be understood as positioning these boys and men at least as alleged combatants or 'terrorists', in which case they are not seen as needing protection. Here, a feminist perspective that takes note of gender is necessary to understand such a situation.

As Charli Carpenter has observed, '"women and children" (but not adult men) are "innocent" and "vulnerable"' (Carpenter 2005: 296) when it comes to the question of who ought to be protected. Such a distinction is problematic as it excludes child soldiers, female combatants, and non-combatant males (Carpenter 2005: 296). But it points to a more significant issue, one that feminist scholars have shed light on for some time: violence is gendered, which may lead to depicting women only as passive, 'as owned and controlled' (Pettman 1992: 61). What does this mean for R2P? It means that, as scholars such as Harris Rimmer and Hilary Charlesworth have demonstrated, R2P should not be regarded as gender-neutral. Instead, R2P's gender dimension for positioning individuals must be considered (Charlesworth 2010; Harris

Rimmer 2015).[38] In studying situations of R2P, asking 'what about women[?]' and 'what role does gender play[?]' (Zalewski 1995) can shed additional analytical light on them, as in situations where only those perceived as male are seen as combatants or terrorists.

The dichotomy between 'terrorists' and 'civilians' also comes to the fore in an analysis by David Miliband: 'the regime of Bashar al-Assad *talks about terrorism, while killing innocent civilians*' (Miliband 2014, emphasis added). This assessment was corroborated through several interview partners, who emphasised this distinction and highlight its importance for understanding what was happening in Syria (Interview A2: 251, 273; Interview A3: 196–197; Interview A4: 39–40, 42, 44–46; Interview A6: 344). As one interviewee remarked, in Syria, a 'narrative of a war on terror ... superseded R2P' (Interview A2: 251). All these remarks clearly illustrate this dichotomy.

In the following years, UNSC resolutions mainly focused on humanitarian matters, making it harder for Russia and China to veto them (Ralph and Gifkins 2017: 647). In February 2014, the UNSC unanimously passed UN Resolution 2139 (UN DPI 2014; UNSC 2014c). For a long time, the fallout after the Libyan situation affected the Council's ability to come together (Brunnée and Toope 2014: 15; Paris 2014: 587). Notably, Australia, Luxembourg, and Jordan were penholders for Resolution 2139. This allowed them to act as an 'honest broker' and to include, through Jordan, the AL's perspective (Interview A10: 108–195). Despite the resolution passing, Russia did not move away from their perspective when the Russian presentative stated that 'there was strong provision in the text calling on all parties to break with terrorists. It underscored the need for opposition groups to take on responsibilities, *support the fight against terrorism*, and pool efforts with the Government to solve that problem' (UN DPI 2014, emphasis added).

The positioning of individual human beings as terrorists also came to the fore in Ja'Afari's statement on behalf of Syria: 'others ... had objected eight times to having the Council denounce terrorist acts that had taken the lives of innocent civilians .... Terrorists, including those associated with Al-Qaeda, were [the] main reason for Syrians' suffering' (UN DPI 2014). Rejecting this positioning once again, the United Kingdom's representative reiterated their perception about who those individual human beings in Syria were and how they participated in the conflict: 'it had been nearly three years since the

[38] See also the special issue on R2P and Sexual and Gender Based Violence, published in *Global Responsibilty to Protect* (2012). Furthermore Outi Donovan has pointed to the importance of taking into account gender when studying "localised protection" in the context of post-intervention Libya (Donovan 2021).

Syrian people had stood up to demand their rights. Since then, Al-Assad had perpetuated one of the worst humanitarian situations the world had ever seen, including widespread violations of human rights' (UN DPI 2014). Again the appearance of individual human beings through positioning them as innocent victims and guilty terrorists is clearly visible in the discourse. This demonstrates how the attribution of certain positions within a discourse strongly matters for whether and how to act in a specific situation – in this case, ongoing violence within a country.

Things did not improve in Syria or the UNSC in the next months. Apart from calls for humanitarian aid, the Council remained inactive. Another double veto by China and Russia (UNSC 2014a) stopped an attempt to refer the situation in Syrian to the ICC (Albania et al. 2014). As it became clear that humanitarian aid remained difficult and Resolution 2139 had not improved the situation (Secretary General 2014), the Security Council passed Resolution 2165 (UNSC 2014d). In the resolution, humanitarian aid transports were authorised to cross conflict lines without consent. It was sufficient to notify the Syrian authorities (UNSC 2014d). Following the resolution, diplomats took the floor to reiterate how they perceived the individual human being in Syria as innocent individual human beings who needed protection and aid or guilty terrorists that needed to be fought (UNSC 2014b). Later resolutions on Syria have dealt with the growing problem of terrorist attacks by Daesh (Security Council Report 2018). The exception is Resolution 2235, on opening an investigation into chemical weapon attacks in Syria, passed on 7 August 2015. The resolution 'condemns' the killing and injuring of civilians and 'stresses' the need to hold those individual human beings accountable (UNSC 2015a: 1). Again, we see a precise positioning of certain individual human beings as potentially guilty for actions prohibited, leading to the request to hold them accountable.

In December 2015, the UN Security Council passed two other resolutions on the situation in Syria. Resolution 2254 (UNSC 2015b) outlines 'the sequence of events that the international community deems necessary to end the Syrian crisis: UN-mediated political talks, a national ceasefire, and a two-year timeline to achieve a Syrian political transition' (What's in Blue 2016). The UNSC passed the second Resolution on 22 December 2015. Resolution 2258 focused on protecting the civilian population and reiterated the Syrian government's responsibility to protect its population and supported the ongoing diplomatic process (UNSC 2015c). In both resolutions, the dichotomy mentioned above between guilty terrorists, who have to be fought, and innocent civilians in need of protection, comes to the fore. As can be seen here, these opposed positionings have an actual effect on how the UNSC acts.

Between 2016 and 2020, the UNSC passed several more resolutions. Briefings and reports remain ongoing (Security Council Report 2021), as does the attempt for a political solution (Karahamad 2021). I refrain from a detailed analysis here. Generally speaking, the resolutions deal with a wide range of issues, including chemical weapons, humanitarian aid delivery, evacuation of civilians, support for ongoing negotiations, or attempts to find political solutions for the conflict. A detailed analysis of these resolutions would also require discussing the developments and conflicts in Syria since 2016 in some detail. For the sake of not making this chapter any longer than it already is, because the earlier resolutions provide sufficient material for the analysis, and because the patterns observed in the analysis of the earlier resolutions reappear here as well, I refrain from delving deeper into them. What did the analysis reveal?

The analysis revealed that the UNSC members position individual human beings in Syria either as innocent civilians or guilty terrorists, leading to a situation in which a common ground for actions is difficult to find. When the actors in the UNSC agreed on the positioning of individual human beings as civilians, resolutions could pass when they were about humanitarian aid or evacuation. If there was disagreement, resolutions failed to make it to the chamber of the UNSC, or if they were tabled, they were vetoed (Akbarzadeh and Saba 2019: 544–549, offer an analysis of several vetoed Resolutions on Syria). In concluding this chapter, Section 6.5 summarises the individual human being's position in the discourse of protection, comparing the insights from the analyses of Libya and Syria. The section also offers a summary of the chapter and provides answers to the two research questions.

6.6 CONCLUSION

The chapter analysed the discourse on protection to answer two questions: First, how does the individual human being appear in the discourse on protection? Second, how does this matter for global politics? To this end, Section 6.2 presented an overview of the development of R2P in the last twenty years. Section 6.3 typologised and critically assessed the extensive literature on R2P. Section 6.4 offered a reading of R2P that centred on the individual human being. Section 6.5 presented the analysis of the discourse on protection in debates about Libya and Syria.

Both of the analyses of the situations in Libya and Syria provided a clear answer to the chapter's first question of how the individual human being appears in the discourse on protection. It does so in two positions. The first position is that of the innocent individual human being, worthy and in need of protection. The second position is that of the guilty individual human being, a terrorist, who should not receive protection. The analytical framework helps to shed light on those appearances and positionings, conceptualising how different actors perceive the participation of individual human beings and position them in the discourse. The heuristics of innocence and guilt help to bring to the fore an underlying dichotomy in those positions.

The analysis of the discourse on the situation in Libya revealed an intersubjectively shared positioning of those participating in the protests as innocent individual human being and hence worthy of protection.[39] As a result, the UNSC authorised the use of force to protect individual human beings from mass atrocities in Libya. This insight offers an additional explanation of the one provided by existing research to the international community's swift action. And despite the legitimate critique of NATO's implementation of Resolution 1973 and the subsequent regime change in Libya that followed, I hold that Libya was a successful application of R2P, preventing a potential genocide in Benghazi and stopping war crimes and crimes against humanity. It also became clear that a post-conflict plan should be in place when the international community decides to intervene. If not, the intervention will have unintended consequences, as the developments in Libya demonstrate.

The analysis of Syria revealed a very different situation. Here the attempts of the United States, the United Kingdom, France, and others to have the Security Council speak out against human rights violations and the killing of innocent individual human beings in Syria failed (see Erameh 2017: 519–523, for an analysis of R2P and Syria from a human rights perspective). As the chapter demonstrated, there are several explanations for the differences between Libya and Syria, including the effect of the Libyan intervention on possible actions in Syria (Brockmeier et al. 2016: 125). Over time, more fundamental issues emerged: debates about terrorism, different perceptions about conflict parties, and – this is what my analysis offers as an additional explanation – a disagreement about whether the victims of violence in Syria were innocent individual human beings in need of protection or whether they were participating in actions that legitimised violence against them under the laws of war. In reconstructing these different positions in which the individual human being appears in the discourse, the value added of the method of positioning analysis comes to the fore.

What I do not answer in this chapter is the question about the validity of these positions. These positions may be challenged both ethically and

39 There is, however, as Anne Peters is right to point out, no legal right of protecting based on R2P (Peters 2016: 250).

legally.[40] Now, in some instances, there is debate, as we saw in Syria. In other cases, but not the ones I discuss here, authorities such as courts may say something about individual human beings' positions. Independent fact-finding commissions or civil society actors may also confirm or falsify specific claims (Rankin 2018). What I offer here is something different. I reconstruct how the relevant actors perceive individual human beings' participation and position them accordingly. And I demonstrate the consequences of these positioning: what happens if there is agreement and what happens if there is disagreement. This constitutes another value added by the approach presented here.

The chapter's second question is concerned with how this appearance and positioning matters for global politics. The question can be answered in two parts: First, studying the consequences of the different positionings. Second, reflecting on the effect of the discourse on protection for states and the international community. So, what are the consequences of different positionings? If actors share a positioning, they can act to protect, as we saw in Libya. If they do not, very little happens, as we still see in Syria.[41] The question of how the individual human being is positioned and how they participate, for example, innocent victims, civilians, innocent bystanders, fighters, supporters of the regime or the opposition, and so on, remains contested – making the question of who needs to be protected and who does not one of continuous debates. These are social constructions based on the diverging interpretations, assessments, and positioning of who these individual human beings are. And what does this analysis mean for R2P as well as states and the international community? The Libyan case demonstrated that R2P could open a pathway towards protection. Actors still discuss and refer to sovereignty. However, they no longer see it as absolute but rather as conditional. Both states and the international community have a responsibility to protect. They cannot shield themselves behind references to non-interference or sovereignty. And if they do, others challenge them.

R2P opened discursive spaces in which actors can focus on the individual human being, no longer bound to the 'strictly humanitarian vision implicit in traditional debates on humanitarian intervention [that] made it tempting to reduce those who benefited from an international intervention to pure bodies in need, human "matter" waiting to be rescued' (Mégret 2010: 49). R2P

[40] I am thankful to one of the anonymous readers of the manuscript for pointing this out.

[41] Exceptions exist, but these are geared towards organisations where all actors agree that the individuals in questions are terrorists such as in the case of members of Daesh (Chulov 2015; Birkenkötter 2016).

facilitates discussing actions to stop war crimes, crimes against humanity, genocide, and ethnic cleansing and at times even serves as a reference point to act against such crimes (Weiss 2014: 18; Thakur 2015: 23). This may sound little, but looking back at the discussions of the 1990s where the term 'genocide' was not even uttered out of fear for having to act in any way, naming genocide and other core crimes as what they are is undoubtedly a step forward. R2P as a norm exerts influence even in situations such as Syria (Glanville 2016: 194–196), it has normative power as it allows actors to use it as a reference point for debates about protection measures (for a critical view on such a perspective, see Pradetto 2015: 48). It empowers individual human beings and focuses on their protection.[42]

But Syria demonstrates that just because R2P exists, this does not mean the problem of mass atrocity crimes is solved. Constructivist scholars noted some time ago that 'norms are what actors make of them; and we would add that they are as "good" (read: just, fair and legitimate) as what actors make them out to be' (Wiener and Puetter 2009: 4). It is easy to blame R2P for failures, but as Jennifer Welsh reminds us, failures should be prescribed to actors, not to norms like R2P (Welsh 2016b: 3). Christian Tomuschat rightly notes: 'There are no easy solutions in cases like Libya and Syria. R2P does not lead a way out of the legal and ethical dilemmas' (Tomuschat 2014: 27, my translation). But R2P has changed the language we use to talk about mass atrocities (Ainley 2015: 50). Doing so allows us to position individual human beings as worthy of protection independent of their status or location. This result answers how the individual human being's appearance and positioning as worthy of protection matters for global politics. It is a precondition for politics of protection that does not rely solely on the state where the individual human being happens to be present or whose citizenship it has. In the future, it may serve as a foundation for claims against states and the international community if they fail to uphold their R2P.

[42] With thanks to Bastian Loges for suggesting this point.

7

Killing the Individual Human Being via Drones

On 21 February 2010, a drone strike in the Uruzgan Province in Afghanistan killed several civilians and injured more. During the conversation between the various people involved in the drone strikes (screeners, the drone crew, military personal in Afghanistan), the screeners identified one of the individual human beings on the ground as a child. A report on the incident states: 'the Predator sensor responds "bullsh*t, where?" The Predator pilot follows with "at least one child .... Really? assisting the MAM [military-aged-male] uh, that means he's guilty' (USFOR 2010: 13).[1]

'One morning in late September 2011, a group of American drones took off from an airstrip the C.I.A. had built in the remote southern expanse of Saudi Arabia. The drones crossed the border into Yemen, and were soon hovering over a group of trucks clustered in a desert patch of Jawf Province .... A group of men who had just finished breakfast scrambled to get to their trucks. One was Anwar al-Awlaki, the firebrand preacher, born in New Mexico, who had evolved from a peddler of Internet hatred to a senior operative in Al Qaeda's branch in Yemen .... Two of the Predator drones pointed lasers on the trucks to pinpoint the targets, while the larger Reapers took aim. The Reaper pilots, operating their planes from thousands of miles away, readied for the missile shots, and fired' (Mazetti et al. 2013).

On 17 March 2011, a drone strike took place in Datta Kehl, a town in the Pakistani district of North Waziristan. The missiles hit participants of a *jirga* 'the principal social institution for decision-making and dispute resolution in FATA [Federally Administered Tribal Areas]' (International Human Rights

[1] This chapter is a revised version of an article published in *Behemoth* (Gholiagha 2015a). While it has generally been revised and updated, parts of the article are reproduced here with little changes. This is especially the case for the results of the analysis in Sections 7.4 and 7.5.

and Conflict Resolution Clinic [Stanford Law School] and Global Justice Clinic [NYU School of Law] 2012: 57). As a report on the strike states: 'One of the survivors ... told us that many of the dead appeared to have been killed by flying pieces of shattered rocks. Another witness ... recalled that "everything was devastated. There were pieces – body pieces – lying around. There was lots of flesh and blood"' (International Human Rights and Conflict Resolution Clinic [Stanford Law School] and Global Justice Clinic [NYU School of Law] 2012: 59).

These three stories provide the first glimpse into the chapter's empirical focus: how the United States (US) uses drone strikes to kill (alleged) terrorists in Pakistan, Yemen, and Afghanistan and how this often involves civilian casualties. At times, the strikes are part of an ongoing armed conflict, but often they are not. As the three descriptions indicate, drone strikes raise myriad legal, ethical, moral, and political issues concerning the conditions under which killing an individual human being is acceptable. The chapter aims to answer these and related questions, taking drone strikes and targeted killing operations as a departure point to show how the humanisation of global politics also includes a darker, deadlier, destructive side.

7.1 INTRODUCTION[2]

The norms and bodies of law regulating war stem from a period in which it was predominantly a collective enterprise, characterised by inter-state conflicts (Kaldor 1999; Daase 1999: 11–12; Kaldor 2005: 492; Blum 2014: 52). Today, wars are often fought between states, on the one hand, and non-state armed groups and at times individual human beings, on the other hand (Daase 1999; Kaldor 2005: 492–493; Chamayou 2011: 2; Finkelstein 2012a: v; Blum 2014: 52; Blank 2015: 233; Welsh 2015). War is usually not about killing specific individual human beings (Goppel 2013: 214–215). Indeed, we find the prohibition of assassination already in the Liber Code, generally considered one of the earliest regulations of military combat (Liber 1863: Article 148).[3] However, wars are becoming asymmetrical, and the individual human being has become the focus of targeted killing operations, often conducted by unmanned aerial vehicles (UAV) more commonly known as drones

[2] The chapter has profited greatly from comments by Neil Renic.

[3] The issue of killing specific individuals was also a contentious issue when snipers first began to be part of military combat operations (see Renic 2020: chapter 5, for a discussion on sniping).

(Chamayou 2014: 79–80; Barrinha and da Vinha 2015: 25; Welsh 2019b: 15–16; Renic 2020: chapter 1).[4]

Targeted killing forms part of a significant change in how states and non-state actors alike conduct war. The scope of this change is so significant because targeted killing via drones changes how war is fought and changes agents and the space of war. The technology is 'challenging us to rethink the human in war' (Saura 2019: 5), and drone strikes and targeted killing perhaps even change the nature of war (Singer 2009: 194; Sylvester 2013b: 117; Renic 2020: 11, 192). Wars are conducted in a way where 'armed violence seeks to pursue the prey wherever it might be' (Chamayou 2011: 3). This development is primarily the result of the growing fight against terrorism and terrorists.[5] Despite legal issues (discussed in Section 7.2) as well as ethical and moral issues (discussed in Section 7.3) concerning targeted killing scholars agree that drone strikes and targeted killing operations will persist (Guiora 2013: 9; Franke 2014: 121; Aslam and Rauxloh 2015: 225).

In this asymmetrical war, the individual human being is a focal point. Therefore, the practice of targeted killing via drones constitutes a suitable case to study the humanisation of global politics (see also Chapter 5). This chapter analyses the discourse on the targeted killing of individual human beings via drones. The study of targeted killing via drones is no arbitrary choice. The combination of a modus of war focused more on killing specific individuals and using drones for this endeavour are equally essential parts of understanding what has often been referred to as the individualisation of war.[6] Put differently, drones are a material dimension of the changes we can observe. Without them, the 'radically asymmetric warfare' that characterises these changes would not exist, and the individualisation of war would not be possible (Renic 2019, 2020).

4 Drones are not used in every targeted killing operation, and not every drone is used for targeted killing. This chapter, however, focuses on those cases where drones are used for targeted killing operations. This chapter will therefore not discuss the potential use for drones in protective military operations such as UN peacekeeping operations or R2P missions (Sandvik and Lohne 2014; Kennedy and Rogers 2015; Wiesner 2015). For a general discussion of drone proliferation, see Dan Gettinger (2019).

5 The term 'terrorist' deserves a discussion of a length this chapter cannot provide. I therefore refer to the literature available on this topic (Altman 2012: 3–4; Crawford 2014; Ganor 2014; Henriksen 2014; Reinold 2014; Saul 2014).

6 As pointed to in the introduction, several authors refer to the individualisation of war (Blum 2014; Dill 2019; Welsh 2019b). I take up this notion at the end of this chapter; but for the book's purpose, targeted killing via drones, while without doubt part of an individualisation of war, also constitutes a manifestation of the humanisation of global politics.

This chapter focuses mainly on the US government's use of drone strikes under the Obama administration (January 2009–January 2017). The book's third case study addresses the book's research objective by asking two specific research questions: First, how does the individual human being appear in the discourse on targeted killing? Second, how does this matter for global politics?[7]

Before outlining this chapter's structure, definitions of the two key terms, 'targeted killing' and 'drones', respectively, are needed. As scholars have pointed out, several definitions exist for the term targeted killing, from very narrow definitions to broader ones (Carvin 2012: 543; Goppel 2013: 10–12). Scholars have analysed the different uses and meanings of the term (Schweiger 2019b: 277, 290) and have suggested typologies (Senn and Troy 2017: 185–189).[8] Nils Melzer provides a good definition of targeted killing operations. He defines 'targeted killing' as 'the use of lethal force attributable to a subject of international law with the intent, premeditation and deliberation to kill individually selected persons who are not in the physical custody of those targeting them' (Melzer 2007: 39). The term 'drone' generally refers to a wide range of UAV (Franke 2015: 55). In this chapter, the term 'drone' refers to UAV in a military or covert operational context.

To answer these research questions, this chapter is structured as follows. Sections 7.2 and 7.3 offer a discussion of the literature to identify areas of debate and provide a base for the empirical analysis (see Archambault 2018 for a recent literature review). While there are two separate bodies of literature, that is, one on targeted killing and the other on drones (Gray 2013: 77), I discuss them together given the chapter's concern with using drones in targeted killing operations. Section 7.2 focuses on legal issues, while Section 7.3 focuses on ethical and moral issues. The importance of studying norms and the different meanings, interpretations, contestations, and dynamic relations between them becomes apparent in both sections. Questions of individual and human rights are also prominently featured in both discussions

[7] See Chapter 5 on how these specific questions were derived.

[8] I refrain from using the terms 'assassination' or 'extrajudicial executions' for describing the practice of targeted killing. The issue of assassination is at times discussed in the targeted killing literature to distinguish between assassination and targeted killing. Most, if not all, authors agree that assassination is both morally wrong and legally prohibited (Maxwell 2012: 34; Whetham 2013: 71–73; Sanders 2014: 514; Boyle 2015: 120). Christine Gray notes that '"targeted killing" is generally seen as a neutral term which, unlike "assassination", does not necessarily imply illegality' (Gray 2013: 78). Part of the US strategy in employing this term is also to normalise this practice (Banka and Quinn 2018: 699). But as it is the central term used both by actors and scholars alike, I am also using this term.

of IHRL and IHL. Section 7.4 presents the analysis of the discourse on targeted killing via drones. Section 7.5 identifies three themes in the discourse on targeted killing via drones. Finally, Section 7.6 offers a discussion of the results of the analysis. It also provides a conclusive answer to the two specific research questions of this case study. In short, individual human beings appear as targeted de-humanised bodies and targeted killing via drones fundamentally change wars and therefore strongly affect how global politics deals with them. The following discussion demonstrates in detail how this is the case.

7.2 LEGAL ISSUES

This section provides a critical discussion of legal issues concerning targeted killing and drones. I begin with IHRL before engaging with IHL. The discussion will also demonstrate that – despite the harm individual human beings receive – the experience of the individual human being and the suffering of the victims of drone strikes remains marginalised in the legal and technical debates on targeted killing via drones. This chapter closes this gap by analysing the discourse on targeted killing via drones from a perspective of humanisation, relying on the book's theoretical, conceptual, and analytical framework (Chapters 3 and 5).

The literature on drones and targeted killing discusses two legal frameworks: IHRL and IHL (Strüwer 2010: 61; English and Rauschning 2013; Crawford 2015a: 95–125). The underlying rationale for this distinction is that either targeted killing is part of policing actions, in which case actions must be conducted following IHRL, or it is part of regular warfare, governed by IHL (Strüwer 2010: 61). Here one key difference between the two must be noted. IHRL only allows targeting and killing based on an individual's conduct, for example, because they pose an 'immediate threat to life' and 'there is no other means of preventing the threat from materializing' (Emmerson 2013: 17). Contrary to this, IHL allows targeting based on status, that is, being a combatant (a detailed discussion on this is offered in Section 7.2.2).

The section on legal issues will focus mainly on IHL. The rationale for this is twofold. First, the US government uses IHL as the primary frame of reference when discussing their drone strikes policy. As this case study focuses on the actual practice of drone strikes, it is, therefore, fitting to discuss the legal framework that relevant actors primarily refer to within the discourse. Second, it prevails over IHRL due to its status as *lex specialis* (ICJ 1996: 240; Schmitt 2013: 91; Blum 2014: 53).

7.2.1 *International Human Rights Law*

Most scholars relying on IHRL point out that how the US government under Obama conducted strikes violates IHRL and is thus illegal (Crawford 2014: 264–266; Brunstetter and Jimenez-Barcadi 2015: 189). The following paragraphs will scrutinise this assessment of illegality. There is no doubt that IHRL does apply within armed conflicts (Heyns 2013: 9). Furthermore, it applies without limitations if there is no armed conflict (Schmitt 2013: 109–112). Perhaps the most central human right in the context of drone strikes is the right to life, as codified under Article 6 of the International Covenant on Civil and Political Rights (ICCPR) (von Bernstorff 2016: 6; Corsi 2017: 214). It includes the qualification that life cannot be taken arbitrarily (Heller 2013: 113). Following this qualification of the right to life, it could be argued that under IHRL it would be permissible to use targeted killing if it is not arbitrary. A non-arbitrary killing, however, requires a trial by court sentencing the person to death. Without a trial, without the chance of appeal, without the possibility to plea for mercy, and without the possibility to transform the punishment into a life sentence in prison, such targeted killing violates IHRL (Jahn-Koch and Koch 2014: 301).

Within IHRL, every killing must be justified based on the individual's conduct and the actual threat the person is posing (Heller 2013: 114; Blank 2015: 233). This justification requires, of course, that the identity of the person killed must be known. However, as the empirical analysis of drone strikes in Section 7.3 will demonstrate, the identity of those killed is often unknown. Such killings are then in violation of IHRL, especially when taking place in times of peace (English and Rauschning 2013: 555). In the discourse on targeted killing via drones, Pakistan, where a majority of US drone strikes takes place, switches between condemning the strikes by referring to IHL, IHRL, and *ius ad bellum* (Pakistan Ministry of Foreign Affairs 2015; Interview A9: 29–39, 47–51, 67–78, 99–105). The US government argues that IHL is the correct legal framework, as it is involved in a non-international armed conflict with Al-Qaeda and associate forces (Koh 2010; Brennan 2012; Heller 2013: 109; Obama 2013; Corsi 2017: 213).

Allen Buchanan and Robert Keohane have argued that IHL should be the only body of law applied to targeted killing via drones, as '[t]errorist attacks are more like acts of war than like ordinary crime' (Buchanan and Keohane 2015a: 15). They also claim that there is an advantage of applying IHL, as '[t]here is a law governing it, and there is an impressive consensus that this body of law is authoritative' (Buchanan and Keohane 2015a: 16). Others have criticised this position (Crawford 2015b; Brookman-Byrne 2017: 37). It remains subject to contestation whether targeted killing is governed by IHRL, IHL, or both (Crawford 2014: 270). Gabriella Blum has suggested collapsing IHL and IHRL into a single body of law. The advantage would be that combatants would be seen as individuals; the disadvantage would be that certain collective aspects of warfare would be undermined, that is, organisation and discipline of military units (Blum 2014: 62). Others, such as Jessica Corsi, have argued to assess drone strikes exclusively with reference to IHRL (Corsi 2017).[9] I do not take a normative position on this a priori but choose to focus on IHL for the pragmatic and analytical reasons outlined above.

7.2.2 *International Humanitarian Law*

IHL formalises and legitimises violence and killing in war. IHL also aims to make war more humane and protect those who are not involved in an armed conflict (Wagner 2014: 1409; Peters 2016: 194), with some arguing that both the 'beneficiary and the addressee ought to be the individual' (Dill 2019: 3). The most important legal sources of IHL are the Geneva Conventions, which constitute *ius in bello*. For the discussion on drones and targeted killing, the question of who can be lawfully targeted and killed matters the most. IHL provides an answer to this question based on the principle of distinction, which has been referred to as the 'cardinal rule' for the question of targeting (Heller 2013: 92). Under this principle, parties to a conflict must differentiate between civilians and combatants (Additional Protocol 1 of the Geneva Conventions: Article 48). If in doubt, one must assume that the individual human being in question is a civilian (Markham and Schmitt 2013: 303).

The principle of distinction raises the question of how combatants and civilians are defined. 'Combatants' are members of armed forces who directly participate in hostilities. Therefore, they may be attacked at any time during an armed conflict and killing them does not constitute murder (Gross 2006: 329; Meisels 2012: 923; Renic 2020: 38–43).[10] As Neil Renic explains: 'It is the material threat posed by the combatant that forfeits their right to life and the reciprocal risk *between* combatants that ensures an equal right to kill' (Renic 2019: 411). There are other justifications for killing in war, such as

[9] Human rights may also matter for questions of human rights obligations due to them being used to 'exercise control over territory or persons' (Rosén 2014: 6). A detailed discussion of such questions or questions of extraterritorial human rights obligations is, however, outside the scope of this chapter.

[10] There are exceptions to this such as medical personnel.

contractual ones, where both sides agree on accepting to be targeted in war (Renic 2019: 417).[11]

Concerning the notion of 'civilian', the Geneva Conventions define anyone who is not a combatant as a civilian (Additional Protocol 1 of the Geneva Conventions: Article 50). IHL thus 'produces' the notion of civilians and combatants (Garbett 2015: 148). This production is essentially a result of the principle of distinction, as Helen Kinsella has demonstrated in her genealogy of that principle. She shows how the principle requires us to constantly ask who a civilian and who a combatant is (Kinsella 2011: 198). However, the distinction between combatants and civilians is not a normative one: 'Combatants do not "deserve" to die any more than non-combatants' (Sparrow 2012: 128). Instead, as Helen Kinsella notes, 'the combatant and the civilian are neither natural nor inevitable identities' (Kinsella 2011: 196).

Civilians are defined negatively, meaning that those who are not combatants are considered civilians (Additional Protocol 1 of the Geneva Conventions: Article 50; Kinsella 2011 offers a fascinating genealogy of the concept and the distinction between civilians and combatants). They are generally protected during wartime and, following the principle of distinction, cannot be attacked. However, who is to be protected has been subject to change (Garbett 2015: 68). Additionally, and similar to what can be observed in the other discourses studied in this book, gender matters for understanding the discourse at hand. As Helen Kinsella has demonstrated in this regard, the distinction between civilian and combatant depends on discourses of gender, race, and civilisation (Kinsella 2011: 7, 111–112, 139–140). She also demonstrates, with reference to the work of Judith Gardam (Gardam 1997), that it is also not as neutral as the term 'humanitarian' indicates because combatants are often assumed to be male (Kinsella 2011: 9–10, 2016: 172).[12] Moreover, 'while technically all individuals are guaranteed equal protection under international humanitarian law, termed the principle of non-discrimination, women are granted special protections owing to their special needs which are held to be a consequence of their biological sex' (Kinsella 2016: 175). In short, IHL 'is gendered and sexed' (Kinsella 2016: 174). The importance of the sexed and

[11] Relatedly, Janina Dill has discussed whether IHL should include a 'duty of care' in attacking (Dill 2019).

[12] Helen Kinsella refers to the 1999 reprinted version of the 1997 article. There, Judith Garma notes: 'There is, however, a gender dimension to this structure that is distinctive to the law of armed conflict. I have explored this distinction between combatants and non- combatants in earlier work and its assumption as to the value of lives based on gender that permeates the structure of the law of armed conflict' (Gardam 1997: 63).

gendered IHL will also become apparent in the empirical analysis of drone strikes.

There are, however, two limitations on the prohibition against killing civilians in war. First, it is accepted that civilian casualties may occur in war times due to military necessity (Hlavkova 2014: 272) and the limits of intelligence and technology. Second, civilians who directly participate in hostilities can be attacked during the time of their participation (Additional Protocol 1 of the Geneva Conventions: Article 51[3]).

However, the meaning of participation, or specifically 'direct participation', is heavily contested (Melzer 2007: 419–450; Goppel 2013: 111). The term and its meaning have been subject to lengthy debates, and there are different understandings of the meaning of the term (Schmitt 2013: 103). However, the contestation of what is essentially a permissive norm legitimising the killing of civilians if they directly participate in combat is especially relevant in the context of drone strikes. Two issues arise. The first issue concerns the term 'participation' and is concerned with what must take place to qualify for participation. In the case of those being targeted by drones, we often encounter cases in which they may switch between participating as a combatant and not participating. In the latter case, they are protected under their civilian status. This changing type of participation has been described as the 'revolving door effect' (Sanders 2014: 523). The second issue concerns the temporal dimension, which is included through the reference to time in the norm. Again, this is especially the case for individual human beings who are not in a constant combat function, as it is often the case with those targeted in drone strikes (Melzer 2007: 441–447). In these cases, it is necessary for the 'individual to be "caught in the act"' (Schmitt 2013: 104). Again, this demonstrates how difficult and challenging the application of the relevant law can be.

To circumvent the issue of terrorist fighters who constantly switch between the categories of civilian and combatant, the US government has suggested that there exists another category, that of the 'enemy combatant' or 'unlawful combatant'. The debate on these terms is evidence for the 'contestedness ... of the distinction between combatants and civilians' (Venzke 2009: 156). In the view of the US government, the 'enemy combatant' is neither a combatant nor a civilian and thus would not be protected under the Geneva Conventions (Sands 2006: 392; Strüwer 2010: 54; Sanders 2014: 523). The US government basically wanted to ensure that they could be targeted and killed under IHL due to their status, but could not receive any protection granted under the same body of law. The category of 'enemy combatant' was developed under the Bush administration, following the attacks of the 9/11 (Strüwer 2010: 54). However, such a third category does not exist in IHL (Strüwer 2010: 94–102;

Goppel 2013: 122). Under the Obama administration, the term 'belligerents' was used instead of 'enemy combatants' (Goppel 2013: 82–83), but legally this does not change anything. Instead, the Obama administration tried to introduce and normalise a term in the discourse that sounded like a legal term but had no defined legal meaning, thereby trying to legalise and normalise the practice of targeted killing via drones (Pratt 2019). In this context, Anna Goppel points to the critical fact that such a third category 'would provide states with a broad justification of targeted killings of terrorists' (Goppel 2013: 209). A third category would dissolve the combatant/civilian distinction and raise legal and moral issues concerning the rules of targeting within wars.

The principle of proportionality (Article 51[5] Additional Protocol I Geneva Conventions) is the second relevant concept within IHL to assess drone strikes and is only present in IHL and not in IHRL. The principle manifests 'itself in three ways: the proportionality of a military's response to an adversary's military actions, the proportionality of a military action in relation to the anticipated military advantage to be gained and proportionality in reprisals' (Carvin 2015: 131). As will become evident in the analysis below, actors within the discourse on targeted killing via drones often refer to the principle of proportionality, and it is used for the assessment of drone strikes. IHL and its principles work reasonably well within symmetrical warfare. This is not the case within asymmetric warfare situations (Pacho and Bodnar 2012: 195; May 2013: 58–59; Sanders 2014: 521). Grégoire Chamayou even goes so far as to claim that drones change an asymmetrical war into a one-sided war that cannot be governed under IHL anymore (Chamayou 2014: 25, 155). Having defined key terms and concepts within IHL relevant to the discourse on targeted killing via drones, the following paragraphs discuss in which types of armed conflicts IHL applies.[13]

7.2.2.1 IHL in Different Types of Armed Conflicts

International law knows two types of armed conflicts: international armed conflicts (IAC) and non-international armed conflicts (NIAC) (Hlavkova 2014:

[13] Here it must be noted that proportionality and thus killing civilians as part of a military operations is only acceptable in IHL not in IHRL. As Cordula Droege explains: 'Also, the principle of proportionality in humanitarian law is different from proportionality in human rights law. Indeed, human rights law requires that the use of force be proportionate to the aim to protect life. Humanitarian law requires that the incidental loss of civilian life, injury to civilians, damage to civilian objects, or a combination thereof caused by an armed attack must not be excessive in relation to the *concrete and direct military advantage* anticipated' (Droege 2007: 345–346, emphasis in original). I owe this point and the reference to Neil Renic.

252), defined most authoritatively in the judgement of the ICTY Appeals Chamber on the merits in the *Tadic* case (ICTY 1995; Hlavkova 2014: 253; Brookman-Byrne 2017: 7–10). In a nutshell, what matters in assessing the existence of an armed conflict are several factors: geographical scope, temporality, and intensity of fighting (ICTY 1995: section A). The ICTY held that 'the temporal and geographical scope of internal and international armed conflicts extends beyond the exact time and place of hostility'. The court also noted an intensity requirement, understood as 'protracted, large-scale violence' (ICTY 1995: paragraph 70).

These questions of the existence and the type of armed conflicts matter for assessing the drone strikes. For example, as Christian Enemark points out, drone strikes in Pakistan and Yemen cannot be assessed under IHL because the United States is not at war with these countries (Enemark 2014: 373). However, the US government has argued that it is in a non-international armed conflict with Al Qaeda and their 'associated forces' (Obama 2013), claiming to be in 'global armed conflict' or a global NIAC (Brookman-Byrne 2017: 6, 11). If these arguments would be accepted, targeted killing operations could be legal under two conditions. First, the person to be killed must be a member of a group actively fighting, and in the case of a civilian, they must directly participate in hostilities (Heyns 2013: 13; Hlavkova 2014: 277). Second, force must be used proportionally (Goppel 2013: 147; Heyns 2013: 14; Hlavkova 2014: 259).

However, both civilians and combatants remain undefined in the treaty law that applies to NIAC (Sanders 2014: 522), although there are different approaches through which a distinction can be made (Bissonnette 2016: 133–150). Furthermore, IHL does not offer clear guidelines on targeting in these conflicts (Heller 2015: 232). It follows that there exists no general principle protecting civilians under IHL that could be put into meaningful practice (Hlavkova 2014: 256). In this context, claims by the US government to apply targeting rules under IHL in NIAC following a logic of analogy have been refuted by some scholars (Heller 2015: 234). In addition, several armed conflicts cannot be identified as either international or non-international and, therefore, analytically, 'fall in the hinterland' (Ohlin 2013: 30). As this brief discussion on types of conflicts reveals, the unclear legal situation makes a legal assessment of most drone strikes difficult. These difficulties become even more complex when questions of *ius ad bellum* come into play. Sections 7.2.2.2 and 7.2.2.3 provide a discussion on the *ius ad bellum*, focusing on self-defence and the notion of imminent threats, on the one hand, and sovereignty, territorial integrity, and government consent, on the other hand.

7.2.2.2 Self-Defence and Imminent Threats

Self-defence is one of the two exceptions from the prohibition of the use of force enshrined within the UN Charter (United Nations 1945: Article 51). Following the attacks on 9/11, the UN Security Council passed two resolutions condemning the attacks against the United States, recognising the collective and individual right of self-defence (UNSC 2001a, 2001b). Similarly, NATO activated Article 5 of the Washington Treaty, by which an attack against one member state is considered an attack against all member states (NATO 2021). As a result of these developments, it is accepted today that Article 51 UN Charter does include the right of self-defence against armed non-state actors (Ruettershoff 2015: 145). Since then, the US government has consistently argued that the 'war against terror' is an act of self-defence. The events of 9/11 led to a change from 'law-enforcement paradigm' to 'law of war paradigm', which also produced tensions between the two paradigms (Maxwell 2012: 36–38; Ruettershoff 2015: 136–139). These changes and tensions make a legal assessment of targeted killing via drones even more difficult. In addition, scholars have noted that self-defence requires temporal limits and does not last forever (Brooks 2014: 93). Therefore, it is safe to assume that more than twenty years after 9/11, an argument of self-defence against the attack is no longer possible (Goppel 2013: 191). The legitimation found in the 2010 US National Security Strategy is based on the fact that the United States sees itself 'at war with a specific network, al-Qa'ida, and its terrorist affiliates' (US President 2010: 20). This assessment is a cornerstone of the US government's legal arguments during the Obama administration to defend its drone strike policy (Gray 2013: 80).[14]

Self-defence furthermore requires the existence of an 'imminent threat'. Since the destruction of the *Caroline* in 1837, an imminent threat had been understood as a situation where the threat occurs at the moment of engagement, with overwhelming force, and no time to discuss alternative means of defence (Whetham 2013: 77–78). However, today the US government 'appears to construe *lack* of knowledge of a future attack as the justification for using force' (Brooks 2014: 94). Christine Gray points out that the US government 'clearly stretches "imminence" beyond any normal understanding of the word' (Gray 2013: 93). Neil Renic notes that the understanding of imminence by the Obama administration assumed that past conduct was sufficient to assume an imminent threat from such a person without the need for evidence of an

[14] Dennis Schmidt and Luca Trenta (2018: 217) identify four types of self-defence that can be identified in the practice of actors: 'reactive', 'interceptive', 'pre-emptive', and 'preventive'.

actual attack in the immediate future (Renic 2020: 178–180). Others point to a changed meaning of the term over time (Schmidt and Trenta 2018: 243).

Furthermore, the usual definition of 'imminence' 'is at odds with the narrative depiction of the Obama administration's drones programme, which shows a deliberate, non-hurried process to identify potential targets with the president's direct input before the drone strike occurs' (Boyle 2015: 112). While the Obama administration's position on self-defence notably had a strong focus on selected individuals, targeting them wherever they are located (Boyle 2015: 111), scholars have argued that a threat against a state usually requires more than one individual human being (Ohlin 2012: 63). Such arguments are evidence for the difficulty of the US government to formulate a precise legal framework for their drone strikes based on *ius ad bellum* arguments. Therefore, it is questionable whether the reference to an imminent threat can be used to provide a legal framework for drone strikes. However, as the analysis in Section 7.4 will demonstrate, the reference to imminent threats is regularly made within the discourse on targeted killing via drones (Birdsall 2018: 256–257).

There are arguments that targeted killing can be legitimised as an act of self-defence (Gross 2006: 323; Henriksen 2014: 216). Against those arguments, Christine Gray points to an important discrepancy in arguments made by the United States as 'the legal basis for the use of force outside the hot battlefield rests on both the existence of an armed conflict and the right of self-defence' (Gray 2013: 83). In addition, Jody Williams clarifies that attacks in Pakistan based on a self-defence argument cannot be upheld because it was not responsible for 9/11. The same holds for Yemen and Somalia (Williams 2011: 17–18). Others have refuted the notion of ongoing self-defence as well (Heller 2015: 254). However, if self-defence arguments cannot be upheld, drone strikes constitute a potentially illegal attack on a sovereign state's territory. To provide legal grounds for a targeted killing operation in a foreign state would thus require that violations of territorial integrity are somehow legitimate. The straightforward option is that the foreign state's government has given its consent alternative is the so-called unwilling and unable test. The following paragraphs discuss both concepts.

7.2.2.3 Sovereignty, Territorial Integrity, and Government Consent

Government consent is based on the idea of 'intervention by invitation' and is discussed by several scholars in the context of drone strikes (Heyns 2013: 2017; Henriksen 2014: 215; Byrne 2016; Heyns et al. 2016: 797–800). Such consent is necessary to justify the violation of territorial integrity because a 'blanket reference to the existence of an armed conflict is not enough' (Henriksen 2014: 234). Pakistan provides an excellent example to illustrate this issue because public statements and leaked government communication are available on government consent. However, Pakistan's position remains inconsistent, with the prime minister publicly denouncing the drone strikes while secretly applauding them as long as the 'right people' are killed (Shaw and Akther 2012: 1491; Gray 2013: 103; Chowdhury and Duvall 2014: 209; Reinold 2014: 176–177). While there might have been oral consent at the beginning of the 'war on terror' for these strikes (Interview A9: 175–188), given public written statements by the government stating no consent (Pakistan Ministry of Foreign Affairs 2015), these oral agreements are no longer valid. This raises the question of whether consent must be public or if secret consent is sufficient. There is no clear answer to this (Orr 2011: 730; Gray 2013: 103; Henriksen 2014: 236). Thus, government consent could de jure provide a solution for the sovereignty issue, but as the Pakistan case illustrates, it does not produce a de facto solution.

The 'unwilling and unable test' is applied in situations in which an armed group operating within a state attacks another state. As Ashley Deeks explains, 'the question is whether the state in which the group is operating (the "territorial state") will agree to suppress the threat on the victim state's behalf' (Deeks 2012: 487). If the territorial state is either unwilling or unable, the state suffering from the attack can use the necessary force to stop the threat (Deeks 2012: 487–488). The test is regularly referred to in statements on drone strikes (Gray 2013: 98) used by the US government (Obama 2013; Boyle 2015: 110), it 'is widely supported in the literature, and it is also mentioned in two 2013 UN reports' (Henriksen 2014: 229).

However, Deeks points out that the test lacks substance and is so general that it cannot serve as a helpful method (Deeks 2012: 546, 488). Despite these difficulties, the US government applies this test to its targeted killing actions in Pakistan. However, combined with the broad definition of imminence the US government uses (see Section 7.2.2.2), the outcome of the test becomes irrelevant, as the result is identical. Either there is consent, or there is no consent. In the latter case, this can be read as Pakistan being unable or unwilling (Brooks 2014: 98). Hence, the unwilling and unable test does not provide a de facto solution for violating territorial integrity.[15] Having discussed vital issues in the

[15] Jochen von Bernstorff has made the important observation that the United States would probably not make use of this practice in Brussels or the capital of its other NATO allies, indicating the arbitrary nature of the way the US administration operates in this context (von Bernstorff 2016: 4).

ius ad bellum pertaining to targeted killing operations via drones, we now proceed to Section 7.2.2.4, which engages with the related topic of the geographical scope of conflicts. The topic of the geographical scope of a conflict is relevant, as actors within the discourse on targeted killing often refer to the term 'battlefield' and thereby imply the existence of a specific defined physical space in which drone strikes take place.

7.2.2.4 Geographical Scope

War no longer occurs within the confined space of carefully selected battlefields or frontlines (Baggiarini 2015: 137). This is especially true in asymmetric conflicts in which most drone strikes occur (Lubell and Derejko 2013: 73). This raises issues concerning the applicability of IHL. Two options exist to determine the geographical scope of an armed conflict. The state's borders in which the conflict occurs or the areas of actual combat define the geographical scope. Both options have weaknesses. The state-border option does not account for the fact that conflicts usually do not occur on the whole territory. The combat-based option raises questions on determination and measurements, that is, how much combat must occur to turn an area into a battle zone and how this is measured (Lubell and Derejko 2013: 66; Hlavkova 2014: 277). Additionally, IHL is not clear on defining the geographical scope in which it applies (Lubell and Derejko 2013: 68, 86–97; Heller 2013: 111). However, this does not result in an unlimited battlefield (Peron 2011: 84; Lubell and Derejko 2013: 68–87).

Yet, in practice, geographical considerations seem of little relevance (Pacho and Bodnar 2012: 194). In fact, in 2004, then US Secretary of Defence Rumsfeld signed 'a secret order, allowing attacks against Al Qaeda cells all over the world, including countries with which the US is not at war' (Reinold 2014: 175, my translation). Moreover, under President Bush, a 'Worldwide Attack Matrix' was developed (Renic 2020: 164). Such a development is also acknowledged by the Special Rapporteur of the United Nations Secretary-General on Extrajudicial, Summary or Arbitrary Executions, Christof Heyns, when he argues that in the future, more and more states will be able 'to pursue targets far removed from what would traditionally be seen as zones of armed conflict' (Heyns 2013: 4). Relatedly, Alexandria Nylen has suggested that the US government has used the idea of 'frontier territories' for the areas in which they conduct drone strikes with the aim of 'manufacturing … legality' (Nylen 2020: 637, 645).

Therefore, space and geography add to the complex environment in which the US government conducts drone strikes, with existing law raising more questions than providing answers. Section 7.2.3, on legal issues, summarises what international law does and does not tell us.

7.2.3 *Summary of Legal Issues*

As Anna Leander notes, 'writing and commenting on the usage of drones is replete with talk about the extent to which drones challenge and change law' (Leander 2013: 812). How can one conceptualise these challenges and changes? As the discussion above demonstrated, the answer within the legal literature is that it depends on how one evaluates the drone strikes and the nature of the conflicts in which they occur. It also depends on the interpretation of certain principles of IHL and other legal regimes and issues discussed above (Casey-Maslen 2014: 382–383). In addition, difficulties arise regarding whether the US drone strikes are categorised as single incidents or a series of strikes. In the former case, a case-by-case evaluation would be necessary; in the latter case, the evaluation would be on all strikes taken together. This makes it extremely difficult to categorise US drone strikes legally (Brooks 2014: 95; Enemark 2014: 370).[16]

In this context, I also would like to briefly discuss the attempts of the Obama administration to legitimise the practice through normalisation (Pratt 2019) and norm entrepreneurship (Birdsall 2018: 243). These attempts have led to a certain amount of contestation. In her work on debates about targeted killing on the international level, analysing UN debates on targeted killing, Elisabeth Schweiger, focusing on both Israel and the United States, finds that the practice is generally condemned, with more outspoken critique towards Israel in the UNSC. In contrast, the critique of US drone strikes is primarily voiced in the HRC (Schweiger 2019a: 757). Others have pointed to similar challenges to the US drone strike policy through UN institutions such as the

[16] In addition, it must be noted that the United States has not signed Protocol I to the Geneva Convention, but they do accept the general principles (Markham and Schmitt 2013: 301). Here, it must be noted that it might be possible to create a legal framework for drone strikes under IHL, under the following three conditions. First, the killing is conducted in accordance with the principles of distinction and proportionality. Second, the operation takes place on the territory of one of the parties in an International Armed Conflict (Goppel 2013: 109). And third, the individual killed must be a combatant (Goppel 2013: 109) or be a civilian taking directly part in conducting hostilities at the time of the attack. Outside of such an IHL framework, strikes would be governed by IHRL, where it is either assessed entirely illegal (Williams 2011: 14) or at the very least limited to a very few exceptional cases (Wagner 2015: 12–13). Others have argued for a 'holistic' approach, suggesting that for a drone strike to be legal it must fulfil the norms of IHL, IHRL, and *ius ad bellum* (Heyns et al. 2016: 795). Others have provided policy analysis in an attempt to clarify the applicable rules (Davis et al. 2016).

Special Rapporteur on Extrajudicial, Summary or Arbitrary Executions (Schmidt and Trenta 2018: 220–221) or debates at the HRC (Cutler 2017: 55–57). While these critical voices exist, the Obama administration by and large retained its legal position, making only changes to how the policy is implemented but did not stop the actual practice.[17]

International law, therefore, leaves us in limbo when trying to assess the practice of targeted killing. Justifications shift between the law of war and fight against criminals, between *ius in bello* and *ius ad bellum* (Blank 2015: 233). As the detailed discussion of the literature demonstrated, international law does not provide a clear answer to whether targeted killing operations are generally legal or illegal. It is only possible to assess individual strike ex post. While scholars such as Allen Buchanan and Robert Keohane have taken a contrary view to this assessment, when they suggest developing an informal legal 'Drone Accountability Regime' (Buchanan and Keohane 2015a, 2015b), others are more critical of such a proposal (Crawford 2015b; Dill 2015b). This uncertainty and ambiguity within international law create the need to discuss ethical and moral questions. Section 7.3 discusses these questions.

7.3 ETHICAL AND MORAL ISSUES

The lack of answers provided by legal debates necessitate the discussion of ethical and moral issues[18] at stake in the debate on targeted killing and the use of drones (Strawser 2013: 10–17; Cook 2016). Such debates often 'focus on consequences of such strikes' (Waddington 2015: 118). Here two views exist. One view claims that drone strikes and targeted killing operations are problematic because of the civilian casualties they cause. The other view favours targeted killing and drone strikes because they reduce civilian casualties compared to alternatives. As will become clear from the empirical analysis in Section 7.4, both views rely on the interpretation of limited and potentially flawed data about civilian casualties. They are therefore only of limited value in the analysis of drone strikes. The following paragraphs discuss four topics that refer to moral and ethical issues. The four topics are relevant for analysing the discourse on targeted killing via drones, as the empirical analysis in

[17] As in Chapter 6, I do not further investigate these legal or ethical challenges to the positionings. As one of the anonymous readers pointed out, this would be highly interesting. I agree, but as already stated in the previous chapters, this analysis is primarily about the positioning by the relevant actors. In the case of the US drone strikes, this means I focus on the positioning undertaken by the US government, more specifically the Obama administration.

[18] Following Neil Renic, 'ethics are agent-centred' while moral questions concern 'the potential targets … of violence' (Renic 2020: 7–8).

Section 7.4 will demonstrate. These topics are distance, surrender, the notion of 'cleanness' of drone strikes, and the growing absence of humans in direct combat.

Distance. Drones are used to kill from a relatively long distance, which prima facie seems unproblematic for two reasons. First, 'some of the worst atrocities of modern times have been carried out at close quarters by men armed with rifles and machetes' (Sparrow 2012: 119). Second, military development has always attempted to expand the distance between combatant and target, from the crossbow to the cruise missile. However, the way distance plays a role in drone strikes challenges the reasoning that they are just the next step in expanding the distance between combatant and target. First, drones can be redirected at any time. They are not a 'fire and forget' weapon. They can hover over a target, and operators can watch individual human beings for weeks before a strike is conducted. Second, there is 'a distinctive spatial relationship between drone operators and their target' (Williams 2015: 93). Drones create intimacy due to the direct relationship between attacker and attacked (Krasmann 2014: 30; Williams 2015: 106) while being far away at the same time. Thus, they do not fit into the usual categories of weapons and cannot be compared to other weapons or means of killing (Additional Protocol 1 of the Geneva Conventions; Chamayou 2014: 126–127). In this context, Laura Saura has suggested that part of the violence exerted by drone strikes is located before the strike, in the 'very *decision* to reach-towards' (Saura 2019: 10, emphasis in original). Moreover, Neil Renic demonstrates in his analysis of asymmetrical warfare that drones have crossed a 'threshold of military imbalance located at the *structural*, inter-belligerent level of war' (Renic 2020: 159, emphasis in original).

Surrender. Under IHL, combatants have a right to surrender. Within an interaction between two combatants in a theatre of war, the intent to surrender or the act of surrender is most often visible. The combatant wishing to surrender may even be able to communicate their intent. As John Williams rightly points out, targeted killing grants autonomy to individual human beings targeted by specially selecting them. At the same time, the individual human being has no chance to surrender anymore, thereby losing the very autonomy targeted killing operations via drones bestow upon them (Williams 2015: 103). Several scholars have criticised this lack of the option to surrender (Finkelstein 2012b: 172; Jahn-Koch and Koch 2014: 293; Williams 2015: 103). It also contributes to the de-humanisation of those individual human beings targeted (see Section 7.5).

'Cleanness'. Drone strikes and targeted killings are also informed by a 'logic of efficiency' (Dill 2015a: 308), in which morality or ethics have little if any place. They have been described as 'clean kills' (Benjamin 2013: 201), referring to the alleged precision of these strikes. Such a notion is reminiscent of the term 'clean bombs'. But as Carol Cohn rightly notes with reference to nuclear bombs, 'anyone who has seen pictures of Hiroshima burn victims or tried to imagine the pain of hundreds of glass shards blasted into flesh may find it perverse beyond imagination to hear a class of nuclear devices matter-of-factly referred to as "clean bombs"' (Cohn 1987: 691). Likewise, Medea Benjamin writes, 'drone attacks are 'clean' because they are not meant to detain, or disarm, or capture. They are meant to kill ... on the spot' (Benjamin 2013: 201). As part of the apparent 'cleanness' of these strikes, the language used in government documents is also often bare of any reference to violence as becomes evident in a leaked document by the Central Intelligence Agency (CIA) on 'high-value targeting' (CIA 2009; Goetz and Winkler 2014).[19] Violence is simply rationalised or pushed aside, presenting a 'legal-scientific approach to conflict' (Carvin and Williams 2015: 202) instead, thereby avoiding discussion on ethical and moral issues. Bonds has described the specific form of violence as 'humanized violence', which is, amongst other things, characterised by a 'humanitizing discourse between governments and human rights organizations, which is devoid of questions about the morality or wisdom of military violence but instead focuses on a narrow set of issues such as the acknowledgement of deaths or questions about 'proportionality' (Bonds 2019: 440).

Absence of Humans. Prima facie, it may sound attractive that soldiers do not have to go into war when machines can do it, putting fewer human lives at risk.[20] As Bradley Strawser argues, 'it's unclear how trying to better protect one's soldiers, particularly those fighting for a just cause ... can be intrinsically wrong to do' (Strawser 2013: 11). His argument is prima facie convincing. However, as Neil Renic has demonstrated in a detailed analysis of asymmetrical warfare, there is a threshold of risk-reduction where too much risk-reduction on one side 'undermine[s] the *structural* reciprocity of risk' (Renic 2020: 43, emphasis in original) between the belligerent parties, which leads to situations where 'unproblematic killing' becomes 'problematic killing' (Renic 2020: 27). In addition, this shift of risk leads to a further de-

[19] The move towards high-value targeting relates to a revisionist version of just war, which assumes that war is nothing special and thus does not require specific morality. Killing in war is morally not different to killing outside of war and only ought to be based on an individual's conduct not its status (Rodin 2008: 47; Frowe 2014: 123). I owe this insight to Neil Renic, who kindly also alerted me to the respective references.

[20] Cornelius Friesendorf offers an analysis of the relationship between the norms to protect civilians in war and to protect soldiers in war (Friesendorf 2019).

humanisation of warfare (Gholiagha 2015a; Renic 2020: 52–54; Kronfeldner 2021 for an overview of de-humanisation studies).

Two main issues contraindicate a de-humanised war. First, the growing use of robotic warfare and the lower risk for human soldiers as a result of this may lower the threshold of going to war (Sparrow 2012: 127), and it raises the question of whether '"war" is going on at all' (Enemark 2014: 366). Second, scholars have argued for the necessity of 'interpersonal' relationships in wartime and the need to recognise the opponent as a human being (Nagel 1972: 136; Sparrow 2012: 124). Furthermore, the technological characteristics of drones and the operational factor that individual human beings are killed from a remote location by personnel who are not in a theatre of war massively undermines the 'interpersonal' relationship. Some scholars argue that it remains an interpersonal relationship, pointing to 'evidence that drone operators feel a surprising degree of intimacy with their targets' (Boyle 2015: 106), but others disagree (Chamayou 2014: 117–123). A better conceptualisation of the distance issue is presented by Grégoire Chamayou, who demonstrates how drones are distant and close at the same time (Chamayou 2014: 126–127). With ever-better technology, the 'human role will be likely to slowly diminish' (Anderson and Waxman 2013: 2), but already today, drones have de-humanised war (Barrinha and da Vinha 2015: 25).[21]

The empirical analysis in Section 7.4 will demonstrate that drone strikes, especially so-called signature strikes and follow-up strikes, are problematic not only legally but also from an ethical and moral perspective (Waddington 2015: 126–128). Yet, as the discussion of the literature demonstrated, the confinement to legal debates alone will not provide the necessary answers to the questions that drone strikes and targeted killing operations create. However, there is no definite answer in ethical and moral considerations concerning targeted killing via drones either. Therefore, Section 7.4 provides a positioning analysis of the discourse on targeted killing via drones to better understand targeted killing via drones.

7.4 ANALYSIS

This section provides an analysis of the discourse on targeted killing via drones. It relies on the theoretical and conceptual framework developed in Chapter 3 and the analytical framework developed in Chapter 5.[22] As in the

[21] A related discussion has been whether this type of warfare and violence constitute cowardice (Renic 2020: 169).

[22] An earlier version of this analysis has been published elsewhere (Gholiagha 2015a).

previous case study, innocence and guilt guide the analysis as heuristics. The central approach is a positioning analysis of the discourse on targeted killing via drones. To quickly recall, positioning analysis focuses on the different positions that actors assign themselves or assign to others; the analysis then reconstructs those positionings. Following the conceptual and theoretical framework developed in Chapter 3, the analysis also uses the concept of participants and considers norms, language, gender, body, and individual and human rights.

As outlined in the introduction to this chapter, the specific research question guiding the analysis is how the individual human being appears in the discourse on targeted killing? To answer this question, the analysis is structured in five sections. Section 7.4.1 offers an overview of the US practice of targeted killing operations via drones under the Obama administration. Section 7.4.2 provides an assessment of the civilian casualties caused by drone strikes and assesses the debate on the extent of these casualties. Section 7.4.3 identifies the documents on which the analysis focuses. The analysis itself is presented in Section 7.4.4. Section 7.5 structures the results of the analysis in three themes that are contextualised with reference to the literature.

7.4.1 *Overview of Drone Strikes during the Obama Administration*

Targeted killing has become a practice of warfare, with the United States conducting targeted killing operations as part of their 'war on terror' following 9/11.[23] The Obama administration, on which I focus here, has employed what has been called the 'Yemen Model', 'which included the mixture of drone strikes and targeted killing of top al-Qaida leaders' (Cutler 2017: 2). The Obama administration based any legal argument concerning targeted killing and drone strikes on the Authorization of the Use of Military Force (AUMF) from 14 September 2001 (Sanders 2014: 518; Boyle 2015: 108). The AUMF 'introduced broad military logical to the CIA's counterterrorism' (Pratt 2019: 735). At the beginning of the use of drone strikes by the US government, two distinct drone programmes existed, a military one, commanded by the Joint Special Operations Command (JSOC), and a clandestine one by the CIA (Williams 2011: 6; Boyle 2015: 118). The JSOC leads the operations in

[23] The focus on the United States stems from the fact that it is the only country that has admitted openly to conduct large-scale targeted killing operations via drones. Other countries either have made no statement or have made statements clearly stating that they do not engage in such action. One example for the latter category is Germany (English and Rauschning 2013: 539). Drones (both armed and unarmed) are, however, on the rise, with more and more countries developing, planning to develop, or acquiring them (Franke 2015: 52–53; Gettinger 2019).

Afghanistan, Somalia, and Yemen, while the CIA undertakes the operations in Pakistan and some of the Yemen operations (Blank 2015: 232; Woods 2015: 96). However, the military and CIA program have become increasingly intertwined (Williams 2011: 7).[24]

In the following discussion of strikes and civilian casualties, I focus on Yemen and Pakistan.[25] In Yemen, the first drone strike took place in 2002 (Williams 2011: 3; Renic 2019: 420) against 'Abu Ali al-Harethi, a senior al-Qaeda leader and suspect in the bombing of the U.S.S. Cole' (Brunstetter and Jimenez-Barcadi 2015: 181). The following data taken from *The Long War Journal* delivers some insights into the strikes in Yemen. For 2002, it only lists the already mentioned strike. The two next strikes were registered in 2009. For 2010, four strikes are listed. In 2011, the number grew to ten; 2012 sees a peak of forty-two strikes. The number declines again with twenty-six strikes in 2013 and twenty-three strikes in 2014. There were also twenty-three strikes in 2015. Finally, in 2016 there were forty-four strikes (Long War Journal 2021).

For Pakistan, *The Long War Journal* lists the number of strikes between 2004 and 2007 at 11. In 2008 alone, there were 35 strikes. In 2009 there were already 53 strikes, and 2010 had a peak of 117 strikes. Numbers declined after that with 64 strikes in 2011, 46 strikes in 2012, 28 strikes in 2013, and 24 strikes in 2014. Finally, in 2015 11 strikes were conducted, and in 2016, 3 (Long War Journal 2021). While strike numbers are usually somewhat similar across the variety of databases available (see Plaw 2013: 126–153, for a good overview), the number of casualties and the combatant-civilian ratio is usually much more contested and varies. Having provided an overview of the US government's current drone strike and targeted killing practices, Section 7.4.2 discusses civilian casualties of drone strikes.

7.4.2 *Civilian Casualties*

Killing of civilians during warfare cannot always be prevented (see Section 7.2). However, drone strikes have led to a situation where civilian casualties in far greater numbers than before are accepted if one specific individual human being can be killed. The NGO Reprieve reports a case in which the killing of one specific individual, which required several strikes until they were killed, caused the death of 164 other individuals, amongst them 11 children (Reprieve 2014: 2). This acceptance of civilian casualties for the sake of killing a single

[24] Later in his term, President Obama decided to shift most operations to JSOC, a decision his successor President Trump reversed (Renic 2020: 164).

[25] For Somalia, see Max Brookman-Byrne (2017: 31–37) and Brendon Cannon (2020: 773–800).

specific individual human being was even pushed further by the Obama administration, when it was decided that every 'military age male' (MAM) within a strike zone was counted as a combatant, with innocence only to be proven ex post (Casey-Maslen 2014: 399). Such a practice, without any doubt, is a war crime. Of course, here already, the importance of studying language becomes clear. The phrase 'military age male' is intriguing because it is not a legal concept. Furthermore, it has an obvious link to perceived biological sex and debates about sex and gender in IHL (Kinsella 2016).

As Christine Gray notes, this allowed the Obama administration 'to claim that a very low number of civilians have been killed by drone strikes' (Gray 2013: 99). Andrea Birdsall takes similar note of the low numbers of civilian casualties and points to 'the idea that all military-aged men were considered combatants' (Birdsall 2018: 258) but points out that policy guidelines say otherwise (Birdsall 2018: 258). Indeed, at least from May 2013 onwards, the available documents did reject the idea of all military-aged men being combatants (Obama 2013; Office of the Press Secretary 2013; Casey-Maslen 2014: 399).

However, a drone strike against an individual human being almost always takes into account the death of innocent civilians (Williams 2011: 21). Marc Thiessen notes that these innocent civilians' 'only sin is that they are married to, or the children of, a terrorist' (Thiessen 2010). This observation points to the fact that, in debates about innocence, the (perceived) sex of those targeted matters. This is not new but can be traced back to historical conflicts (Kinsella 2011: 94).[26] CIA director Panetta declared that 'the operations have been very effective because they have been very precise in terms of hitting targets with a minimum of collateral damage' (cited in Williams 2011: 10). Likewise, Brennan, at the time adviser to US President Obama on anti-terrorism, claimed in June 2011 that there were no civilian casualties in drone strikes in Pakistan. This, however, is, as leaked US government documents prove, not true (Woods and Serle 2011; Woods 2015: 99–101). NGOs have also documented civilian casualties for Pakistan and Yemen (Amnesty International 2013; Human Rights Watch 2013; Reprieve 2014; Open Society Justice Initiative 2015). Finally, as Thomas Gregory notes, civilian casualties happen because individuals 'happen to be in the wrong place at the wrong time' (Gregory 2017: 219).

Christof Heyns suggests that accountability must be a guiding principle as part of any drone strike requesting that 'civilian casualties must be determined and should be disclosed' (Heyns 2013: 22). Unfortunately, his request, as well

[26] Helen Kinsella also offers more detailed discussion of the discourse on innocence with regard to the distinction between civilian and combatants (Kinsella 2011: e.g., 172–173, 185–186, 196).

meaning as it is, will most likely not be put into practice. Civilian casualties are hardly documented due to the danger such documentation would pose to access sites of strikes. Yet the very few pictures that exist (Ackermann 2011) are evidence of civilian casualties taking place, regardless of statements arguing the contrary. Even if one is to argue that civilian casualties are low, as Brian Williams does (Williams 2013: 89–120), each killed as innocent civilians are individual human beings who have become targets. Whether this was intentional and foreseeable or unintentional and unforeseeable does not matter to them.

Jessica Corsi (2017) describes how several civilians from Yemen and Pakistan, who had lost family members through drone strikes or lived in areas where drone strikes took place, testified before the US Congress in 2013. They spoke about the civilian casualties and the fear the drone operations caused. These statements can be understood as acts of self-positioning in which those who participate (unwillingly) in the discourse on drone strikes position themselves or those they lost as innocent victims (Corsi 2017: 206).

In April 2016, President Obama acknowledged that civilian casualties occurred during drone strikes (Cutler 2017: 59). Furthermore, in July 2016, he signed Executive Order 13732 (US President 2016; see also Birdsall 2018: 259) on the 'United States Policy on Pre- and Post-Strike Measures To Address Civilian Casualties in U.S. Operations Involving the Use of Force', which acknowledges civilian casualties take place and promises more transparency about them, measures to reduce and prevent them, and a commitment to pay condolence payments in case of civilian casualties (US President 2016; see also Bähring 2017; Gregory 2020).

In terms of the numbers of civilian casualties, a complete account is impossible to provide due to the clandestine nature of the operations. However, various sources have data available (Columbia Law School Human Rights Clinic 2012; NBC 2013; Sanders 2014: 516; Waddington 2015: 121; Cutler 2017: 48–49; Renic 2019: 423). For Pakistan, *The Long War Journal* lists 2,789 combatants and 158 civilians killed between January 2006 and June 2016 (Roggio 2016). For Yemen, it lists 830 'enemies' and 118 civilians killed between 2002 and January 2017 (Roggio and Barry 2017).[27] Leonard Cutler

[27] The US government provided total numbers for all drone strikes in 'areas outside of active hostilities', which includes at least Pakistan, Yemen, and Somalia between 20 January 2009 and 31 December 2015. Here they list a total of 473 strikes, between 2,372–2,581 killed combatants and 64–116 non-combatants (Director of National Intelligence 2016: 1).

(2017: 49) provides an overview of numbers based on the Bureau of Investigative Journalism. Between June 2005 and November 2016, he cites 424–966 civilians killed in Pakistan. For Yemen, between November 2002 and November 2016, he cites 65–101 civilians killed. Yet, despite the availability of different databases, accurate drone strike casualties are challenging to put together, and there is no single authoritative source for them. Given the clandestine nature of the strikes, scholars will most likely never have a total death toll available

This brief discussion on civilian casualties and the debate around 'military-aged men' already demonstrates the importance of gender in analysing drone strikes, a point that will become clear further below. Section 7.4.3 identifies the documents for the positioning analysis and contextualises them. Furthermore, the time frame for the analysis is defined.

7.4.3 *Documents for the Analysis and Time Frame of Analysis*

The majority of the documents for the analysis consist of public government documents and speeches aimed at the public. Due to the limited access to information and documents on this topic, this relatively small number of documents is complemented by relying on secondary literature on this topic, including a detailed newspaper article on a specific targeted killing. To gain further insights, I conducted two expert interviews. Finally, I use a declassified document concerning a specific drone strike in Afghanistan. By choosing documents from different sources and aimed at different audiences, a broader picture of the discourse can be painted (Hansen 2006: 82–87). The time frame of analysis spans from 2010 to 2016, covering the largest parts of the two Obama administration terms (January 2009–January 2017), except for using one historical document from 1981.[28] Table 7.1 provides an overview of the documents.

[28] In addition to documents and interviews conducted, the analysis in this chapter also relies on field notes from the Expert Meeting of the Convention on Conventional Weapons on Lethal Autonomous Weapon Systems (LAWS) in May of 2014. I am grateful to Cecylia Lynch, Joel Oesterreich and Joel Davis from ISA Headquarters for the support in organising this participation. I would also like to thank Bantan Nugroho, Head of the Convention on Conventional Weapons Implementation Support Unit at Geneva, Mary Wareham from Human Rights Watch, and Peter Asaro from the International Committee for Robot Arms Control, and the Campaign to Stop Killer Robots.

TABLE 7.1. *Documents for the analysis of the discourse on targeted killing via drones*

Document name	Source	Date
Executive Order 12333	President of the United States	4 December 1981
'Lawfulness of a Lethal Operation directed against a US Citizen Who is a senior Operational Leader of Al-Qaeda or an Associated Force'	US Department of Justice	16 July 2010
The Obama Administration and International Law	Harald Koh	25 March 2010
Memorandum 'Executive Summary for AR 15-6 Investigation, 21 February 2010 CIVCAS incident in Uruzgan Province'	US Forces in Afghanistan (USFOR)	3 April 2010
The Efficacy and Ethics of U.S. Counterterrorism Strategy	John Brennan	30 April 2012
Remarks by the President at the National Defense University	Barack Obama	23 May 2013
How a U.S. Citizen Came to Be in America's Cross Hairs	Mazetti, Mark; Savage, Charlie; Shane, Scott	9 March 2013
Joint Targeting	Joint Chiefs of Staff	31 March 2013
Interview A1	Interview conducted by the author	5 April 2014
Interview A9	Interview conducted by the author	16 May 2015
Executive Order 13732	President of the United States	7 July 2016

Source: Gholiagha

7.4.4 *Positioning Analysis: General Drone Strike Policy and Selected Drone Strikes*

In this section, I conduct a positioning analysis of the general drone strike policy of the United States and an analysis of three specific strike types: direct strikes, signature strikes, and follow-up strikes. This approach allows engagement with all three kinds of strikes and for comparing their respective characteristics. Furthermore, I selected the examples based on available data and literature, ensuring sufficient material for a positioning analysis. A positioning analysis of general documents identified above is presented before engaging with the positioning analysis of the three strike types.

7.4.4.1 Targeted Killing: General Drone Strike Policy

While targeted killing via drones is a relatively new way of killing specific individual human beings, the assassination of foreign political leaders has been debated for much longer. However, this older debate on assassination provides some relevant insight into the general topic of killing individual human beings deemed a 'risk' or a 'threat' to US security. The foundational document on assassination by the US government is the Executive Order 12333 from 4 December 1981 (President of the United States 1981). The document itself prohibits assassinations (for further analyses, see Großklaus 2017: 273–274; Pratt 2019: 732). However, and this is what makes this document so interesting, as Theresa Reinold (2014: 175) has noted, the following qualification was made in a memorandum of law that was not made public at the time:

> Acting consistent with the Charter of the United Nations, a decision by the President to employ clandestine, low visibility or overt military force would not constitute assassination if U.S. military forces were employed against the combatant forces of another nation, a guerrilla force, or *a terrorist or other organization whose actions pose a threat to the security of the United States* (Parks 1989: 8, emphasis added).

The language of this memorandum closely resembles language used within public statements made by US officials during the Obama administration on targeted killing, as will be demonstrated in the following.[29] The first public statement by a high-profile US government representative on targeting and killing individual human beings with drones was given on 25 March 2010 by Koh, at that time legal adviser at the US Department of State. Koh outlined that the principles of distinction and proportionality would always be upheld in these kinds of operations (Koh 2010). He also used a mixed legitimisation for those strikes, referring to an ongoing war and self-defence (Koh 2010). Koh also outlined that 'targeting individual[s]' was something good, stating that it 'serves to narrow the focus when force is employed and to avoid broader harm to civilians and civilian objects' (Koh 2010). Two years later, Brennan, then assistant to the president for Homeland Security and Counterterrorism, gave a speech on targeted killing via drones (Brennan 2012). In his remarks, Brennan outlined publicly that the US government was indeed conducting strikes

[29] Simon Pratt has pointed out that the Obama administration aimed at differentiating between assassinations, which it still saw as illegal under US law, and targeted killing operations, which it aimed at providing with a legal framework (Pratt 2019: 740). In the context of assessing the targeted killing practice, Jeremy Waldron has pointed to in his view the most problematic part of it, which is the use of 'death list' and 'death squads', making the practice 'homicidal' (Waldron 2016: 293).

against specific individual human beings via drones intending to kill them (Brennan 2012). He described the strikes as legal and ethical, in conformity with IHL, and strategically the right choice (Brennan 2012). While Brennan refers to legal aspects, there is a shift in the speech to policy issues, as Christine Gray notes with reference to the following passage (Gray 2013: 96):

> Of course, the law only establishes the outer limits of the authority in which counterterrorism professionals can operate. Even if we determine that it is lawful to pursue the terrorist in question with lethal force, it doesn't necessarily mean we should. There are, after all, literally *thousands of individuals* who are part of al-Qa'ida, the Taliban, or associated forces – thousands. Even if it were possible, going after every single one of *these individuals* with lethal force would neither be wise nor an effective use of our intelligence and counterterrorism resources .... *Rather, we conduct targeted strikes because they are necessary to mitigate an actual ongoing threat – to stop plots, prevent future attacks, and save American lives* (Brennan 2012, emphasis added).

In his speech, Brennan positions individual human beings as legitimate targets, but he refrains from making any determination of guilt or innocence. In fact, following his remarks, he refutes the suggestion that the notions of guilt or innocence have any play in the decision for a drone strike, 'we are not a court, we're not trying to determine guilt or innocence, and then carry out a strike in retaliation' (Brennan 2012). However, this is not the case. As the discussion of civilian casualties demonstrated, the US government operates with what has been termed by Michael Boyle as 'guilt by association', which he holds to be unjustifiable (Boyle 2013: 6–7). He notes, 'the result of the "guilt by association" approach has been a gradual loosening of the standards by which the US selects targets for drone strikes' (Boyle 2013: 7). Others also point to the use of the innocence–guilt dichotomy (Blum 2014: 59) or use it themselves (Interview A9: 119, 205). Likewise, Oliver Kessler and Wouter Werner demonstrate how innocence and guilt are ascribed and, therefore, lethal actions against those deemed guilty are legitimised (Kessler and Werner 2008: 296–297).

US President Obama outlined the US drone strike policy in more detail in a speech on 23 May 2013 (Obama 2013). He begins with positioning US civilians and terrorists as two groups within a new kind of war that began with the attacks on 9/11. At the same time, he positions Muslims as innocent and victims of terrorist attacks. He describes the strikes as effective, proven by intelligence, and as legal, as evident by reference to just war criteria. Finally, Obama positioned those targeted as terrorists, guilty not of past actions but constituting an imminent threat (Obama 2013; see Cutler 2017: 65–75, for an analysis). Obama claims that 'we are choosing the course of action least likely to result in the loss of *innocent life*' (Obama 2013, emphasis added). In sum, his speech positioned those targeted as guilty terrorists while those protected by the strikes as innocent civilians. The apparent precision of the weapons causes fewer civilian casualties, thereby protecting individuals positioned in the discourse as innocent.

Obama weighs the numbers of civilian casualties of drone strikes against the actual and possible number of civilian casualties if the terrorists continue their attacks due to the lack of drone strikes. Thereby, he constructs a justification of the targeted killing of those individual human beings thought to be guilty of posing a threat while positioning those protected from this future threat as innocent individual human beings.[30] Thus, again, references to guilt and innocence are visible, and there is an underlying understanding that the use of drones leads to a distinction between those who need to be protected, that is, the innocent, and those who need to be killed to protect, that is, the guilty (Allinson 2015: 117).

Over time, more documents have been released, either due to the Freedom of Information Act or due to decisions by the US government. (Nylen 2020: 656–659, offers an overview of publicly available documents from 2010 to 2016). One of them was entitled 'Procedures for Approving Direct Action against Terrorist Targets Located Outside the United States and Areas of Active Hostilities' from May 2013 (US President 2013). The Department of Defence also implemented the procedures (see Gregory 2017: 212–236, for an analysis).[31]

The positioning analysis of these general statements and documents demonstrates that individual human beings in the discourse on targeted killing appear as legitimate targets based on assertions of threat and guilt in the discourse (Blum 2014: 73; Shah 2015: 185). The underlying positioning of guilty terrorists and innocent civilians takes place at times with reference to the law, at times with reference to ethics, and at times with reference to strategy (Brunstetter and Jimenez-Barcadi 2015: 186). While the discussion above was situated on a more general level, Section 7.4.4.2 provides a more specific discussion of strike types. The literature and documents available allow identifying three strike types: direct strikes, signatures strikes, and follow-up strikes. For each of the three strike types, I offer a brief discussion and conduct a positioning analysis.

30 It has been noted that the rules outlined in 2013 have been applied inconsistently from the beginning, with exceptions and waivers granted for certain battlefields, for example, in Pakistan and Yemen (Timm 2015).

31 The term 'outside areas of active hostilities' has no legal meaning but is used by the US administration nevertheless (Brookman-Byrne 2017: 4, 38).

7.4.4.2 Direct Strikes

Direct strikes are targeted killing operations directed at individual human beings identified as 'high value' (CIA 2009: 1; Schmitt 2013: 100).[32] Because of their nature, they have also been termed 'named killings' (Gross 2006: 324) or 'personalised strikes' (Williams 2015: 96–97). The selection process of those individual human beings is mainly kept secret. However, it is known that so-called 'kill lists' are maintained and updated with the input of various agencies and government bodies (Martin 2015: 159; Waldron 2016: 293). The process of target definition for such high-value targets is rather complex, as it 'involves weekly secure video teleconferences managed by the Pentagon in which over 100 government officials analyse the biographies of suspected terrorists and subsequently submit a list of targets to the President' (Barrinha and da Vinha 2015: 24). This complex and time-consuming process defies any claims of imminence (see Section 7.2). There would be no time for such a long and complex procedure in case of an imminent threat. The drone strikes themselves are then conducted through a procedure called 'kill chain', which 'consists of target identification, dispatching forces or weapons to the target, the decision and order to attack the target, and finally the destruction of the target' (Wilcox 2015: 139–140). The following provides a positioning analysis of a direct strike that was the result of such a procedure.

The strike used in the following as an example is well documented. This is primarily due to the availability of the so-called drone-memo (see Heller 2014 for a detailed legal analysis), which was released following a Freedom of Information Act request by the *New York Times* (Cutler 2017: 53–55). The memo was written in preparation to kill a specific individual human being, a US citizen named Anwar al-Awlaki (also Anwar al-Aqulaqi), through a CIA operation (Chesney 2010; Mazetti et al. 2013: 1; Cutler 2017: 50–53; Gregory 2017: 212–236). The analysis of the memo demonstrates that the justification to kill al-Awlaki was based on the justice department's assessment of him as a 'legitimate target' (Office of the Assistant Attorney General 2010: 20–21). The Attorney General provided further legitimation in a letter to the then-chairman of the US Senate Committee on Judiciary, Senator Patrick J. Leahy, in May 2013. In the letter, the Attorney General positioned

[32] The number of low-level targets is, as far as this can be assessed, much higher than the number of high-level targets (Barrinha and da Vinha 2015: 23; Gregory 2015b: 204–205; Wilcox 2015: 15; Renic 2019: 423, 2020: 176;). As Neil Renic notes, what constitutes a 'high-value' target and a level of threat that warrants (from the perspective of the United States) an attack has been lowered over time (Renic 2020: 177–180).

Americans as 'innocent' who were the target of potential future actions of al-Awlaki, which may lead to their death (Office of the Attorney General 2013: 2).[33]

The memo concludes that al-Awlaki can be killed legitimately because the killing occurs as part of an ongoing armed conflict, and it constitutes an act of self-defence (Mazetti et al. 2013: 3). Here it becomes evident that the memo combines justifications for lethal force available in different legal regimes. The legal distinction between combatants and civilians in IHL becomes irrelevant in the memo when al-Awlaki is positioned as a target; at that moment, it does not matter anymore whether he is a civilian, a combatant, or a belligerent. He is simply a participant and becomes positioned as a legitimate target. As Claire Garbett notes, 'civilians are an "agentic" category of persons' (Garbett 2015: 158), an argument that can also be made with reference to combatants. Targets, however, are not 'agentic' anymore, as they become the object of action by others, as the following quote from a newspaper report in the *New York Times* on the killing demonstrates. Here the drones and the pilots are agents who actively do something. Targeting and killing are specific acts (Interview A1: 49–51). The target is only 'pinpointed'. Here, individual human beings are only described as 'targets'.

> *Two of the Predator drones pointed lasers on the trucks to pinpoint the targets,* while the larger Reapers took aim. The Reaper pilots, operating their planes from thousands of miles away, readied for the missile shots, and fired (Mazetti et al. 2013: 1, emphasis added).

The quote does not even reveal that individual human beings are killed. 'Targets' could also refer to objects, not human beings. This indicates a dehumanisation of the individual human being that will be revisited in detail further below. By targeting an individual human being, they are 'constructed in the eye of the observer' (Krasmann 2014: 33, my translation). For the assessment of the strike, it is essential to know that the attack was carried out against 'a group of men who had just finished breakfast' (Mazetti et al. 2013: 1). Al-Awlaki had become the target of an attack without being aware of it and thus had no chance to surrender (see Section 7.2). At the time of the attack, al-Awlaki was not actively involved in hostilities. If he is categorised as a combatant (Maxwell 2012: 58–59), he can, of course, be killed nevertheless. If he is identified as a civilian (Finkelstein 2012b: 159), his killing was unlawful,

[33] Because al-Awlaki was a US citizen, certain legal questions had to be discussed (Office of the Assistant Attorney General 2010: 22). A number of domestic lawsuits were brought against the US administration concerning the strike (Crawford 2013: 405; Weill 2016: 49–67).

given the legal framework discussed in Section 7.2. In addition to this problem, the long period of over one year between the memo legitimising the strike and the actual strike, which took place on 30 September 2011, raises the issue of how imminent the threat al-Awlaki posed could be (see Section 7.2).

The direct strike against al-Awlaki demonstrates how the US administration uses contested legal arguments to position individual human beings as guilty terrorists and, in doing so, blurs the distinction between combatants and civilians. This is in accordance with a more general observation on so-called new wars (Kaldor 1999, 2005, 2013), where the distinction between combatants and civilians is blurred, making clear legal assessment difficult if not impossible (Kaldor 2005: 492; Gross 2006: 328). Furthermore, this new method of warfare leads to an asymmetrical relation between attackers and attacked (Renic 2019, 2020). Those who are attacked are positioned as targets without knowledge. The death of other, innocent individual human beings is accepted, often amounting to clear violations of principles of proportionality when applying IHL and murder when targeted killings occur outside the context of armed conflicts, falling under IHRL (see Section 7.2).

7.4.4.3 Signature Strikes

Signature strikes differ from direct strikes as the targeted person is not identified (Martin 2015: 160) but instead chosen based on specific characteristics, known as 'signatures' (Casey-Maslen 2014: 393). The majority of strikes conducted by the United States fall, at least within Pakistan, under this category (Jahn-Koch and Koch 2014: 297; Sanders 2014: 523). Part of the signature strike is to use a so-called pattern-of-life analysis (Peron 2011: 90–91; Casey-Maslen 2014: 393; Williams 2015: 97). Certain patterns of life or signatures then legitimise that someone can be targeted. As Christian Enemark notes, 'in the words of one senior U.S. official (speaking anonymously): "We might not always have their names but . . . these are people whose actions over time have made it obvious that they are a threat"' (Enemark 2014: 373). Put differently, individual human beings are selected as a target because they participate in various activities or practices that are deemed as indicating terrorist activities.

Some have pointed out that signature strikes could lower the risk of misidentification, as they allow targeting via membership of a group like Al Qaeda, who is being targeted (Buchanan and Keohane 2015a: 22). And as Christine Gray points out, such signature strikes as such would be within the realms of the law when taking place in an armed conflict and all necessary conditions under IHL are complied with (Gray 2013: 100). However, if this is not the case, they are difficult to argue for (Gray 2013: 100).

One central point of critique of signature strikes is the reliance on the pattern-of-life analysis (Franz 2017: 112). Jody Williams questions whether 'fallible human beings from thousands of miles away can – by "pattern of life" assessments through surveillance – decide that someone (or someones) are legitimate targets for extrajudicial execution?' (Williams 2011: 12). Furthermore, the de-humanising effect of such strikes is highlighted, pointing out the use of algorithm-based decisions (Krasmann 2014: 39; see also Schwarz 2016: 61, 64). Susanne Krasmann argues that such procedures make the targeted person 'faceless' (Krasmann 2014: 40, my translation). Furthermore, scholars have pointed out that such strikes carry a greater risk of leading to civilian casualties by falsely identifying targets and that it may violate the principle of distinction and proportionality (Boyle 2015: 114–115).[34]

An example of a signature strike gone wrong is the attack on a group of civilians travelling together for safety reasons (Gregory 2015a), known as the Uruzgan incident, named after the Afghan province in which it took place (USFOR 2010). The signature 'large group of people travelling together in cars' was interpreted by the data analyst as signalling a combatant group (Hall 2014: 68). As Derek Gregory rightly observes, 'the crew of the Predator interpreted more or less everything they saw on their screens as indicative of hostile intent' (Gregory 2015a). How the drone crew discussed the possible presence of children provides an example of this kind of interpretation. A disclosed conversation[35] of the drone crew demonstrates that 'the suggestion that there might be children present was then quickly reinterpreted as being evidence of possible adolescents. That in turn morphed into "possibly military age males"' (Martin 2015: 164). This is an apt example of how language is used to position individual human beings as guilty targets by shifting their position in the discourse from innocent civilians to individual human beings who pose a threat, thereby legitimising lethal force. The reference to military-aged males is illustrative of the importance of considering gender and sex in analysing the language used in the discourse about drone strikes.

Another example of a signature strike gone wrong occurred in February of 2002 when three men were killed near the city of Kost in Afghanistan. At the

[34] The practice of signature strikes also raised questions within the United States, for example, in the form of a letter by twenty-six members of the Congress, who sent a letter to Obama raising their concerns with signature strikes (Members of Congress 2012).

[35] Reproduced in parts in an article by Jamie Allinson in *International Political Sociology* (Allinson 2015: 122–123). As Jamie Allinson notes, 'The MAM belongs to a population understood as, by definition, illegitimate, if not dubiously human' (Butler 2004: 91). Jamie Allinson refers to Judith Butler' work on 'precarious life', where Judith Butler discusses the question of who counts as human (Butler 2004: 91). The notion of de-humanisation is discussed in more detail below.

time of the attack, it was believed that they were three Taliban, one of them possibly Osama bin Laden, due to the height of one of the men.[36] It later turned out that these were three civilians (Benjamin 2013: 91–94; Heller 2013: 89–90; Martin 2015: 145). In a press conference, a week after the attack, the following conversation between two government spokespersons and a reporter took place:

> Reporter: You said you don't know who is killed in the attack, whether civilians or Taliban?
>
> Pentagon spokesperson 1: No [inaudible] I am sorry.
>
> Pentagon spokesperson 2: We don't know exactly who it was.
>
> Pentagon spokesperson 1: We don't know the identity of the individuals involved
>
> Reporter: But you are convinced they are Taliban?
>
> Pentagon spokesperson 1: Now we are convinced that, uhm [pauses, looks up, breathes heavily]
>
> Pentagon spokesperson 2: We are convinced it was an appropriate target – based on the observation based on the information that it was an appropriate target. We do not know yet who exactly who it was' (C-SPAN 2002, my transcription).

This extract illustrates that despite the complexity of military decision-making and the number of actors involved in a single strike, there is a certain simplicity to the actual decision of killing individual human beings. This simplicity boils down to positioning those killed as legitimate targets based on a few selected signatures assigned. As Kevin Heller notes, 'many of the signatures on which the United States relies are legally suspect' (Heller 2013: 92), including the signature of 'military-age male in area of known terrorist activity' (Heller 2013: 97).[37] In addition, carrying weapons is customary in

[36] I do not discuss bin Laden's killing here, as he was not killed through a drone strike, but of course his killing is a central event in debates about assassination (Jose 2017a, 2017b).

[37] The legal assessment of the signatures provided by Kevin Heller (2013: 94–103), assuming *arguendo* that those strikes are at least in principle legal, demonstrates that the reliance on signatures can be illegal in some cases, where signatures do not conform to rules of targeting in IHL. In other cases, the killing might have been legal but only if the assigned signatures hold up to be true, which is not always the case as the examples discussed demonstrate. This is also due to the lack of evidence that is often displayed in those strikes. As Kevin Heller argues, in absence of evidence, signature strikes cannot be conducted as 'the attacker must presume that the target is a civilian' (Heller 2013: 103). Others go further, refuting the principal assumption that those strikes could be legal even if IHL principles were to be upheld (which they are often not) (Heyns 2013: 15; Council of Europe 2015: 4, 15). Signature strikes furthermore raise a range of legal issues that cannot and are not resolved within IHL (Heller 2013: 119). In 2015, a signature strike led to the clearly unintended killing of two hostages of Taliban forces. This is a

many of the regions in which drone strikes occur; thus, the presence of weapons is problematic for assessing an actual threat. The military-age male signature is an interesting one from a gender aspect. As Charli Carpenter discusses in the context of protecting civilians, 'women and children' are traditionally framed as 'innocent' and 'vulnerable', while adult men are not. This, however, is problematic, as this does neither include female combatants and child soldiers nor civilian males (Carpenter 2005: 296). Hence, men are constructed as 'killable combatants' and women as 'accidental killings', because the latter are seen as innocent (Wilcox 2015: 160; Beier 2021). Signature strikes are conducted within the same complex commando structure and with a similar number of actors than those involved in other strikes (Gregory 2015a). This, however, must be juxtaposed with the fact that at times the decision to kill is based on information and data that is interpreted wrongly or even flawed to begin with.

As the analysis of signature strikes reveals, guilt or innocence are assigned to individual human beings based on the analysis of at times questionable data and contested signatures. This leads to the positioning of individual human beings in the discourse as guilty terrorists or innocent civilians. Because of this positioning, the individual human being in those signature strikes appears as a target positioned as guilty and as a non-target when positioned as innocent. Once the individual human being appears as a target in the discourse, they become killable (Wilcox 2015: 156). As is the case with direct strikes, the positioning and the consequential appearance in the discourse leads to harm for the individual human being. This empirical result becomes analytically graspable through the notion of humanisation and reference to the concept of participant developed in this book because it can account for the appearance of the individual human being in discourses of international relations (see Chapter 1). Section 7.4.4.4 discusses follow-up strikes as the third distinct strike type identified.

7.4.4.4 Follow-up Strikes

Follow-up strikes are the third specific strike type. They are, for example, conducted against mourners at a funeral or against people coming to a scene of a recent drone strike – therefore the name – to aid the wounded and recover the dead (Casey-Maslen 2014: 395; Baggiarini 2015: 138). Some scholars are less critical of follow-up strikes (Williams 2013: 164–168). Yet Christof Heyns is relatively straightforward again, assessing such strikes as illegal under IHL and

sad illustration for the limits of such strikes and the margin of error, which is inherit in this type of strike (Boone and Kirchgaessner 2015; Richter 2015).

IHRL (Heyns 2013: 15). As the Bureau of Investigative Journalism notes in one of its reports, 'a three month investigation including eye witness reports has found evidence that at least 50 civilians were killed in follow-up strikes when they had gone to help victims. More than 20 civilians have also been attacked in deliberate strikes on funerals and mourners' (Woods and Lamb 2012). The following describes such an attack on a funeral. It was conducted in 2009 aiming to kill Baitullah Mehsud (Williams 2013: 2–10).

The CIA had killed Khwaz Wali Mehsud on 23 June 2009 with a drone strike. To target Baitullah Mehsud, they decided to target Kwhaz Whali Mehsud's funeral. As Stuart Casey-Maslen notes: 'They planned to use his [Kwhaz Whali Mehsud's, SG] body "as bait" to target Baitullah Mehsud, who was expected to attend Kwhaz Wali Mehsud's funeral. Up to 5,000 people attended the funeral, including not only Taliban fighters but many civilians. US drones struck again, killing up to eighty-three people' (Casey-Maslen 2014: 397). Baitullah Mehsud was not killed then but at yet another attack on 5 August 2009, in which several family members and a bodyguard were also killed (Williams 2011: 11; Renic 2020: 1–2). What we can see here in this short description of this follow-up strike is a positioning of one individual human being, Khwaz Wali Mehsud, first as a target, and then, after being killed, as 'bait' to attract yet another individual human being, Baitullah Mehsud, to the funeral to kill him. The dead body of Khwaz Wali Mehsud thus becomes fully de-humanised. He is no longer a target, as he is dead. However, he now becomes something different, a dead body used as bait to kill another individual human being.[38] Even if one were to argue that an already killed person could be used for such a task, the fact that a larger number of innocent bystanders and mourners are also foreseeably killed and injured raises strong ethical, moral, and legal problems (see Sections 7.2 and 7.3). Having provided a position analysis of the discourse on targeted killing via drones, the final part of the analysis identifies three themes in the discourse on targeted killing via drones.

7.5 THREE THEMES IN THE DISCOURSE ON TARGETED KILLING VIA DRONES

The positioning analysis conducted above has reconstructed how individual human beings are positioned in the discourse on targeted killings via drones. On an aggregated level, these positionings can be summarised into three themes: targets, bodies, and de-humanisation, which are derived from the

[38] As Thomas Gregory has demonstrated, dismembering already killed bodies is a specific form of violence (Gregory 2016).

material and the empirical analysis. As the following presentation of the themes demonstrates, the literature on drones and targeted killings identifies these themes, thereby validating the results of the empirical analysis.

7.5.1 *Theme I: Targets*

As Amos Guiora argues, an individual human being identified as a legitimate target '"enters" a category whereby chances of a targeted killing are significant' (Guiora 2013: 54). Amos Guiora describes the result of the appearance of the individual human being in the discourse on targeted killing via drones, which was reconstructed in the positioning analysis. The individual human being 'enters' the category of a target. Their (alleged) participation in a conflict or their potential future participation in an activity considered a threat position them as a target and thus positions them in the cross-hair of the missile. At this moment, the prior status of the targeted individual human being becomes irrelevant. It does not matter whether they had been classified as combatants or civilians. The term 'target' is omnipresent in the discourse on targeted killing via drones, as the analysis above has demonstrated. It is also often referred to more generally in the discourse on the 'war on terror' (Weber 2005: 4). The term 'target' also appears in the description of weapon systems used, for example, 'the MQ-1 Predator . . . is employed . . . against *dynamic execution targets*' (Casey-Maslen 2014: 385–386, emphasis added). It is also the key term in a publication by the Joint Chiefs of Staff on 'Joint Targeting' from 2013, defining the process of targeting and characteristics of 'targets' (Joint Chiefs of Staff 2013).

In addition, Amos Guiora argues that when targets 'are not narrowly defined [this] creates an operational environment whereby anyone killed – regardless of whether intended or unintended – is considered a legitimate target' (Guiora 2013: 6). Thus, the theme of targets raises the issue of potentially unlimited killing. The word 'target' blurs the distinction between innocent civilians and combatants, who can be lawfully killed in a war (Chamayou 2014: 159). Instead, killing occurs based on the idea that an individual human being who has been guilty of an attack in the past will also be guilty of future attacks that have to be prevented or are guilty by posing an (apparent) imminent threat. The terminology of threats is also 'used today to cover over the Schmittian concept of absolute enmity' (Chamayou 2014: 4). Others disagree, claiming that targeting is based on status or conduct 'without any determination of fault or culpability' (Sassóli 2014: 332–333). However, as Michael Gross rightly argues, naming someone as a target, 'assigns guilt . . . . In doing so, named killing places war itself beyond convention' (Gross 2006: 326). Guilt also appears in a de-classified document concerning the Uruzgan incident (see above). Here, in a conversation amongst the drone crew, concerning the possibility of the presence of children, the drone pilot states that the child is 'assisting the MAM, uh, that means he's [*sic*] *guilty*' (USFOR 2010: 13, emphasis added). Gender plays an important role here, too; and as Lauren Wilcox notes, it also 'appears *after* the missile strikes as a kind of Turing test to determine whether the algorithmic and visual processes of target identification were correct, as the presence of bodies of "military-aged men" are taken as indications that combatants have been killed' (Wilcox 2017: 21).

Closely related to the reference to targets is the so-called soda-straw effect, 'meaning that operators tend to "zoom in" to focus on an increasingly narrow area around the target' (Martin 2015: 158).[39] As a result, individual human beings are 'translated into statistical and *targeted* calculations' (Shaw and Akther 2012: 1505, emphasis added). The reference to targets is the first of three themes identified by the positioning analysis conducted above. The second theme, the language of the body, is discussed next.

7.5.2 *Theme II: Bodies*

Bodies are the second theme reconstructed in the positioning analysis of the discourse on targeted killing via drones. Bodies are what drone operators target, often not knowing the specific identity of the individual human being they are about to kill (Sylvester 2013b: 67; Gregory 2015b: 209). While bodies within IR theory are often seen as purely biological (Wilcox 2015: 2), they have been a recurring theme in feminist and constructivist literature (Wendt 1992: 402; Butler 1993; Fierke 2013; Onuf 2013: 82; Wilcox 2015). Bodies have 'increasingly become the target of political control, rationalisation and discipline' (Fierke 2013: 21). Karin Fierke furthermore argues that the meaning attached to the body is an instance 'of world-making in which the same material object/subject is constituted differently within two worlds' (Fierke 2013: 65). While in the world of a drone pilot, the body represents a legitimate target, in the world of those living in areas where drone strikes take place, the body might belong to a family member.

How does this understanding of a body matter for how we can understand targeted killing via drones? As Lauren Wilcox rightly notes, 'bodies that are killed by drones are made killable by drones; that is, they exist as bodies to be

39 This points to the larger topic of visuality and the relevance of seeing and images in the context of war. I do not have the space here to discuss these topics in detail but luckily others have done so (Bousquet 2018; Grayson and Mawdsley 2019).

killed only by virtue of their representation on the screens of the UAV assemblages' (Wilcox 2015: 156). Lauren Wilcox introduces the dichotomy between 'unintended dead' and 'targeted bodies' (Wilcox 2015: 151). This is a similar notion to the guilty terrorist who is targeted and the innocent civilians who are killed as 'collateral damage' as I have reconstructed in the positioning analysis. The theme of the body comes especially to the fore in signature strikes and follow-up strikes.

Signature strikes are not only a specific strike type; they are also specific with regard to the notion of the body. Signature strikes target bodies, as their target selection is not based on the identity of a specific individual human being but the behaviour and appearance of some*body*. In all strike types, bodies are destroyed, but by destroying the body, 'the very individuality of the human being' (Gregory 2015b: 208) is destroyed. The same holds for follow-up strikes, where the bodies of killed individual human beings attract first responders or mourners, who are then killed in a follow-up strike. Reconstructing how the reference to the body is used in the discourse of targeted killing via drones to position individual human beings as the above analysis has done is therefore relevant not only analytically but also normatively, as our individuality is what makes us human and 'the body undone (blown apart, torn to pieces) loses its individuality' (Cavarero 2008: 9). Thus, the focus on the body is important when we study violence in the form of drone strikes or war more generally (Gregory 2015b: 209; Wilcox 2017: 24; Saura 2019; Narozhna 2021). The third theme identified by the analysis of the discourse on targeted killing is that of de-humanisation.

7.5.3 *Theme III: De-humanisation*

The growing distance produced by drones, especially in viewing individual human beings from far above and far away, leads to de-humanisation (Finkelstein 2012b: 174; Wagner 2014: 1410; Sandvik and Lohne 2014: 155; Shah 2015: 209). Drone victims became 'faceless' (Mayer 2009; Carvin 2012: 553) and are, as a result, often not visible in the discourse. As Sikander Shah notes, 'this invisibility is a symptom of the conceptualisation of drone victims as "*inhuman*" and therefore unworthy of coverage' (Shah 2015: 207, emphasis added). This theme of de-humanisation also comes to the fore when US government officials like Brennan state that drone strikes 'eliminate the cancerous tumor' (cited in Gregory 2015b: 204). As Elke Schwarz rightly argues with reference to such metaphors:

> The narrative of military intervention as a 'therapeutic' procedure that remedies the unhealthy aspects of a specific society in turn renders violence as something good and intrinsically moral. Thus, using biologically grounded metaphors, civilian casualties and targeted assassinations can be fully justified by the biopolitical mandate for survival (Schwarz 2016: 67).

Drone victims' identities are often either not revealed or not known. The way decisions to kill an individual human being are made leads to a further de-humanisation of individual human beings (Shah 2015: 196), who appear as targets within the discourse, as the analysis in this chapter revealed. IHL aims at humanising war (Wagner 2014: 1409). However, targeted killing via drones may have the effect that those who participate forget that real human beings are part of these strikes, both as attacker and victim (Williams 2011: 24).

However, this development towards a de-humanised war is not entirely new but has always been part of warfare, especially by 'Western' states (Carvin and Williams 2015: 208). De-humanisation does not only appear in the more abstract discourse but is also visible within specific strikes. This is illustrated by the following description after a (hypothetical) strike: 'As the smoke cleared, the CIA drone operators would have doubtless seen many "squirters" (i.e. survivors fleeing the explosions) as well as numerous dead and dying people lying scattered around the detonation zone (known as "bugsplats" in CIA parlance)' (Williams 2013: 6). Note that the terms 'squirters' and 'bugsplats' are usually not used to describe individual human beings.[40] Others have argued that 'bugsplat' actually is a technical term describing the shape of an exploding bomb (Pincus 2014). As McNeal explains, 'bombs do not explode in a perfect circle but are flattened on one side, similar to the shape of a bug that hits a windshield. A 'bugsplat' refers to the shape of the planning tool used as an overlay to predict a collateral effect radius' (McNeal 2012: 337). Contrary to this technical use, a Pakistani artist has employed the term in a project labelled #NotABugSplat (Shah 2015: 203). As a CNN article explains, 'the project is a reaction to the dehumanizing nature of drone warfare' (Saifi 2014). This project can also be seen as an act of self-positioning. This apparent tension between the two uses of the term reveals the contested nature of the

[40] 'Squirter' stems from the verb to squirt, which refers to 'eject or spirt out water' according to the Oxford English Dictionary. 'Bugsplats' makes an obvious reference to bugs, with splats meaning 'to land with a sharp smacking sound, or with a sound as of slapping and splashing' (Oxford English Dictionary). Both terms thus clearly refer not to actions usually used to describe actions of individual human beings.

discourse on the de-humanisation of drone strikes and targeted killing.[41] However, the practice of targeted killing produces results that at times make it impossible to say whether remains found are human at all. This is evident in the following quote: 'A doctor who has treated drone victims described how "[S]kin is burned so that *you can't tell cattle from human*"' (International Human Rights and Conflict Resolution Clinic [Stanford Law School] and Global Justice Clinic [NYU School of Law] 2012: 94, emphasis added). While there is no doubt that individual human beings are being killed, during the whole process, that is, before the killing, during the killing, and after the killing, the individual human being is de-humanised.

There is, however, a possibility of ex post re-humanisation taking place when a drone target becomes a drone victim. This process requires the 'drone *target* . . . to go through a series of recategorisations in order to become a fully grievable drone *victim*' (Shah 2015: 201, emphasis in original). Becoming a victim is a process of social construction (Shah 2015: 199). Of course, the dichotomy of target and victim is an example of the aforementioned innocence–guilt dichotomy. Targets, as outlined above, are positioned as guilty in the discourse on targeted killing via drones. Victims, however, are positioned as innocent individual human beings who have been harmed (see Chapter 4). The work of international NGOs and domestic civil society actors to bring drone strikes before courts (Craig 2014; Brühl 2015; European Center for Constitutional and Human Rights 2017) is an excellent example of attempts to re-humanise targets of drone strikes as victims. It can be understood as an attempt of representation and self-representation, with 'those who gain representation, especially self-reprezentation [*sic*], have a better chance of being humanised, and those who have no chance to represent themselves, run a greater risk of being treated as less than human, regarded as less than human, or indeed, not regarded at all' (Butler 2004: 141). Attempts to have targets legally acknowledged as victims are, therefore, a specific form of re-humanisation. It can also be understood as a posthumous attempt of self-positioning, conducted by others representing the killed individual human being.

To sum up, drone strikes de-humanise warfare and individual human beings alike. That drone operators develop close feelings about their targets does not stop the de-humanisation effect (Baggiarini 2015: 139) because, in constructing humans, we also produce the inhuman (Butler 1993: 8; Fierke 2013: 85). The positioning of individual human beings as targets in the

[41] I owe the insight that contradictions within a discourse are telling of underlying contestations to Lauren Wilcox.

discourse, the use of signatures, the fact that at times it is only known that some*body* was killed, but the identity of that individual human being remains unknown, are all part of the de-humanisation of warfare through targeted killing via drones. Having provided the positioning analysis of the discourse on targeted killing via drones, Section 7.6 provides a conclusive summary.

7.6 CONCLUSION: THE INDIVIDUAL HUMAN BEING AS A TARGETED DE-HUMANISED BODY

This chapter began with two specific research questions guiding this chapter. First, how does the individual human being appear in the discourse on targeted killing via drones? Second, how does this appearance matter for global politics? The following conclusion will present the results of this chapter conclusively to demonstrate how the research conducted on targeted killing via drones provides valuable insights into the humanisation of global politics, in which this book is ultimately interested.

Targeted killing via drones means the loss of life and the ultimate end for individual human beings in global politics (International Human Rights and Conflict Resolution Clinic [Stanford Law School] and Global Justice Clinic [NYU School of Law] 2012: 108). As Lauren Wilcox notes, 'there are no civilians in precision war, there are only *individuals* who, by a variety of processes, have been targeted for death rained by above' (Wilcox 2015: 160, emphasis added). With reference to Judith Butler's work, drone strikes raise the question of who counts as human and who does not (Butler 2004: 20). As the analysis has demonstrated, targets do not count as individual human beings anymore. Instead, they appear in the discourse on targeted killing via drones as targeted de-humanised bodies (see also Wilcox 2015: 151). Targeted killing of individual human beings via drones also places the individual outside of the law (Crosston 2014: 6). Certain individuals are 'acceptable' targets (Allinson 2015: 120) within this discourse, based on assertions of guilt. The legal protection combatants and civilians enjoy is not granted to these targeted de-humanised bodies; their legal protection is destroyed (Owens 2008: 527). Hannah Arendt has referred to this as 'kill[ing] the juridical person in man [*sic*] ... by putting certain categories of people outside the protection of the law' (Arendt 1969 [1958]: 447). The discourse on targeted killing via drones thus opens a discursive space, in which the individual human being appears as a de-humanised targeted body, making the killing of individual human beings in a de-humanised war possible in the first place. This brings up the second research question of this chapter: How does this matter for global politics?

The practice of targeted killing via drones has deteriorating effects on what Antje Wiener calls, 'the most familiar principles of constitutionalism [which] are the rule of law, democracy, sovereignty and individual rights' (Wiener 2011: 268), as the discussion of legal, as well as ethical and moral issues and the empirical analysis clearly demonstrated. Furthermore, targeted killing via drones changes the way war is conducted. The case study has demonstrated that discussing law and ethics alone does not sufficiently grasp the practice of targeted killing via drones. As the study *Living Under the Drones* demonstrated, 'US drone strike policies cause considerable and under-accounted-for harm to the daily lives of ordinary civilians, beyond death and physical injury' (International Human Rights and Conflict Resolution Clinic [Stanford Law School] and Global Justice Clinic [NYU School of Law] 2012: 7; see also Amnesty International 2013). As a result of all these changes, the practice of targeted killing affects 'the ideas, norms, and rules of the global international order' (Senn and Troy 2017: 176).

The case study has reconstructed the discourse on targeted killing via drones to demonstrate how this affects individual human beings in global politics, thereby taking up calls by feminist scholars, such as Christine Sylvester, for the necessity to study war from a personal perspective (Sylvester 2013a: 619–620). Focusing on the individual human being in the discourse on targeted killing via drones allows for studying the disruptions of everyday civil life the drone strikes have caused (Crawford 2015b: 43; Boyle 2015: 116). More importantly, warfare conducted through targeted killing operations by drones constitutes an increasingly individualised war that is at the same time more and more de-humanised. The argument that the individual human being in the discourse on targeted killing via drones appears as a targeted de-humanised body allows understanding the simultaneous individualisation and de-humanisation of drone warfare. And it demonstrates the dark, destructive, and deadlier side of humanisation.

8

The Individual Human Being as a Theoretical Category

A Conclusion and an Outlook

The Hague, 6 May 2021. The ICC Trial Chamber IX judges sign a document sentencing Dominic Ongwen to imprisonment for twenty-five years for war crimes and crimes against humanity. Once an innocent victim forced to become a child soldier, he is now a guilty perpetrator (ICC 2021d, see also Chapter 4).

New York, 6 May 2021. The High Representative for Disarmament Affairs, Ms Izumi Nakamitsu, briefs the UNSC on new evidence on the use of chlorine gas in Syria in 2018 and the slow and lacking implementation of the destruction of existing stock (High Representative of Disarmament Affairs 2021).

Washington, DC, 1 May 2021.The Biden Administration releases a retracted version of drone strikes rules under the Trump administration. According to news reports, the administration 'began a review of how both Obama- and Trump-era policies had worked – both on paper and in practice – with an eye toward developing its own policy' (Savage 2021).

8.1 SUMMARY AND RESULTS

This book opened with three examples of the humanisation of global politics, each example stemming from the discourse on prosecution, protecting, and killing, respectively. The three examples above stem from the same discourse, but they are much more recent. The examples demonstrate that the humanisation of global politics is an ongoing process. Individual human beings continue to appear in discourses of global politics in various positions. Moreover, they participate in various forms in discourses of global politics. The book provided a theorisation and conceptualisation of this humanisation.

In addition, it has provided an interdisciplinary analysis of the humanisation of global politics, bringing together IL and IR scholarship.[1]

In providing the theorisation and an interdisciplinary analysis of the humanisation of global politics, the book has overcome the double mismatch identified in the book's introduction. The first mismatch manifested in the observations in global politics about the growing humanisation, on the one hand, and a lack of theorising this humanisation in IR theory, on the other hand. The second mismatch manifested itself in comparing the two disciplines concerned with global politics: IR theory and IL. While the latter entails a strong focus on the individual human being in global politics, the former missed (so far) a theorisation of the humanisation of global politics. In this final chapter, I will summarise the book, take note of the advantage of its interdisciplinary approach, and present its central results. I also discuss the contribution and added value provided by this book. Furthermore, I outline the implications of the book's result for IR, IL, and global politics, and I close with an outlook on future research.

8.1.1 *Summary*

Throughout seven chapters, the book has described the humanisation of global politics, identified it as a relevant topic of study for both IR and IL scholars, and suggested a conceptual, theoretical, and analytical framework to study it. Furthermore, the book provided evidence for three connected arguments: first, a conceptual and theoretical framework developed from feminism and constructivist approaches in IR and IL scholarship enables scholars to study the humanisation of global politics; second, the conceptual argument, namely, that the individual human being in global politics should be conceptualised as socially constructed; and third, the empirical argument that the appearance of the individual human being in discourses of global politics results from participation in and acts of positioning the individual human being within these discourses. The book also provided a critical assessment of IR and IL scholarship concerning the humanisation of global politics, discussing numerous approaches and concepts in detail and outlining their conceptual, analytical, and theoretical weaknesses and strengths in studying the humanisation of global politics.

Three in-depth cases studies, guided by a novel analytical framework, provided a detailed analysis of the humanisation of global politics and the

1 The chapter has profited immensely from comments and feedback by Mitja Sienknecht.

appearance of the individual human being in three discourses of global politics: prosecution, protecting, and killing. Each case studied answered two specific research questions: First, how does the individual human being appear in the respective discourse? Second, how does this matter for global politics? The case study on prosecution demonstrated that the individual human being appeared in the discourse as an innocent victim or a guilty perpetrator. The analysis revealed how this opens a discursive space in international politics in which politics of prosecution become possible. The third purpose was to demonstrate how innocence and guilt as two concepts within the discourse on prosecution were applied as heuristics in the subsequent two case studies. The book then moved from empirics to methodology, embedding the two heuristics into a larger analytical framework to analyse the two subsequent case studies on protection and killing. That framework also made positioning analysis fruitful for the study of discourses of global politics. Although positioning analysis is not a type of discourse analysis in the narrower sense, this approach allowed for uncovering interactions and intersubjective or juxtaposed positionings of the individual human being within the discourses studied.

The two subsequent case studies constituted a return to empirics. They provided insights into the discourse on protection in the context of R2P and the discourse on killing in targeted killing operations via drones. In the case of R2P, the case study demonstrated that the individual human being's protection hinges on the position as an innocent civilian worthy of protection. When states agree on such positioning, as initially was the case in Libya, protection is possible. When they disagree, as was and still is the case in Syria, protection becomes much harder to provide. The case study on drone strikes revealed three themes within the discourse: targets, bodies, and de-humanisation. Taken together, they constituted the foundation for the appearance of the individual human being in the discourse on targeted killing via drones as a de-humanised targeted body. As a result, a discursive space opened in which individual human beings are positioned as guilty and hence as 'legitimate' targets or innocent and hence as non-targets. The oscillation between theory and empirics through an abductive research logic and analytical framework that embedded results from the empirical analysis of one case into other cases allowed me to fully take advantage of the book's interdisciplinary approach, which I summarise below.

8.1.2 *The Advantage of Interdisciplinarity*

From the outset, the book was an interdisciplinary endeavour to scrutinise the humanisation of global politics that mainly had been assessed from a perspective of international law. However, contrary to such an exclusive legal perspective, the book took up an interdisciplinary perspective by arguing that the humanisation of global politics, while often taking place with reference to international law, should not be analysed from a legal perspective alone. To this end, the book employed insights from international law and discussed IL literature in detail and combined it with insights from the IR literature. In doing so, the book used 'a range of lenses to understand interacting and overlapping dimensions of reality' (Lang Jr. et al. 2013: 3–4). Of course, such an interdisciplinary approach comes not without challenges but can be an advancement for both disciplines when conducted with care. Therefore, I want to summarise what insights this book has produced for interdisciplinary approaches that draw on IR and IL.

On a theoretical level, I demonstrated how the humanisation of global politics was neither fully graspable through a focus on either IR theory or IL alone. Instead, as evident from the theoretical and conceptual frameworks the book developed, combining insights from both disciplines provides a broader and better understanding of global politics as a field of study. This insight also became visible in the three subsequent case studies. The first case study on ICL and the work of the ICC were situated within international law. Nevertheless, as the case study demonstrated, an interdisciplinary approach that considered the humanisation of global politics provided insights into the social construction of the individual human being, either as a victim or a perpetrator, in the discourse on prosecution. In the case study on protection and R2P, an interdisciplinary perspective allowed for transcending debates about the legal characterisation of the R2P. At the same time, the case study provided important insights for IR theory on some of the legal qualities R2P entails, such as the connection with ICL or questions of authority over the use of force. Finally, in the third case study on targeted killing via drones, a strong legal discourse was scrutinised from a perspective of IR theory, demonstrating how gaps left in the legal debate could be filled with insights from IR theory.

To sum up, an interdisciplinary approach that wants to work with IL and IR must consider the respective insights of both disciplines. At the same time, scholars should not shy away from advancing the one with insights from the other and, more importantly, transcend disciplinary boundaries and categories when the objective of the research or the field of study requires doing so. In Section 8.1.3, I present the book's central results.

8.1.3 *Positions, Participation, and the Socially Constructed Individual Human Being*

The central result of the book is the insight that the social construction of the individual human being in global politics takes place through the positioning of the individual human being in discourses of global politics and the participation of individual human beings in global politics. This result allows us to answer the two guiding research questions of this book. First, how should we conceptualise the humanisation of global politics? Second, how can the individual human being be included in IR theory as a category of its own? The following provides a conclusive answer to both questions.

- Result 1: We can conceptualise the humanisation of global politics via the positions of the individual human being in discourses of international relations and by identifying the discursive spaces created through the appearance in and the participation of the individual human being in discourses of global politics.
- Result 2: The reconstruction of the appearance of the individual human being in discourses of global politics facilitates the inclusion of the individual human being as a category of IR theory.

These results warrant further elaboration. To recall, the ontological assumption of this book was that we live in a 'world of our making' (Onuf 1989), which is part of our socially constructed reality (Berger and Luckmann 1967 [1966]: 1). Given this constructivist assumption, we should equally conceptualise all actors and entities as social constructions. As outlined in Chapters 1 and 2, constructivist research has done precisely this except for transferring the idea of social construction to the individual human being (Weinert 2015 is a notable exception).

Critics could point out that when choosing approaches with an ontological foundation rooted in the belief that reality is socially constructed (Berger and Luckmann 1967 [1966]: 1), the result cannot be anything but a social construction. This critique can be refuted on several grounds. First, the empirical results resulted from a data-driven reconstructive analysis guided by an abductive research logic. I neither deductively tested a hypothesis, nor did I draw insight inductively from data. Instead, I worked with an abductive approach, oscillating between theoretical insight and empirical research to conduct theory-guided research and advance IR theory at the same time. Second, the discussion of IR theory and IL scholarship demonstrated that alternative theoretical approaches and conceptions of the individual human being have analytical shortcomings. Therefore, the book presents an alternative conceptual and theoretical framework that provides sufficient guidance for the research while simultaneously facilitating constant reflection of the research and its results.[2]

[2] Matthew Weinert discusses a similar circularity challenge in the context of humanisation (Weinert 2015: 16–17).

The case studies have all demonstrated that individual human beings participate – albeit to varying degrees – in those discourses of global politics (on prosecution, protection, and killing, respectively). They are both positioned by others as well as by themselves. Hence, they appear within these discourses as an entity on their own. This appearance always entails a 'social' moment because it requires recognising this positioning by others, either by agreement or disagreement. This social moment also comes to the fore in references to participants and participation. Such an argument is similar to constructivist arguments on the necessity of intersubjectivity and discursive decisions for the validation of norms (Kratochwil 1984a: 707–708; Wiener 2018: 15).

Here I like to note that while demonstrating that the individual human being in global politics is an entity on its own, the results seem to indicate that the individual human being remains an object of state actions: being prosecuted, being protected, and killed.[3] While the observation is correct, the interpretation is not. The fact that the individual human being is the direct addressee of prosecution, protection, and killing already defies the argument that they are mere objects. For this reason, I have suggested using the term participants (Higgins 1994: 50). This is in line with an understanding of global politics as relational (Jackson and Nexon 1999: 293) and as inter-national (Wiener 2008: 1, 2014a: 6–7).[4]

The appearance of the individual human being within the discourse takes place via discourse-specific positions. Therefore, our knowledge about the individual human being in global politics depends on examining and analysing this positioning. Positioning, the book argues, is understood as an act of social construction through the interaction of entities (Jackson and Nexon 1999: 293). Different positionings were analysed in detail in the three case studies. Table 8.1 lists for each of the three discourses studied (a) the positioning of the individual human being in the specific discourse studied that demonstrates how the individual human being appears in the specific discourse, (b) which discursive space is opened via this positioning, and (c) the relevance for global politics. The positionings and the discursive spaces identified in each of the three case studies are understood as specific social constructions of the individual human being in global politics.

[3] I am thankful to Judith Renner and Bastian Loges for raising this point – independently of each other.

[4] Future research may be able to shed more light on the question of how, through the humanisation of global politics, both the study of global politics and global politics itself change. Below, I outline some possible implications.

TABLE 8.1. *The social construction of the individual human being: Three cases*

Discourse	Positioning: How does the individual human being appear in the discourse?	Discursive space	Relevance for global politics
Prosecution	Individual human being appears as guilty perpetrator or innocent victim	Discursive space in which politics of prosecution becomes possible and innocent victims may be able to experience justice	Allows discussing and at times enacting the punishment of those guilty of serious international crimes. Allows delivering justice to the victims of such crimes
Protection	Individual human being appears as innocent civilian worthy of protection or as guilty terrorist or combatant not worthy of protection	Discursive space in which the individual human being is positioned as worthy of protection and a politics of protection becomes possible or protection fails because individuals are not positioned as worthy of protection	Allows discussing and at times enacting a politics of protection, ranging from humanitarian aid to military force
Targeted Killing via Drones	Individual human being appears as an innocent civilian who should not be killed (if possible) or as a guilty terrorist who should be killed	Discursive spaces in which the individual human being is positioned as a target or non target and becoming killable or not killable	Allows the killing of specific individual human beings and sparing the life of other specific individual human beings

Source: Gholiagha

8.2 CONTRIBUTION AND VALUE ADDED

Four contributions stand out in this book. First, regarding the value added on the level of theory, the book contributed to filling a gap within IR theory by incorporating the individual human being as a theoretical category beyond their earlier assigned role as the 'carrier' of ideas, norms, and identities (Krell 2009: 377, my translation). It therefore contributed to an agentic constructivism (Sikkink 2011a, 2011b: 237; Lantis 2016: 387; Zimmermann et al. 2017: 691; Wiener 2017) as well as to calls of feminist scholars such as Christine Sylvester who argued that 'in IR, individuals are studied using someone else's script, not their own, which might be a reason why IR is on the back foot when it comes to anticipating people as stakeholders, actors, and *participants* in international relations' (Sylvester 2013a: 614, emphasis added). The book provides a conceptualisation of the individual human being in global politics as a socially constructed entity (see also Weinert 2015), thus allowing us to understand how the 'carrier' of ideas, norms, and identity (Krell 2009: 377, my translation) comes into being. Doing so enables IR theory to study the individual human being as a being and as a participant in global politics, not as the objects or subjects of others. Such an approach enables IR scholars to conceptualise and theorise the humanisation of global politics alongside legal scholarship on the humanisation of international law (Meron 2006; Teitel 2011; Peters 2014, 2016).

Second, the book provided a detailed study of the humanisation of global politics, departing from feminist and critical constructivist approaches in IR. Concerning feminist approaches, the book has demonstrated the necessity for IR scholars to consider feminist approaches and feminist perspective to global politics, something many others have, of course, done before (Alcoff 1987; Zalewski 1995; Enloe 2014; Tickner and True 2018; Kinsella and Shepherd 2019). Concerning constructivist approaches, the book identified some weaknesses in constructivist approaches: either constructivist approaches were too close to realism, basing their notion of the human being on a realist understanding of human nature and focused too much on the state and collective actors (e.g., Wendt 1992), or they were too close to liberalism, assuming the individual human being as a given entity who enters into social interactions already constituted (e.g., Risse 2000). This book further developed critical constructivism by strengthening the focus on agency (Hofius et al. 2014; Wiener 2014a; Wiener 2017; Gholiagha et al. 2021). Thus, the book refutes both conventional versions of constructivism. By demonstrating how the individual human being in global politics can be integrated into the study of global politics, and especially constructivist IR as a social construction, the book has advanced the study of global politics. This reconstruction of the individual human being in global politics also allows ascribing agency to the individual human being in global politics, demonstrating how the individual human being participates in global politics (Higgins 1994: 49; Sylvester 2013a: 614).

Third, conceptually, the book contributed by introducing a conceptual framework for studying the humanisation of global politics. The framework combined feminist and constructivist IR approaches with IL approaches, drawing on concepts such as gender and body, norms and language, rights and duties, and positions and participation. The conceptual framework allowed me to grasp the appearance of the individual human being in discourses of global politics. Not all concepts were referred to explicitly in every part of each analysis. However, throughout the book, the theoretical and conceptual framework's added value became evident. Notions of gender and sex, and the human body, played an important role, especially in studying discourses on protection and killing. Individual and human rights mattered in all three discourses, as they constituted an important part of each discourse. Norms mattered equally, as actors drew on them, contested them, or debated their meanings in the respective discourses. The importance of language came to the fore throughout the book in form, especially when analysing the various discourses, debates, and documents. Finally, positions and participants as concepts guided the analysis alongside the heuristics of innocence and guilt. The book, relying on the concept of participants (Higgins 1978–1979, 1994), and developing it further, provides a way to break out of the 'intellectual prison' constituted by the subject/object dichotomy (Higgins 1994: 49) in which both scholars of IR and IL often find themselves. As discussed in detail in Chapter 2, the notion of subjects and objects does not help grasp the appearance of the individual human being in global politics. On the contrary, it ascribes mere passive roles to certain actors, who become the 'object' of actions by other 'subjects'. Participation highlights the agency of those involved in global politics and that individual human beings are participants in global politics alongside other actors.

Fourth, on a methodological level, the book provided an interpretative methodological framework, enabling the reconstruction of processes of social construction. Such a framework facilitates accessing a wide range of data types, such as documents, interviews, legal texts, and news reports. Such a methodological framework is, of course, also applicable to other processes of construction. Furthermore, the book demonstrated how IR theory could study the individual human being in global politics without falling into the trap of methodological individualism or relying on pre-given theoretical conceptions of the individual human being. Related to this, the concept of discursive spaces (Holzscheiter 2010: 143, 146, 178, 184; Wiener 2014b; Papamichail and Partis-Jennings 2016; Parks 2018) is the place where participants can discuss moral questions of agency (Erskine 2008: 704) and hence can be analysed by scholars of global politics. It is here where human beings 'form a world between them' (Arendt 1990 [1963]: 175), a 'world of our making' (Onuf 1989). Understanding that this mutual constitution is a process of social construction allows us to analytically access and thereby understand the mutual constitution of each other.

Here, I would like to point to something this book has not done in terms of positioning. While this book has focused on positioning and participation in discourses of global politics and has studied the positioning predominantly undertaken by states or international institutions, it has also considered how, for example, in drone strikes, the crews of a drone position individual human beings and how the principle of distinction is of relevance here. It has, however, not studied these moments of mutual recognition in detail. Matthew Weinert (2015), who has offered such a detailed study and explains how recognising others as humans matters for our understanding of humanity, demonstrates how these issues also matter for questions of global politics and the international order:

> the full actualization of one's humanity – that is, individuality and status as human with dignity – requires recognition qua human by other human beings. Recognition may sometimes be the result of other processes to make others human, which this study examined. In this fundamental, basic sense, we constitute each other. How we mutually constitute one another is, centrally, the problem not only of personhood and interpersonal relations but, ultimately, of international relations and world order (Weinert 2015: 18).

The issue of recognition relates to whether the positioning of individual human beings is accepted or challenged by others.[5] Throughout this book, I have pointed to instances of challenges to specific positions. The case study on prosecution provides the most obvious example. An individual positioned as guilty may challenge this positioning by claiming their innocence. The defence team will also be part of this challenge. These challenges can also be found in the other case studies. For example, in the case study on protection, members of the UNSC did not agree on the positioning of individual human beings in the case of Syria, challenging each other's positioning. In the case study on killing, challenging positioning before strikes is, in most cases, impossible due to the clandestine nature of the operations. Al-Awlaki may be the only exception to this, where relatives of al-Awlaki tried to challenge the decision to kill him before a US court (Weill 2016: 54). However, we can see that NGOs try to challenge the positioning of individual human beings through human rights litigation, albeit ex post and often postmortem.

[5] I am thankful to one of the anonymous readers of the original manuscript for pointing me to this issue.

However, discussing these challenges does not entail an externalist judgement of whether this positioning is appropriate or convincing.[6] I am not interested in such an externalist analysis. Instead, I have attempted to demonstrate how the positioning matters for how the individual human being appears in the respective discourse. In doing so, I have taken an internalist perspective (Kreuder-Sonnen and Zürn 2020: 243). It is here that I need to admit to one apparent weakness in my work concerning self-positioning. While I have included the analysis of acts of self-positioning wherever possible and feasible, this remains limited. Conceptually and methodologically, positioning always entails both positionings through others and self-positioning. However, a study of self-positioning in detail would require additional empirical material I have not included for various reasons. For example, in the case of drone strikes, interviews with survivors of drone strikes or relatives of those killed would have been necessary. Where possible, I have relied on secondary sources that include such material. In the case of the ICC and the cases studied, interviews with those appearing before the court would have provided ideal material. Again, where possible, I relied on secondary sources and court documents to provide at least a glimpse into speech acts that included self-positioning. The same holds for the case study on protection. I hope myself or perhaps others may be able to remedy this omission in future work.

Finally, the book has contributed to the study of global politics on an empirical level. Specifically, the book has contributed to a better understanding of three related security discourses on prosecution and ICL and the ICC, protection and the R2P, and killing individuals, especially with drone strikes. In doing so, these analyses also contributed to growing literature on the individualisation of war (Blum 2014; Dill 2019; Renic 2019; Welsh 2019b; Renic 2020), the growing research on issues of human protection (Bellamy 2016; Erameh 2017; Rhoads and Welsh 2019), and the existing and continuously growing body of work on the individual in ICL (Osiel 2014; Gil Gil and Maculan 2015; Stolk 2018; Mégret 2018, 2019; Mégret and Giles Samson 2019; Jessberger and Geneuss 2020).

8.3 THE HUMANISATION OF GLOBAL POLITICS: IMPLICATIONS FOR IR, IL, AND GLOBAL POLITICS

In this book, I have argued that the conceptualisation of the humanisation of global politics is possible by studying the appearance through reconstructing

[6] A point suggested by one of the anonymous readers.

individual human beings' (self)-positioning in global politics and conceptualising individual human beings as participants in global politics. As I further demonstrated, such an approach allows us to understand processes and developments within global politics. In the following, I outline the implications of the book's results for IR and IL and global politics.

8.3.1 *Implications for IR and IL*

The individual human being takes up a central position as a participant. This matters for IR theory and IL scholars regardless of their specific interests because individuals matter in global politics. As this book demonstrated, they also should matter for IR scholars. Based on this argument, in the following, I will outline the implications this argument has for studying global politics on a normative, analytical, and theoretical level.

On a normative level, the argument allows us 'to better understand our interhuman ties, to expose inequalities and "human wrongs", to promote our empowerment and allay our common fears' (Aalto 2011: 178). Once we acknowledge the individual human being in global politics, we can genuinely assess good and evil done by and done to individual human beings. Only then can we evaluate policies aimed at helping individual human beings, be it in the realm of security, development, or humanitarianism. Prosecution, protection, and killing are existential issues for individual human beings. Therefore, understanding how these practices matter for global politics is an important normative contribution of this book. Furthermore, a focus on the individual human being prevents us as scholars from building our assessments on structural aspects or collective aspects alone. Thus, it allows IR theory to overcome the strong focus on structural and material aspects of global politics. It allows scholars of IL to engage with the individual human being outside of the subject-object dichotomy.

On an analytical level, studying the humanisation of global politics and including this into IR theory 'provides added value by sharpening the analytical and explanatory potential of IR' (Aalto 2011: 178). Whatever its research focus may be, IR theory ought to take the individual human being as a participant of global politics into account. This book has prepared the ground for this shift and demonstrated the applicability and feasibility of focusing on the individual human being in global politics. Furthermore, such an approach allows scholars of IR theory to cross interdisciplinary boundaries by having a shared research focus not only with IL but also with disciplines such as ethnography, anthropology, philosophy, and sociology. The same holds for IL. Finally, considering the political dimension of the humanisation of global politics allows scholars of IL to apply their analysis to issues that are not exclusively of legal nature.

On a theoretical level, theorising the humanisation of global politics by conceptualising the individual human being as a social construction allows us to deepen the understanding of our world. It adds the individual human being as a category of its own to IR theory. In doing so, the individual human being becomes observable through IR theory as they are neither seen as given nor reduced to a biological entity with a fixed 'nature'. Such a perspective bears a solid linkage to the feminist IR theory. To recall, it was feminist scholars who argued that understanding gender as socially constructed (Harding 1986: 647; Alcoff 1987: 120; Brown 1988: 473; Butler 1993: 8, 1999: 9) allowed for an advancement of IR theory. Similarly, the insight of the social construction of the individual human being advanced IR theory. The theoretical innovation this book offers means that the individual human being does not need to be bracketed any longer within IR theory.

8.3.2 *Implications for Global Politics*

The overall aim of this book has been to understand the humanisation of global politics. However, there is no doubt that the humanisation of global politics also affects both structures and actors of global politics.[7] In terms of the effects on the structure of global politics, the rise of legal treaties that protect individual human beings or grant them more rights and better means of protecting these rights or legal means of redress in case of violations is perhaps an excellent example for those structural changes. The ICC is the most recent and most obvious example here. It also affects how states – individually or collectively – deal with alleged perpetrators of mass atrocity crimes. Moreover, it has led to structural changes within states, introducing means to prosecute such crimes. We have also witnessed discussions about new human rights, such as the right to water (Reiners 2021a, 2021b). Such developments constitute another case of structural changes to global politics on the level of rights individual human beings have. Furthermore, the book has also highlighted changes to the meaning of norms such as non-interference or sovereignty due to the humanisation of global politics.

Finally, on the level of structure, I would like to discuss the notion of power, albeit very briefly. Power has not been part of the book's framework or of the empirical analysis I have conducted.[8] This omission is not due to neglect.

7 I am thankful to one of the anonymous readers for this insight.

8 I am thankful to one of the anonymous readers for asking me about power.

Instead, the analytical focus of this book lies elsewhere. The book has been concerned with processes of social construction and the humanisation of global politics. This process involves actors often seen as 'powerful' (e.g., the UN Security Council or specific states) but also actors often depicted as 'powerless' (e.g., victims of drone strikes). Focusing on power does not, therefore, in my view, provide a useful analytical lens to the question the book is concerned with (see Guzzini 1993 for the question of how power can and cannot contribute to IR). There is, however, an interesting question that could be a focus of work that is built upon the present one: 'Who or what has the power to push their position and define the individual in different global forums?'[9] I would, however, suggest that such a work would make use of a feminist understanding of power, as articulated by J. Ann Tickner, with reference to Hannah Arendt: 'Hannah Arendt, frequently cited by feminists writing about power, defines power as the human ability to act in concert, or to take action in connection with others who share similar concerns' (Tickner 1991: 33). However, this would be a very different analysis and hence a different book.

In terms of actors, we also see changes, for example, concerning international organisations and states. But international organisations have also begun to change how they engage with individual human beings by taking their rights, needs, and views unmediated through states into account (Zürn and Heupel 2017; Dingwerth et al. 2019; Dingwerth and Witt 2020). States can also not shield interference from the outside when they violate individual human being's rights, as the debate on R2P has demonstrated. For example, sovereignty is conditioned on protecting the population on the territory of a state (Annan 1999; Peters 2009; Orford 2011). But non-state actors such as businesses have begun to pay more attention to human rights questions (for many, see Ruggie 2007). In sum, the humanisation of global politics affects structures and actors of global politics alike in various ways, all of which may be subject to further studies. In Section 8.4, I would like to give an outlook on further research.

8.4 OUTLOOK ON FURTHER RESEARCH

Having developed theoretical, conceptual, and analytical frameworks capable of reconstructing the appearance of the individual human being in discourses of global politics, the most obvious research project that could follow from this

9 I have taken the liberty to take this question from one of the reader's reports, because I think it is an important question and well phrased.

book is to extend the analysis to additional discourses. For example, climate change and discussion about 'climate refugees' and climate migration (Nash 2019) would be a good case study providing an additional discourse in which the appearance, positioning, and participation of individual human beings is central to the discourse. Other cases could be drawn from the discourse on refugee protection, for example, by studying the appearance, positioning, and participation of refugees and internally displaced persons within the discourse on refugee protection (Orchard 2014; Bradley 2019). An additional case study in this context could be developed from the ongoing debate about the rescue at sea operations and normative tensions between the duty to rescue at sea, the obligation to prevent smuggling, and border and immigration control (Ghezelbash et al. 2018; Cusumano 2019). The heuristics of innocence and guilt could also be applied to a broader range of discourses to see whether they yield further insights that would remain undiscovered otherwise. Finally, on a more abstract theoretical level, the humanisation of global politics could be investigated further, relying on a broader interdisciplinary framework, including work from philosophy, ethics, and international political theory.

Furthermore, two research topics could be developed out of the case studies. First, from the case study on targeted killing, a research project focusing on autonomous weapon systems and their effect and influence on the future of warfare could be further investigated (Bhuta et al. 2016; Ekelhof 2017; Bode and Huelss 2018). Here, especially the issues of political and legal questions stemming from the potential deployment of such weapons could be studied in a research project at the nexus of IHL, IHRL, and IR theory. In this context, the possibility of non-human actors within global politics and their role also comes to the fore (Cudworth and Hobden 2013a, 2013b; Wilcox 2017). Second, the ongoing contestation of R2P could constitute a second research project that could be developed from the case studies; here, the focus could lie on the discursive spaces opened by R2P. Within this project, the role of the EU in advancing R2P could be critically juxtaposed with the position of the BRICS and other non-state actors on these issues (Staunton and Ralph 2020; Hunt and Orchard 2020a).

The empirical analysis in this book is interpretative. There are good reasons for this. Participation, interactions, meaning, positions, and discourse lend themselves more to an interpretative and qualitative methodology than a positivist or quantitative one. Furthermore, the aim to understand the humanisation of global politics rather than to explain it or its effects also led me to choose an interpretative approach. In future research, the idea of the humanisation of global politics and the concepts of positions and participations could nevertheless be studied with a more quantitative approach (although the constructivist ontology may not provide a good foundation for positivist approaches). More specifically, quantitative text analysis, especially in combination with interpretative approaches, can facilitate the study of larger amounts of texts.

To conclude, the book has provided an in-depth analysis of the humanisation of global politics and has contributed to IR theory by incorporating the individual human being as a theoretical category of their own. At the same time, the book has opened up IR towards studying the individual human being in global politics within various discourses, contexts, events, and developments. Global politics are not the exclusive realm of nations or states, nor is there an international community where the individual human being has no place. Instead, global politics are the realm of every individual human being walking the face of this earth. In this spirit, Pami Aalto has argued that 'international studies painting images of international interactions without noting how the very constitution of the international would never have been possible without human beings, would be a very strange endeavour, both in the academic and normative sense' (Aalto 2011: 196–197). Individual human beings have not only made this world and are continuing to do so. Individual human beings also make themselves in this process. This book contributed to incorporating this important insight into IR theory by providing an empirical study of instances of the social construction of the individual human being in global politics. The book has also demonstrated the relevance of studying the humanisation of global politics from an interdisciplinary perspective, bringing together work from scholars of IR and IL. Finally, as the examples at the beginning of this conclusion demonstrate, the issues and topics this book has engaged with remain relevant and relate to ongoing developments in global politics. I hope this book provides a foundation for such research in the future.

Appendices

OVERVIEW OF INTERVIEWS

The empirical analysis in this book relies in part on interviews conducted in 2014 in New York and Geneva. Given that some interview partners requested full anonymity I granted the maximum level of anonymity to all interview partners and hence only refer to the interviews in the text by a number. The following constitutes a list of the interviews conducted.

- UN staff member of the UN Office for the Coordination of Humanitarian Affairs
- UN Staff member of the UN Department for Political Affairs (today UN Department for Political and Peacebuilding Affairs)
- Diplomat from the Australian Mission to the UN
- Diplomat from the German Mission to the UN
- Diplomat from the Liechtenstein Mission to the UN
- Pakistani officials
- Member of the ICISS
- UN Official
- Staff members of the Coalition for the International Criminal Court
- Staff member of the International Coalition for the Responsibility to Protect

References

Aalto, Pami (2011). The human subject in international studies: An outline for interdisciplinary research programmes. In Aalto, Pami, Harle, Vilho, and Moisio, Sami, eds., *International Studies*. London; New York: Palgrave Macmillan, 178–206.

Acharya, Amitav (2004). How ideas spread: Whose norms matter? Norm localization and institutional change in Asian regionalism. *International Organization*, 58(2), 239–275.

(2011). Norm subsidiarity and regional orders. *International Studies Quarterly*, 55(1), 95–123.

Ackelsberg, Martha A. (1992). Feminist analyses of public policy. *Comparative Politics*, 24(4), 477–493.

Ackelsberg, Martha A., and Diamond, Irene (1987). Gender and political life: New directions in political science. In Hess, Beth B., and Ferree, Myra M., eds., *Analyzing Gender: A Handbook of Social Science Research*. Newbury Park: SAGE, 504–525.

Ackermann, Spencer (2011). Rare Photographs Show Ground Zero of the Drone War. *Wired*. www.wired.com/2011/12/photos-pakistan-drone-war/.

Adediran, Bolarinwa (2017). Implementing R2P: Towards a regional solution? *Global Responsibility to Protect*, 9(4), 459–487.

Adler, Emanuel (2013). Constructivism in international relations: Sources, contributions, and debates. In Carlsnaes, Walter, Risse, Thomas, and Simmons, Beth A., eds., *Handbook of International Relations*. 2nd ed. London: SAGE , 112–144.

Adler, Emanuel, and Pouliot, Vincent (2011). International practices. *International Theory*, 3(1), 1–36.

Adler-Nissen, Rebecca, and Pouliot, Vincent (2014). Power in practice: Negotiating the international intervention in Libya. *European Journal of International Relations*, 20(4), 889–911.

African Union Assembly (2008). Decision on the Situation in Kenya Following the Presidential Election of 27 December 2007. (Assembly/AU/Dec.187[X]). https://au.int/sites/default/files/decisions/9562-assembly_en_31_january_2_february_2008_auc_tenth_ordinary_session_decisions_and_declarations.pdf.

(2013). Twenty-First Ordinary Session. https://au.int/sites/default/files/decisions/9654-assembly_au_dec_474-489_xxi_e.pdf.

African Union Peace and Security Council (2011). Communique of the 265th Meeting of the Peace and Security Council. (PSC/PR/COMM.2[CCLXV]). www.peaceau.org/uploads/communique-libya-eng.pdf.

Africanews (2021). Interim Government Assumes Power in Libya. www.africanews.com/2021/03/16/interim-government-assumes-power-in-libya/.

Agerberg, Mattias, and Kreft, Anne-Kathrin (2020). Gendered conflict, gendered outcomes: The politicization of sexual violence and quota adoption. *Journal of Conflict Resolution*, 64(2–3), 290–317.

Ainley, Kirsten (2008). Individual agency and responsibility for atrocity. In Jeffery, Renée, ed., *Confronting Evil in International Relations: Ethical Responses to Problems of Moral Agency*. Vol 1. New York: Palgrave Macmillan, 37–70.

(2011). Excesses of responsibility: The limits of law and the possibilities of politics. *Ethics & International Affairs*, 25(4), 407–431.

(2015). The Responsibility to Protect and the International Criminal Court: Counteracting the crisis. *International Affairs*, 91(1), 37–54.

Aistrope, Tim, Gifkins, Jess, and Taylor, N. A. J. (2018). The Responsibility to Protect and the question of attribution. *Global Change, Peace & Security*, 30(1), 1–20.

Akbarzadeh, Shahram, and Saba, Arif (2019). UN paralysis over Syria: The responsibility to protect or regime change? *International Politics*, 56(4), 536–550.

Albania; Andorra; Australia; Austria; Belgium; Botswana; Bulgaria; Canada; Central African Republic; Chile; Côte d'Ivoire; Croatia; Cyprus; Czech Republic; Democratic Republic of the Congo; Denmark; Estonia; Finland; France; Georgia; Germany; Greece; Hungary; Iceland; Ireland; Italy; Japan; Jordan; Latvia; Libya; Liechtenstein; Lithuania; Luxembourg; Malta; Marshall Islands; Mexico; Monaco; Montenegro; Netherlands; New Zealand; Norway; Panama; Poland; Portugal; Qatar; Republic of Korea; Republic of Moldova; Romania; Samoa; San Marino; Saudi Arabia; Senegal; Serbia; Seychelles; Slovakia; Slovenia; Spain; Sweden; Switzerland; The former Yugoslav Republic of Macedonia; Turkey; Ukraine; United Arab Emirates; United Kingdom of Great Britain and Northern Ireland; United States of America (2014). Draft Resolution. (S/2014/348). www.securitycouncilreport.org/atf/cf/%7B65BFCF9B-6D27-4E9C-8CD3-CF6E4FF96FF9%7D/s_2014_348.pdf.

Alcoff, Linda (1987). Justifying feminist social science. *Hypatia*, 2(3), 107–120.

(1988). Cultural feminism versus post-structuralism: The identity crisis in feminist theory. *Signs*, 13(3), 405–436.

Aljazeera (2014). Mixed Reactions to ICC Decision on Kenyatta. www.aljazeera.com/news/2014/12/6/mixed-reactions-to-icc-decision-on-kenyatta.

(2021). Libya Talks Make Progress towards New Temporary Government: UN. www.aljazeera.com/news/2021/1/17/libya-talks-make-progress-towards-new-temporary-government-un.

Allinson, Jamie (2015). The necropolitics of drones. *International Political Sociology*, 9(2), 113–127.

Allott, Philip (1992). Reconstituting humanity—New international law. *European Journal of International Law*, 3(2), 219–252.

Almagro, Maria M. de (2018). Lost boomerangs, the rebound effect and transnational advocacy networks: A discursive approach to norm diffusion. *Review of International Studies*, 44(4), 672–693.

Alter, Karen J. (2020). Comprehending global governance: International regime complexity vs. Global constitutionalism. *Global Constitutionalism – Human Rights, Democracy and the Rule of Law*, 9(2), 413–423.
Alter, Karen J., and Meunier, Sophie (2009). The politics of international regime complexity. *Perspective on Politics*, 7(1), 13–24.
Altman, Andrew (2012). Introduction. In Finkelstein, Claire, Ohlin, Jens D., and Altman, Andrew, eds., *Targeted Killing: Law and Morality in an Asymmetrical World*. Oxford: Oxford University Press, 1–27.
Alvarez, José E. (2008). The schizophrenia of R2P. In MacDonald, Euan, and Alston, Philip, eds., *Human Rights, Intervention, and the Use of Force*. Oxford: Oxford University Press, 275–284.
Alvesson, Mats, and Sandberg, Jörgen (2011). Generating research questions through problematization. *Academy of Management Review*, 36(2), 247–271.
(2013). *Constructing Research Questions*. London: SAGE.
Ambos, Kai (2013). Expanding the focus of the 'African criminal court'. In Schabas, William A., McDermott, Yvonne, and Hayes, Niamh, eds., *The Ashgate Research Companion to International Criminal Law: Critical Perspectives*. Surrey; Burlington, VT: Ashgate, 499–529.
Amnesty International (2013). 'Will I Be Next?' US Drone Strikes in Pakistan. https://www.amnestyusa.org/wp-content/uploads/2017/04/asa330132013en.pdf.
Anderson, Kenneth, and Waxman, Matthew C. (2013). Law and Ethics for Autonomous Weapon Systems: Why a Ban Won't Work and How the Laws of War Can. (Research Paper No. 2013-11). https://scholarship.law.columbia.edu/cgi/viewcontent.cgi?article=2804&context=faculty_scholarship.
Aning, Kwesi, and Edu-Afful, Fiifi (2016). African agency in R2P: Interventions by African Union and ECOWAS in Mali, Cote d'Ivoire, and Libya. *International Studies Review*, 18(1), 120–133.
Annan, Kofi (1999). Two concepts of sovereignty. *The Economist*, 18 September 1999.
Arab League (2011). The Outcome of the Council of the League of Arab States Meeting at the Ministerial Level in Its Extraordinary Session on the Implications of the Current Events in Libya and the Arab Position. http://responsibilitytoprotect.org/Arab%20League%20Ministerial%20level%20statement%2012%20march%202011%20-%20english%281%29.pdf.
Arbour, Louise (2008). The Responsibility to Protect as a duty of care in international law and practice. *Review of International Studies*, 34(3), 445–458.
(2013). Entmachtet die Großmächte. *Die ZEIT*, 14 November 2013.
Archambault, Emil (2018). Review article: Targeted killing, technologies of violence, and society. *Millennium: Journal of International Studies*, 47(1), 142–152.
Arendt, Hannah (1951). *The Origins of Totalitarianism*. New York: Harcourt, Brace and Company.
(1963). *Eichmann in Jerusalem*. New York: The Viking Press.
(1969 [1958]). *The Origins of Totalitarianism*. 2nd enlarged ed. Cleveland; New York: Meridian.
(1990 [1963]). *On Revolution*. London: Penguin.
(1998 [1958]). *The Human Condition*. 2nd ed. Chicago: University of Chicago Press.
Ashley, Richard K. (1984). The poverty of neorealism. *International Organization*, 38 (2), 225–286.

Aslam, Wali, and Rauxloh, Regina (2015). Conclusions. In Aaronson, Mike, Aslam, Wali, Dyson, Tom, and Rauxloh, Regina, eds., *Precision Strike Warfare and International Intervention*. Oxon: Routledge, 225–233.

Auchter, Jessica (2016). Paying attention to dead bodies: The future of security studies? *Journal of Global Security Studies*, 1(1), 36–50.

Aukerman, Miriam J. (2002). Extraordinary evil, ordinary crime: A framework for understanding transitional justice. *Harvard Human Rights Journal*, 15, 39–96.

Aust, Helmut P. (2017). 'The system only dreams in total darkness': The future of human rights law in the light of algorithmic authority. *German Yearbook of International Law*, 60, 1–15.

Babbitt, Eileen F. (2017). Responsibility to Protect: Time to reassess. *Journal of Human Rights Practice*, 9(3), 431–435.

Baggiarini, Bianca (2015). Drone warfare and the limits of sacrifice. *Journal of International Political Theory*, 11(1), 128–144.

Bahrain; Colombia; Egypt; France; Germany; Jordan; Kuwait; Libya; Morocco; Oman; Portugal; Qatar; Saudi Arabia; Togo; Tunisia; Turkey; United Arab Emirates; United Kingdom and United States of America (2012). Draft Resolution. (S/2012/77). www.securitycouncilreport.org/atf/cf/%7B65BFCF9B-6D27-4E9C-8CD3-CF6E4FF96FF9%7D/Syria%20S2012%2077.pdf.

Bähring, Jill (2017). Individual Redress and State Responsibility the Law and Politics of Compensation Payments and Their Application to Drone Strike Victims. Master Thesis, Vrije Universiteit Amsterdam.

Bain, William (2010). Responsibility and obligation in the 'Responsibility to Protect'. *Review of International Studies*, 36(Special Issue S1), 25–46.

Ban, Ki-Moon (2009). Implementing the Responsibility to Protect. (A/63/677). www2.ohchr.org/english/bodies/chr/special/docs/17thsession/SG_reportA_63_677_en.pdf.

Banka, Andris, and Quinn, Adam (2018). Killing norms softly: US targeted killing, quasi-secrecy and the assassination ban. *Security Studies*, 27(4), 665–703.

Baranovsky, Vladimir, and Mateiko, Anatoly (2016). Responsibility to Protect: Russia's approaches. *The International Spectator*, 51(2), 49–69.

Barnett, Michael N. (2012). International paternalism and humanitarian governance. *Global Constitutionalism – Human Rights, Democracy and the Rule of Law*, 1(3), 485–521.

Barrinha, Andre, and da Vinha, Luis (2015). Dealing with risk. In Aaronson, Mike, Aslam, Wali, Dyson, Tom, and Rauxloh, Regina, eds., *Precision Strike Warfare and International Intervention*. Oxon: Routledge, 14–32.

Bartelson, Jens (1995). *A Genealogy of Sovereignty*. Cambridge: Cambridge University Press.

BBC (2010). *Kenya Election Violence: ICC Names Suspects*. www.bbc.com/news/world-africa-11996652.

(2013). *Syria Crisis: Russia and China Step up Warning over Strike*. www.bbc.com/news/world-us-canada-23845800.

(2014). *Syria conflict: UN concerned over Homs detentions*. www.bbc.com/news/world-middle-east-26131742.

Beier, J. Marshall (2021). 'This changes things': Children, targeting, and the making of precision. *Cooperation and Conflict*. Online First, 1–16.

Bell, Duncan (2012). The dawn of biopolitical IR? *International Studies Review*, 14(4), 653–656.

Bellamy, Alex J. (2006). Whither the Responsibility to Protect? Humanitarian intervention and the 2005 world summit. *Ethics & International Affairs*, 20(2), 143–169.

(2008). The Responsibility to Protect and the problem of military intervention. *International Affairs*, 84(4), 615–639.

(2009). *Responsibility to Protect—The Global Effort to End Mass Atrocities*. Cambridge: Polity Press.

(2010). The Responsibility to Protect—five years on. *Ethics & International Affairs*, 24(2), 143–169.

(2011a). *Global Politics and the Responsibility to Protect*. Oxford; New York: Routledge.

(2011b). Libya and The Responsibility to Protect: The exception and the norm. *Ethics & International Affairs*, 25(3), 263–269.

(2014). The Responsibility to Protect and the problem of regime change. In Scheid, Don E., ed., *The Ethics of Armed Humanitarian Intervention*. Cambridge: Cambridge University Press, 166–186.

(2015). *The Responsibility to Protect: A Defense*. 1st ed. Oxford: Oxford University Press.

(2016). The humanisation of security? Towards an international human protection regime. *European Journal of International Security*, 1(1), 112–133.

(forthcoming). *Syria Betrayed: Atrocities, War, and the Failure of International Diplomacy*. New York: Columbia University Press.

Bellamy, Alex J., and McLoughlin, Stephen (2018). *Rethinking Humanitarian Intervention*. London: Palgrave.

Bellamy, Alex J., and Reike, Ruben (2010). The Responsibility to Protect and international law. *Global Responsibility to Protect*, 2(3), 267–286.

Benhabib, Seyla (2007). Twilight of sovereignty or the emergence of cosmopolitan norms? Rethinking citizenship in volatile times. *Citizenship Studies*, 11(1), 19–36.

Benjamin, Medea (2013). *Drone Warfare*. London: Verso.

Bensouda, Fatou (2014). Gender justice and the ICC: Progress and reflections. *International Feminist Journal of Politics*, 16(4), 538–542.

Berenskötter, Felix (2018). Deep theorizing in international relations. *European Journal of International Relations*, 24(4), 814–840.

Berger, Peter L., and Luckmann, Thomas (1967 [1966]). *The Social Construction of Reality*. First Anchor Books Edition. New York: Anchor Books.

Besson, Samantha (2009). The authority of international law – Lifting the state veil. *Sydney Law Review*, 31(3), 343–380.

(2010). Theorizing the sources of international law. In Besson, Samantha, and Tasioulas, John, eds., *The Philosophy of International Law*. Oxford: Oxford University Press, 163–185.

Besson, Samantha, and Tasioulas, John, eds. (2010). *The Philosophy of International Law*. Oxford: Oxford University Press.

Bhuta, Nehal, Beck, Susanne, Geiß, Robin, Liu, Hin-Yan, and Kreß, Claus, eds. (2016). *Autonomous Weapons Systems: Law, Ethics, Policy*. Cambridge: Cambridge University Press.

Biersteker, Thomas J., and Weber, Cynthia, eds. (1996). *State Sovereignty as Social Construct*. Cambridge: Cambridge University Press.

Birckenbach, Hanne-Magret (1991). Paradigmen der internationalen Politik: Eine Kritik aus der Perspektive feministischer Friedensforschung. *Blätter für deutsche und internationale Politik*, 2(8), 959–970.

Birdsall, Andrea (2018). Drone warfare in counterterrorism and normative change: US policy and the politics of international law. *Global Society*, 32(3), 241–262.

Birkenkötter, Hannah (2016). Ein Erfolgreicher Jahresabschluss? Zur Syrien-Resolution des UN-Sicherheitsrats. https://jungeunforschung.wordpress.com/2016/01/04/ein-erfolgreicher-jahresabschluss-zur-syrien-resolution-des-un-sicherheitsrats/.

(2020). International law as a common language across spheres of authority? *Global Constitutionalism – Human Rights, Democracy and the Rule of Law*, 9(2), 318–342.

Birkenkötter, Hannah, and Kaya, Berkan (2022). The ICJ in an age of inter-legality: A survey of its case law in the new millennium. *German Yearbook of International Law*, 63(1), 421–450.

Birmingham, Peg (2003). Holes of oblivion: The banality of radical evil. *Hypatia*, 18, 80–113.

Bissonnette, Camille M. (2016). The definition of civilians in non-international armed conflicts. *Journal of International Humanitarian Legal Studies*, 7(1), 129–155.

Blank, Laurie R. (2015). Targeted killing. In Johnson, James T., and Patterson, Eric D., eds., *The Ashgate Research Companion to Military Ethics*. Farnham: Ashgate, 231–243.

Blatter, Joachim K., Janning, Frank, and Wagemann, Claudius (2007). *Qualitative Politikfeldanalyse*. Wiesbaden: VS Verlag für Sozialwissenschaften.

Bleiker, Roland, and Hutchison, Emma (2008). Fear no more: Emotions and world politics. *Review of International Studies*, 34(S1), 115–135.

Blum, Gabriella (2014). The individualization of war: From war to policing in the regulation of armed conflicts. In Sarat, Austin, Douglas, Lawrence, and Umphrey., Martha M., eds., *Law and War*. Stanford: Stanford University Press, 48–83.

Blumer, Herbert (1954). What is wrong with social theory? *American Sociological Review*, 29(1), 3–10.

Boateng, Oheneba A. (forthcoming). *Africa's Homegrown Humanitarianism: Regional Responses Versus Global Governance*. London; New York: Routledge.

Bode, Ingvild, and Huelss, Hendrik (2018). Autonomous weapons systems and changing norms in international relations. *Review of International Studies*, 44 (3), 393–413.

Bogner, Alexander, Littig, Beate, and Menz, Wolfgang (2014). *Interviews mit Experten: Eine Praxisorientierte Einführung*. Wiesbaden: Springer.

Bogner, Alexander, and Menz, Wolfgang (2009). Das theoriegenerierende Experteninterview: Erkenntnisinteresse, Wissensformen, Interaktionen. 3rd ed. In Bogner, Alexander, Littig, Beate, and Menz, Wolfgang, eds., *Experteninterviews*. Wiesbaden: VS Verlag für Sozialwissenschaften, 61–98.

Bonafé, Beatrice I. (2013). Coordinating concurrent legal orders in the prosecution of international crimes. *Global Constitutionalism – Human Rights, Democracy and the Rule of Law*, 2(2), 316–344.

Bonds, Eric (2019). Humanitized violence: Targeted killings and civilian deaths in the US war against the Islamic State. *Current Sociology*, 67(3), 438–455.

Boone, Jon, and Kirchgaessner, Stephanie (2015). Pakistan Uses Hostage Killings to Underline Risk of US Drone Strikes. *The Guardian*. www.theguardian.com/world/2015/apr/24/pakistan-us-hostage-killings-drone-strikes-weinstein-lo-porto.

Bousquet, Antoine J. (2018). *The Eye of War: Military Perception from the Telescope to the Drone*. Minneapolis: University of Minnesota Press.

Bower, Adam (2019). Contesting the International Criminal Court: Bashir, Kenyatta, and the status of the nonimpunity norm in world politics. *Journal of Global Security Studies*, 4(1), 88–104.

Boyle, Michael J. (2013). The cost and consequences of drone warfare. *International Affairs*, 89(1), 1–29.

(2015). The legal and ethical implications of drone warfare. *The International Journal of Human Rights*, 19(2), 105–126.

Bradley, Megan (2019). Unresolved and unresolvable? Tensions in the refugee regime. *Ethics & International Affairs*, 33(1), 45–56.

Brennan, John O. (2012). The Efficacy and Ethics of U.S. Counterterrorism Strategy. www.wilsoncenter.org/event/the-efficacy-and-ethics-us-counterterrorism-strategy.

Brock, Lothar (1999). Normative Integration und kollektive Handlungskompetenz auf internationaler Ebene. *Zeitschrift für Internationale Beziehungen*, 6(2), 323–347.

(2013). Dilemmata des internationalen Schutzes von Menschen vor innerstaatlicher Gewalt. Ein Ausblick. In Daase, Christopher, and Junk, Julian, eds., *Die Friedenswarte: Journal of International Peace and Organization*, 88(1–2), 163–185.

Brockmeier, Sarah, Stuenkel, Oliver, and Tourinho, Marcos (2016). The impact of the Libya intervention debates on norms of protection. *Global Society*, 30(1), 113–133.

Brookman-Byrne, Max (2017). Drone use 'outside areas of active hostilities': An examination of the legal paradigms governing US covert remote strikes. *Netherlands International Law Review*, 64(1), 3–41.

Brooks, Rosa (2014). Drones, and the international rule of law. *Ethics & International Affairs*, 28(1), 83–103.

Brown, Anne M. (2002a). *Human Rights and the Borders of Suffering*. Manchester; New York: Manchester University Press.

Brown, Chris (2002b). *Sovereignty, Rights and Justice: International Political Theory Today*. Cambridge: Polity Press.

(2009). Structural realism, classical realism and human nature. *International Relations*, 23(2), 257–270.

Brown, Chris, and Ainley, Kirsten (2009). *Understanding International Relations*. 4th ed. Hampshire; New York: Palgrave Macmillan.

Brown, Sarah (1988). Feminism, international theory, and international relations of gender inequality. *Millennium: Journal of International Studies*, 17(3), 461–475.

Brühl, Jannis (2015). Recht und Ramstein. *Süddeutsche Zeitung*, 28 May 2015.

Brunnée, Jutta, and Toope, Stephen J. (2010a). *Legitimacy and Legality in International Law*. Cambridge: Cambridge University Press.

(2010b). The Responsibility to Protect and the use of force: Building legality? *Global Responsibility to Protect*, 2(3), 191–212.

(2014). The Rule of Law in an Agnostic World: The Prohibition on the Use of Force and Humanitarian Exceptions. https://papers.ssrn.com/sol3/papers.cfm?abstract_id=2547022.

Brunstetter, Daniel R., and Jimenez-Barcadi, Arturo (2015). Clashing over drones: The legal and normative gap between the united states and the human rights community. *The International Journal of Human Rights*, 19(2), 176–198.

Buchanan, Allen (2003). Reforming the international law of humanitarian intervention. In Holzgrefe, Jeff L. and Keohane, Robert O., eds., *Humanitarian Intervention: Ethic, Legal and Political Dilemmas*. Cambridge: Cambridge University Press, 130–173.

(2010). The legitimacy of international law. In Besson, Samantha, and Tasioulas, John, eds., *The Philosophy of International Law*. Oxford: Oxford University Press, 79–96.

Buchanan, Allen, and Keohane, Robert O. (2015a). Toward a drone accountability regime. *Ethics & International Affairs*, 29(1), 15–37.

(2015b). Toward a drone accountability regime: A rejoinder. *Ethics & International Affairs*, 25(1), 67–70.

Buitelaar, Tom, and Hirschmann, Gisela (2021). Criminal accountability at what cost? Norm conflict, UN peace operations and the International Criminal Court. *European Journal of International Relations*, 27(2), 548–571.

Bumke, Christian (2009). Menschenbilder des Rechts. *Jahrbuch des Öffentlichen Rechts der Gegenwart*, 57, 125–148.

Bünte, Marco (2009). Myanmar und die Frage der externen Intervention: Von der „Responsibility to Protect" zum humanitären Dialog. *Die Friedenswarte: Journal of International Peace and Organization*, 84(1), 125–141.

Burchill, Scott (2009). Liberalism. In Burchill, Scott, Linklater, Andrew, Devetak, Richard, Donnelly, Jack, Nardin, Terry, Paterson, Matthew, Reus-Smit, Christian, and True, Jacqui, eds., *Theories of International Relations*. 4th ed. Hampshire; New York: Palgrave Macmillan, 57–85.

Burger, Julian, and Kapron, Mary (2017). Drug policy and indigenous peoples. *Health and Human Rights Journal*, 19(1), 269–278.

Burke-White, William W. (2008). Implementing a policy of positive complementarity in the Rome system of justice. *Criminal Law Forum*, 19(1), 59–85.

Buss, Doris (2016). International criminal courts. In Steans, Jill, and Tepe-Belfrage, Daniela, eds., *Handbook on Gender in World Politics*. Cheltenham: Edward Elgar, 162–170.

Butler, Judith (1993). *Bodies That Matter: On the Discursive Limits of 'Sex'*. New York; London: Routledge.

(1999). *Gender Trouble*. 2nd ed. New York; London: Routledge.

(2004). *Precarious Life*. London; New York: Verso.

Buzan, Barry, and Hansen, Lene (2009). *The Evolution of International Security Studies*. Cambridge: Cambridge University Press.

Byers, Michael, and Chesterman, Simon (2003). Changing the rules about the rules? Unilateral humanitarian intervention and the future of international law. In Holzgrefe, Jeff L. and Keohane, Robert O., eds., *Humanitarian Intervention: Ethic, Legal and Political Dilemmas*. Cambridge: Cambridge University Press, 177–203.

Byrne, Max (2016). Consent and the use of force: An examination of 'intervention by invitation' as a basis for US drone strikes in Pakistan, Somalia and Yemen. *Journal on the Use of Force and International Law*, 3(1), 97–125.

Cacciatori, Mattia (2018). When kings are criminals: Lessons from ICC prosecutions of African presidents. *International Journal of Transitional Justice*, 12(3), 386–406.
Campbell, Kirsten (2013). The making of global legal cultures and international criminal law. *Leiden Journal of International Law*, 26(1), 155–172.
Cannon, Brendon J. (2020). What's in it for us? Armed drone strikes and the security of Somalia's federal government. *Small Wars & Insurgencies*, 31(4), 773–800.
Capasso, Matteo (2014). The Libyan drawers: 'stateless society', 'humanitarian intervention', 'logic of exception' and 'traversing the phantasy'. *Middle East Critique*, 23 (4), 387–404.
Carpenter, R. Charli (2005). 'Women, children and other vulnerable groups': Gender, strategic frames and the protection of civilians as a transnational issue. *International Studies Quarterly*, 49(2), 295–334.
Carver, Terrell (2016). Sex, gender, and sexuality. In Steans, Jill, and Tepe-Belfrage, Daniela, eds., *Handbook on Gender in World Politics*. Cheltenham: Edward Elgar Publishing, 58–65.
Carvin, Stephanie (2012). The trouble with targeted killing. *Security Studies*, 21(3), 529–555.
(2015). Getting drones wrong. *The International Journal of Human Rights*, 19(2), 127–141.
Carvin, Stephanie, and Williams, Michael J. (2015). *Law, Science, Liberalism and the American Way of Warfare*. Cambridge: Cambridge University Press.
Casey-Maslen, Stuart (2014). The use of armed drones. In Casey-Maslen, Stuart, ed., *Weapons under international human rights law*. Cambridge: Cambridge University Press, 382–407.
Cavarero, Adriana (2008). *Horrorism: Naming Contemporary Violence*. New York: Columbia University Press.
Celermajer, Danielle, and Lefebvre, Alexandre (2020a). Introduction: Bringing the subject of human rights into focus. In Celermajer, Danielle, and Lefebvre, Alexandre, eds., *The Subject of Human Rights*. Stanford: Stanford University Press, 1–25.
Celermajer, Danielle, and Lefebvre, Alexandre eds. (2020b). *The Subject of Human Rights*. Stanford: Stanford University Press.
Chamayou, Grégoire (2011). The manhunt doctrine. *Radical Philosophy*, 169, 2–6.
(2014). *Ferngesteuerte Gewalt*. Wien: Passagen Verlag.
Chandler, David (2004). The Responsibility to Protect? Imposing the 'liberal peace'. *International Peacekeeping*, 11(1), 59–81.
(2010). Born posthumously: Rethinking the shared characteristics of the ICC and R2P. *Finnish Yearbook of International Law*, 21, 5–13.
Chappell, Louise A. (2016). *The Politics of Gender Justice at the International Criminal Court: Legacies and Legitimacy*. Oxford; New York: Oxford University Press.
Charlesworth, Hilary (2010). Feminist reflections on the Responsibility to Protect. *Global Responsibility to Protect*, 2(3), 232–249.
(2016). Gender and international law. In Steans, Jill, and Tepe-Belfrage, Daniela, eds., *Handbook on Gender in World Politics*. Cheltenham: Edward Elgar Publishing, 137–144.
Charlesworth, Hilary, and Chinkin, Christine (2000). *The Boundaries of International Law: A Feminist Analysis*. Manchester: Manchester University Press.

Checkel, Jeffrey T. (1998). The constructivist turn in international relations. *World Politics*, 50(2), 324–348.

Chesney, Robert (2010). Who may be killed? Anwar al-Awlaki as a case study in the international legal regulation of lethal force. In Schmitt, Michael N., Arimatsu, Louise, and McCormack, Tim, eds., *Yearbook of International Humanitarian Law – 2010*. The Hague: T. M. C. Asser Press, 3–60.

Chowdhury, Arjun, and Duvall, Raymond (2014). Sovereignty and sovereign power. *International Theory*, 6(2), 191–223.

Chulov, Martin (2015). Syria peace talks pin hopes for end to war on Iran and Saudi Arabia. *The Guardian*, 30 March 2015.

CIA (2009). CIA Best Practices in Counterinsurgency. http://wikileaks.org/cia-hvt-counterinsurgency.

Clarke, Kamari M. (2009). *Fictions of Justice*. Cambridge; New York: Cambridge University Press.

Close, Joseph (2020). The ICC Refrains from Affirming a General Ban on Amnesties in the Gaddafi Admissibility Appeal Decision. https://internationallaw.blog/2020/04/20/the-icc-refrains-from-affirming-a-general-ban-on-amnesties-in-the-gaddafi-admissibility-appeal-decision/.

Cloward, Karisa (2016). *When Norms Collide*. Oxford: Oxford University Press.

Cohen, Jean L. (2004). Whose sovereignty? Empire versus international law. *Ethics & International Affairs*, 18(3), 1–24.

Cohn, Carol (1987). Sex and death in the rational world of defense intellectuals. *Signs*, 12(4), 687–718.

Columbia Law School Human Rights Clinic (2012). Counting Drone Strike Deaths. https://web.law.columbia.edu/sites/default/files/microsites/human-rights-institute/files/COLUMBIACountingDronesFinal.pdf.

Commission of Inquiry into Post-Election Violence (2008). Report of the Commission of Inquiry into Post-Election Violence. https://digitalcommons.law.seattleu.edu/cgi/viewcontent.cgi?article=1004&context=tjrc-gov.

Conley-Zilkic, Bridget (2014). Who is the subject of atrocities prevention? *Global Responsibility to Protect*, 6(4), 430–452.

Cook, Martin L. (2016). Ethical issues in targeting. In Ducheine, Paul A., Schmitt, Michael N., and Osinga, Frans P., eds., *Targeting: The Challenges of Modern Warfare*. The Hague; Heidelberg; New York: T. M. C. Asser Press; Springer, 147–158.

Corsi, Jessica L. (2017). Drone deaths violate human rights: The applicability of the ICCPR to civilian deaths caused by drones. *International Human Rights Law Review*, 6(2), 205–241.

Council of Europe (2015). Drones and Targeted Killings: The Need to Uphold Human Rights and International Law. (Doc. 13731). http://assembly.coe.int/nw/xml/XRef/X2H-Xref-ViewPDF.asp?FileID=21580&lang=en.

Cox, Robert W. (1981). Social forces, states and world orders: Beyond international relations theory. *Millennium: Journal of International Studies*, 10(2), 126–155.

Craig, Katherine (2014). Tod vom Himmel. *Süddeutsche Zeitung*, 26 July 2014.

Crawford, Emily (2014). Terrorism and targeted killings under international law. In Saul, Ben, ed., *Research Handbook on International Law and Terrorism*. Cheltenham; Northhampton: Edward Elgar, 250–270.

(2015a). *Identifying the Enemy*. Oxford: Oxford University Press.
Crawford, James R., and Watkins, Jeremy (2010). International responsibility. In Besson, Samantha, and Tasioulas, John, eds., *The Philosophy of International Law*. Oxford: Oxford University Press, 283–298.
Crawford, Neta C. (2000). The passion of world politics: Propositions on emotion and emotional relationships. *International Security*, 24(4), 116–156.
(2013). *Accountability for Killing*. Oxford: Oxford University Press.
(2015b). Accountability for Targeted Drone Strikes Against Terrorists? *Ethics & International Affairs*, 25(1), 39–49.
Crilly, Rob (2018). Gaddafi's son saif 'to run for Libyan president' in 2018 elections. *The Telegraph*, 20 March 2018.
Crossley, Noele (2020). Consistency, protection, responsibility. *Global Governance: A Review of Multilateralism and International Organizations*, 26(3), 473–499.
Crosston, Matthew (2014). Pandora's presumption: Drones and the problematic ethics of techno-war. *Journal of Strategic Security*, 7(4), 1–24.
C-SPAN (2002). Defense Department Briefing. www.c-span.org/video/?168635-1/defense-department-briefing.
Çubukçu, Ayça (2013). The Responsibility to Protect: Libya and the problem of transnational solidarity. *Journal of Human Rights*, 12(1), 40–58.
Cudworth, Erika, and Hobden, Stephen (2013a). Complexity, ecologism, and posthuman politics. *Review of International Studies*, 39(3), 643–664.
(2013b). Of parts and wholes: International relations beyond the human. *Millennium: Journal of International Studies*, 41(3), 430–450.
Cunliffe, Philip (2016). From ISIS to ICISS: A critical return to the Responsibility to Protect report. *Cooperation and Conflict*, 51(2), 233–247.
Cunliffe, Philip, and Kenkel, Kai M. (2016). Rising powers and intervention: Contested norms and shifts in global order. *Cambridge Review of International Affairs*, 29(3), 807–811.
Cusumano, Eugenio (2019). Migrant rescue as organized hypocrisy: EU maritime missions offshore Libya between humanitarianism and border control. *Cooperation and Conflict*, 54(1), 3–24.
Cutler, Leonard (2017). *President Obama's Counterterrorism Strategy in the War on Terror: An Assessment*. New York: Palgrave Macmillan.
Daase, Christopher (1999). *Kleine Kriege – Große Wirkung*. Baden-Baden: Nomos Verlagsgesellschaft.
(2013). Die Legalisierung der Legitimität – Zur Kritik der Schutzverantwortung als emerging norm. In Daase, Christopher, and Junk, Julian, eds., *Die Friedenswarte: Journal of International Peace and Organization*, 88(1–2), 41–62.
Dalhaus, Nora (2015). The *responsibility while protecting*—Brazil's attempt to frame the R2P debate. In Staack, Michael, and Krause, Dan, eds., *Schutzverantwortung in der Debatte*. Opladen; Berlin; Toronto: Verlag Barbara Budrich, 217–228.
Davies, Bronwyn, and Harré, Rom (1990). Positioning: The discursive production of selves. *Journal for the Theory of Social Behaviour*, 20(1), 43–63.
Davis, Lynn E., McNerney, Michael J., and Greenberg, Michael D. (2016). Clarifying the Rules for Targeted Killing: An Analytical Framework for Policies Involving Long-Range Armed Drones. C www.rand.org/pubs/research_reports/RR1610.html.

de Búrca, Gráinne (2010). The European Court of Justice and the international legal order after Kadi. *Harvard International Law Journal*, 51(1), 1–49.

de Vos, Christian M. (2020). *Complementarity, Catalysts, Compliance: The International Criminal Court in Uganda, Kenya, and the Democratic Republic of Congo*. Cambridge: Cambridge University Press.

de Waal, Alexander (2013). African roles in the Libyan conflict of 2011. *International Affairs*, 89(2), 365–379.

de Wet, Erika (2006). The international constitutional order. *International & Comparative Law Quarterly*, 55(1), 55–76.

de Wet, Erika, and Vidmar, Jure (2013). Conflicts between international paradigms: Hierarchy versus systemic integration. *Global Constitutionalism - Human Rights, Democracy and the Rule of Law*, 2(2), 196–217.

Deeks, Ashley S. (2012). 'Unwilling or unable': Toward a normative framework for extraterritorial self-defense. *Virginia Journal of International Law*, 52(3), 483–550.

deGuzman, Margaret M. (2012). How serious are international crimes? The gravity problem in international criminal law. *Columbia Journal of Transnational Law*, 51, 18–68.

Deitelhoff, Nicole (2006). *Überzeugung in der Politik: Grundzüge einer Diskurstheorie internationalen Regierens*. Frankfurt am Main: Suhrkamp Verlag.

(2009). The discursive process of legalization: Charting islands of persuasion in the ICC case. *International Organization*, 63(1), 33–65.

Deitelhoff, Nicole, and Zimmermann, Lisbeth (2019). Norms under challenge: Unpacking the dynamics of norm robustness. *Journal of Global Security Studies*, 4(1), 2–17.

(2020). Things we lost in the fire: How different types of contestation affect the robustness of international norms. *International Studies Review*, 22(1), 51–76.

Della Porta, Donatella, and Keating, Michael (2008a). How many approaches in the social sciences? An epistemological introduction. In Della Porta, Donatella, and Keating, Michael, eds., *Approaches and Methodologies in the Social Sciences*. Cambridge: Cambridge University Press, 19–39.

(2008b). Introduction. In Della Porta, Donatella, and Keating, Michael, eds., *Approaches and Methodologies in the Social Sciences*. Cambridge: Cambridge University Press, 1–15.

Deng, Francis M., Kimaro, Sadikiel, Lyons, Terrence, Rothschild, Donald, and Zartman, W. I. (1996). *Sovereignty as Responsibility: Conflict Management in Africa*. Washington, DC: Brookings.

Diez, Thomas, Bode, Ingvild, and Fernandes da Costa, Aleksandra (2011). *Key Concepts in International Relations*. London: SAGE.

Dill, Janina (2015a). *Legitimate Targets?* Cambridge: Cambridge University Press.

(2015b). The informal regulation of drones and the formal legal regulation of war. *Ethics & International Affairs*, 25(1), 51–58.

(2019). Do attackers have a legal duty of care? Limits to the 'individualization of war'. *International Theory*, 11(1), 1–25.

Dingwerth, Klaus,and Witt, Antonia (2020). Towards a Typology of Pathways: The Rise of People-Centred Norms in the Legitimation of Global Governance Organizations. Paper presented at the IB-Sektionstagung 7.–9.10.2020 Freiburg (online). On file with author.

Dingwerth, Klaus, Witt, Antonia, Lehmann, Ina, Reichel, Ellen, and Weise, Tobias (2019). *International Organizations Under Pressure*. 1st ed. Oxford: Oxford University Press.

Director of National Intelligence (2016). Summary of Information Regarding U.S. Counterterrorism Strikes Outside Areas of Active Hostilities. www.dni.gov/files/documents/Newsroom/Press%20Releases/DNI+Release+on+CT+Strikes+Outside+Areas+of+Active+Hostilities.PDF.

Dixon, Martin (2007). *Textbook on International Law*. 6th ed. Oxford; New York: Oxford University Press.

(2013). *Textbook on International Law*. 7th ed. Oxford: Oxford University Press.

Doezema, Jo (2005). Now you see her, now you don't: Sex workers at the UN trafficking protocol negotiation. *Social & Legal Studies*, 14(1), 61–89.

Dombrowski, Peter (1998). Fragmenting identities, shifting loyalties: The influence of individualisation on global transformations. *Global Society*, 12(3), 363–388.

Donnelly, Jack (2007). The relative universality of human rights. *Human Rights Quarterly*, 29(2), 281–306.

(2009). Realism. In Burchill, Scott, Linklater, Andrew, Devetak, Richard, Donnelly, Jack, Nardin, Terry, Paterson, Matthew, Reus-Smit, Christian, and True, Jacqui, eds., *Theories of International Relations*. 4th ed. Hampshire: Palgrave Macmillan, 31–56.

Donovan, Outi (2021). Trading freedoms for protection: Gender and localised protection in Libya. *Global Responsibility to Protect*, 13(4), 458–480.

Doty, Roxanne L. (1993). Foreign policy as social construction: A post-positivist analysis of U.S. counterinsurgency policy in the Philippines. *International Studies Quarterly*, 37(3), 297–320.

Douven, Igor (2011). Peirce on Abduction. http://plato.stanford.edu/entries/abduction/peirce.html.

Dresing, Thorsten, and Pehl, Thorsten (2015). Manual (On) Transcription: Transcription Conventions, Software Guides and Practical Hints for Qualitative Researchers. www.audiotranskription.de/english/manual-on-transcription.htm.

Droege, Cordula (2007). The interplay between international humanitarian law and international human rights law in situations of armed conflict. *Israel Law Review*, 40(2), 310–355.

Drumbl, Mark A. (2005). Collective violence and individual punishment: The criminality of mass atrocity. *Northwestern University Law Review*, 99(2), 539–610.

du Plessis, Max, and Louw, Antoinette (2011). Justice and the Libyan Crisis: The ICC's Role Under Security Council Resolution 1970. https://reliefweb.int/sites/reliefweb.int/files/resources/Full_Report_1087.pdf.

Dunford, Robin, and Neu, Michael (2019). The Responsibility to Protect in a world of already existing intervention. *European Journal of International Relations*, 25(4), 1080–1102.

Dunne, Timothy, Kurki, Milja, and Smith, Steve, eds. (2020). *International Relations Theories*. 5th ed. Oxford: Oxford University Press.

Dunoff, Jeffrey L., and Pollack, Mark A. (2013). International law and international relations: Introducing an interdisciplinary dialogue. In Dunoff, Jeffrey L., and Pollack, Mark A., eds., *Interdisciplinary Perspectives on International Law and International Relations*. Cambridge: Cambridge University Press, 3–32.

Eckes, Christina (2013). Individuals in a pluralist world: The implications of counter-terrorist sanctions. *Global Constitutionalism – Human Rights, Democracy and the Rule of Law*, 2(2), 218–236.

Edkins, Jenny, and Pin-Fat, Véronique (1999). The subject of the political. In Edkins, Jenny, Persram, Nalini, and Pin-Fat, Véronique, eds., *Sovereignty and Subjectivity*. Boulder; London: Lynne Rienner, 1–18.

Efrat, Asif (2015). Cross-national interviewing at international conferences: How to make the most of a unique research opportunity. *International Studies Perspectives*, 16(3), 302–311.

Ekelhof, Merel A. (2017). Complications of a common language: Why it is so hard to talk about autonomous weapons. *Journal of Conflict & Security Law*, 22(2), 311–331.

Emmerson, Ben (2013). Report of the Special Rapporteur on the Promotion and Protection of Human Rights and Fundamental Freedoms While Countering Terrorism. (A/68/389). https://digitallibrary.un.org/record/759181?ln=en.

Endoh, Fabrice T. (2020). African Union and the politics of selective prosecutions at the International Criminal Court. *African Journal of International Criminal Justice*, 6(1), 3–32.

Endoh, Fabrice T., and Mbao, M. L. Melvin (2016). Political dynamics in Kenya's post-electoral violence: Justice without peace or political compromise? *African Security Review*, 25(3), 275–287.

Enemark, Christian (2014). Drones, risk, and perpetual force. *Ethics & International Affairs*, 28(3), 365–381.

Engelkamp, Stephan, Glaab, Katharina, and Graf, Antonia, eds. (2021). *Kritische Normenforschung in den Internationalen Beziehungen*. 1. Auflage; Baden-Baden: Nomos; Nomos Verlagsgesellschaft.

Engelkamp, Stephan, Glaab, Katharina, and Renner, Judith (2012). In der Sprechstunde. *Zeitschrift für Internationale Beziehungen*, 19(2), 101–128.

(2013). Ein Schritt vor, zwei Schritte zurück? Eine Replik auf Nicole Deitelhoff und Lisbeth Zimmermann. *Zeitschrift für Internationale Beziehungen*, 20(2), 105–118.

English, Nicholas, and Rauschning, Tim (2013). The procurement and use of armed UAVs by the German military in international and German law. *German Yearbook of International Law*, 56, 539–555.

Enloe, Cynthia (2014). *Bananas, Beaches and Bases: Making Feminist Sense of International Politics*. 2nd ed. Berkley; Los Angeles; London: University of California Press.

Epstein, Charlotte (2013). Theorizing agency in Hobbes's wake: The rational actor, the self, or the speaking subject? *International Organization*, 67(2), 287–316.

Erameh, Nicholas I. (2017). Humanitarian intervention, Syria and the politics of human rights protection. *The International Journal of Human Rights*, 21(5), 517–530.

Erskine, Toni (2008). Locating responsibility: The problem of moral agency in international relations. In Reus-Smit, Christian, and Snidal, Duncan, eds., *The Oxford Handbook of International Relations*. Oxford: Oxford University Press, 699–707.

European Center for Constitutional and Human Rights (2017). Litigating Drone Strikes: Challenging the Global Network of Remote Killing. https://www.ecchr.eu/fileadmin/Publikationen/Litigating_Drone_Strikes_PDF.pdf.

Evers, Miles M. (2020). Just the facts: Why norms remain relevant in an age of practice. *International Theory*, 12(2), 220–230.

Fabri, Hélene R. (2008). Human rights and state sovereignty: Have the boundaries been significantly redrawn. In MacDonald, Euan, and Alston, Philip, eds., *Human Rights, Intervention, and the Use of Force*. Oxford: Oxford University Press.

Fairclough, Norman, and Wodak, Ruth (1997). Critical Discourse Analysis. In van Dijk, Teujn Adrianus, ed., *Discourse as Social Interaction*. London: SAGE, 258–285.

Fann, Kuni T. (1970). *Peirce's Theory of Abduction*. The Hague: Martinus Nijhoff.

Farer, Tom. (2003). Humanitarian intervention before and after 9/11: Legality and legitimacy. In Holzgrefe, Jeff L., and Keohane, Robert O., eds., *Humanitarian Intervention: Ethic, Legal and Political Dilemmas*. Cambridge: Cambridge University Press, 53–89.

Faude, Benjamin, and Fuß, Julia (2020). Coordination or conflict? The causes and consequences of institutional overlap in a disaggregated world order. *Global Constitutionalism – Human Rights, Democracy and the Rule of Law*, 9(2), 268–289.

Fehl, Caroline (2018). Navigating Norm Complexity: A Shared Research Agenda for Diverse Constructivist Perspectives. (HFSK Working Papers No. 41). www.hsfk.de/fileadmin/HSFK/hsfk_publikationen/PRIF_WP_41.pdf.

(2019). Bombs, trials, and rights: Norm complexity and the evolution of liberal intervention practices. *Human Rights Quarterly*, 41(4), 839–915.

Fierke, Karin M. (2001). Critical methodology and constructivism. In Fierke, Karin M., and Jørgensen, Knud E., eds., *Constructing International Relations*. Armonk; London: M. E. Sharpe, 115–135.

(2010). Constructivism. In Dunne, Timothy, Kurki, Milja, and Smith, Steve, eds., *International Relations Theories: Discipline and Diversity*. 2nd ed. Oxford: Oxford University Press, 177–194.

(2013). *Political Self-Sacrifice*. Cambridge: Cambridge University Press.

Fierke, Karin M., and Jørgensen, Knud E. (2001). Introduction. In Fierke, Karin M., and Jørgensen, Knud E., eds., *Constructing International Relations*. Armonk; London: M. E. Sharpe, 3–10.

Finkelstein, Claire (2012a). Preface. In Finkelstein, Claire, Ohlin, Jens D., and Altman, Andrew, eds., *Targeted Killing*. Oxford: Oxford University Press, v–x.

(2012b). Targeted Killing as Preemptive Action. In Finkelstein, Claire, Ohlin, Jens D., and Altman, Andrew, eds., *Targeted Killing*. Oxford: Oxford University Press, 156–182.

Finnemore, Martha (1996). Constructing Norms of Humanitarian Intervention. In Katzenstein, Peter J., ed., *The Culture of National Security. Norms and Identity in World Politics*. New York: Columbia University Press, 153–185.

Finnemore, Martha, and Sikkink, Kathryn (1998). International norm dynamics and political change. *International Organization*, 52(4), 887–917.

Fischer-Lescano, Andreas, and Teubner, Gunther (2004). Regime-collisions. *Michigan Journal of International Law*, 25(4), 999–1046.

Flick, Uwe (2003). Design und Prozess qualitativer Forschung. In Flick, Uwe, von Kardorff, Ernst, and Steinke, Ines, eds., *Qualitative Forschung*. 2nd ed. Reinbek bei Hamburg: Rowohlt Taschenbuch Verlag GmbH, 252–265.

Flick, Uwe, Kardorff, Ernst von, and Steinke, Ines, eds. (2003). *Qualitative Forschung*. 2nd ed. Reinbek bei Hamburg: Rowohlt Taschenbuch Verlag GmbH.

Flonk, Daniëlle, Jachtenfuchs, Markus, and Obendiek, Anke S. (2020). Authority conflicts in internet governance: Liberals vs. Sovereigntists? *Global Constitutionalism – Human Rights, Democracy and the Rule of Law*, 9(2), 364–386.

Flynn, Gregory, and Farrell, Henry (1999). Piecing together the democratic peace: The CSCE, norms and the 'construction' of security in post-cold war Europe. *International Organization*, 53(3), 505–535.

Føllesdal, Andreas (2020). Survey article: The legitimacy of international courts. *Journal of Political Philosophy*, 28(4), 476–499.

Forsythe, David P. (2013). 'Political trials'? The UN Security Council and the development of international criminal law. In Schabas, William A., McDermott, Yvonne, and Hayes, Niamh, eds., *The Ashgate Research Companion to International Criminal Law: Critical Perspectives*. Surrey; Burlington: Ashgate, 475–497.

(2018). *Human Rights in International Relations*. Cambridge: Cambridge University Press.

France; Germany; Portugal; and United Kingdom (2011). Draft Resolution 04.10.2015. www.securitycouncilreport.org/atf/cf/%7B65BFCF9B-6D27-4E9C-8CD3-CF6E4FF96FF9%7D/Syria%20S2011%20612.pdf.

Franke, Ulrich and Roos, Ulrich (2013). Einleitung: Zu den Begriffen 'Weltpolitik' und 'Rekonstruktion'. In Franke, Ulrich, and Roos, Ulrich, eds., *Rekonstruktive Methoden der Weltpolitikforschung*. Baden-Baden: Nomos Verlagsgesellschaft, 7–29.

Franke, Ulrike E. (2014). Drones, drone strikes, and US policy: The politics of unmanned aerial vehicles (review essay). *Parameters*, 44(1), 121–130.

(2015). The global diffusion of unmanned aerial vehicles (UAVs), or 'drones'. In Aaronson, Mike, Aslam, Wali, Dyson, Tom, and Rauxloh, Regina, eds., *Precision Strike Warfare and International Intervention*. Oxon: Routledge, 52–72.

Frankenberg, Gunter (2011). Down by law: Irony, seriousness, and reason. *German Law Journal*, 12(1), 300–337.

Franz, Nina (2017). Targeted killing and pattern-of-life analysis: Weaponised media. *Media, Culture & Society*, 39(1), 111–121.

Freeden, Michael, and Stears, Marc (2013). Liberalism. In Freeden, Michael, Sargent, Lyman T., and Stears, Marc, eds., *The Oxford Handbook of Political Ideologies*. Oxford: Oxford University Press, 329–347.

Freyberg-Inan, Annette (2004). *What Moves Man*. Albany: State University of New York Press.

Frick, Marie-Luisa (2021). Dehumanization and human rights. In Kronfeldner, Maria, ed., *The Routledge Handbook of Dehumanization*. Abingdon; Oxon; New York: Routledge, 187–200.

Friedrichs, Jörg (2009). From positivist pretense to pragmatic practice: Varieties of pragmatic methodology in IR scholarship. In Hellmann, Gunther, ed., *International Studies Review*. 11(3), Pragmatism and International Relations, 645–648.

Friedrichs, Jörg, and Kratochwil, Friedrich V. (2009). On acting and knowing: How pragmatism can advance international relations research and methodology. *International Organization*, 63(4), 701–731.

Friesendorf, Cornelius (2019). Selbstschutz und Fremdschutz als Normenkonflikt? *Zeitschrift für Internationale Beziehungen*, 26(1), 59–88.
Frost, Mervyn, and Lechner, Silviya (2016). Understanding international practices from the internal point of view. *Journal of International Political Theory*, 12(3), 299–319.
Frowe, Helen (2014). *Defensive Killing*. 1st ed. Oxford: Oxford University Press.
Fujii, Lee A. (2018). *Interviewing in Social Science Research*. New York; Abingdon; Oxon: Routledge.
Fuller, Lon L. (1964). *The Morality of Law*. New Haven: Yale University Press.
Fung, Courtney J. (2020). Rhetorical adaptation, normative resistance and international order-making: China's advancement of the responsibility to protect. *Cooperation and Conflict*, 55(2), 193–215.
Gallagher, Adrian (2013). *Genocide and Its Threat to Contemporary International Order*. Houndmills; Basingstoke; Hampshire; New York: Palgrave Macmillan.
(2016). Conceptualizing humanity in the English school. *International Theory*, 8(2), 341–364.
Gallagher, Adrian, and Ralph, Jason (2013). Syria: Can Legitimacy for Intervention Be Found in a Uniting for Peace Resolution? www.bss.leeds.ac.uk/2013/09/05/syria-can-legitimacy-for-intervention-be-found-in-a-uniting-for-peace-resolution/.
Ganor, Boaz (2014). Identifying the enemy in counterterrorism operations – A comparison of the Bush and Obama administrations. *International Law Studies*, 90, 341–360.
Garbett, Claire (2015). *The Concept of the Civilian*. Oxford; New York: Routledge.
García Iommi, Lucrecia (2020). Whose justice? The ICC 'Africa problem'. *International Relations*, 34(1), 105–129.
Gardam, Judith (1997). Women and the law of armed conflict: Why the silence? *International and Comparative Law Quarterly*, 46(1), 55–80.
Garwood-Gowers, Andrew (2015). R2P ten years after the world summit: Explaining ongoing contestation over pillar III. *Global Responsibility to Protect*, 7(3–4), 300–324.
Gegout, Catherine, and Suzuki, Shogo (2020). China, Responsibility to Protect, and the case of Syria. *Global Governance: A Review of Multilateralism and International Organizations*, 26(3), 379–402.
Geneva Conventions Protocol Additional to the Geneva Conventions of 12 August 1949, and Relating to the Protection of Victims of International Armed Conflicts (Protocol I) (1977). www.icrc.org/applic/ihl/ihl.nsf/Treaty.xsp?action=openDocument&documentId=D9E6B6264D7723C3C12563CD002D6CE4.
George, Terry (2004). *Hotel Rwanda*. Sydney: MGM Distributions.
Gerges, Fawaz A. (2016). *ISIS: A History*. Princeton: Princeton University Press.
Gettinger, Dan (2019). The Drone Databook. https://dronecenter.bard.edu/projects/drone-proliferation/databook/.
Gevers, Christopher (2020). Africa and international criminal law. In Heller, Kevin J., Mégret, Frédéric, Nouwen, Sarah M., Ohlin, Jens D., and Robinson, Darryl, eds., *The Oxford Handbook of International Criminal Law*. Oxford: Oxford University Press, 154–193.
Ghezelbash, Daniel, Moreno-Lax, Violeta, Klein, Natalie, and Opeskin, Brian (2018). Securitization of search and rescue at sea: The response to boat migration in the

Mediterranean and offshore Australia. *International & Comparative Law Quarterly*, 67(2), 315–351.

Gholiagha, Sassan (2013). From Kosovo to Syria—Why R2P Is of No Use If the UN Security Council Is Unable to Act Together. https://verfassungsblog.de/from-kosovo-to-syria-why-r2p-is-of-no-use-if-the-un-security-council-is-unable-to-act-together/.

(2014a). Die Responsibility to Protect und Souveränität. In Volk, Christian, and Kuntz, Friederike, eds., *Der Begriff der Souveränität in der transnationalen Konstellation*. Baden-Baden: Nomos Verlagsgesellschaft, 198–214.

(2014b). The Responsibility to Protect: Words, deeds, and humanitarian interventions – A review essay. *Journal of International Political Theory*, 10(3), 361–370.

(2015a). Individualized and yet dehumanized? Targeted killing via drones. *Behemoth*, 8(2), 128–153.

(2015b). To prevent 'future Kosovos and future Rwandas': A critical constructivist view on the responsibility to protect. *International Journal of Human Rights*, 19(8), 1074–1097.

Gholiagha, Sassan, Hansen-Magnusson, Hannes, and Hofius, Maren (2021). Meaning-in-use: Zum Verhältnis von Normativität und Normalität in der Normenforschung. In Engelkamp, Stephan, Glaab, Katharina, and Graf, Antonia, eds., *Kritische Normenforschung in Deutschland. Neue Wege in den Internationalen Beziehungen*. Baden-Baden: Nomos Verlagsgesellschaft, 221–249.

Gholiagha, Sassan, Holzscheiter, Anna, and Liese, Andrea (2020a). Activating norm collisions: Interface conflicts in international drug control. *Global Constitutionalism – Human Rights, Democracy and the Rule of Law*, 9(2), 290–317.

(2020b). *When Norms Collide: The COVID-19 Pandemic and Difficult Choices on the Hierarchy of Norms and Values*. Duck of Minerva. www.duckofminerva.com/2020/05/when-norms-collide-the-covid-19-pandemic-and-difficult-choices-on-the-hierarchy-of-norms-and-values.html.

Gholiagha, Sassan, and Loges, Bastian (2020). Telling the story of R2P: The emplotment of R2P in the UN Security Council's debates on Libya. In Hunt, Charles T., and Orchard, Phil, eds., *Constructing the Responsibility to Protect*. Abingdon; Oxon; New York: Routledge, 69–88.

Gholiagha, Sassan, and Wiener, Antje (2013). Responsibility to Protect. https://verfassungsblog.de/responsibility-to-protect-a-political-science-perspective-on-the-international-law-section-of-the-coalition-agreement/.

Giddens, Anthony (1993). *New Rules of Sociological Method*. 2nd ed. Stanford: Stanford University Press.

Gifkins, Jess (2016). R2P in the UN Security Council: Darfur, Libya, and beyond. *Cooperation and Conflict*, 5(2), 148–165.

Gil Gil, Alicia, and Maculan, Elena (2015). Current trends in the definition of 'perpetrator' by the International Criminal Court: From the decision on the confirmation of charges in the *Lubanga* case to the *Katanga* judgment. *Leiden Journal of International Law*, 28(2), 349–371.

Gildemeister, Regine (2003). Geschlechterforschung (gender studies). In Flick, Uwe, von Kardorff, Ernst, and Steinke, Ines, eds., *Qualitative Forschung*. 2nd ed. Reinbek bei Hamburg: Rowohlt Taschenbuch Verlag GmbH, 213–223.

Gillespie, Alex, and Cornish, Flora (2014). Sensitizing questions: A method to facilitate analyzing the meaning of an utterance. *Integrative Psychological & Behavioral Science*, 48(4), 435–452.
Giumelli, Francesco, and Costa Buranelli, Filippo (2020). When states and individuals meet: The UN ombudsperson as a 'contact point' between international and world society. *International Relations*, 34(1), 46–66.
Glanville, Luke (2014). Armed humanitarian intervention and the problem of abuse after Libya. In Scheid, Don E., ed., *The Ethics of Armed Humanitarian Intervention*. Cambridge: Cambridge University Press, 148–165.
(2016). Does R2P matter? Interpreting the impact of a norm. *Cooperation and Conflict*, 51(2), 184–199.
Global Centre for the Responsibility to Protect (2021). UN Security Council Resolutions and Presidential Statements Referencing R2P. www.globalr2p.org/resources/un-security-council-resolutions-and-presidential-statements-referencing-r2p/.
Goetz, John, and Winkler, Willi (2014). Die kalte Sprache des gezielten Tötens. *Süddeutsche Zeitung*, 19 December 2014.
Gómez-Mera, Laura (2016). Regime complexity and global governance: The case of trafficking in persons. *European Journal of International Relations*, 22(3), 566–595.
Goppel, Anna (2013). *Killing Terrorists*. Berlin: de Gruyter.
Gorlick, Brian (2000). Human rights and refugees: Enhancing protection through international human rights law. *Nordic Journal of International Law*, 69(2), 117–177.
Gorski, Simone (2011). Individuals in International Law. In *Max Planck Encyclopedia of Public International Law*. https://opil.ouplaw.com/home/mpil.
Gött, Henner (2013). Die Lehre von den Völkerrechtssubjekten und die Entfaltung der internationalen Rechtsordnung. www.juwiss.de/die-lehre-von-den-volkerrechtssubjekten-und-die-entfaltung-der-internationalen-rechtsordnung/.
Grant, Rebecca (1991). The source of gender bias in international relations theory. In Grant, Rebecca, and Newland, Kathleen, eds., *Gender and International Relations*. Bloomington; Indianapolis: Indiana University Press, 8–26.
Grant, Rebecca, and Newland, Kathleen (1991). Introduction. In Grant, Rebecca, and Newland, Kathleen, eds., *Gender and International Relations*. Bloomington; Indianapolis: Indiana University Press, 1–7.
Gray, Christine (2008). *International Law and the Use of Force*. 3rd ed. Oxford: Oxford University Press.
(2013). Targeted killings: Recent US attempts to create a legal framework. *Current Legal Problems*, 66(1), 75–106.
Grayson, Kyle, and Mawdsley, Jocelyn (2019). Scopic regimes and the visual turn in international relations: Seeing world politics through the drone. *European Journal of International Relations*, 25(2), 431–457.
Gregory, Derek (2015a). Angry Eyes (1). http://geographicalimaginations.com/2015/10/01/angry-eyes-1/.
Gregory, Thomas (2012). Potential lives, impossible deaths. *International Feminist Journal of Politics*, 14(3), 327–347.
(2015b). Drones, targeted killings, and the limitations of international law. *International Political Sociology*, 9(3), 197–212.

(2016). Dismembering the dead: Violence, vulnerability and the body in war. *European Journal of International Relations*, 22(4), 944–965.

(2017). Targeted killings: Drones, noncombatant immunity, and the politics of killing. *Contemporary Security Policy*, 38(2), 212–236.

(2020). The costs of war: Condolence payments and the politics of killing civilians. *Review of International Studies*, 46(1), 156–176.

Grieco, Joseph, Ikenberry, G. J., and Mastanduno, Michael (2019). *Introduction to International Relations: Perspectives, Connections, and Enduring Questions*. London: Macmillan; Red Globe Press.

Gromes, Thorsten, and Dembinski, Matthias (2019). Practices and outcomes of humanitarian military interventions: A new data set. *International Interactions*, 45(6), 1032–1048.

Gross, Michael L. (2006). Assassination and targeted killing: Law enforcement, execution or self-defence? *Journal of Applied Philosophy*, 23(3), 323–335.

Großklaus, Mathias (2017). Friction, not erosion: Assassination norms at the fault line between sovereignty and liberal values. *Contemporary Security Policy*, 38(2), 260–280.

Gubrium, Jaber F., Holstein, James A., Marvasti, Amir B., and McKinney, Amir B., eds. (2012). *The SAGE Handbook of Interview Research: The Complexity of the Craft*. Thousand Oaks: SAGE.

Guiora, Amos N. (2013). *Legitimate Target*. Oxford: Oxford University Press.

Guzzini, Stefano (1993). Structural power: The limits of neorealist power analysis. *International Organization*, 47(3), 443–478.

(2000). A reconstruction of constructivism in international relations. *European Journal of International Relations*, 6(2), 147–182.

Haacke, Jürgen (2009). Myanmar, the Responsibility to Protect, and the need for practical assistance. *Global Responsibility to Protect*, 1(2), 156–184.

Habermas, Jürgen (1999). Bestialität und Humanität: Ein Krieg an der Grenze zwischen Recht und Moral. *Die ZEIT*, 29 April 1999.

Haddad, Bassam (2015). Four Years on: Now Easy Answers in Syria (Part 1). www.jadaliyya.com/Details/31890/Four-Years-On-No-Easy-Answers-in-Syria-Part-1.

Hafner-Burton, Emily (2013). *Making Human Rights a Reality*. Princeton: Princeton University Press.

Hahn, Kristina, and Holzscheiter, Anna (2013). The ambivalence of advocacy: Representation and contestation in global NGO advocacy for child workers and sex workers. *Global Society*, 27(4), 497–520.

Hailbronner, Kay (2007). Der Staat und der Einzelne als Völkerrechtssubjekt. In Graf Vitzthum, Wolfgang, ed., *Völkerrecht*. 4th ed. Berlin: de Gruyter, 217–325.

Hakimi, Monica (2014). Toward a legal theory on the Responsibility to Protect. *The Yale Journal of International Law*, 39(2), 247–280.

Halberstam, Daniel, and Stein, Eric (2009). The United Nations, the European Union, and the King of Sweden: Economic sanctions and individual rights in a plural world order. *Common Market Law Review*, 46, 13–72.

Hall, Stephanie (2014). Help wanted: American drone program needs multifaceted support to be effective. *Journal of Strategic Security*, 7(4), 57–80.

Hammady, Omar (2018). What went wrong with Libya's failed elections. *Foreign Policy*. https://foreignpolicy.com/2022/02/18/libya-elections-2021-postponed/.

Hanrieder, Tine (2011). The false promise of the better argument. *International Theory*, 3(3), 390–415.
Hansen, Lene (2006). *Security as Practice*. Oxford; New York: Routledge.
Hansen-Magnusson, Hannes (2020). *International Relations as Politics among People*. Abingdon; Oxon; New York: Routledge.
Hansen-Magnusson, Hannes, and Vetterlein, Antje, eds. (2020). *The Rise of Responsibility in World Politics*. Cambridge: Cambridge University Press.
Harding, Sandra (1986). The instability of the analytical categories of feminist theory. *Signs*, 11(4), 645–664.
Harper, Douglas (2021a). Guilty. www.etymonline.com/word/guilty.
(2021b). Innocence.www.etymonline.com/word/innocence.
Harré, Rom, and van Langenhove, Luk, eds. (1999a). *Positioning Theory: Moral Contexts of Intentional Action*. Malden, MA: Blackwell.
(1999b). The dynamics of social episodes. In Harré, Rom, and van Langenhove, Luk, eds., *Positioning Theory: Moral Contexts of Intentional Action*. Malden: Blackwell, 1–13.
Harris Rimmer, Susan (2015). Is the Responsibility to Protect doctrine gender-neutral. In Thakur, Ramesh, and Maley, William, eds., *Theorising the Responsibility to Protect*. Cambridge: Cambridge University Press, 266–284.
Hartsock, Nancy C. (1987). The feminist standpoint: Developing the ground for a specifically feminist historical materialism. In Harding, Sandra, ed., *Feminism and Methodology: Social Science Issues*. Bloomington; Indianapolis: Indiana University Press, 157–180.
Hay, Colin (2002). *Political Analysis*. Houndmills; Basingstoke; Hampshire; New York: Palgrave Macmillan.
Hehir, Aidan (2010). The Responsibility to Protect: 'sound and fury signifying nothing'? *International Relations*, 24(2), 218–239.
(2011). The Responsibility to Protect in international political discourse: Encouraging statement of intent or illusory platitudes? *The International Journal of Human Rights*, 15(8), 1331–1348.
(2012). *The Responsibility to Protect*. Houndsmill: Palgrave Macmillan.
(2016). Assessing the influence of the Responsibility to Protect on the UN Security Council during the Arab Spring. *Cooperation and Conflict*, 51(2), 166–183.
(2018a). *Hollow Norms and the Responsibility to Protect*. Cham: Palgrave Macmillan.
(2018b). The lack of 'responsibility' in the Responsibility to Protect. In Ulbert, Cornelia, Finkenbusch, Peter, Sondermann, Elena, and Debiel, Tobias, eds., *Moral Agency and the Politics of Responsibility*. London; New York: Routledge, 71–84.
Hehir, Aidan, and Pattison, James (2016). Introduction: The Responsibility to Protect after the Arab Spring. *Cooperation and Conflict*, 51(2), 141–147.
Helfferich, Cornelia (2011). *Die Qualität qualitativer Daten*. 4th ed. Wiesbaden: VS Verlag für Sozialwissenschaften.
Heller, Joseph (1961). *Catch-22*. New York: Simon and Schuster.
Heller, Kevin J. (2006). The shadow side of complementarity: The effect of article 17 of the Rome Statute on national due process. *Criminal Law Forum*, 17(3–4), 255–280.

(2013). 'One hell of a killing machine'. *Journal of International Criminal Justice*, 11 (1), 89–119.

(2014). Let's Call Killing Al-Awlaki What It Still Is – Murder. http://opiniojuris.org/2014/06/23/lets-call-killing-al-awlaki-still-murder/?utm_source=rss&utm_medium=rss&utm_campaign=lets-call-killing-al-awlaki-still-murder.

(2015). The use and abuse of analogy in IHL. In Ohlin, Jens David, eds, *Theoretical Boundaries of Armed Conflict and Human Rights*. Cambridge: Cambridge University Press, 232–286.

Henriksen, Anders (2014). Jus ad bellum and American targeted use of force to fight terrorism around the world. *Journal of Conflict and Security Law*, 19(2), 211–250.

Herborth, Benjamin (2004). Die via media als konstitutionstheoretische Einbahnstraße. *Zeitschrift für Internationale Beziehungen*, 11(1), 61–87.

(2012). The elusive nature of human nature: Hidden essentialism and the flight from social theory. *International Studies Review*, 14(4), 660–663.

Heupel, Monika, and Zürn, Michael, eds. (2017). *Protecting the Individual from International Authority: Human Rights in International Organizations*. Cambridge: Cambridge University Press.

Heyns, Christof (2013). The Report of the Special Rapporteur on Extrajudicial, Summary or Arbitrary Executions. (A/68/382). https://documents-dds-ny.un.org/doc/UNDOC/GEN/N13/473/63/pdf/N1347363.pdf.

Heyns, Christof, Akande, Dapo, Hill-Cawthorne, Lawrence, and Chengeta, Thompson (2016). The international law framework regulating the use of armed drones. *International & Comparative Law Quarterly*, 65(4), 791–827.

Hiéramente, Mayeul (2013). Wahlen in Zeiten der Strafverfolgung. *Die Friedenswarte: Journal of International Peace and Organization*, 88(1–2), 187–205.

Higgins, Rosalyn (1978). Conceptual thinking about the individual in international law. *British Journal of International Studies*, 4(1), 1–19.

(1978–1979). Conceptual thinking about the individual in international law. *New York Law School Law Review*, 24, 11–29.

(1994). *Problems and Process*. Oxford: Clarendon.

High Representative of Disarmament Affairs (2021). Briefing to the Security Council on the Implementation of Security Council Resolution 2118 (2013) On the Elimination of the Chemical Weapons Programme of the Syrian Arab Republic. https://front.un-arm.org/wp-content/uploads/2021/05/05.06.21-Briefing-to-the-Security-Council-on-the-implementation-of-Security-Council-resolution-2118-2013-on-the-elimination-of-the-chemical-weapons-programme-of-the-Syrian-Arab-Republic–2.pdf.

Hill, Christopher (1999). 'Where are we going?' international relations and the voices from below. *Review of International Studies*, 25(1), 107–122.

Hillebrecht, Courtney (2020). International criminal accountability and the domestic politics of resistance: Case studies from Kenya and Lebanon. *Law & Society Review*, 54(2), 453–486.

Hinnebusch, Raymond (2020). Proxy wars and spheres of influence in post-ISIS Syria. *IEMEd Mediterranean Yearbook 2020*, 78–83.

Hinnebusch, Raymond, and Saouli, Adham, eds. (2020). *The War for Syria: Regional and International Dimensions of the Syrian Uprising*. Abingdon; Oxon; New York: Routledge.

Hlavkova, Monika (2014). Reconstructing the civilian/combatant divide: A fresh look at targeting in non-international armed conflict. *Journal of Conflict and Security Law*, 19(2), 251–278.

Hobbes, Thomas (1966 [1651]). *Leviathan*. Neuwied; Berlin: Hermann Luchterhand Verlag GmbH.

Hobbs, Patricia (2020). The catalysing effect of the Rome Statute in Africa: Positive complementarity and self-referrals. *Criminal Law Forum*, 31(3), 345–376.

Hofius, Maren (2015). Constituting Community, Practicing Boundaries: European Union Diplomacy in Ukraine. PhD Thesis, University of Hamburg.

(2020). Towards a 'theory of the gap': Addressing the relationship between practice and theory. *Global Constitutionalism – Human Rights, Democracy and the Rule of Law*, 9(1), 169–182.

Hofius, Maren, Wilkens, Jan, Hansen-Magnusson, Hannes, and Gholiagha, Sassan (2014). Den Schleier lichten? Kritische Normenforschung, Freiheit und Gleichberechtigung im Kontext des 'Arabischen Frühlings'. *Zeitschrift für Internationale Beziehungen*, 21(2), 85–105.

Hollis, Martin, and Smith, Steve (1990). *Explaining and Understanding International Relations*. Oxford: Clarendon Press.

Hollway, Wendy (1984). Gender difference and the production of subjectivity. In Henriques, Julian, Urwin, Cathy, Hollway, Wendy, Venn, Couze, and Walkerdine, Valerie, eds., *Changing the Subject*. London; New York: Methuen, 227–263

Holmes, Marcus, Jordan, Richard, and Parajon, Eric (2021). Assessing the renaissance of individuals in international relations. *PS: Political Science & Politics*, 542(2), 214–219.

Holmes, Marcus, and Wheeler, Nicholas J. (2020). Social bonding in diplomacy. *International Theory*, 12(1), 133–161.

Holzgrefe, Jeff L., and Keohane, Robert O., eds. (2003). *Humanitarian Intervention: Ethic, Legal and Political Dilemmas*. Cambridge: Cambridge University Press.

Holzscheiter, Anna (2005). Discourse as capability: Non-state actors' capital in global governance. *Millennium: Journal of International Studies*, 33(3), 723–746.

(2010). *Children's Rights in International Politics*. Basingstoke: Palgrave Macmillan.

(2014). Between communicative interaction and structures of signification: Discourse theory and analysis in international relations. *International Studies Perspectives*, 15(2), 142–162.

(2016). Representation as power and performative practice: Global civil society advocacy for working children. *Review of International Studies*, 42, 205–226.

(2017a). The Politics of Age: Children and Older Persons as Contested Subjects in International Human Rights Law-Making. Conference paper presented at the 5th open section conference of the German Political Science Association (DVPW) IR Section, 4–6 October 2017, Bremen. On file with author.

(2017b). Was vom arguing übrigblieb .... *Zeitschrift für Internationale Beziehungen*, 24(1), 143–159.

Holzscheiter, Anna, Gholiagha, Sassan, and Liese, Andrea (2022). Advocacy coalitions and norm collisions: Insights from international drug control, human trafficking, and child labour. *Global Society*, 36(1), 25–48.

Hoover, Joseph (2012). Reconstructing responsibility and moral agency in world politics. *International Theory*, 4(2), 233–268.

Hopgood, Stephen (2017). Human rights on the road to nowhere. In Hopgood, Stephen, Snyder, Jack, and Vinjamuri, Leslie, eds., *Human Rights Futures*. Cambridge: Cambridge University Press, 283–310.

Hopgood, Stephen, Snyder, Jack, and Vinjamuri, Leslie, eds. (2017a). *Human Rights Futures*. Cambridge: Cambridge University Press.

(2017b). Introduction: Human rights past, present, and future. In Hopgood, Stephen, Snyder, Jack, and Vinjamuri, Leslie, eds., *Human Rights Futures*. Cambridge: Cambridge University Press, 1–23.

Hülsse, Rainer (2007). Creating demand for global governance: The making of a global money-laundering problem. *Global Society*, 21(2), 155–178.

Human Rights Council (2011). The Current Human Rights Situation in the Syrian Arab Republic in the Context of Recent Events. (A/HRC/RES/S-16/1). https://undocs.org/A/HRC/RES/S-16/1.

(2012). Report of the International Commission of Inquiry on Libya. www.ohchr.org/Documents/HRBodies/HRCouncil/RegularSession/Session19/A.HRC.19.68.pdf.

Human Rights Watch (2013). 'Between a Drone and Al-Qaeda" - the Civilian Cost of US Targeted Killings in Yemen. www.hrw.org/sites/default/files/report_pdf/yemen1013web.pdf.

Hunt, Charles T. (2016). Emerging powers and the Responsibility to Protect: Non-linear norm dynamics in complex international society. *Cambridge Review of International Affairs*, 29(3), 870–890.

Hunt, Charles T., and Orchard, Phil, eds. (2020a). *Constructing the Responsibility to Protect*. Abingdon; Oxon; New York: Routledge.

(2020b). Introduction: Consolidation and contestation of the Responsibility to Protect. In Hunt, Charles T. and Orchard, Phil, eds., *Constructing the Responsibility to Protect*. Abingdon; Oxon; New York: Routledge.

Hunt, Lynn (2007). *Inventing Human Rights: A History*. 1st ed. New York: W. W. Norton & Company.

ICC (2009). *Warrant of Arrest for Omar Hassan Ahmad Al Bashir*. www.icc-cpi.int/iccdocs/doc/doc639078.pdf.

(2010a). *Situation in the Republic of Kenya*. (ICC-01/09). www.icc-cpi.int/iccdocs/doc/doc854287.pdf.

(2010b). *Second Warrant of Arrest for Omar Hassan Ahmad Al Bashir*. www.icc-cpi.int/en_menus/icc/situations%20and%20cases/situations/situation%20icc%200205/related%20cases/icc02050109/court%20records/chambers/ptci/Pages/95.aspx.

(2011a). *Decision on the 'Prosecutor's Application Pursuant to Article 58 as to Muammar Mohammed Abu Minyar GADDAFI, Saif Al-Islam GADDAFI and Abdullah ALSENUSSI'*. www.icc-cpi.int/iccdocs/doc/doc1101337.pdf.

(2011b). *Decision on the Prosecutor's Application for Summons to Appear for William Samoei Ruto, Henry Kiprono Kosgey and Joshua Arap Sang*. www.icc-cpi.int/CourtRecords/CR2011_02585.PDF.

(2011c). *Decision on the Prosecutor's Application for Summonses to Appear for Francis Kirimi Muthaura, Uhuru Muigai Kenyatta and Mohammed Hussein Ali*. www.icc-cpi.int/CourtRecords/CR2011_02586.PDF.

(2013). *Decision on the Admissibility of the Case Against Abdullah Al-Senussi*. (ICC-01/11-01/11). www.icc-cpi.int / CourtRecords/ CR2013_07445.PDF.
(2014). *Notice of Withdrawal of the Charges Against Uhuru Muigai Kenyatta*. (ICC-01/09-02/11). www.icc-cpi.int / CourtRecords/ CR2014_09939.PDF.
(2015). *Case Information Sheet: Situation in the Republic of Kenya – the Prosecutor vs Uhuru Muigai Kenyatta*. (ICC-PIDS-CIS-KEN-02-014/15_Eng). www.icc-cpi.int / CaseInformationSheets/ kenyattaEng.pdf.
(2019a). *Case Information Sheet: Situation in Libya – the Prosecutor V. Saif Al-Islam Gaddafi*. www.icc-cpi.int / CaseInformationSheets/ gaddafiEng.pdf.
(2019b). *Crime of Aggression – Amendments Ratification*. https:// asp.icc-cpi.int / en_menus/ asp/ crime%20of%20aggression/ Pages/ default.aspx.
(2019c). *Decision on the 'Admissibility Challenge by Dr. Saif Al-Islam Gadafi Pursuant to Articles 17(1)©, 19 and 20(3) Of the Rome Statute'*. www.icc-cpi.int / Pages/ record.aspx ? docNo= ICC-01/11-01/11-662.
(2020a). *Kenya*. www.icc-cpi.int / kenya.
(2020b). *Libya*. www.icc-cpi.int / libya.
(2020c). *Situations under Investigation*. www.icc-cpi.int / pages/ situation.aspx.
(2020d). *Judgment on the Appeal of Mr Saif Al-Islam Gaddafi Against the Decision of Pre-Trial Chamber I Entitled 'Decision on the "Admissibility Challenge by Dr. Saif Al-Islam Gadafi Pursuant to Articles 17(1)©, 19 and 20(3) Of the Rome Statute"' of 5 April 2019*. www.icc-cpi.int / Pages/ record.aspx ? docNo= ICC-01/11-01/11-695.
(2021a). *Afghanistan*. www.icc-cpi.int / afghanistan.
(2021b). *Ongwen Case*. www.icc-cpi.int / uganda/ ongwen.
(2021c). *Situation in Uganda in the Case of the Prosecutor v. Dominic Ongwen*. www .icc-cpi.int / CourtRecords/ CR2021_01026.PDF.
(2021d). *The Prosecutor v. Dominic Ongwen*. www.icc-cpi.int / CourtRecords/ CR2021_04230.PDF.
ICISS (2001). *The Responsibility to Protect*. Ottawa: International Development Research Centre.
ICJ (1951). *Reservations on the Convention on the Prevention and Punishment of the Crime of Genocide. I.C.J. Reports*. www.icj-cij.org / docket/ files/ 12/ 4285.pdf.
(1996). *Legality of the Threat or Use of Nuclear Weapons. I.C.J. Reports*. www.icj-cij .org / docket/ files/ 95/ 7495.pdf.
(2001). *LaGrand Case (Germany v. United States of America). I.C.J. Reports*. www .icj-cij.org / docket/ files/ 104/ 7736.pdf.
(2007). *Case Concerning Application of the Convention on the Prevention and Punishment of the Crime of Genocide. I.C.J. Reports*. http:// www.icj-cij.org / docket/ files/ 91/ 13685.pdf.
(2021). *Application of the Convention on the Prevention and Punishment of the Crime of Genocide (The Gambia v. Myanmar)*. www.icj-cij.org / en/ case/ 178.
ICRtoP (2009). *General Assembly Debate on the Responsibility to Protect and Informal Interactive Dialogue*. www.responsibilitytoprotect.org / index.php/ component/ content/ article/ 35- r2pcs- topics/ 2493- general- assembly- debate- on- the- respon sibility- to- protect- and- informal- interactive- dialogue- .
ICTY (1995). *PROSECUTOR V.DUSKO TADIC A/k/a 'DULE'*. www.icty.org / x/ cases/ tadic/ acdec/ en/ 51002.htm.

(2001). *Prosectur v. Dragoljub Kunarac Radomir Kovac and Zoran Vukovic*. www.icty.org/x/cases/kunarac/tjug/en/kun-tj010222e.pdf.

Ignatieff, Michael (2017). Human rights, global ethics, and the ordinary virtues. *Ethics & International Affairs*, 31(1), 3–16.

Independent International Commission on Kosovo (2000). *The Kosovo Report*. Oxford: Oxford University Press.

International Crisis Group (2019). Averting an ISIS Resurgence in Iraq and Syria. (Middle East report No 207). https://d2071andvipowj.cloudfront.net/207-averting-an-isis-resurgence.pdf.

International Human Rights and Conflict Resolution Clinic (Stanford Law School) and Global Justice Clinic (NYU School of Law) (2012). Living Under Drones: Death, Injury, and Trauma to Civilians from US Drone Practices in Pakistan. https://law.stanford.edu/wp-content/uploads/sites/default/files/publication/313671/doc/slspublic/Stanford_NYU_LIVING_UNDER_DRONES.pdf.

Ipsen, Knut, Menzel, Eberhard, and Epping, Volker (2004). *Völkerrecht*. 5th ed. München: Beck.

Isiksel, Türküler (2010). Fundamental rights in the EU after Kadi and Al Barakaat. *European Law Journal*, 16(5), 551–577.

Isiksel, Türküler, and Thies, Anne (2013). Introduction. *Global Constitutionalism – Human Rights, Democracy and the Rule of Law*, 2(2), 151–159.

Jabareen, Yosef (2009). Building a conceptual framework: Philosophy, definitions, and procedure. *International Journal of Qualitative Methods*, 8(4), 49–62.

Jackson, Patrick T. (2011). *The Conduct of Inquiry in International Relations*. London; New York: Routledge.

Jackson, Patrick T., and Nexon, Daniel H. (1999). Relations before states: Substance, process and the study of world politics. *European Journal of International Relations*, 5(3), 291–332.

Jackson, Robert (2007). *Sovereignty*. Cambridge: Polity Press.

Jacobi, Daniel (2015). On the social (re)construction of the human in world politics. In Jacobi, Daniel, and Freyberg-Inan, Annette, eds., *Human Beings in International Relations*. Cambridge: Cambridge University Press, 247–265.

Jacobi, Daniel, and Freyberg-Inan, Annette (2012). The forum: Human being(s) in international relations. *International Studies Review*, 14(4), 645–665.

(2015a). *Human Beings in International Relations*. Cambridge: Cambridge University Press.

(2015b). Introduction. In Jacobi, Daniel, and Freyberg-Inan, Annette, eds., *Human Beings in International Relations*. Cambridge: Cambridge University Press, 1–31.

Jacobs, Dov (2013). A shifting scale of power: Who is in charge of the charges at the International Criminal Court. In Schabas, William A., McDermott, Yvonne, and Hayes, Niamh, eds., *The Ashgate Research Companion to International Criminal Law: Critical Perspectives*. Surrey; Burlington: Ashgate, 205–222.

Jacobson, David (1997). *Rights across Borders. Immigration and the Decline of Citizenship*. Baltimore; London: Johns Hopkins University Press.

Jaeger, Hans-Martin (1996). Konstruktionsfehler des Konstruktivismus in den Internationalen Beziehungen. *Zeitschrift für Internationale Beziehungen*, 3(2), 313–340.

Jahn-Koch, Ingrid, and Koch, Michael (2014). Bewaffnete Drohnen – Teufelszeug oder Waffen wie andere? Eine völkerrechtliche Überprüfung. In Delbrück, Jost, Heinz, Ursula, Odendahl, Kerstin, Matz-Lück, Nele, and von Arnauld, Andreas, eds., *Aus Kiel in die Welt. Kiel's Contribution to International Law: Essays in Honour of the 100th Anniversary of the Walther-Schücking Institut for International Law.* Berlin: Duncker & Humblot, 265–315.

Jarvis, Samuel (2018). Assessing the Responsibility to Protect's motivational capacity: The role of humanity. *Journal of International Political Theory*, 14(1), 107–124.

Jawad, Rana (2017). What Next for Saif Al-Islam Gaddafi? www.bbc.com/news/world-africa-40246964.

Jessberger, Florian, and Geneuss, Julia, eds. (2020). *Why Punish Perpetrators of Mass Atrocities?* New York: Cambridge University Press.

Job, Brian L. (2016). Evolution, retreat or rejection: Brazil's, India's and China's normative stances on R2P. *Cambridge Review of International Affairs*, 29(3), 891–910.

Johnson, Toni A. (2016). LGBTI rights: The international context. In Steans, Jill, and Tepe-Belfrage, Daniela, eds., *Handbook on Gender in World Politics*. Cheltenham: Edward Elgar, 153–161.

Joint Chiefs of Staff (2013). Joint Targeting. www.aclu.org/files/dronefoia/dod/drone_dod_jp3_60.pdf.

Jose, Betcy (2017a). Bin Laden's targeted killing and emerging norms. *Critical Studies on Terrorism*, 10(1), 44–66.

(2017b). Not completely the new normal: How human rights watch tried to suppress the targeted killing norm. *Contemporary Security Policy*, 38(2), 237–259.

Juma, Monica K. (2009). African mediation of the Kenyan post-2007 election crisis. *Journal of Contemporary African Studies*, 27(3), 407–430.

Jurkovich, Michelle (2020). What isn't a norm? Redefining the conceptual boundaries of 'norms' in the human rights literature. *International Studies Review*, 22, 693–711.

Kaldor, Mary (1999). *New & Old Wars*. Stanford: Stanford University Press.

(2005). Old wars, cold wars, new wars, and the war on terror. *International Politics*, 42(4), 491–498.

(2013). In defence of new wars. *Stability*, 2(1), 1–16.

Kaleck, Wolfgang (2012). *Mit zweierlei Maß*. Berlin: Wagenbach.

Karahamad, Mustafa (2021). *Counter-Terrorism for Peace* – Syria between the Russian-Led Coercive Peace and the United States' Withdrawal. https://blog.prif.org/2021/02/24/counter-terrorism-for-peace-syria-between-the-russian-led-coercive-peace-and-the-united-states-withdrawal/.

Katzenstein, Peter J. (1996). Introduction: Alternative perspectives on national security. In Katzenstein, Peter J., ed., *The Culture of National Security: Norms and Identity in World Politics*. New York: Columbia University Press, 1–32.

Kaukoranta, Päivi (2010). Finnish perspectives on the ICC and R2P. *Finnish Yearbook of International Law*, 21, 15–19.

Kaul, Hans-Peter (2013). Der Internationale Strafgerichtshof: Ein Spielball der Politik? Friedrich-Ebert-Stiftung. Internationale Tagung: 'Staatspräsidenten vor Gericht: Die Verfahren gegen amtierende Regierungschefs aus Afrika als Meilenstein für die internationale Strafjustiz?', Berlin 5 November 2013.

Keck, Margaret E., and Sikkink, Kathryn (1998). *Activities beyond Borders*. Ithaca; London: Cornell University Press.

Kelle, Udo (1996). Die Bedeutung theoretischen Vorwissens in der Methodologie der Grounded Theory. In Strobl, Rainer, and Böttger, Andreas, eds., *Wahre Geschichten?* Baden-Baden: Nomos Verlagsgesellschaft, 23–47.

Keller, Reiner (2005). Analysing discourse: An approach from the sociology of knowledge. *Forum Qualitative Social Research*, 6(3), 32.

Kennedy, Caroline, and Rogers, James I. (2015). Virtuous drones? *The International Journal of Human Rights*, 19(2), 211–227.

Kennedy, David (2016). *A World of Struggle: How Power, Law, and Expertise Shape Global Political Economy*. Princeton; Oxford: Princeton University Press.

Kennedy, David W. (1988). A new stream of international law scholarship. *Wisconsin International Law Journal*, 7(1), 1–49.

Kennedy, Duncan, and Klare, Karl E. (1984). A bibliography of critical legal studies. *The Yale Law Journal*, 94(2), 461–490.

Keohane, Robert O. (1991). International relations theory: Contributions of a feminist standpoint. In Grant, Rebecca, and Newland, Kathleen, eds., *Gender and International Relations*. Bloomington; Indianapolis: Indiana University Press, 41–50.

Kersavage, Kathryn (2014). The 'Responsibility to Protect' our answer to 'never again'? *International Affairs Forum*, 5(1), 23–41.

Kersten, Mark (2014a). Does Russia have a 'Responsibility to Protect' Ukraine? Don't buy it. *The Globe and Mail*, 4 March 2014.

(2014b). The Lesson the ICC Shouldn't Learn in the Wake of Kenyatta. http://justiceinconflict.org/2014/12/07/the-lesson-the-icc-shouldnt-learn-in-the-wake-of-kenyatta/.

(2015). The Responsibility to Protect Doctrine Is Faltering. Here's Why … www.washingtonpost.com/news/monkey-cage/wp/2015/12/08/the-responsibility-to-protect-doctrine-is-failing-heres-why/.

(2016). *Justice in Conflict*. Oxford: Oxford University Press.

(2018). A fatal attraction? The UN Security Council and the relationship between R2P and the International Criminal Court. In Handmaker, Jeff, and Arts, Karin, eds., *Mobilising International Law for 'Global Justice'*. Cambridge: Cambridge University Press, 142–162.

(2021). The Life and Trials of Dominic Ongwen: A JiC Symposium. https://justiceinconflict.org/2021/02/01/the-life-and-trials-of-dominic-ongwen-a-jic-symposium/.

Kessler, Oliver, and Werner, Wouter (2008). Extrajudicial killing as risk management. *Security Dialogue*, 29(2–3), 289–307.

Kettemann, Matthias C. (2013). *The Future of Individuals in International Law*. The Hague: Eleven International.

Kinsella, Helen M. (2011). *The Image before the Weapon: A Critical History of the Distinction between Combatant and Civilian*. Ithaca; London: Cornell University Press.

(2016). 'With all the respect due to their sex': Gender and international humanitarian law. In Steans, Jill, and Tepe-Belfrage, Daniela, eds., *Handbook on Gender in World Politics*. Cheltenham: Edward Elgar, 171–178.

Kinsella, Helen M., and Shepherd, Laura J. (2019). 'Well, what is the feminist perspective on international affairs?': Theory/practice. *International Affairs*, 95 (6), 1209–1213.

Kirby, Paul (2015). Ending sexual violence in conflict: The preventing sexual violence initiative and its critics. *International Affairs*, 91(3), 457–472.

Kjeldgaard-Pedersen, Astrid (2018). *The International Legal Personality of the Individual*. Oxford: Oxford University Press.

Klotz, Audie (2008). Case Selection. In Klotz, Audie, and Prakash, Deepa, eds., *Qualitative Methods in International Relations*. Houndsmill: Palgrave Macmillan, 43–58.

Koh, Harold H. (2010). The Obama Administration and International Law. https://2009-2017.state.gov/s/l/releases/remarks/139119.htm.

Kornprobst, Markus (2011). The agent's logic of action: Defining and mapping political judgement. *International Theory*, 3(1), 70–104.

Korobov, Neill (2001). Reconciling theory with method: From conversation analysis and critical discourse analysis to positioning analysis. *Forum Qualitative Social Research*, 2(3), 36.

Koschut, Simon (2020). A critical perspective on emotions in international relations. In Roach, Steven C., ed., *Handbook of critical international relations*. Cheltenham; Northampton: Edward Elgar, 72–89.

Kranz, Jerzey (2008). Der Kampf um den Frieden und sein besonderer Facilitator – Anmerkungen zur Georgienkrise. *Archiv des Völkerrechts*, 46(4), 481–501.

Krasmann, Susanne (2014). Der Aufstieg der Drohnen. *WestEnd – Neue Zeitschrift für Sozialforschung*, 11(1), 25–43.

Krasner, Stephen D. (1993). Westphalia and all that. In Goldstein, Judith, and Keohane, Robert O., eds., *Ideas and Foreign Policy*. Ithaca: Cornell University Press, 235–264.

(1996). Sovereignty and intervention. In Lyons, Gene M., and Mastanduno, Michael, eds., *Beyond Westphalia?* Baltimore; London: The Johns Hopkins University Press, 228–249.

(1999). *Sovereignty*. Princeton: Princeton University Press.

Kratochwil, Friedrich V. (1984a). The force of prescriptions. *International Organization*, 38(4), 685–708.

(1984b). Thrasymmachos revisited: On the relevance of norms and the study of law for international relations. *Journal of International Affairs*, 37(2), 343–356.

(1989a). *Rules, Norms, and Decisions: On the Conditions of Practical and Legal Reasoning in International Relations and Domestic Affairs*. Cambridge: Cambridge University Press.

(2000). How do norms matter? In Byers, Michael, ed., *The Role of Law in International Politics*. Oxford; New York: Oxford University Press, 35–68.

(2001). Constructivism as an approach to interdisciplinary study. In Fierke, Karin M., and Jørgensen, Knud E., eds., *Constructing International Relations*. Armonk; London: M. E. Sharpe, 13–35.

(2008). Constructivism: What it is (not) and how it matters. In Della Porta, Donatella, and Keating, Michael, eds., *Approaches and Methodologies in the Social Sciences*. Cambridge: Cambridge University Press, 80–98.

(2014). *The Status of Law in World Society: Meditations on the Role and Rule of Law*. Cambridge: Cambridge University Press.

Kratochwil, Friedrich V., and Ruggie, John G. (1986). International organization: A State of the Art on an Art of the State. *International Organization*, 40(4), 753–775.

Krell, Gert (2009). *Weltbilder und Weltordnung*. 4th ed. Baden-Baden: Nomos Verlagsgesellschaft.

Kreuder-Sonnen, Christian (2020). *Emergency Powers of International Organizations: Between Normalization and Containment*. Oxford: Oxford University Press.

Kreuder-Sonnen, Christian, and Zürn, Michael (2020). After fragmentation: Norm collisions, interface conflicts, and conflict management. *Global Constitutionalism - Human Rights, Democracy and the Rule of Law*, 9(2), 241–267.

Krisch, Nico, Corradini, Francesco, and Reimers, Lucy L. (2020). Order at the margins: The legal construction of interface conflicts over time. *Global Constitutionalism – Human Rights, Democracy and the Rule of Law*, 9(2), 343–363.

Kronfeldner, Maria (2021). Introduction: Mapping dehumanization studies. In Kronfeldner, Maria, ed., *The Routledge Handbook of Dehumanization*. Abingdon; Oxon; New York: Routledge, 1–36.

Krook, Mona L., and True, Jacqui (2012). Rethinking the life cycles of international norms: The United Nations and the global promotion of gender equality. *European Journal of International Relations*, 18(1), 103–127.

Kruse, Jan (2014). *Qualitative Interviewforschung: Ein Integrativer Ansatz*. 2nd ed. Weinheim: Beltz Juventa.

Kumm, Mattias (2010). How does European Union law fit into the world of public law? Costa, Kadi, and three concepts of public law. In Wiener, Antje, and Neyer, Jügern, eds., *Political Theory of the European Union*. Oxford: Oxford University Press, 111–138.

Kuntz, Friederike (2018). Aporias: The International Relation, Interrelated Sovereigns, the Human Individual, and Power-Knowledge. PhD Thesis, University of Bielefeld.

Kurtz, Gerrit, and Rotmann, Philipp (2016). The evolution of norms of protection: Major powers debate the Responsibility to Protect. *Global Society*, 30(1), 3–20.

Labonte, Melissa (2016). R2P's status as a norm. In Bellamy, Alex J., and Dunne, Tim, eds., *The Oxford Handbook of the Responsibility to Protect*. Oxford: Oxford University Press, 133–150.

Landolt, Laura K. (2004). (Mis)constructing the third world? *Third World Quarterly*, 25 (3), 579–591.

Lang, Anthony F. Jr. (2009). Conflicting rules: Global constitutionalism and the Kosovo intervention. *Journal of Intervention and State Building*, 3(2), 185–204.

(2011). Punishing genocide: A critical reading of the International Court of Justice. In Vernon, Richard, and Issacs, Tracey, eds., *Accountability for Collective Wrongdoing*. Cambridge: Cambridge University Press, 92–118.

Lang, Anthony F. Jr., Kumm, Mattias, Wiener, Antje, Tully, James, and Maduro, Miguel P. (2013). Interdisciplinarity: Challenges and opportunities. *Global Constitutionalism – Human Rights, Democracy and the Rule of Law*, 2(1), 1–5.

Lang Anthony F. Jr., and Williams, John (2005). Between international politics and international ethics. In Lang, Anthony F. Jr., and Williams, John, eds., *Hannah*

Arendt and International Relations. New York; Houndsmill: Palgrave Macmillan, 221–232.

Langlois, Anthony F. (2018). International political theory and LGBTQ rights. In Brown, Chris, and Eckersley, Robyn, eds., *The Oxford Handbook of International Political Theory*. Oxford: Oxford University Press, 370–382.

Lantis, Jeffrey S. (2016). Agentic constructivism and the proliferation security initiative: Modeling norm change. *Cooperation and Conflict*, 51(3), 384–400.

Lantis, Jeffrey S., and Wunderlich, Carmen (2018). Resiliency dynamics of norm clusters: Norm contestation and international cooperation. *Review of International Studies*, 44(03), 570–593.

Lauterpacht, Hersch (1946). The Grotian tradition in international law. *British Year Book of International Law*, 23, 1–53.

Leander, Anna (2013). Technological agency in the co-constitution of legal expertise and the US drone program. *Leiden Journal of International Law*, 26(4), 811–831.

Lebow, Richard N. (2003). *The Tragic Vision of Politics: Ethics, Interest and Orders*. Cambridge: Cambridge University Press.

(2012). The palette of human nature. *International Studies Review*, 14(4), 646–649.

Lee, Steven P. (2010). The moral distinctiveness of genocide. *Journal of Political Philosophy*,

Legro, Jeffrey W. (1997). Which norms matter? *International Organization*, 51(1), 31–63.

Liber, Francis (1863). Instructions for the Government of Armies of the United States in the Field (Lieber Code). https://ihl-databases.icrc.org/applic/ihl/ihl.nsf/xsp/.ibmmodres/domino/OpenAttachment/applic/ihl/ihl.nsf/A25AA5871A04919BC12563CD002D65C5/FULLTEXT/IHL-L-Code-EN.pdf.

Liese, Andrea (2009). Exceptional necessity: How liberal democracies contest the prohibition of torture and ill-treatment when countering terrorism. *Journal of International Law and International Relations*, 5(1), 17–48.

Lindenmayer, Elisabeth, and Kaye, Josie L. (2009). *A Choice for Peace? The Story of Forty-One Days of Mediation in Kenya*. New York: International Peace Institute. www.ipinst.org/wp-content/uploads/publications/kenyamediation_epub.pdf.

Linklater, Andrew (2011). *The Problem of Harm in World Politics*. Cambridge: Cambridge University Press.

Liste, Philip (2020). The Workings of Power in Transnational Law. (Transnational Law Institute Research Paper Series, King's College London, Paper 24/2020). https://ssrn.com/abstract=3756985.

Lobasz, Jennifer K. (2019). *Constructing Human Trafficking*. Cham: Palgrave Macmillan.

Loges, Bastian (2013). *Schutz als neue Norm in den internationalen Beziehungen*. Wiesbaden: Springer.

(2020). Vom Verantwortungsgefühl zur Verantwortungsübernahme: Die Schutzverantwortung der Vereinten Nationen aus Sicht des emotional turn. In Koschut, Simon, ed., *Emotionen in den Internationalen Beziehungen*. Baden-Baden: Nomos Verlagsgesellschaft, 99–120.

Long War Journal (2021). US Airstrikes in the Long War. www.longwarjournal.org/us-airstrikes-in-the-long-war.

Luban, David (2010). Fairness to rightness: Jurisdiction, legality, and the legitimacy of international criminal law. In Besson, Samantha, and Tasioulas, John, eds., *The Philosophy of International Law*. Oxford: Oxford University Press, 569–588.

Lubell, Noam, and Derejko, Nathan (2013). A global battlefield? *Journal of International Criminal Justice*, 11(1), 65–88.

Lucas, George R. Jr. (2014). Revisiting armed humanitarian intervention. In Scheid, Don E., ed., *The Ethics of Armed Humanitarian Intervention*. Cambridge: Cambridge University Press, 26–45.

Luchterhandt, Otto (2008). Völkerrechtliche Aspekte des Georgien-Krieges. *Archiv des Völkerrechts*, 46(4), 435–480.

Lucius-Hoene, Gabriele, and Deppermann, Arnulf (2014). *Rekonstruktion narrativer Identität*. 2nd ed. Wiesbaden: VS Verlag für Sozialwissenschaften.

Luck, Edward C. (2015). R2P at ten: A new mindset for a new era? *Global Governance: A Review of Multilateralism and International Organizations*, 21(4), 499–504.

Lynch, Cecilia (2014). *Interpreting International Politics*. New York; Oxon: Routledge.

MacDonald, Euan, and Alston, Philip (2008). Sovereignty, human rights, security: Armed intervention and the foundational problem of international law. In MacDonald, Euan, and Alston, Philip, eds., *Human Rights, Intervention, and the Use of Force*. Oxford: Oxford University Press, 1–31.

Macleod, Christopher (2012). An alternative approach to the harm of genocide. *POLITICS*, 23(3), 197–206.

Malito, Debora V. (2017). The Responsibility to Protect what in Libya? *Peace Review*, 29(3), 289–298.

(2019). Morality as a catalyst for violence: Responsibility to Protect and regime change in Libya. *Politikon*, 46(1), 104–121.

Mallavarapu, Siddharth (2015). Colonialism and the Responsibility to Protect. In Thakur, Ramesh, and Maley, William, eds., *Theorising the Responsibility to Protect*. Cambridge: Cambridge University Press, 305–322.

(2020). 'After fragmentation': Notes from the global south. *Global Constitutionalism - Human Rights, Democracy and the Rule of Law*, 9(2), 424–436.

March, James G., and Olsen, Johan P. (1989). *Rediscovering Institutions*. New York: Free Press.

Markham, Christopher J., and Schmitt, Michael N. (2013). Precision air warfare and the law of armed conflict. *Israel Yearbook on Human Rights*, 43, 297–319.

Marlier, Grant, and Crawford, Neta C. (2013). Incomplete and imperfect institutionalisation of empathy and altruism in the 'Responsibility to Protect' doctrine. *Global Responsibility to Protect*, 5(4), 397–422.

Martin, Craig (2015). A means-methods paradox and the legality of drone strikes in armed conflict. *The International Journal of Human Rights*, 19(2), 142–175.

Maunganidze, Ottilia A., and Du Plessis, Anton (2015). The ICC and the AU. In Stahn, Carsten, ed., *The Law and Practice of the International Criminal Court*. Oxford: Oxford University Press, 65–83.

Maxwell, Mark (2012). Rebutting the civilian presumption: Playing whack-a-mole without a mallet. In Finkelstein, Claire, Ohlin, Jens D., and Altman, Andrew, eds., *Targeted Killing*. Oxford: Oxford University Press, 31–59.

May, Larry (2013). Targeted killings and proportionality in law. *Journal of International Criminal Justice*, 11(1), 47–63.

Mayer, Jane (2009). The predator war: What are the risks of the C.I.A.'s covert drone program? *The New Yorker*, 26 October 2009.

Mazetti, Mark, Savage, Charlie, and Shane, Scott (2013). How a U.S. Citizen came to be in america's cross hairs. *The New York Times*, 9 March 2013.

Mburu, Daniel M. (2018). The lost Kenyan duel: The role of politics in the collapse of the International Criminal Court cases against Ruto and Kenyatta. *International Criminal Law Review*, 18(6), 1015–1047.

McCorquodale, Robert (2004). An inclusive international legal system. *Leiden Journal of International Law*, 17, 477–504.

(2006). The individual and the international legal system. In Evans, Malcolm D., ed., *International Law*. Oxford: Oxford University Press. 2nd ed. 307–332.

(2017). Sources and the subjects of international law: A plurality of law-making participants. In Besson, Samantha, and D'Aspremont, Jean, eds., *The Oxford Handbook of the Sources of International Law*. Oxford: Oxford University Press, 749–768.

McCourt, David M. (2016). Practice theory and relationalism as the new constructivism. *International Studies Quarterly*, 60(3), 475–485.

McElroy, Damien (2012). Colonel Gaddafi Died After Being Stabbed with Bayonet, Says Report. www.telegraph.co.uk/news/worldnews/africaandindianocean/libya/9613394/Colonel-Gaddafi-died-after-being-stabbed-with-bayonet-says-report.html.

McNeal, Gregory S. (2012). Are targeted killings unlawful? In Finkelstein, Claire, Ohlin, Jens D., and Altman, Andrew, eds., *Targeted Killing*. Oxford: Oxford University Press, 326–346.

Mearsheimer, John J. (2010). Structural realism. In Dunne, Timothy, Kurki, Milja, and Smith, Steve, eds., *International Relations Theories: Discipline and Diversity*. 2nd ed. Oxford: Oxford University Press, 77–94.

Meggido, Tamar (2019). Beyond fragmentation: On international law's integrationist forces. *The Yale Journal of International Law*, 44, 115–147.

Mégret, Frédéric (2010). ICC, R2P, and the international community's evolving interventionist toolkit. *Finnish Yearbook of International Law*, 21, 21–51.

(2017). The subjects of international criminal law. In Kastner, Philipp, ed., *International criminal law in context*. London: Routledge, 28–45.

(2018). The repentant defendant and the potential of international criminal justice. *Contemporary Justice Review*, 21(4), 432–454.

(2019). 'Bring forth the accused!' defendant attitudes and the intimate legitimacy of the international criminal trial. *Arizona Journal of International & Comparative Law*, 36(3), 397–476.

Mégret, Frédéric, and Giles Samson, Marika (2013). Holding the line on complementarity in Libya: The case for tolerating flawed domestic trials. *Journal of International Criminal Justice*, 11(3), 571–589.

Mégret, Frédéric, and Giles Samson, Marika (2019). Defiance, defence, repentance and what lies between. *Journal of International Criminal Justice*, 17(1), 151–177.

Mégret, Frédéric, and Scalia, Damiel (2019). Foreword. *Journal of International Criminal Justice*, 17(1), 101–103.

Meisels, Tamar (2012). In defense of the defenseless: The morality of the laws of war. *Political Studies*, 60(4), 919–935.

Melzer, Nils (2007). *Targeted Killing*. Zürich; Basel; Genf: Schulthess Juristische Medien AG.
Members of Congress (2012). Letter to President Obama. http://goodtimesweb.org/covert-operations/2014/Ltr-to-President-Obama-Sig-Strikes-06-12-2012.pdf.
Meron, Theodor (2006). *The Humanization of International Law*. Leiden: Nijhoff.
Michaels, Ralf, and Paulwelyn, Joost (2011). Conflict of norms or conflict of laws. *Duke Journal of Comparative & International Law*, 22, 349.
Michel, Torsten (2018). Of particles and humans: The question of 'human being' in Alexander Wendt's quantum mind and social science. *Millennium: Journal of International Studies*, 47(1), 114–127.
Miliband, David (2014). Syria May Be Lost, but We Must Stand by Its Victims. www.rescue.org/blog/david-miliband-syria-may-be-lost-we-must-stand-its-victims-commentary.
Milliken, Jennifer (1999). The study of discourse in international relations: A critique of research and methods. *European Journal of International Relations*, 5(2), 225–254.
(2001). Discourse Study: Bringing Rigor to Critical Theory. In Fierke, Karin M., and Jørgensen, Knud E., eds., *Constructing International Relations*. Armonk; London: M. E. Sharpe, 136–159.
Mills, Kurt (2015). Bashir in South Africa: Defeat, Victory or Both for International Criminal Justice? https://justiceinconflict.org/2015/06/16/bashir-in-south-africa-defeat-victory-or-both-for-international-criminal-justice/.
Mills, Kurt, and Bloomfield, Alan (2018). African resistance to the International Criminal Court: Halting the advance of the anti-impunity norm. *Review of International Studies*, 44(1), 101–127.
Moe, Louise W., and Geis, Anna (2020). From liberal interventionism to stabilisation: A new consensus on norm-downsizing in interventions in Africa. *Global Constitutionalism – Human Rights, Democracy and the Rule of Law*, 9(2), 387–412.
Moravcsik, Andrew (2008). The new liberalism. In Reus-Smit, Christian, and Snidal, Duncan, eds., *The Oxford Handbook of International Relations*. Oxford: Oxford University Press, 234–254.
Moreno-Lax, Violeta, and Papastavridis, Efthymios, eds. (2017). *Boat Refugees and Migrants at Sea*. Leiden; Boston: Brill Nijhoff.
Morgenthau, Hans J. (1954). *Politics among Nations*. New York: Knopf.
(1962). *The Decline of Democratic Politics*. Chicago; London: University of Chicago Press.
Morris, Justin (2013). Libya and Syria: R2P and the spectre of the swinging pendulum. *International Affairs*, 89(5), 1265–1283.
(2016). The Responsibility to Protect and the use of force: Remaking the procrustean bed? *Cooperation and Conflict*, 51(2), 200–215.
Morse, Janice M. (2012). The implications of interview type and structure in mixed-method designs. In Gubrium, Jaber F., Holstein, James A., Marvasti, Amir B., and McKinney, Amir B., eds., *The SAGE Handbook of Interview Research: The Complexity of the Craft*. Thousand Oaks: SAGE, 193–206.
Moyn, Samuel (2014). *Human Rights and the Uses of History*. London; New York: Verso.

Müller, Harald (1994). Internationale Beziehungen als kommunikatives Handeln. *Zeitschrift für Internationale Beziehungen*, 1(1), 15–44.

Murphy, Liam (2010). International responsibility. In Besson, Samantha, and Tasioulas, John, eds., *The Philosophy of International Law*. Oxford: Oxford University Press, 299–315.

Mutua, Makau (2016). *Human Rights Standards*. Albany: State University of New York Press.

Nagel, Thomas (1972). War and Massacre. *Philosophy & Public Affairs*, 1(2), 123–144.

Nahlawi, Yasmine (2019). Overcoming Russian and Chinese vetoes on Syria through Uniting for Peace. *Journal of Conflict and Security Law*, 24(1), 111–143.

Narozhna, Tanya (2021). The lived body, everyday and generative powers of war: Toward an embodied ontology of war as experience. *International Theory*, Online First, 1–23.

Nash, Sarah L. (2019). *Negotiating Migration in the Context of Climate Change: International Policy and Discourse*. Bristol; Chicago: Bristol University Press.

NATO (1999a). NATO's Role in Relation to the Conflict in Kosovo. www.nato.int/kosovo/history.htm.

(1999b). Statement on Kosovo Issued by the Heads of State and Government Participating in the Meeting of the North Atlantic Council in Washington, D.C. (Press Release S-1(99) 062). www.nato.int/cps/en/natolive/official_texts_27441.htm?selectedLocale=en.

(2021). Collective Defence – Article 5. www.nato.int/cps/ar/natohq/topics_110496.htm?.

Navarrete-Frías, Carolina, and Thoumi, Francisco E. (2005). Illegal Drugs and Human Rights of Peasants and Indigenous Communities: The Case of Peru. https://unesdoc.unesco.org/ark:/48223/pf0000140241.

NBC (2013). CIA Didn't Always Know Who It Was Killing in Drone Strikes, Classified Documents Show. www.nbcmiami.com/news/national-international/natl-cia-didnt-always-know-who-drone-strikes-killed/2039518/.

Neuman, William L. (2006). Field Research. In Neuman, William L., ed., *Social research methods*. 6th ed. Boston: Pearson, 378–417.

Neumann, Iver B. (1996). Self and other in international relations. *European Journal of International Relations* 2, 139–174.

(2002). Returning practice to the linguistic turn: The case of diplomacy. *Millennium: Journal of International Studies*, 31(3), 627–651.

(2008). Discourse analysis. In Klotz, Audie, and Prakash, Deepa, eds., *Qualitative Methods in International Relations*. Houndsmill: Palgrave Macmillan, 61–77.

Newman, Edward (2001). Human security and constructivism. *International Studies Perspectives*, 2(3), 239–251.

Nichols, Lionel (2015). *The International Criminal Court and the End of Impunity in Kenya*. Cham; Heidelberg; New York; Dordrecht; London: Springer.

Niemann, Holger, and Schillinger, Henrik (2017). Contestation 'all the way down'? The grammar of contestation in norm research. *Review of International Studies*, 43(01), 29–49.

Nijman, Janne E. (2004). *The Concept of International Legal Personality*. The Hague: T. M. C. Asser Press.

Norgaard, Carl A. (1962). *The Position of the Individual in International Law*. Copenhagen: Munksgaard.

Nuñez-Mietz, Fernando G. (2018). Legalization and the legitimation of the use of force: Revisiting Kosovo. *International Organization*, 72(3), 725–757.

Nylen, Alexandria J. (2020). Frontier justice: International law and 'lawless' spaces in the 'war on terror'. *European Journal of International Relations*, 26(3), 627–659.

Obama, Barack (2013). Remarks by the President at the National Defense University. https://obamawhitehouse.archives.gov/the-press-office/2013/05/23/remarks-president-national-defense-university.

Obama, Barack, Cameron, David, and Sarkozy, Nicolas (2011). Libya's pathway to peace. *The New York Times*, 14 April 2011.

Office of the Assistant Attorney General (2010). Memorandum for the Attorney General: Re: Applicability of Federal Criminal Laws and the Constitution to Contemplated Lethal Operations Against Shayk Anwar Al-Aulaqi. https://fas.org/irp/agency/doj/olc/aulaqi.pdf.

Office of the Attorney General (2013). Letter to Senator Patrick J. Leahy. www.justice.gov/slideshow/AG-letter-5-22-13.pdf.

Office of the Press Secretary (2013). Fact Sheet: U.S. Policy Standards and Procedures for the Use of Force in Counterterrorism Operations Outside the United States and Areas of Active Hostilities. www.whitehouse.gov/the-press-office/2013/05/23/fact-sheet-us-policy-standards-and-procedures-use-force-counterterrorism.

Office of the Prosecutor (2010a). Prosecutor's Application Pursuant to Article 58 as to Francis Kirimi Muthaura, Uhuru Muigai Kenyatta and Mohammed Hussein Ali. www.icc-cpi.int/iccdocs/doc/doc1050845.pdf.

(2010b). Prosecutor's Application Pursuant to Article 58 as to William Samoei Ruto, Henry Kiprono Kosgey and Joshua Arap Sang. www.icc-cpi.int/iccdocs/doc/doc1050835.pdf.

(2013). Policy Paper on Preliminary Examinations. www.icc-cpi.int/iccdocs/otp/otp-policy_paper_preliminary_examinations_2013-eng.pdf.

OHCHR (n.d.a). Human Rights Bodies – Complaints Procedures. www.ohchr.org/en/hrbodies/tbpetitions/pages/hrtbpetitions.aspx.

(n.d.b). World Conference on Human Rights, Vienna, 1993. www.ohchr.org/en/aboutus/pages/viennawc.aspx.

Ohlin, Jens D. (2012). Targeting Co-Belligerents. In Finkelstein, Claire, Ohlin, Jens D., and Altman, Andrew, eds., *Targeted Killing*. Oxford: Oxford University Press, 60–89.

(2013). Is *Jus in Bello* in Crisis? *Journal of International Criminal Justice*, 11(1), 27–45.

(2015). Co-perpetration. In Stahn, Carsten, ed., *The Law and Practice of the International Criminal Court*. Oxford: Oxford University Press, 517–537.

Onuf, Nicholas G. (1989). *World of Our Making*. Columbia: University of South Carolina Press.

(2013). *Making Sense, Making Worlds*. Oxford; New York: Routledge.

(2016). Constructivism at the crossroads; or, the problem of moderate-sized dry goods. *International Political Sociology*, 10(2), 115–132.

OPCW (2015). Member State – Syria. https://www.opcw.org/about-us/member-states/syria.

Open Society Justice Initiative (2015). Death by Drone: Civilian Harm Caused by U.S. Targeted Killings in Yemen. www.justiceinitiative.org/uploads/1284eb37-f380-4400-9242-936a15e4de6c/death-drones-report-eng-20150413.pdf.

Orchard, Phil (2014). *A Right to Flee*. Cambridge: Cambridge University Press.

(2020). Contestation, norms and the Responsibility to Protect as a regime. In Hunt, Charles T., and Orchard, Phil, eds., *Constructing the Responsibility to Protect*. Abingdon; Oxon; New York: Routledge, 28–49.

Orend, Brian (2014). Post-intervention. In Scheid, Don E., ed., *The Ethics of Armed Humanitarian Intervention*. Cambridge: Cambridge University Press, 224–242.

Orford, Anne (2011). *International Authority and the Responsibility to Protect*. Cambridge: Cambridge University Press.

Organisation of Islamic Cooperation (2011). Final Communique Issued by the Emergency Meeting of the Committee of Permanent Representatives to the Organization of the Islamic Conference on the Alarming Developments in Libyan Jamahiriya. https://reliefweb.int/report/libya/final-communique-issued-emergency-meeting-committee-permanent-representatives.

Orr, Andrew C. (2011). Unmanned, unprecedented, and unresolved: The status of American drone strikes in Pakistan under international law. *Cornell International Law Journal*, 44(3), 729.

Osiel, Mark (2014). Who are atrocity's 'real' perpetrators, who its 'true' victims and beneficiaries? *Ethics & International Affairs*, 28(03), 281–297.

Owens, Patricia (2007). *Between War and Politics*. Oxford: Oxford University Press.

(2008). Humanity, sovereignty, and the camps. *International Politics*, 45, 522–530.

(2012). Human security and the rise of the social. *Review of International Studies*, 38, 547–567.

Pacheco-Vega, Raul (2018). Writing Theoretical Frameworks, Analytical Frameworks and Conceptual Frameworks. www.raulpacheco.org/2018/09/writing-theoretical-frameworks-analytical-frameworks-and-conceptual-frameworks/.

Pacho, Irmina, and Bodnar, Adam (2012). Targeted killings (drone strikes) and the European convention on human rights. *Polish Yearbook of International Law*, 32 (189–208).

Pakistan Ministry of Foreign Affairs (2015). Pakistan Condemns US Drone Strike in North Waziristan. http://mofa.gov.pk/pakistan-condemns-us-drone-strike-in-north-waziristan/.

Panke, Diana, and Petersohn, Ulrich (2012). Why international norms disappear sometimes. *European Journal of International Relations*, 18(4), 719–742.

Papamichail, Andeas, and Partis-Jennings, Hannah (2016). Why common humanity? Framing the responsibility to protect as a common response. *International Politics*, 53(1), 83–100.

Pape, Robert A. (2012). When duty calls. *International Security*, 37(1), 41–80.

(2015). Response to Roland Paris Article. *International Peacekeeping*, 22(1), 9–10.

Paris, Roland (2014). The 'Responsibility to Protect' and the structural problems of preventive humanitarian intervention. *International Peacekeeping*, 21(5), 569–603.

Parks, Louise (2018). Spaces for local voices? A discourse analysis of the decisions of the convention on biological diversity. *Journal of Human Rights and the Environment*, 9(2), 141–170.

Parks, W. Hays (1989). Memorandum of Law Subject: Executive Order 12333 and Assassination. (DAJA-IA (27-1A)). https://sites.duke.edu/lawfire/files/2019/01/ParksMemo1989.pdf.

Parlett, Kate (2011). *The Individual in the International Legal System*. Cambridge: Cambridge University Press.

Partzsch, Lena (2014). *Die neue Macht von Individuen in der globalen Politik*. Baden-Baden: Nomos Verlagsgesellschaft.

(2017). Powerful individuals in a globalized world. *Global Policy*, 8(1), 5–13.

Pattison, James (2011). The ethics of humanitarian intervention in Libya. *Ethics & International Affairs*, 25(3), 271–277.

(2017). Perilous noninterventions? The counterfactual assessment of Libya and the need to be a responsible power. *Global Responsibility to Protect*, 9(2), 219–228.

Patton, Michael Q. (1990). *Qualitative Evaluation and Research Methods*. 2nd ed. Newbury Park; London: SAGE.

Pecquet, Julian (2015). Emails to Hillary Contradict French Tale on Libya War. www.al-monitor.com/pulse/originals/2015/06/libya-gadhafi-french-spies-rebels-support.html.

Pedde, Nicola (2017). The Libyan conflict and its controversial roots. *European View*, 16(1), 93–102.

Peltner, Anne (2017). Competing norms and foreign policy change: Humanitarian intervention and British foreign policy. *International Politics*, 54(6), 745–759.

Percy, Sarah (2019). What makes a norm robust: The norm against female combat. *Journal of Global Security Studies*, 4(1), 123–138.

Peron, Alcides Eduardo dos Reis (2011). The 'surgical' legitimacy of drone strikes? *Journal of Strategic Security*, 7(4), 81–93.

Peters, Anne (2006). Compensatory constitutionalism: The function and potential of fundamental international norms and structures. *Leiden Journal of International Law*, 19(3), 579–610.

(2009). Humanity as the A and Ω of sovereignty. *European Journal of International Law*, 20(3), 513–544.

(2011). Das subjektive internationale Recht. *Jahrbuch des Öffentlichen Rechts der Gegenwart*, 59, 411–456.

(2014). *Jenseits Der Menschenrechte*. Tübingen: Mohr Siebeck.

(2016). *Beyond Human Rights: The Legal Status of the Individual in International Law*. Cambridge: Cambridge University Press.

Peters, Daniel (2015). Der 'perfekte Sturm' in Libyen und die Implementierung der Schutzverantwortung – Vom begrenzten Nutzen einer kriterienbasierten Entscheidungsfindung. In Staack, Michael, and Krause, Dan, eds., *Schutzverantwortung in der Debatte*. Opladen; Berlin; Toronto: Verlag Barbara Budrich, 161–180.

Pettman, Jan J. (1992). A feminist perspective on peace and security. *Interdisciplinary Peace Research*, 4(2), 58–71.

Pfeiffer, Sven (2013). Rights of indigenous peoples and the international drug control regime: The case of traditional coca leaf chewing. *Göttingen Journal of International Law*, 5(1), 287–324.

Phillips, Christopher (2020). *The Battle for Syria: International Rivalry in the New Middle East*. New Haven; London: Yale University Press.

Pincus, Walter (2014). Are Predator Drones a Technological Tipping Point in Warfare? www.washingtonpost.com/world/are-predator-drones-a-technological-tipping-point-in-warfare/2011/04/19/AFmC6PdE_story.html.

Plaw, Avery (2013). Counting the dead: The proportionality of predation in Pakistan. In Strawser, Bradley J., ed., *Killing by Remote Control*. Oxford: Oxford University Press, 126–153.

Pollack, Mark A. (2020). *International Relations Theory and International Courts and Tribunals*. https://ssrn.com/abstract=3634791.

Pouliot, Vincent (2008). The logic of practicality: A theory of practice of security communities. *International Organization*, 62(2), 257–288.

(2010). *International Security in Practice: The Politics of NATO-Russia Diplomacy*. New York: Cambridge University Press.

Pradetto, August (2015). R2P, der Regimewechsel in Libyen und die Nichtintervention in Syrien: Durchbruch oder Sargnagel für die Schutzverantwortung. In Staack, Michael, and Krause, Dan, eds., *Schutzverantwortung in der Debatte*. Opladen; Berlin; Toronto: Verlag Barbara Budrich, 15–54.

Pratt, Simon F. (2019). Norm transformation and the institutionalization of targeted killing in the US. *European Journal of International Relations*, 25(3), 723–747.

(2020). From norms to normative configurations: A pragmatist and relational approach to theorizing normativity in IR. *International Theory*, 12(1), 59–82.

President of the Security Council (2011). *Statement by the President of the Security Council*. (S/PRST/2011/16). www.securitycouncilreport.org/atf/cf/%7B65BFCF9B-6D27-4E9C-8CD3-CF6E4FF96FF9%7D/Syria%20%20SPRST%202011%2016.pdf.

President of the United States (1981). Executive Order 12333. www.archives.gov/federal-register/codification/executive-order/12333.html.

Price, Richard (2019). Syria and the chemical weapons taboo. *Journal of Global Security Studies*, 4(1), 37–52.

Prügl, Elisabeth (2012). Feminism and the figure of man. *International Studies Review*, 14(4), 656–660.

Quashigah, Kofi (2010). The future of the International Criminal Court in African crisis and its relationship with the R2P project. *Finnish Yearbook of International Law*, 21, 89–99.

Radice, Henry (2016). The Responsibility to Protect as humanitarian negotiation: A space for the 'politics of humanity'? *International Politics*, 53(1), 101–117.

Rajkovic, Nikolas M. (2010). 'Global law' and governmentality: Reconceptualizing the 'rule of law' as rule 'through' law. *European Journal of International Relations*, 18 (1), 29–52.

Ralph, Jason (2018). What should be done? Pragmatic constructivist ethics and the Responsibility to Protect. *International Organization, International Organization*, 72(1), 173–203.

Ralph, Jason, and Gifkins, Jess (2017). The purpose of United Nations Security Council practice: Contesting competence claims in the normative context created by the Responsibility to Protect. *European Journal of International Relations*, 23(3), 630–653.

Randelzhofer, Albrecht (1999). The legal position of the individual under present international law. In Randelzhofer, Albrecht, and Tomuschat, Christian, eds.,

State Responsibility and the Individual. The Hague; London; Boston: Martinus Nijhoff, 231–242.

Rankin, Melinda (2018). The future of international criminal evidence in new wars? The evolution of the commission for international justice and accountability (CIJA). *Journal of Genocide Research*, 20(3), 392–411.

Reike, Ruben (2014). The 'responsibility to prevent'. *Ethics & International Affairs*, 28 (4), 451–476.

Reiners, Nina (2021a). Despite or because of contestation? How water became a human right. *Human Rights Quarterly*, 43(2), 329–343.

(2021b). *Transnational Lawmaking Coalitions for Human Rights*. Cambridge: Cambridge University Press.

Reinold, Theresa (2014). Transnationaler Terrorismus und Souveränität. In Volk, Christian, and Kuntz, Friederike, eds., *Der Begriff der Souveränität in der transnationalen Konstellation*. Baden-Baden: Nomos Verlagsgesellschaft, 165–188.

Renic, Neil C. (2019). Justified killing in an age of radically asymmetric warfare. *European Journal of International Relations*, 25(2), 408–430.

(2020). *Asymmetric Killing: Risk Avoidance, Just War, and the Warrior Ethos*. New York: Oxford University Press.

Renner, Judith (2013). *Discourse, Normative Change and the Quest for Reconciliation in Global Politics*. Manchester; New York: Manchester University Press.

Reprieve (2014). You Never Die Twice: Multiple Kills in the US Drone Program. https://reprieve.org/wp-content/uploads/sites/2/2020/07/Report_YouNeverDieTwice_2014.pdf.

Reus-Smit, Christian (2001). Human rights and the social construction of sovereignty. *Review of International Studies*, 27, 519–538.

(2013). *Individual Rights and the Making of the International System*. Cambridge: Cambridge University Press.

Rhoads, Emily P., and Welsh, Jennifer (2019). Close cousins in protection: The evolution of two norms. *International Affairs*, 95(3), 597–617.

Richter, Nicolas (2015). Glasaugen sehen schlecht. *Süddeutsche Zeitung*, 25 April 2015.

Ringmar, Erik (2014). The search for dialogue as a hindrance to understanding: Practices as inter-paradigmatic research program. *International Theory*, 6(1), 1–27.

Risse, Thomas (2000). 'Let's argue!': Communicative action in world politics. *International Organization*, 54(1), 1–39.

(2003). Konstruktivismus, Rationalismus und Theorien Internationaler Beziehungen - warum empirisch nichts so heiß gegessen wird, wie es theoretisch gekocht wurde. In Hellmann, Gunther, Wolf, Klaus D., and Zürn, Michael, eds., *Die neuen Internationalen Beziehungen: Forschungsstand und Perspektiven der Internationalen Beziehungen in Deutschland*. Baden-Baden: Nomos Verlagsgesellschaft, 99–132.

Risse, Thomas, Ropp, Stephen C., and Sikkink, Kathryn (1999a). *The Power of Human Rights: International Norms and Domestic Change*. Cambridge: Cambridge University Press.

Robinson, Darryl (2013). A cosmopolitan liberal account of the International Criminal Court. *Leiden Journal of International Law*, 26(1), 127–153.

Robinson, Fiona (2008). The importance of care in the theory and practice of human security. *Journal of International Political Theory*, 4(2), 167–188.

Rodin, David (2008). The moral inequality of soldiers: Why jus in bello asymmetry is half right. In Rodin, David, and Shue, Henry, eds., *Just and Unjust Warriors: The Moral and Legal Status of Soldiers*. Oxford: Oxford University Press, 44–68.

Rodley, Nigel (2015). 'Humanitarian intervention'. In Weller, Marc, ed., *The Oxford Handbook of The Use of Force in International Law*. Oxford: Oxford University Press, 775–796.

Roff, Heather M. (2013). *Global Justice, Kant, and the Responsibility to Protect*. Oxon: Routledge.

Roggio, Bill (2016). Charting the Data for US Airstrikes in Pakistan, 2004–2017. https://web.archive.org/web/20170109075551/; www.longwarjournal.org/pakistan-strikes.

Roggio, Bill, and Barry, Bob (2017). Charting the Data for US Airstrikes in Yemen, 2002–2015. https://web.archive.org/web/20170201091440/http://www.longwarjournal.org/yemen-strikes.

Rosén, Frederik (2014). Extremely stealthy and incredibly close: Drones, control and legal responsibility. *Journal of Conflict and Security Law*, 19(1), 1–19.

Rosert, Elvira (2019a). Norm emergence as agenda diffusion: Failure and success in the regulation of cluster munitions. *European Journal of International Relations*, 25 (4), 1103–1131.

(2019b). Salience and the emergence of international norms: Napalm and cluster munitions in the inhumane weapons convention. *Review of International Studies*, 45(1), 77–99.

Roxin, Claus (2008). *Täterschaft und Tatherrschaft*. 8th ed. Berlin: de Gruyter.

(2011). Crimes as part of organized power structure. *Journal of International Criminal Justice*, 9(1), 193–205.

Ruettershoff, Tobias (2015). Terrorising terrorist – The *jus ad bellum* of drone operations in Pakistan. In Aaronson, Mike, Aslam, Wali, Dyson, Tom, and Rauxloh, Regina, eds., *Precision Strike Warfare and International Intervention*. Oxon: Routledge, 133–151.

Ruggie, John G. (1998). What makes the world hang together? Neo-utilitarianism and the social constructivist challenge. *International Organization*, 52(4), 855–885

(2007). Business and human rights: The evolving international agenda. *American Journal of International Law*, 101(4), 819–840.

Russett, Bruce (2010). Liberalism. In Dunne, Timothy, Kurki, Milja, and Smith, Steve, eds., *International Relations Theories: Discipline and Diversity*. 2nd ed. Oxford: Oxford University Press, 95–115.

Saba, Arif, and Akbarzadeh, Shahram (2021). The ICC and R2P: Complementary or contradictory? *International Peacekeeping*, 28(1), 84–109.

SáCouto, Susana, and Clearly, Katherine (2008). The gravity threshold of the International Criminal Court. *American University International Law Review*, 23, 807–854.

Saifi, Sophia (2014). Not a 'Bug Splat': Artists Give Drone Victims a Face in Pakistan. http://edition.cnn.com/2014/04/09/world/asia/pakistan-drones-not-a-bug-splat/.

Sanders, Rebecca (2014). Legal frontiers: Targeted killing at the borders of war. *Journal of Human Rights*, 13(4), 512–536.

Sandholtz, Wayne (2019). Norm contestation, robustness, and replacement. *Journal of Global Security Studies*, 4(1), 139–146.

Sands, Phillipe (2006). Lawless world: The cultures of international law. *Texas International Law Journal*, 41(3), 387–398.

(2016a). *East West Street*. London: Weidenfeld & Nicolson.

(2016b). Reflections on international judicialization. *The European Journal of International Law*, 27(4), 885–900.

Sandvik, Kristin B., and Lohne, Kjersti (2014). The rise of the humanitarian drone: Giving content to an emerging concept. *Millennium: Journal of International Studies*, 43(1), 145–164.

Sassóli, Marco (2014). Autonomous weapons and international humanitarian law: Advantages, open technical questions and legal issues to be clarified. *International Law Studies*, 90, 308–340.

Saul, Ben, ed. (2014). *Research Handbook on International Law and Terrorism*. Cheltenham; Northhampton: Edward Elgar.

Saura, Laura (2019). Drones, the Body, and the Human in War: Targeted Killing as 'Almost-Touch'. EISA Pan-European Conference on International Relations, Sofia, Bulgaria. On file with author

Savage, Charlie (2021). Trump's secret rules for drone strikes outside war zones are disclosed. *The New York Times*, 1 May 2021.

Schabas, William A. (2013). The short arm of international criminal law. In Schabas, William A., McDermott, Yvonne, and Hayes, Niamh, eds., *The Ashgate Research Companion to International Criminal Law: Critical Perspectives*. Surrey; Burlington: Ashgate, 387–405.

(2020). The dynamics of the Rome conference. In deGuzman, Margaret M., and Oosterveld, Valerie, eds., *The Elgar Companion to the International Criminal Court*. Cheltenham: Edward Elgar, 3–19.

Scharf, Michael P. (1999). The amnesty exception to the jurisdiction of the International Criminal Court. *Cornell International Law Journal*, 32(3), 507–527.

Schiff, Benjamin N. (2008). *Building the International Criminal Court*. Cambridge; New York: Cambridge University Press.

Schmidt, Averell, and Sikkink, Kathryn (2019). Breaking the ban? The heterogeneous impact of US contestation of the torture norm. *Journal of Global Security Studies*, 4(1), 105–122.

Schmidt, Dennis R., and Trenta, Luca (2018). Changes in the law of self-defence? Drones, imminence, and international norm dynamics. *Journal on the Use of Force and International Law*, 5(2), 201–245.

Schmidt, Hajo (2015). Instrumente der Re-Legimitierung des Krieges oder Vehikel der Kriegsächtung: Eine Betrachtung der R2P aus friedensethischer Sicht. In Staack, Michael, and Krause, Dan, eds., *Schutzverantwortung in der Debatte*. Opladen; Berlin; Toronto: Verlag Barbara Budrich, 139–160.

Schmitt, Michael N. (2013). Extraterritorial lethal targeting: Deconstructing the logic of international law. *Columbia Journal of Transnational Law*, 52(1), 77–112.

Schmitter, Philippe (2008). The design of social and political research. In Della Porta, Donatella, and Keating, Michael, eds., *Approaches and Methodologies in the Social Sciences*. Cambridge: Cambridge University Press, 263–295.

Schoch, Bruno (2014). Die Libyen-Intervention: Warum Deutschlands Enthaltung im Sicherheitsrat falsch war. In Beestermöller, Gerhard, ed., *Libyen: Missbrauch der Responsibility to Protect?* Baden-Baden: Nomos Verlagsgesellschaft, 115–138.

Schreuer, Christoph (1993). The waning of the sovereign state: Towards a new paradigm for international law? *European Journal of International Law*, 4(1), 447–471.

Schulz, Philipp (2018). Displacement from gendered personhood: Sexual violence and masculinities in northern Uganda. *International Affairs*, 94(5), 1101–1119.

Schwarz, Elke (2016). Prescription drones: On the techno-biopolitical regimes of contemporary 'ethical killing'. *Security Dialogue*, 47(1), 59–75.

Schwedler, Jillian (2013). Puzzle. *Qualitative and Multi-Method Research*, 11(2), 27–30.

Schweiger, Elisabeth (2019a). 'Targeted killing' and the lack of acquiescence. *Leiden Journal of International Law*, 32(4), 741–757.

(2019b). The lure of novelty: 'Targeted killing' and its older terminological siblings. *International Political Sociology*, 13(3), 276–295.

Scott, Joan W. (1991). The evidence of experience. *Critical Inquiry*, 17(4), 773–797.

Secretary General (2014). Implementation of Security Council resolution 2139 (2014). (S/2014/295). www.securitycouncilreport.org/atf/cf/%7B65BFCF9B-6D27-4E9C-8CD3-CF6E4FF96FF9%7D/s_2014_295.pdf.

Security Council Report (2018). Syria: Chronology of Events. www.securitycouncilreport.org/chronology/syria.php.

(2021). Syria. www.securitycouncilreport.org/syria/.

Sehmi, Anushka (2018). 'Now that we have no voice, what will happen to us?' – Experiences of victim participation in the Kenyatta case. *Journal of International Criminal Justice*, 16(3), 571–591.

Seibel, Wolfgang (2013). Libyen, das Prinzip der Schutzverantwortung und Deutschlands Stimmenthaltung im UN-Sicherheitsrat bei der Abstimmung über Resolution 1973 am 17. März 2011. In Daase, Christopher, and Junk, Julian, eds., *Die Friedenswarte: Journal of International Peace and Organization*. 88(1–2), 87–115.

Selth, Andrew (2008). Even paranoids have enemies: Cyclone Nargis and Myanmar's fears of invasion. *Contemporary Southeast Asia: A Journal of International and Strategic Affairs*, 30(3), 379–402.

Senn, Martin, and Troy, Jodok (2017). The transformation of targeted killing and international order. *Contemporary Security Policy*, 38(2), 175–211.

Sewell Jr., William H. (1992). A theory of structure: Duality, agency and transformation. *American Journal of Sociology*, 98(1), 1–29.

Shah, Sikander A. (2015). *International Law and Drone Strikes in Pakistan*. Oxon: Routledge.

Shaw, Ian Graham Ronald, and Akther, Majed (2012). The unbearable humanness of drone warfare in FATA, *Pakistan. Antipode*, 44(4), 1490–1509.

Shaw, Malcolm N. (2003). *International Law*. 5th ed. Cambridge: Cambridge University Press.

(2021). *International Law*. 9th ed. Cambridge: Cambridge University Press.

Shepherd, Laura J. (2011). Sex, security and superhero(in)es: From 1325 to 1820 and beyond. *International Feminist Journal of Politics*, 13(4), 504–521.

(2017). *Gender, UN Peacebuilding, and the Politics of Space*. New York: Oxford University Press.

Shesterinina, Anastasia (2016). Evolving norms of protection: China, Libya and the problem of intervention in armed conflict. *Cambridge Review of International Affairs*, 29(3), 812–830.

Sienknecht, Mitja (2021). Rebel with a cause: Rebel responsibility in intrastate conflict situations. In Hansen-Magnusson, Hannes, and Vetterlein, Antje eds., *The Routledge Handbook on Responsibility in International Relations*. London: Routledge, 271–287.

Sikkink, Kathryn (2011a). Beyond the Justice Cascade: How Agentic Constructivism Could Help Explain Change in International Politics. Revised Paper from a Keynote Address, Millennium Annual Conference, October 22, 2011, 'Out of the Ivory Tower: Weaving the Theories and Practice of International Relations', London School of Economics, to Be Presented at the Princeton University IR Colloquium, November 21, 2011. On file with author.

(2011b). *The Justice Cascade*. 1st ed. New York; London: W. W. Norton & Company.

(2017). *Evidence for Hope: Making Human Rights Work in the 21st Century*. Princeton: Princeton University Press.

Simma, Bruno, and Paulus, Andreas L. (1998). The 'international community': Facing the challenge of globalization. *European Journal of International Law*, 9(2), 266–277.

Simmons, Beth A., and Jo, Hyeran (2019). Measuring norms and normative contestation: The case of international criminal law. *Journal of Global Security Studies*, 4 (1), 18–36.

Singer, Peter W. (2009). *Wired for War*. London: Penguin.

Sjoberg, Laura (2016). The gender of violence in war and conflict. In Steans, Jill, and Tepe-Belfrage, Daniela, eds., *Handbook on Gender in World Politics*. Cheltenham: Edward Elgar, 197–205.

(2020). Quantum ambivalence. *Millennium: Journal of International Studies*, 030582982097171.

Smeulers, Alette (2020). A criminological approach to the ICC's control theory. In Heller, Kevin J., Mégret, Frédéric, Nouwen, Sarah M., Ohlin, Jens D., and Robinson, Darryl, eds., *The Oxford Handbook of International Criminal Law*. Oxford: Oxford University Press, 379–399.

Smith, Karen E. (2010). *Genocide and the Europeans*. New York: Cambridge University Press.

Solomon, Ty, and Steele, Brent J. (2017). Micro-moves in international relations theory. *European Journal of International Relations*, 23(2), 267–291.

Sparrow, Robert (2012). Robotic weapons and the future of war. In Tripodi, Paolo, and Wolfendale, Jessica, eds., *New wars and new soldiers*. Farnham Surrey; England; Burlington: Ashgate, 117–133.

Srivastava, Swati (2020). Varieties of social construction. *International Studies Review*, 22(3), 325–346.

Stahn, Carsten (2012). Libya, the International Criminal Court and complementarity: A test for 'shared responsibility'. *Journal of International Criminal Justice*, 10(2), 325–349.

(2014). Between law-breaking and law-making: Syria, humanitarian intervention and 'what the law ought to be'. *Journal of Conflict and Security Law*, 19(1), 25–48.

(2015). Introduction: More than a court, less than a court, several courts in one? In Stahn, Carsten, ed., *The Law and Practice of the International Criminal Court*. Oxford: Oxford University Press, lxxxiii–c.

Stamnes, Eli (2009). 'Speaking R2P' and the prevention of mass atrocities. *Global Responsibility to Protect*, 1(1), 70–89.

Staunton, Eglantine, and Ralph, Jason (2020). The Responsibility to Protect Norm cluster and the challenge of atrocity prevention: An analysis of the European Union's strategy in Myanmar. *European Journal of International Relations*, 26(3), 660–686.

Steans, Jill, and Tepe-Belfrage, Daniela, eds. (2016). *Handbook on Gender in World Politics*. Cheltenham: Edward Elgar.

Stearns, Scott (2011). African Union Says ICC Prosecutions Are Discriminatory. www.voanews.com/africa/african-union-says-icc-prosecutions-are-discriminatory.

Stephen, Chris (2015). Gaddafi's son Saif al-Islam sentenced to death by court in Libya. www.theguardian.com/world/2015/jul/28/saif-al-islam-sentenced-death-by-court-in-libya-gaddafi-son.

Sterling-Folker, Jennifer (2010). Neoliberalism. In Dunne, Timothy, Kurki, Milja, and Smith, Steve, eds., *International Relations Theories: Discipline and Diversity*. 2nd ed. Oxford: Oxford University Press, 116–134.

Stern, Maria (2016). Poststructuralist feminism in world politics. In Steans, Jill, and Tepe-Belfrage, Daniela, eds., *Handbook on Gender in World Politics*. Cheltenham: Edward Elgar, 33–40.

Stimmer, Anette (2019). Beyond internalization: Alternate endings of the norm life cycle. *International Studies Quarterly*, 63(2), 270–280.

Stimmer, Anette, and Wisken, Lea (2019). The dynamics of dissent: When actions are louder than words. *International Affairs*, 95(3), 515–533.

Stolk, Sofia (2018). A sophisticated beast? On the construction of an 'ideal' perpetrator in the opening statements of international criminal trials. *European Journal of International Law*, 29(3), 677–701.

Stone Sweet, Alec (2011). Managing difference: Constitutional pluralism and transnational rights protection. In Raube, Kolja, and Sattler, Annik, eds., *Difference and Democracy*. Frankfurt am Main; New York: Campus Verlag, 227–244.

(2012). A cosmopolitan legal order: Constitutional pluralism and rights adjudication in Europe. *Global Constitutionalism – Human Rights, Democracy and the Rule of Law*, 1(1), 53–90.

Strauss, Ekkehard (2009). *The Emperor's New Clothes? The United Nations and the Implementation of the Responsibility to Protect*. 1st ed. Baden-Baden: Nomos Verlagsgesellschaft.

Strawser, Bradley J. (2013). Introduction: The moral landscape of unmanned weapons. In Strawser, Bradley J., ed., *Killing by Remote Control*. Oxford: Oxford University Press, 3–24.

Strüwer, Elisabeth (2010). *Zum Zusammenspiel von humanitären Völkerrecht und den Menschenrechten am Beispiel des Targeted Killing*. Bonn: Peter Lang Internationaler Verlag der Wissenschaften.

Suddaby, Roy (2006). From the editors: What grounded theory is not. *Academy of Management Journal*, 49(4), 633–642.

Sylvester, Christine (2013a). Experiencing the end and afterlives of international relations/theory. *European Journal of International Relations*, 19(3), 609–626.

(2013b). *War as Experience*. Oxon: Routledge.

Tacheva, Blagovesta, and Brown, Garrett W. (2015). Global constitutionalism and the Responsibility to Protect. *Global Constitutionalism – Human Rights, Democracy and the Rule of Law*, 4(3), 428–467.
Teitel, Ruti (2011). *Humanity's Law*. Oxford: Oxford University Press.
(2013). Response. *Ethics & International Affairs*, 27(2), 233–234.
Téson, Fernando R. (2014). The moral basis of armed humanitarian intervention revisited. In Scheid, Don E., ed., *The Ethics of Armed Humanitarian Intervention*. Cambridge: Cambridge University Press, 61–77.
Tétreault, Mary A., and Lipschutz, Ronnie D. (2005). *Global Politics as If People Mattered*. Lanham: Rowman & Littlefield.
Thakur, Ramesh (2015). R2P's 'Structural' Problems: A Response to Roland Paris. *International Peacekeeping*, 22(1), 11–25.
(2016). The Responsibility to Protect at 15. *International Affairs*, 92(2), 415–434.
Thies, Anne (2013). EU membership of the WTO: *Global Constitutionalism – Human Rights. Democracy and the Rule of Law*, 2(2), 237–261.
Thiessen, Marc A. (2010). Dead terrorists tell no tales. *Foreign Policy*, 8 February 2010.
Tickner, J. Ann (1991). Hans Morgenthau's principle of political realism: A feminist reformulation. In Grant, Rebecca, and Newland, Kathleen, eds., *Gender and International Relations*. Bloomington; Indianapolis: Indiana University Press, 27–40.
Tickner, J. Ann, and Sjoberg, Laura (2010). Feminism. In Dunne, Timothy, Kurki, Milja, and Smith, Steve, eds., *International Relations Theories: Discipline and Diversity*. 2nd ed. Oxford: Oxford University Press, 195–212.
Tickner, J. Ann, and True, Jacqui (2018). A century of international relations feminism: From World War I women's peace pragmatism to the women, peace and security agenda. *International Studies Quarterly*, 62(2), 221–233.
Timm, Trevor (2015). America's Drone Policy Is All Exceptions and No Rules. www.theguardian.com/commentisfree/2015/jun/20/americas-drone-policy-all-exceptions-no-rules-yemen.
Todorov, Tzvetan (2014). The Responsibility to Protect and the war in Libya. In Scheid, Don E., ed., *The Ethics of Armed Humanitarian Intervention*. Cambridge: Cambridge University Press, 46–58.
Tomuschat, Christian (1993). Obligations arising for states without or against their will. *Recueil des Cours*, 241(IV), 195–374.
(2014). Die Rechtmäßigkeit der Resolution 1973 (2011) des UN-Sicherheitsrates. In Beestermöller, Gerhard, ed., *Libyen: Missbrauch der Responsibility to Protect?* Baden-Baden: Nomos Verlagsgesellschaft, 13–29.
Tourinho, Marcos, Stuenkel, Oliver, and Brockmeier, Sarah (2016). 'Responsibility while protecting': Reforming R2P implementation. *Global Society*, 30(1), 134–150.
Towns, Ann E. (2010). *Women and States – Norms and Hierarchies in International Society*. Cambridge: Cambridge University Press.
Trahan, Jennifer (2017). The International Criminal Court's Libya case(s) – The need for consistency with international human rights as to due process and the death penalty. *International Criminal Law Review*, 17(5), 803–843.
True, Jacqui (2009). Feminism. In Burchill, Scott, Linklater, Andrew, Devetak, Richard, Donnelly, Jack, Nardin, Terry, Paterson, Matthew, Reus-Smit,

Christian, and True, Jacqui, eds., *Theories of International Relations*. 4th ed. Hampshire: Palgrave Macmillan, 237–259.

True, Jacqui, and Wiener, Antje (2019). Everyone wants (a) peace: The dynamics of rhetoric and practice on 'women, peace and security'. *International Affairs*, 95(3), 553–574.

Tushnet, Mark (1991). Critical legal studies: A political history. *The Yale Law Journal*, 100(5), 1515–1544.

Ulbert, Cornelia (2012). Vom Klang vieler Stimmen: Herausforderungen 'kritischer' Normenforschung. *Zeitschrift für Internationale Beziehungen*, 19(2), 129–139.

UN Diplomatic Conferences of Plenipotentiaries on the Establishment of the International Criminal Court Rome Statute of the International Criminal Court. (1998). https://undocs.org/en/A/CONF.183/9.

UN DPI (2011). Security Council Approves 'No-Fly Zone' over Libya, Authorizing 'All Necessary Measures' to Protect Civilians, by Vote of 10 in Favour with 5 Abstentions. (SC/10200). www.un.org/News/Press/docs/2011/sc10200.doc.htm.

(2014). Security Council Unanimously Adopts Resolution 2139 (2014) To Ease Aid Delivery to Syrians, Provide Relief from 'Chilling Darkness'. www.un.org/News/Press/docs/2014/sc11292.doc.htm.

UNDP (1994). Human Development Report. http://hdr.undp.org/sites/default/files/reports/255/hdr_1994_en_complete_nostats.pdf.

UNGA (1948a). Convention on the Prevention and Punishment of the Crime of Genocide. https://treaties.un.org/doc/Publication/UNTS/Volume%2078/volume-78-I-1021-English.pdf.

(1948b). Universal Declaration of Human Rights. (A/RES/217). www.un.org/en/ga/search/view_doc.asp?symbol=A/RES/217(III).

(1950). Uniting for Peace. (377 (V)). www.un.org/en/sc/repertoire/otherdocs/GAres377A%28v%29.pdf.

United Nations (1945). UN Charter. www.un.org/en/documents/charter/.

(2003a). United Nations Operation in Somalia I. www.un.org/en/peacekeeping/missions/past/unosomi.htm.

(2003b). United Nations Operation in Somalia II. www.un.org/en/peacekeeping/missions/past/unosom2.htm.

(2005a). Basic Principles and Guidelines on the Right to a Remedy and Reparation for Victims of Gross Violations of International Human Rights Law and Serious Violations of International Humanitarian Law. (A/Res/60/147). https://undocs.org/A/RES/60/147.

(2005b). Outcome Document of the 2005 World Summit. (A/RES/60/1). https://undocs.org/A/RES/60/1.

(2014). Security Council Unanimously Adopts Resolution Condemning Violent Extremism, Underscoring Need to Prevent Travel, Support for Foreign Terrorist Fighters. www.un.org/press/en/2014/sc11580.doc.htm.

(2020). UN Salutes New Libya Ceasefire Agreement That Points to 'A Better, Safer, and More Peaceful Future'. https://news.un.org/en/story/2020/10/1076012.

UNSC (1991). Resolution 688. (S/RES/688). https://undocs.org/S/RES/688(1991).

(1992a). Resolution 767. (S/RES/767). https://undocs.org/S/RES/767(1992).

(1992b). Resolution 794. (S/RES/794). https://undocs.org/S/RES/794(1992).

(1993a). Resolution 814. (S/RES/814). https://undocs.org/S/RES/814(1993).

(1993b). Resolution 819. (S/RES/819). https://undocs.org/S/RES/819(1993).
(1994a). Resolution 918. (S/RES/918). https://undocs.org/S/RES/918(1994).
(1994b). Resolution 925. (S/RES/925). https://undocs.org/S/RES/925(1994).
(1998). Resolution 1199. (S/RES/1199). https://undocs.org/S/RES/1199(1998).
(2001a). Resolution 1368. (S/Res/1368). https://undocs.org/S/RES/1368(2001).
(2001b). Resolution 1373. (S/RES/1373). https://undocs.org/S/RES/1373(2001).
(2006a). Resolution 1674. (S/RES/1674). https://undocs.org/S/RES/1674(2006).
(2006b). Resolution 1706. (S/RES/1706). https://undocs.org/S/RES/1706(2006).
(2011a). 6491st Meeting. (S/PV.6491). https://undocs.org/S/PV.6491.
(2011b). 6498th Meeting. https://undocs.org/S/PV.6498.
(2011c). 6627th Meeting. (S/PV.6627).
(2011d). Resolution 1970. https://undocs.org/S/RES/1970(2011).
(2011e). Resolution 1973. (S/RES/1973). https://undocs.org/S/RES/1973(2011).
(2011f). Security Council Approves 'No-Fly Zone' over Libya, Authorizing 'All Necessary Measures' to Protect Civilians, by Vote of 10 in Favour with 5 Abstentions. (SC/10200). www.un.org/press/en/2011/sc10200.doc.htm.
(2012a). 6711th Meeting. (S/PV.7611). https://undocs.org/S/PV.6711.
(2012b). Resolution 2042. (S/RES/2042). https://undocs.org/S/RES/2042(2012).
(2012c). Resolution 2043. (S/RES/2043). https://undocs.org/S/RES/2043(2012).
(2012d). Resolution 2059. (S/RES/2059). https://undocs.org/S/RES/2059(2012).
(2013a). Resolution 2100. (S/RES/2100). https://undocs.org/S/RES/2100(2013).
(2013b). Resolution 2118. (S/RES/2118). https://undocs.org/S/RES/2118(2013).
(2013c). Resolution 2121. (S/RES/2121). https://undocs.org/S/RES/2121(2013).
(2014a). 7180th Meeting. (S/PV.7180). https://undocs.org/S/PV.7180.
(2014b). 7216th Meeting. (S/PV.7216). https://undocs.org/S/PV.7216.
(2014c). Resolution 2139. (S/RES/2139). https://undocs.org/S/RES/2139(2014).
(2014d). Resolution 2165. (S/RES/2165). https://undocs.org/S/RES/2165(2014).
(2015a). Resolution 2235. (S/RES/2235). https://undocs.org/S/RES/2235(2015).
(2015b). Resolution 2254. (S/RES/2254). https://undocs.org/S/RES/2254(2015).
(2015c). Resolution 2558. (S/RES/2258). https://undocs.org/S/RES/2258(2015).

US President (2010). National Security Strategy. https://obamawhitehouse.archives.gov/sites/default/files/rss_viewer/national_security_strategy.pdf.
(2013). Procedures for Approving Direct Action Against Terrorist Targets Located Outside the United States and Areas of Active Hostilities. www.justice.gov/oip/foia-library/procedures_for_approving_direct_action_against_terrorist_targets/download.
(2016). Executive Order 13732 of July 1, 2016: United States Policy on Pre- and Post-Strike Measures to Address Civilian Casualties in U.S. Operations Involving the Use of Force. www.govinfo.gov/content/pkg/FR-2016-07-07/pdf/2016-16295.pdf.

USFOR (2010). Executive Summary for AR 15-6 Investigation, 21 February 2010 CIVCAS Incident in Uruzgan Province. http://cryptome.org/2012/03/creech-savagery.pdf.

van Beers, Britta, Corrias, Luigi, and Werner, Wouter, eds. (2014). *Humanity across International Law and Biolaw*. Cambridge: Cambridge University Press.

van Langenhove, Luk, and Harré, Rom (1999). Introducing positioning analysis. In Harré, Rom, and van Langenhove, Luk, eds., *Positioning Theory: Moral Contexts of Intentional Action*. Malden: Blackwell, 14–31.

van Sliedregt, Elies (2015). Perpetration and participation in article 25(3). In Stahn, Carsten, ed., *The Law and Practice of the International Criminal Court*. Oxford: Oxford University Press, 499–516.

Vasiliev, Sergey (2014). The Making of International Criminal Law. https://papers.ssrn.com/sol3/papers.cfm?abstract_id=2518406.

Vennesson, Pascal (2008). Case studies and process tracing: Theories and practice. In Della Porta, Donatella, and Keating, Michael, eds., *Approaches and Methodologies in the Social Sciences*. Cambridge: Cambridge University Press, 223–239.

Venzke, Ingo (2009). Legal contestation about 'enemy combatants'. *Journal of International Law & International Relations*, 5(1), 155–184.

Verlage, Christopher (2009). *Responsibility to Protect: Ein neuer Ansatz im Völkerrecht zur Verhinderung von Völkermord, Kriegsverbrechen und Verbrechen gegen die Menschlichkeit*. Tübingen: Mohr Siebeck.

(2013). Die Sicherheitsratsresolution 1973 zum Fall Libyen – Ein Meilenstein für die völkerrechtliche Verankerung der Responsibility to Protect. In Daase, Christopher, and Junk, Julian, eds., *Die Friedenswarte: Journal of International Peace and Organization*. 88(1–2), 63–86.

Vetterlein, Antje, and Hansen-Magnusson, Hannes (2020). The rise of responsibility in world politics. In Hansen-Magnusson, Hannes, and Vetterlein, Antje, eds., *The Rise of Responsibility in World Politics*. Cambridge: Cambridge University Press, 8–37.

Vetterlein, Antje, and Wiener, Antje (2013). Gemeinschaft Revisited: Die sozialen Grundlagen internationaler Ordnung. *Leviathan*, 41(Sonderband 28/2013), 78–103.

Volk, Christian (2010). The decline of order: Hannah Arendt and the paradoxes of the nation-state. In Benhabib, Seyla, ed., *Politics in Dark Times: Encounters with Hannah Arendt*. Cambridge: Cambridge University Press, 173–197.

von Arnauld, Andreas (2009). Souveränität und Responsibility to Protect. *Die Friedenswarte: Journal of International Peace and Organization*, 84(1), 11–52.

(2011). Die Rückkehr des Bürgers. *Jahrbuch des Öffentlichen Rechts der Gegenwart*, 59, 497–519.

(2015). Werdende Norm oder politisches Konzept? In Staack, Michael, and Krause, Dan, eds., *Schutzverantwortung in der Debatte*. Opladen; Berlin; Toronto: Verlag Barbara Budrich, 55–76.

von Bernstorff, Jochen (2016). Drone strikes, terrorism and the zombie: On the construction of an administrative law of transnational executions. *ESIL Reflections*, 5(7), 1–6.

Waddington, Conway (2015). Drones. In Aaronson, Mike, Aslam, Wali, Dyson, Tom, and Rauxloh, Regina, eds., *Precision Strike Warfare and International Intervention*. Oxon: Routledge, 114–132.

Wagner, Markus (2014). The dehumanization of international humanitarian law. *Vanderbilt Journal of Transnational Law*, 47(5), 1371–1424.

(2015). Unmanned Aerial Vehicles. http://ssrn.com/abstract=2584652.

Waldron, Jeremy (2016). Death squads and death lists: Targeted killing and the character of the state. *Constellations*, 23(2), 292–307.
Walter, Christian (2012). Subjects of International Law. https://opil.ouplaw.com/view/10.1093/law:epil/9780199231690/law-9780199231690-e1476.
Waltz, Kenneth N. (1959). *Man, the State, and War*. New York: Columbia University Press.
(1979). *Theory of International Politics*. New York: McGraw-Hill.
Weber, Cynthia (1994). Review. *The American Political Science Review*, 88(4), 1049–1051.
(1995). *Simulating Sovereignty – Intervention, the State and Symbolic Exchange*. Cambridge: Cambridge University Press.
Weber, Max (2015 [1921]). *Soziologische Grundbegriffe*. Tübingen; Berlin: Mohr Siebeck.
Weber, Samuel (2005). *Targets of Opportunity*. New York: Fordham University Press.
Weerdesteijn, Maartje, and Holá, Barbora (2020). 'Tool in the R2P toolbox'? Analysing the role of the International Criminal Court in the three pillars of the Responsibility to Protect. *Criminal Law Forum*, 31(3), 377–414.
Weill, Sharon (2016). Reducing the security gap through national courts: Targeted killings as a case study. *Journal of Conflict and Security Law*, 21(1), 49–67.
Weinert, Matthew S. (2015). *Making Human*. Ann Arbor: University of Michigan Press.
Weiss, Thomas G. (2007). *Humanitarian Intervention: Ideas in Action*. Cambridge; Malden: Polity Press.
(2011). RtoP alive and well after Libya. *Ethics & International Affairs*, 25(3), 287–292.
(2014). Military humanitarianism: Syria hasn't killed it. *The Washington Quarterly*, 37(1), 7–20.
Weiss, Thomas G., and Burke, Martin J. (2014). The Security Council and ad hoc tribunals: Law and politics, peace and justice. In Popovski, Vesselin, and Fraser, Trudy, eds., *The Security Council as Global Legislator*. London; New York: Routledge, 214–265.
Weldes, Jutta, and Saco, Diana (1996). Making state action possible. *Millennium: Journal of International Studies*, 25(2), 361–395.
Welsh, Jennifer M. (2011). Civilian protection in Libya: Putting coercion and controversy back into RtoP. *Ethics & International Affairs*, 25(3), 255–262.
(2013). Norm contestation and the Responsibility to Protect. *Global Responsibility to Protect*, 5(4), 365–396.
(2014). Responsibility to Protect and the language of crimes: Collective action and individual culpability. In Scheid, Don E., ed., *The Ethics of Armed Humanitarian Intervention*. Cambridge: Cambridge University Press, 209–223.
(2015). The Individualisation of War: Reconfiguring the Ethics, Law and Politics of Armed Conflict. http://iow.eui.eu/welcome/.
(2016a). The responsibility to prevent: Assessing the gap between rhetoric and reality. *Cooperation and Conflict*, 51(2), 216–232.
(2016b). The Responsibility to Protect at ten: Glass half empty or half full? *The International Spectator*, 51(2), 1–8.
(2019a). Norm robustness and the Responsibility to Protect. *Journal of Global Security Studies*, 4(1), 53–72.

(2019b). The individualisation of war: Defining a research programme. *Annals of the Fondazione Luigi Einaudi*, 53, 9–28.
Welsh, Jennifer M., and Banda, Maria (2010). International law and the Responsibility to Protect: Clarifying or expanding state's responsibility. *Global Responsibility to Protect*, 2(3), 213–231.
Wendt, Alexander (1987). The agent-structure problem in international relations theory. *International Organization*, 41(3), 335–370.
(1992). Anarchy is what states make of it: The social construction of power politics. *International Organization*, 46(2), 391–426.
(1999). *Social Theory of International Politics*. Cambridge: Cambridge University Press.
(2015). *Quantum Mind and Social Science: Unifying Physical and Social Ontology*. Cambridge: Cambridge University Press.
Wenzel, Nicola (2008). *Das Spannungsverhältnis zwischen Gruppenschutz und Individualschutz im Völkerrecht*. Berlin; Heidelberg; New York: Springer.
Wernicke, Christian (2014). Justiz des schlechten Gewissens. *Süddeutsche Zeitung*, 5 February 2014.
What's in Blue (2014). Draft Humanitarian Resolution on Syria and Briefing by Humanitarian Chief. www.whatsinblue.org/2014/02/draft-humanitarian-resolution-on-syria-and-briefing-by-humanitarian-chief.php.
(2016). Syria: Special Envoy to Brief on Political Talks. www.whatsinblue.org/2016/01/syria-special-envoy-to-brief-on-political-talks.php.
Wheeler, Nicholas J. (2002). *Saving Strangers – Humanitarian Intervention in International Society*. Oxford; New York: Oxford University Press.
(2006). The humanitarian responsibility of sovereignty: Explaining the development of a new norm of military intervention for humanitarian purposes in international society. In Welsh, Jennifer M., ed., *Humanitarian Intervention and International Relations*. Oxford; New York: Oxford University Press, 29–52.
Whetham, David (2013). Drones and targeted killing: Angels or assassins? In Strawser, Bradley J., ed., *Killing by Remote Control*. Oxford: Oxford University Press, 69–83
Whitworth, Sandra (1989). Gender in the inter-paradigm debate. *Millennium: Journal of International Studies*, 18(2), 265–272.
(2008). Feminism. In Reus-Smit, Christian, and Snidal, Duncan, eds., *The Oxford Handbook of International Relations*. Oxford: Oxford University Press, 391–407.
Wibben, Annick T. R. (2016). Feminist methodologies and world politics. In Steans, Jill, and Tepe-Belfrage, Daniela, eds., *Handbook on Gender in World Politics*. Cheltenham: Edward Elgar, 66–73.
Wiener, Antje (2003). Die Wende zum Dialog – Konstruktivistische Brueckenstationen und ihre Zukunft. In Hellmann, Gunther, Wolf, Klaus D., and Zürn, Michael, eds., *Die neuen Internationalen Beziehungen: Forschungsstand und Perspektiven der Internationalen Beziehungen in Deutschland*. Baden-Baden: Nomos Verlagsgesellschaft, 133–159.
(2004). Contested compliance: Interventions on the normative structure of world politics. *European Journal of International Relations*, 10(2), 189–234.
(2007). The dual quality of norms and governance beyond the state: Sociological and normative approaches to 'interaction'. *Critical Review of International Social and Political Philosophy*, 10(1), 47–69.

(2008). *The Invisible Constitution of Politics. Contested Norms and International Encounters*. Cambridge: Cambridge University Press.
(2009). Enacting meaning-in-use. Qualitative research on norms and international relations. *Review of International Studies*, 35(1), 175–193.
(2011). Comment: Global constitutionalism and the concept of difference. In Raube, Kolja, and Sattler, Annik, eds., *Difference and Democracy*. Frankfurt am Main; New York: Campus Verlag, 261–275.
(2014a). *A Theory of Contestation*. Heidelberg; New York: Springer.
(2014b). Kontestation in verknüpften Diskursräumen. *Zeitschrift für Internationale Beziehungen*, 21(2), 147–154.
(2017). Agency of the governed in global international relations: Access to norm validation. *Third World Thematics: A TWQ Journal*, 2(5), 709–725.
(2018). *Contestation and Constitution of Norms in Global International Relations*. Cambridge: Cambridge University Press.
Wiener, Antje, and Puetter, Uwe (2009). The quality of norms is what actors make of it: Constructivist research on norms. *Journal of International Law and International Relations*, 5(1), 1–16.
Wiesner, Ina (2015). UAV for R2P? In Aaronson, Mike, Aslam, Wali, Dyson, Tom, and Rauxloh, Regina, eds., *Precision Strike Warfare and International Intervention*. Oxon: Routledge, 152–170.
Wight, Colin (2006). *Agents, Structures, and International Relations*. Cambridge; New York: Cambridge University Press.
Wight, Colin, Hansen, Lene, and Dunne, Tim, eds. (2013). *End of International Relations Theory? A Special Issue. European Journal of International Relations*, 19(3).
Wilcox, Lauren B. (2015). *Bodies of Violence*. Oxford: Oxford University Press.
(2017). Embodying algorithmic war: Gender, race, and the posthuman in drone warfare. *Security Dialogue*, 48(1), 11–28.
Williams, Brian G. (2013). *Predators*. Dulles: Potomac Books.
Williams, Jody (2011). Borderless battlefield: The CIA, the U.S. Military, and drones . *International Journal of Intelligence Ethics*, 2(1), 2–34.
Williams, John (2015). Distant intimacy: Space, drones, and just war. *Ethics & International Affairs*, 29(1), 93–110.
Willmot, Haidi, and Mamiya, Ralph (2015). Mandated to protect: Security Council practice of the protection of civilians. In Weller, Marc, ed., *The Oxford Handbook of The Use of Force in International Law*. Oxford: Oxford University Press, 375–397.
Wilmer, Franke (2002). *The Social Construction of Man, the State, and War*. New York; London: Routledge.
Winston, Carla (2018). Norm structure, diffusion, and evolution: A conceptual approach. *European Journal of International Relations*, 24(3), 638–661.
Woods, Chris (2015). Covert drone strikes and the fiction of zero civilian casualties. In Aaronson, Mike, Aslam, Wali, Dyson, Tom, and Rauxloh, Regina, eds., *Precision Strike Warfare and International Intervention*. Oxon: Routledge, 95–113.
Woods, Chris, and Lamb, Christina (2012). CIA Tactics in Pakistan Include Targeting Rescuers and Funerals. www.thebureauinvestigates.com / stories/ 2012-02-04/ cia-tactics- in- pakistan- include- targeting- rescuers- and- funerals.

Woods, Chris, and Serle, Jack (2011). Secret US Documents Show Brennan's 'No Civilian Drone Deaths' Claim Was False. www.thebureauinvestigates.com/2013/04/11/secret-us-documents-show-brennans-no-civilian-drone-deaths-claim-was-false/.

Worth, Robert F. (2021). Qaddafi's son is alive. And he wants to take Libya back. 30 July 2021. *The New York Times*. www.nytimes.com/2021/07/30/magazine/qaddafi-libya.html.

Yeatman, Anna (2000). Who is the subject of human rights. *American Behavioral Scientist*, 49(9), 1498–1513.

Zalewski, Marysia (1995). 'Well, what is the feminist perspective on Bosnia?'. *International Affairs*, 71(2), 339–356.

Zambakari, Christopher (2016). The misguided and mismanaged intervention in Libya: Consequences for peace. *African Security Review*, 25(1), 44–62.

Zangl, Bernhard, and Zürn, Michael (1996). Argumentatives Handeln bei internationalen Verhandlungen: Moderate Anmerkungen zur post-realistischen Debatte. *Zeitschrift für Internationale Beziehungen*, 3(2), 341–366.

Zaum, Dominik (2007). *The Sovereignty Paradox – The Norms and Politics of International State Building*. Oxford: Oxford University Press.

Zehfuß, Maja (2001). Constructivism and identity: A dangerous liaison. *European Journal of International Relations*, 7(3), 315–348.

Zimmermann, Lisbeth (2017). *Global Norms with a Local Face*. Cambridge: Cambridge University Press.

Zimmermann, Lisbeth, Deitelhoff, Nicole, and Lesch, Max (2017). Unlocking the agency of the governed: Contestation and norm dynamics. *Third World Thematics: A TWQ Journal*, 2(5), 691–708.

Zürn, Michael, and Heupel, Monika (2017). Human rights protection in international organizations: An introduction. In Heupel, Monika, and Zürn, Michael, eds., *Protecting the Individual from International Authority: Human Rights in International Organizations*. Cambridge: Cambridge University Press, 1–39.

Index